Europe's post-war recovery

Western Europe's recovery from World War II was nothing short of miraculous. From the chaos of the war and the crisis of 1947, Europe moved to the most rapid quarter-century of economic growth in her history. The contributors to this volume seek to identify the sources of this singularly successful recovery. That all European countries shared in the miracle suggests that its roots may lie at the international level. The chapters therefore focus on the role played by international institutions – the International Monetary Fund, the World Bank, the European Coal and Steel Community, the European Payments Union, the General Agreement on Tariffs and Trade – and weigh the relative importance of domestic and international factors in Europe's post-war recovery.

This book will be of interest to students of modern European history and to economists interested in economic growth, European economic integration, and reform of the Bretton Woods institutions.

Studies in Monetary and Financial History

Editors: Michael Bordo and Forrest Capie

Europe's post-war recovery

Edited by

BARRY EICHENGREEN

University of California at Berkeley

Published by the Press Syndicate of the University of Cambridge
The Pitt Building, Trumpington Street, Cambridge CB2 1RP
40 West 20th Street, New York, NY 10011-4211, USA
10 Stamford Road, Oakleigh, Melbourne 3166, Australia

First published 1995

A catalogue record for this book is available from the British Library

Library of Congress cataloguing in publication data

Europe's post-war recovery / edited by Barry Eichengreen.
    p.   cm. – (Studies in monetary and financial history)
    ISBN 0 521 48279 8
    1. Europe – Economic conditions – 1945– 2. International economic
relations. 3. Europe – Economic integration. I. Eichengreen, Barry J. II. Series.
HC240.E873   1995
330.94'055 – dc20   94-37937 CIP

ISBN 0 521 48279 8 hardback

Transferred to digital printing 2003

Contents

Contributors

Helge Berger
Department of Economics, University of Munich

Isabelle Cassiers
Department of Economics, Catholic University of Louvain

N.F.R. Crafts
Department of Economics, University of Warwick

Barry Eichengreen
Departments of Economics and Political Science,
University of California, Berkeley

Chiarella Esposito
Department of History, University of Mississippi

John Gillingham
Department of History, University of Missouri

Douglas A. Irwin
Graduate School of Business, University of Chicago

Harold James
Department of History, Princeton University

Lucrezia Reichlin
Observatoire Française de Conjonctures Economiques

Albrecht Ritschl
Volkswirtschaftliches Institut, University of Munich

Gilles Saint-Paul
DELTA

Holger C. Wolf
Department of Economics, New York University

Preface

For many years, the decade following World War II existed in a no-man's land between economics and economic history. The period did not yet qualify as history for a generation of scholars who had lived through it and for whom access to the archives was barred by thirty-year rules and various and sundry bureaucratic obstacles. It was too remote to be of interest to economists whose forays were frustrated by the fact that organizations like the International Monetary Fund only began to generate consistent time series on economic performance in the 1950s.

Recently, however, this began to change. The end of the Cold War heightened interest in the origins of the conflict. The archives opened, due not just to the ineluctable forward march of the thirty-year rule but also because the fall of the Berlin Wall made available new materials. For economists, the Single Market Program and the Maastricht Treaty awakened interest in the post-war origins of European economic integration. The difficulties of economic adjustment in the formerly centrally planned economies of Eastern Europe led to a quest for precedents in Western Europe's successful post-World War II recovery. The 50th anniversary of the Bretton Woods institutions raised the question of whether the time was ripe for their reform and directed attention toward their post-war origins.

The essays collected in this volume speak to these issues. Most of all, however, they seek to clearly depict the contours of Europe's post-war recovery, expose the role of international institutions, and contrast the very different national experiences.

This volume is the fruit of a project initiated by the Association d'économie financière in Paris. I thank Jean-Marie Thiveaud, its director, and Ellen Plois of the Caisse de Dépôts. Marc Uzan provided assistance at a critical stage. Patrick McCartan went above and beyond the call of duty in shepherding the manuscript into print. Additional support for the editorial work was provided by the Center for German and European Studies of the University of California. I am grateful to these individuals and organizations, but most of all to the authors who contributed to the project.

Part I

Introduction and survey

1 Mainsprings of economic recovery in post-war Europe

BARRY EICHENGREEN

1 Introduction

With production stagnating, trade collapsing, and commodity hoarding widespread, the economy teetered on the brink of disaster. Shortages were pervasive, and the overhang of liquid assets threatened runaway inflation. Public officials desperately attempted to consolidate the budget and to shift workers between the public and private sectors without aggravating unemployment and provoking large-scale migration.

Readers might think that this was a description of the crisis in the Soviet Union and its successor states in the 1990s. In fact it could as easily be a portrait of Western Europe in the aftermath of World War II. In 1947, two years after the cessation of hostilities, Europe's recovery was in doubt. The rise of output to prewar levels appeared to be losing momentum. The major economies were suffering open and repressed inflation, disruptive food and raw material shortages, and a binding foreign exchange constraint. Government budgets were in deficit. Trade was collapsing. A large-scale westward movement of economic and political refugees was underway.

Yet by 1948 recovery and adjustment had miraculously resumed. For the next four years the Western European economy expanded at a rate of more than 10 percent per annum. By 1951 production was fully 55 percent above levels reached four years before. Western Europe then embarked on two decades of rapid growth unmatched in its prior or subsequent history.

It is tempting to consider the sources of Western Europe's post-World War II recovery in an effort to identify a recipe that might be applied in post-Cold War Eastern Europe today. While the contributors to this volume search out parallels, they also point to important differences in the two settings. The institutional prerequisites for a smoothly functioning capitalist economy – tax systems, financial systems, legal systems and well-defined property rights – were all in place. For these reasons and others, post-war Western Europe could pursue options not available to the formerly centrally planned economies today. But this very contrast makes it possible to isolate the importance of institutional obstacles to adjustment and recovery in the former Soviet Union. It permits one to ask what options available to Western Europe two generations ago remain infeasible in Eastern Europe until property rights are defined and the relevant institutions are established.

A second way in which the post-World War II Western European experience can shed light on the prospects for the former centrally planned economies derives from the fact that the post-war period was one of far-reaching institutional change at the international level. International initiatives included the Marshall Plan, the European Payments Union (EPU), the European Coal and Steel Community (ECSC), the International Monetary Fund, the World Bank, and the General Agreement on Tariffs and Trade. The question is how prominently these international initiatives figured, relative to domestic policies, in Europe's recovery and growth. Were macroeconomic stabilization, economic liberalization and financial reform necessary and sufficient to inaugurate the golden age of post-World War II economic growth? Or did the transition also hinge on a favorable international climate: exchange rate stability and the rapid expansion of trade, which in turn required an institutional framework for international transactions and the provision of foreign aid? This question speaks to the importance of current industrial country policies toward Eastern Europe and the former Soviet Union – specifically, market access and foreign aid.

These are the issues addressed in the present volume, which, following an introductory section, comes in two parts. The first considers the contribution of international initiatives to the recovery of the Western European economies. The second consists of country studies which weigh the relative importance of domestic and international factors in Europe's post-war recovery.

2 The contribution of this book

Economic growth in post-war Europe emerges from these pages in a new light. The difference is the role of international institutions. Leading studies of the economics of the golden age place relatively little weight on such institutions, focusing instead on domestic factors.[1] Thus, authors stressing the scope for catch-up (viz. Abramovitz, 1989; Barro, 1991) emphasize

---

[1] See Boltho (1982), Graham and Seldon (1990) and Marglin and Schor (1990). This statement should be qualified. The Boltho volume contains a chapter on the effects of the EEC, but this is concerned with a later period than is our focus here. The Graham and Seldon book begins with a chapter on the international environment which enumerates the principal international initiatives of the period. Similarly, Glyn *et al.* in the Marglin and Schor book provide a discussion of the international order.

supply-side factors: rates of population growth, the accumulation of physical and human capital, and imports of technology.[2] Others (viz. Boltho, 1982; Glyn *et al.*, 1990) square the circle by arguing that supply conditions favorable to growth would only have evolved in an environment of stable and buoyant demand. The General Agreement on Tariffs and Trade (GATT) as a vehicle for trade liberalization, the Bretton Woods System as a supplier of exchange rate stability, and the United States as a source of foreign aid and the principal market for the exports of other countries appear fleetingly on the stage, but the role attributed to them is at best ancillary.

There are several reasons for this neglect. First, the earliest analyses singled out international initiatives as key to growth. The post-war growth miracle could not have occurred, according to the authors of these studies, in the absence of the Marshall Plan, the GATT, and the Bretton Woods System.[3] Given exaggerated claims, it was inevitable that a reaction would set in. And once growth slowed in the 1970s without a corresponding change in the structure of international institutions (aside from the demise of the Bretton Woods System of pegged but adjustable exchange rates in 1973), it became harder to sustain the argument that international institutions had fueled Europe's rapid growth. Third, studies seeking to establish the importance of domestic institutions for comparative growth performance (viz. Crafts, 1992; Grier, 1993) produced only mixed results.[4] This negative evidence concerning the role of domestic institutions fed skepticism about the importance of their international counterparts. Finally, hopes that regional initiatives like the European Coal and Steel Community and the European Payments Union would create irresistible momentum for the foundation of a European economic and political union were disappointed. Again, the implication was that the importance of international initiatives had been overdrawn.

Perhaps the stubbornest obstacle to the development of a balanced view of the role of international institutions was the absence of an adequate conceptual framework. Here recent developments in the analysis of institutions, upon which the contributors to this volume build, allow the debate to be advanced. One such development is the literature in economics on institutions as solutions to commitment problems (North, 1993). An insight of this literature is that many economic policy decisions take the form of a prisoner's dilemma. In the same way that prisoners in different interrogation rooms can resist the temptation to confess first only if their partners in crime are credibly committed to doing likewise, the first-best

---

[2] This literature is surveyed in section 3 below.
[3] Citations to the relevant literature are provided starting in section 4.
[4] Holger Wolf's chapter in this volume provides further evidence on this question.

trade policy of liberalization and export orientation might be feasible only if a country's trading partners commit to pursuing the same strategy. In this view, the role of institutions such as the EPU and the ECSC was to provide monitoring technologies, penalties, and rewards that made this commitment to liberalization credible. The creation of a Managing Board and a Joint High Authority allowed national policies to be effectively monitored. The EPU possessed a pool of resources, access to which was conditional on countries carrying out the requisite adjustments. Assessments of the first post-war decade by contributors to this volume generally attach more importance to the EPU and the ECSC than to the IMF, the World Bank, and the GATT. Given this theoretical perspective, their conclusion is logical enough. European countries traded heavily with one another. Many financial transactions were intra-European. Hence, institutions were required to lend credibility to *European* countries' claim that their commitment to openness and liberalization was irreversible. Institutions like the EPU and the ECSC were tailor-made to post-war Europe's needs.

These European institutions did not function in isolation from the rest of the world. How they were integrated into the international order can be illuminated by a second literature, this one on international regimes (Krasner, 1982; Keohane, 1984). By an international regime is meant the norms and understandings, sometimes but not always articulated formally, that helped to mould national policies and foster international cooperation. These norms included the presumption that liberalization would occur in the context of social market economies in which the price system would be used to guide resource allocation and the government would intervene to support public enterprise and provide a social safety net. They included the understanding that liberalization would take place in a non-discriminatory fashion; thus, intra-European liberalization would occur in the context of an ongoing GATT process which insured that barriers to transactions with the rest of the world would be lowered with sufficient speed to prevent damaging the growth prospects of other countries. They included the understanding that any discriminatory effects of the EPU were transitional since European payments arrangements were merely a stepping stone to full implementation of the Bretton Woods Agreement.

It is here that the role of the Marshall Plan can be seen. The United States emerged from World War II as the world's dominant economic power. It possessed an exceptional capacity to make the side payments needed to bring other countries on board when institutional arrangements were designed and to induce its partners to conform to the norms and understandings that buttressed those arrangements. The Marshall Plan was a source of US leverage to prompt liberalization and stabilization on the part of European governments and to encourage their adherence to the norms and understandings of what might be called the Bretton Woods regime. It strengthened the hand of European leaders seeking to control the levers of economic policy and rebuff the opponents of the market economy.

Thus, international institutions and initiatives emerge from these chapters as a key component of Europe's post-war recovery. They were far from the entire story; their role was just to facilitate the operation of the domestic determinants of growth. Inevitably, it is with those domestic determinants that analysis must start.

3 Domestic sources of growth

It is useful to begin by distinguishing two questions. First, what made possible adjustment and recovery following the war? Second, what sustained high growth for two decades? Clearly, these questions are related. Initial conditions put in place during the period of recovery and adjustment could have played a decisive role in the subsequent period of sustained expansion. But there is no reason that a particular factor originating in either the domestic or international sphere should have been equally important to both post-war recovery and subsequent growth. Depending on the time frame, one may want to emphasize very different considerations.

Some authors (Dumke, 1990; Wolf, this volume) highlight the scope that existed for rapid growth simply by putting existing resources back to work. Until roads and bridges were repaired and waterways cleared, it was impossible to get inputs to the factory and outputs to the market. Until skilled workers were demobilized and coal miners were provided food with adequate caloric content, it was difficult to get factories operating again. But much wartime damage, however disruptive, was readily repaired. This was the lesson gleaned from wartime experience with strategic bombing. Once immediate problems were solved, output could rise quickly, as it did across Europe. The strength of the rebound depended, *inter alia*, on the extent of wartime disruption: figure 1.1 documents the correlation across countries between the extent of the output fall from prewar levels to 1947, on the horizontal axis, and the rate of GDP growth between 1947 and 1952, on the vertical one.[5] (The chapter by Wolf explores these connections further.) This correlation survives when the analysis is extended to the mid 1950s, as in figure 1.2. But figure 1.3 shows that the relationship disintegrates when the wartime shortfall is juxtaposed against the long boom of the 1950s and 1960s. The negative slope of the regression line in

---

[5] The data on GDP growth plotted in figure 1.1 are taken from Maddison (1982).

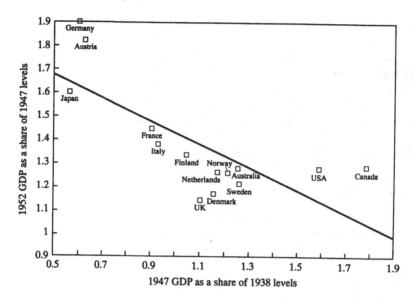

Figure 1.1

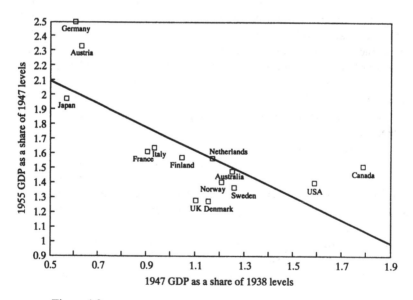

Figure 1.2

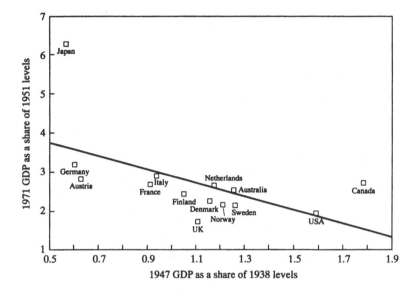

Figure 1.3

figure 1.3 hinges on the inclusion of Japan. When this one country is removed from the sample, the "rubber band effect" disappears. Wartime losses, in other words, have more explanatory power for immediate post-war recovery than for subsequent rates of growth.

Other authors (Olson, 1972) emphasize the advantages of clearing away institutional obstacles to growth. Vested interests in the defeated countries, which according to the Olson thesis had acquired the ability to obstruct the free play of markets and constrain the options available to policymakers, were dislodged by the occupying authorities, inaugurating a period of flexibility and prosperity until new interest groups filled the void. Germany, Austria, and Japan are obvious cases where the victorious powers sought to eradicate existing organizations and install new ones. The argument applies in milder form to countries like France, where individuals and organizations were discredited by collaboration, and the experience of the war prompted constitutional reform.

Historians debate whether vested interests were dislodged or unions in Germany and zaibatsu in Japan, to take two examples, modified their appearance but not their function. They are more skeptical still about the applicability of the hypothesis to other countries. N.F.R. Crafts, in his chapter on Britain, argues that prewar interest groups and associations survived the war and continued to hinder efforts to adapt the economy to the new conditions of the post-war era. Isabelle Cassiers advances a compatible account of the Belgian case, with the additional twist that the Marshall Plan and the European Payments Union actually strengthened conservative tendencies.[6]

Abramovitz (1989) emphasizes not the contrast between prewar and post-war but productivity relative to that of the national economy that was the technological leader. In the aftermath of World War II there existed a significant technology gap between the United States and Western Europe which found reflection in per capita incomes. The depression of the 1930s and the fact that the war was waged on European soil delayed the application there of American innovations. Post-World War II Western Europe could thus close the gap simply by importing existing technology. The literature on convergence (Baumol, 1986; DeLong, 1988) has documented the relatively rapid growth in the post-war are of industrial countries that started with low per capita incomes.[7]

Abramovitz observes that the existence of a technological backlog is not sufficient; countries must be capable of exploiting it. This capability comes partly from investment, since new technology is embodied in physical and human capital. Table 1.1 shows that investment in post-World War II Europe ran at high levels (see also figure 1.4). In every country considered, investment rates were higher in the 1950s and 1960s than in the 1920s and 1930s. Figure 1.5 indicates that the argument applies not just to secular growth but to immediate post-war recovery as well. Excluding Norway (where an exceptionally high investment rate was associated with unusually slow growth), there is a positive association between the investment ratio and the growth rate.[8]

This investment–growth correlation raises an important question of causation. Causality could have run from growth to investment insofar as rapidly growing countries were best able to set aside resources for capital

---

[6] The preceding figures nonetheless highlight a strong correlation between defeated-power status and growth. This thesis would appear to be relevant to both immediate post-war recovery and subsequent growth.

[7] Even if we restrict our attention to 1947–52, countries whose per-capita incomes in 1938 were furthest below that of the US appear to have expanded most quickly. Evidence to this effect is provided by Eichengreen and Uzan (1992).

[8] Data on the investment ratio are taken from OEEC (1954, 1957). The horizontal line superimposed on figure 1.4 shows the regression relationship between investment and growth for the entire sample of countries, while the positively sloped regression line also plotted is estimated after excluding Norway from the sample. On the low returns from investment in Norway, whose government allocated a large share of investment resources toward goals that were, strictly speaking, non-economic, see Eichengreen and Uzan (1992).

Table 1.1. *Non-residential fixed investment as percent of GNP at current prices* (average of ratios for years cited)

	1920–38	1950–60	1960–70
Austria	6.1[a]	16.4	20.2
Belgium		12.4	15.5
Denmark	8.9	14.0	16.9
Finland		19.6	20.0
France	11.8	13.7	17.4
Germany	9.7	16.1	19.3
Greece	7.5[b]	11.7	18.2
Ireland		13.1	15.1
Italy	13.6	15.1	14.5
Netherlands		18.0	20.3
Norway	12.4	23.7[c]	23.8[c]
Sweden	10.5	15.5	17.3
Switzerland		14.1	20.0
UK	5.7	11.6	14.2
Average for Western Europe	9.6	15.4	18.1

Notes: [a]1924–37.
[b]1929–38.
[c]Includes some elements of repair and maintenance excluded by other countries.
Source: Maddison (1976), p. 487.

formation.[9] Even if causality ran primarily from investment to growth, shifting the focus from productivity to investment merely strips another layer off the onion. If investment explains growth, in other words, what explains investment?

One possibility, suggested by Postan (1964) and Kindleberger (1967), is elastic labor supplies and wage moderation. As formulated by Kindleberger, the hypothesis runs as follows. Wage moderation meant profits to be plowed into investment. Where there existed an abundance of underutilized labor in low-productivity sectors (like agriculture) or regions (including neighboring countries), growth would not inflate wages and squeeze profitability. While a complete explanation of the wage moderation that characterized recovery is more complicated than this, it is indisputable that labor–management relations were central to the growth. As Wallich (1955,

---

[9] This is a point made for different periods and countries by World Bank (1993) and Bloomstrom *et al.* (1993).

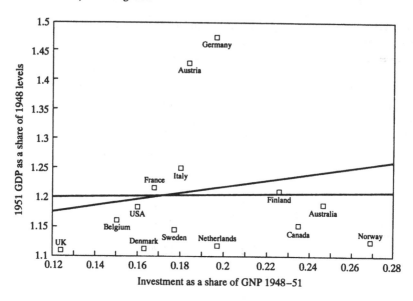

Figure 1.4

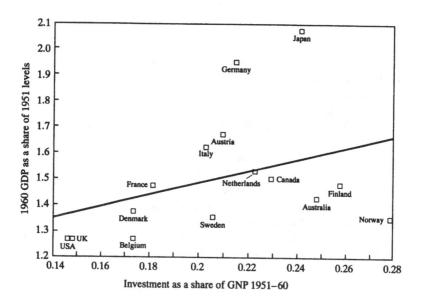

Figure 1.5

pp. 299–300) put the point for Germany:

For the economy as a whole labor's muted and unaggressive policy has been an inestimable advantage. It has, in the first place, made a major contribution to the stability of the new currency . . . in the second place, labor's restraint has helped to make and keep exports competitive . . . the final and probably most decisive contribution, however, has been to the financing of the investment boom. By allowing wages to lag behind profits, labor made it possible for business to engage in large-scale self-financing. The inequality of the income distribution, favoring the higher incomes where proportionately more savings accrue, was the essential condition of the high rate of investment.

Data limitations frustrate efforts to validate this argument for other countries and to ascertain whether it is also applicable to subsequent decades. Insofar as pressure to moderate wages depended on disguised rather than open unemployment and on potential rather than actual migration, it is difficult to measure the pressure on wage formation. For what they are worth, data on the factoral distribution of income assembled by the ILO starting in the 1950s do suggest a correlation between labor's share of national income and both growth (figure 1.6) and investment (figure 1.7).

For investment to take place there must be a demand as well as a supply. The mere existence of investment opportunities does not ensure that funds will be committed to them. If investors fear that their assets will be garnished by hostile governments, they will value liquidity over yield and shun productive opportunities. Figure 1.8 shows that there is a negative correlation between one measure of government hostility toward private property (the share of parliamentary seats held by representatives of communist parties) and the level of investment. Figure 1.9 confirms the existence of a negative correlation between political instability (as measured by the number of significant changes in government) and the investment ratio.[10] Thus, political factors appear to help explain cross-country variations in investment rates during the post-war recovery.

Such reasoning strays from familiar determinants of the level of investment such as aggregate demand. Investment rates were high in post-war Europe, it might be argued, because demand conditions were favorable. Milward (1984) stresses the importance for Europe of the fact that America's post-war recession was mild. Wolf in his chapter emphasizes the favorable impact on Germany of the Korean War boom.[11] Linking this

---

[10] Both political indicators were constructed from data in Taylor and Jodice (1983). Again, these issues are taken up more systematically in Wolf's chapter.

[11] On this point see however Temin (1994).

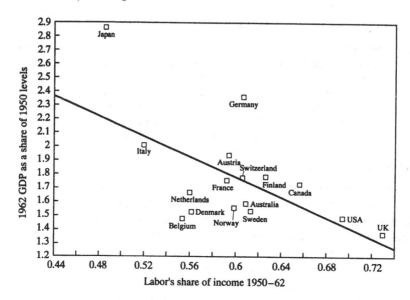

Figure 1.6

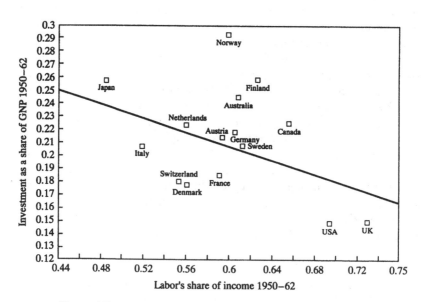

Figure 1.7

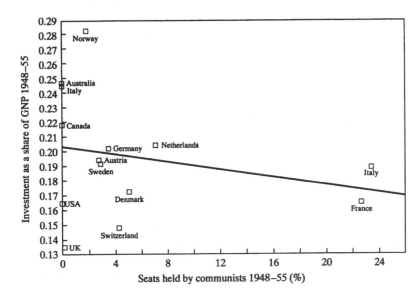

Figure 1.8

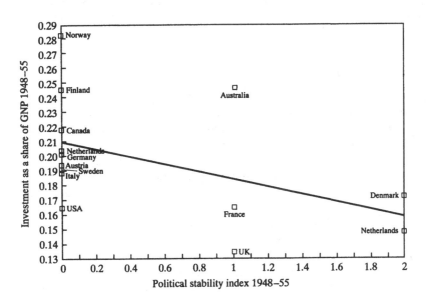

Figure 1.9

argument to the subsequent period of secular growth is more problematic, given the difficulty of seeing why favorable demand shocks should have continued to fall like manna from heaven. One possibility is to follow Boltho (1982) in crediting Keynesian policies with stabilizing demand and sustaining investment and growth. Not only does this overstate the prevalence of Keynesian policies in Europe, especially in the 1950s, however, but it runs up against the question of why if Keynesian policy was so effective before 1971 it should have faltered subsequently.

A reconciliation, offered by DeLong and Eichengreen (1993), is that Keynesian stabilization policy was effective only so long as demand stimulus affected output rather than wages and prices. So long as labor markets were accommodating in Kindleberger's sense, Keynesian policies worked to stabilize production, sustaining investment and growth. But as labor markets tightened, their flexibility declined. Unions began to bargain over real rather than nominal wages. Higher pressure of demand meant higher money wages and prices, not additional output. Stabilization policy lost its potency, the business cycle resurfaced, and investment suffered, especially in recessions.

The preceding explanations for Western Europe's recovery and growth all share a characteristic: they minimize the role of international factors. Trade and integration as engines of growth, pegged exchange rates as a source of monetary stability and an anchor for price expectations, foreign investment and aid as catalysts of growth – none of these considerations figures in the preceding analysis of sources of post-war Europe's economic success. It is to such factors that we now turn.

4 The Marshall Plan

One can distinguish three generations of scholarship on the Marshall Plan, following the genealogy laid out in Lucrezia Reichlin's chapter. The first (Ellis, 1950; Price, 1955) ascribes considerable importance to the US transfer. Marshall aid, it is asserted, critically supplemented domestic sources of investment finance. Depressed European incomes following the war exacerbated the difficulty of mobilizing domestic savings. Savings rates in every European country were lower during the Marshall Plan years than over the subsequent decade (table 1.2). US aid therefore played an important role in topping off Europe's supply of investible funds. New capital equipment, which embodied the latest technology, had a dramatic impact on European productivity. Technical assistance accelerated the transfer of US technology to Western Europe and further boosted growth.

By relaxing the foreign exchange constraint, Marshall aid is also said to have relieved bottlenecks and shortages that threatened to halt European

Table 1.2. *Savings rates in the aftermath of World War II and in the 1950s (in percent)*

Period	1946–51	1948–51	1952–60
Australia	16	20	21
Austria	n.a.	12	23
Belgium	n.a.	n.a.	17
Canada	16	20	21
Denmark	15	23	25
Finland	14	24	27
France	n.a.	18	20
Germany	n.a.	19	27
Italy	15	18	19
Japan	15	18	24
Netherlands	n.a.	20	27
Norway	28	35	34
Sweden	17	21	22
Switzerland	n.a.	10	23
UK	9	13	16
US	14	17	18

Note: Savings rates are calculated as the sum of investment and the current account surplus.
Source: Mitchell (1975, 1983).

recovery in its tracks. Food production was held back by shortages of fertilizer, which was made scarce by shortages of coal. Steel production was hindered by shortages of fuel for firing blast furnaces, supplies of which were interrupted by shortages of timber for reinforcing mine shafts. Textile production was stymied by lack of cotton. Commodities such as these could be purchased from the Western Hemisphere only for dollars and gold. When UNRRA aid was wound down in 1946 and Europe depleted its remaining gold and dollar reserves, the constraint began to bind. Countries could import raw materials only if they exported finished goods, but production for export was impossible unless imported materials were first obtained. Dollar credits were needed to break this logjam, and here the Marshall Plan was key.

Finally, it is argued, Marshall aid expedited infrastructure repair. Workers could function at normal levels only if adequately fed and housed. Post-war diets, in occupied Germany but also elsewhere in Europe, were spartan at best. Travelers in the immediate post-war period were struck mute by mile after mile of ruined houses and apartment buildings. Materials could not be transported to the factory, finished goods to the market, until basic infrastructure was repaired. As one Frenchman described his country:

It was a ravaged France that left its prison. 115 major railroad stations had been destroyed or badly damaged ... We had 12,000 locomotives; 2,800 of them remained. From Paris to Lyon, Marseilles, Toulouse, Nantes, Lille, Nancy, there were no more trains. Canals, riverways, ports were unusable. Electric lines were cut. 3,000 ports had been blown up. Of every ten motor vehicles, nine could no longer run and the tenth was out of fuel. Airplanes? There weren't any.

(Lecerf, 1963, pp. 11–12, cited in Lieberman, 1977).

With Marshall aid, governments could make good this damage.

The second generation of scholars downplayed the importance of the Marshall Plan. Abelshauser (1975, 1991) argued on the basis of German evidence that the program was largely superfluous. Recovery was already underway before US aid came on stream. Germany's supplies of capital and labor were adequate to support growth in the absence of aid. By the summer of 1947 the most serious transportation bottlenecks had been eliminated. A system of production bonuses, along with supplementary rations of bacon, coffee, cigarettes, sugar, and schnapps, boosted coal output. The economy displayed sufficient flexibility to substitute away from imported inputs and to prevent raw material shortages from constraining production.

Milward (1984) similarly insists that recovery commenced prior to the Marshall Plan. European savings were adequate to support sustained growth, and in any case Marshall aid represented no more than 10 percent of European investment over its life span. By 1948, when the Plan commenced, essential transportation and communication links were already repaired, although much cosmetic damage remained. The course of recovery would have been little different, from this point of view, in the absence of US aid.

The technical assistance (TA) component of the Plan received relatively little scrutiny from this second generation of scholars. Recently, Silberman and Weiss (1992) have argued that TA had a powerful impact on productivity in the recipient countries. Crafts in his chapter provides what would appear to be the first systematic test of this hypothesis, for which he finds little support.

Those who downplay the Marshall Plan encounter the most difficulty with the foreign exchange constraint. Borchardt and Buchheim (1991), focusing on the textile industry, argue that Abelshauser exaggerates the scope for substituting away from scarce inputs. If inputs requirements were inflexible, as they suggest, shortages of coal or cotton could have had a major effect. Even in countries like Germany and Italy where Marshall-Plan-financed deliveries of non-food imports were slow to materialize, the knowledge that they would be forthcoming could have encouraged the release of raw material hoards, boosting production.

The logical way of pursuing this point is input–output analysis. DeLong and Eichengreen (1993) use an input–output table for Italy to analyze the impact on production of making available additional supplies of imported coal. They find that the elimination of coal imports would have reduced Italian GDP by only 3.2 percent over the life of the Marshall Plan. Schran (1992), in an analogous exercise for France, finds that the removal of all Marshall-Plan-financed imports would have reduced French output in the program's first year by fully 9 percent. Additional research is needed to determine whether these different magnitudes reflect the different structures of the French and Italian economies, the different commodities considered, or the different periods considered in these analyses. There is no doubt, however, that input–output analysis with its assumption of fixed coefficients overstates the output effect of additional raw material supplies. The question, as the Abelshauser–Borchardt/Buchheim debate reminds us, is the extent.

Milward provides the definitive statement of this revisionist view. He too argues that European economic growth was proceeding smoothly on the eve of the Marshall Plan. The crisis merely reflected governments' overly ambitious investment plans. Investment minus saving, by definition, equals the deficit on current account. Investment programs that strain the availability of domestic savings can be sustained only if financed from abroad. Through the beginning of 1947, according to Milward, European countries, most notably but not only France and Norway, succeeded in financing ambitious investment programs with the help of foreign aid and by parting with international reserves. Then the external constraint began to bind. In the absence of the Marshall Plan, France would have been forced to scale back the Monnet Plan, Norway to moderate its ambitious program of modernization, but recovery and growth would have continued.

The third generation of research on the Marshall Plan accepts the revisionist critique that US aid did not work primarily by stimulating investment, financing infrastructure repair, or alleviating resource bottlenecks. But it suggests that the Marshall Plan encouraged the negotiation of the social contract entailing wage moderation and high profit rates upon which the subsequent generation of rapid growth was based. On the eve of the Plan, Europe was suffering from a marketing crisis in which producers refused to bring goods to the market, and workers and managers limited the effort they devoted to market work. Political instability, commodity shortages and fears of financial chaos encouraged commodity hoarding and withholding of effort. By helping to end the "war of attrition" over income distribution in which capital and labor were engaged, the Marshall Plan facilitated the restoration of financial stability and the liberalization of production and prices. It did so by increasing the size of the distributional pie, reducing the sacrifices required of the parties that compromised. With agreement on distribution, budget balance again became possible. Once budgets were balanced and financial instability no longer loomed, it became possible to relax controls and liberalize prices. Inventories were released, and goods returned to the market. With the danger of confiscatory taxation removed, long-term investments were undertaken.

A contribution of US aid, in this view, was to alter the environment in which economic policy was made. The strings attached to US aid strengthened the hand of those who favored the return to a relatively uncontrolled economy.[12] The Marshall Plan intervened at precisely the juncture when post-World War II Europe was faced with the decision of whether to cultivate or suppress the market. Socialists and communists hostile to the market occupied key positions in the governments of Italy and France. In both countries, centrist parties were able to use Marshall aid as a means of strengthening their positions and weakening that of the communists (Casella and Eichengreen, 1993; Esposito, this volume).[13]

The other way in which the Marshall Plan worked to alter the policy environment was by encouraging European integration. American officials made the coordination of national recovery programs a precondition for aid. They required the recipient governments to develop a joint proposal for how Marshall aid should be divided among them. In response to their

---

[12] This is not to argue that Marshall Plan conditionality was necessarily effective in all its particulars. Chiarella Esposito shows how French and Italian governments were able to exploit divisions within the US policy community and resist policies that the Marshall planners attempted to force upon them.

[13] Whether Marshall aid was as influential elsewhere has yet to be studied, as Reichlin points out in her chapter. There is no question that the Marshall Plan was received differently in different countries. American officials had no doubt that "the purpose of the Marshall Plan was to restore the economies of Europe to the point where free markets could function efficiently," as Kindleberger (1978) observes. These ideas were embraced by Adenauer, Erhard, and the German public. But in other countries the Marshall Plan was seen as consistent with ambitious programs of economic planning. Even in Germany, as Abelshauser notes, the Frankfurt ECA Mission criticized Erhard's reforms as too beholden to the ideology of *laissez-faire*. These views are possible to reconcile when one recalls that Europe's market economy was a social market economy – a market economy with a social safety net. Planning was "indicative": government made suggestions and provided inducements for production and investment without suppressing market signals. The post-war European economy was by no means a pure market economy, but it was freer than the highly planned alternative contemplated in 1947.

prodding, the Europeans established the body that became the Organization for European Economic Cooperation and, later, the OECD. The Marshall planners helped to overcome opposition from the IMF and certain branches of the US government to the creation of a special arrangement to reconstruct intra-European trade and payments named the European Payments Union.

5 The European Payments Union

Post-war Europe's trade was organized on the basis of bilateral agreements. To devote its hard-currency receipts to purchases of dollar-area exports, European country A limited its imports from European country B to claims on country B accumulated contemporaneously through its own export sales. The need to settle in gold and hard currency (i.e., dollars) was thereby avoided.

This bilateralism had costs. European country A in surplus with European country B and in deficit with European country C was prevented from balancing its external accounts in the normal triangular fashion; it was forced to reduce its exports to country B and ration imports from country C until both accounts balanced bilaterally. Insofar as dollars were needed to import badly needed raw materials from the US, each European country had an incentive to further compress its imports from elsewhere in an effort to earn additional dollars. Trade was both distorted and depressed.

The EPU was an attempt to multilateralize Europe's trade. Each member country continued to conduct its trade in Western European currencies through previously existing payments agreements. At the end of each month, net balances with each partner were reported to the Bank for International Settlements (BIS), the EPU's financial agent, and offsetting claims were canceled. Each country was left with claims on or liabilities not to other individual countries but to the union as a whole. It thus made no difference to European governments with which other European country trade was conducted. Only the overall balance of debits and credits in European currencies mattered at the end of the day.

Initially, debts could be financed with credits, but as they grew they had to be settled in dollars and gold. Each country was provided with a quota roughly proportional to its trade. Thus, not only was trade multilateralized, but its volume was stimulated by EPU credit lines.

Intra-European trade expanded vigorously during the EPU's reign. Countries that exhausted their quotas, like West Germany in 1950–1, were relieved of having to adopt draconian measures of deflation by the extension of EPU credit and succeeded in adjusting from debtor to creditor status in the union. The payments union scheme is portrayed as an important step toward the restoration of currency convertibility in 1958.[14]

A more skeptical perspective is that, while preferable to bilateralism, the EPU was inferior to convertibility. Compared to convertibility, the EPU could have created more trade diversion, distorted relative prices, and posed an obstacle to foreign borrowing. Analysis of these issues is sparse. In his contribution to this volume Gilles Saint-Paul attempts for one country, France, to estimate the impact for growth and welfare of the EPU and other policies that limited access to foreign funds, finding that the effects were considerable.

My own chapter on the EPU shows that the union's architects were aware of these problems and went to considerable lengths to minimize negative side effects. To the extent that such problems remained, it becomes important to ask whether the alternative of current account convertibility was also feasible. Janos Kornai (1990) identifies four preconditions for convertibility.[15] The first is a "realistic" exchange rate – i.e., one consistent with balance of payments equilibrium. The question is whether if countries had undertaken somewhat larger devaluations than they did in 1949, the balance of payments would have improved significantly. Polak (1953) shows that the 1949 currency realignments significantly strengthened the trade balances of the devaluing countries. Eichengreen (1993a) demonstrates that devaluations only somewhat larger than those actually undertaken in 1949 would have been sufficient to balance the external accounts.[16]

Kornai's second precondition for viable convertibility is adequate international reserves. European policymakers were preoccupied by the low level of reserves in the 1940s. By the early fifties this situation was much improved, however, partly as a result of devaluation itself; British reserves, for example, rose from $1.3 billion in early September 1949 to $2.4 billion at the end of June 1950. By this point, it is no longer clear that reserves were inadequate to support convertible currencies.

A third precondition for convertibility is the elimination of liquidity overhangs. Monetary overhangs had already been removed by inflation and currency reform in the 1940s (Dornbusch and Wolf, 1990). More

---

[14] See for example Triffin (1957) and Kaplan and Schleiminger (1989).

[15] In fact, he identifies a fifth – hard budget constraints to prevent public enterprises from demanding unlimited quantities of foreign exchange relevant to the formerly centrally planned economies today but not so much to Western Europe in the 1950s.

[16] Currency depreciation exercised a powerful impact on the volume of exports by enhancing domestic competitiveness and switching foreign demands toward European goods. It may have also compressed European import demands, and it reversed prior months' capital outflows.

persistent were overhangs of other liquid assets, namely foreign holdings of domestic interest-bearing obligations. The sterling area and other overseas regions had accumulated vast sterling balances during the war. Even a small disturbance to the international accounts might prompt these holders of sterling to liquidate their balances, undermining any attempt to restore convertibility. This danger was acute so long as questions remained about the state of British fiscal policy. But the same argument hardly applied to countries that did not share Britain's debtor status.[17] Moreover, the British economy, not to mention other European economies, was in a stronger position in 1950 than three years before. Sterling balances as a share of British GNP had been considerably reduced by growth, inflation, and prior liquidation.

A fourth and final precondition for convertibility is wage discipline. In fact, one of the most remarkable features of the 1950s was the stability of unit labor costs. In many countries, workers allowed real wage increases to lag behind productivity to provide incentives and resources for investment. In the Netherlands, unions allowed wages to lag behind productivity "so that industry could earn profits which would pay for expansion and modernization of the productivity apparatus" (Windmuller, 1969, pp. 350–1). Even in Britain, the Trades Union Congress cooperated with management and with the Conservative governments that ruled from 1951, moderating its wage claims. It is hard to argue that lack of labor-market discipline precluded an early move to convertibility.

Thus, for some countries, like Belgium, the case considered in the chapter by Cassiers, convertibility was clearly a viable option from the beginning of the EPU period. Harold James argues that the same quickly became true for Germany. My own work (Eichengreen, 1993a) suggests that this was soon true for much of Europe, once the impact on the German balance of payments of the Korean War had passed and Britain's problem of sterling balances began to recede.

If not the infeasibility of convertibility, what then made the EPU attractive? European countries when contemplating the adoption of outward-oriented policies faced a coordination problem. Dropping trade barriers and transferring resources into sectors producing exportable goods would be advantageous only if other countries did likewise, opening their markets to the exports of trading partners. Promises by other countries that they too were committed to trade liberalization and restructuring might not suffice if that commitment could be reneged upon.

---

[17] This view was argued by a number of observers such as Harrod (1947), Hazlitt (1947), and Haberler (1948).

Helge Berger and Albrecht Ritschl, in their chapter on Germany, suggest that the EPU provided a commitment technology to solve these problems. It limited the conditions under which quantitative restrictions might be used. Its Code of Liberalization established a pre-announced schedule for their removal. The EPU Managing Board, was not a supranational entity to which sovereign powers were ceded; it only monitored member country policies and recommended corrective actions. But its leverage was buttressed by the institutions with which it worked hand in glove. Its accounts were managed by the Bank for International Settlements, and it worked in tandem with the Organization for European Economic Cooperation. The Marshall Plan authorities, overcoming opposition from other US quarters, backed up the operation of the payments union. They provided working capital to underwrite its operation, together with an implicit threat that countries which failed to play by its rules might jeopardize their access to Marshall aid. This lent credibility to Germany's stated commitment to free international trade and European integration and encouraged the participating countries to move simultaneously toward the restoration of current account convertibility.

6 The European Coal and Steel Community

Along with the European Payments Union, the most conspicuous step toward European integration was the European Coal and Steel Community (ECSC). The Schuman Plan, out of which the Community grew, proposed a customs union with a common external tariff for coal and steel alone. French steel producers were assured of access to German coal and coke, German steel producers of access to French iron ore, on equal terms. Prior to the Plan's adoption, discriminatory pricing by coal producers and railways had placed wedges of as much as 60 percent between domestic and export prices of coal and ore. The Schuman Plan anticipated the elimination of such discriminatory pricing and freight rates.

A Joint High Authority was established to rationalize and modernize production through the coordination of national investment plans. Europe's steel industry had suffered from chronic overcapacity between the wars and had supported prices through the establishment of an International Steel Cartel. Post-war governments' ambitious investment plans implied that the overcapacity problem would soon re-emerge. The coal and steel authority was consequently empowered to coordinate the rationalization of national investment plans and to provide transitional protection for those national industries, like Italy's, least able to compete.

The measures ultimately adopted were more modest than those initially envisioned. Existing coal distribution organizations were retained. Italy was allowed to protect its high-cost industry. Although coal prices were harmonized and dual pricing was ended, differential national and international rail freight rates remained until 1957 (Diebold, 1959).

Did the ECSC enhance or diminish the efficiency of European production? Freer trade in the products of the coal and steel industries of the members of the Community should have enhanced efficiency. Insofar as national industries were highly concentrated, competition across borders should have helped to dissipate monopoly rents and apply market discipline. (Even German coal and steel firms, which were broken up, or "deconcentrated," in 1950–1, "remained associated by numerous personal and business links" (Milward, 1984, p. 412), including the traditional one of interlocking directorships.) In practice, however, trade hardly proved free. The High Authority was subjected to pressure to insulate the weak against competitive winds, as John Gillingham's chapter recounts. Steps to coordinate adjustment proved fertile ground for measures to maintain an "orderly market." It is hard to argue that the ECSC significantly accelerated the liberalization of Europe's coal and steel market or that it heightened efficiency through competition.

But trade there nevertheless was. One thing the ECSC thereby accomplished was to provide a solution to "the Ruhr problem" that had plagued Europe through the ages. It guaranteed France access to the coal of the Ruhr and Germany to the iron ore of Lorraine. It served as a commitment mechanism insuring the irreversibility of policies of market access, if not of unfettered competition. As Gillingham puts it, it was based on a new idea, "supra-nationality." Members transferred sovereign powers to an international entity with the authority to influence domestic policies toward the industry. Resisting its edicts would have jeopardized a host of post-war political and economic understandings, which deterred participating countries from succumbing to the temptation. In this way the ECSC helped to coordinate the principal European countries' steps toward freer trade and to promote acceptance in France and elsewhere in Europe of Germany's re-entry into the international economy.[18]

The benefits of the ECSC could have also resided in the impetus it provided for further integration. Spillovers from functional integration in areas like coal and steel to a common market and ultimately to political union were forecast by Haas (1958). John Gillingham's retrospective vision is more skeptical. Contrary to Haas's *ex ante* theorizing, he finds little *ex post* evidence of integrationist spillovers. The ECSC hardly provided a

---

[18] Isabelle Cassiers's chapter emphasizes the extent to which the ECSC and the European Payments Union were designed to meet the needs of France and Germany, the large countries of continental Europe, benefitting smaller countries like Belgium less than proportionately.

model for the structure of its successor, the European Economic Community. Insofar as the ECSC mattered for the course of European integration, it did so in a more diffuse way, by keeping alive the idea and the momentum and by schooling European negotiators in the art of integrationist diplomacy.

7 The IMF and the World Bank

A conspicuous contrast between the post-World War I period and the aftermath of World War II was the creation at Bretton Woods in 1944 of institutions to oversee international monetary and financial affairs. Post-World War I monetary and financial reconstruction had been haphazard and, ultimately, unsuccessful. Foreign investment by the United States was organized on an *ad hoc* basis. Long-term lending to war-torn Europe was delayed; rather than promoting post-war reconstruction, it got underway only in 1924–5 after the basis for reconstruction had already been laid and the risks of foreign investment had been reduced. US lending was interrupted in 1928 by the Wall Street boom, setting the stage for Europe's depression. The laboriously reconstructed interwar gold standard had operated unsatisfactorily, neither guaranteeing price stability nor facilitating balance of payments adjustment, and collapsing on the first occasion it was tested.

To avoid a repetition of these events, negotiators at Bretton Woods created the International Monetary Fund to oversee the operation of a system of pegged but adjustable exchange rates and the International Bank for Reconstruction and Development to organize lending for reconstruction in Europe and economic development in other parts of the world. Most accounts attach little weight to the activities of the two organizations in their first decade of operation. Although the Bank extended more credit to Europe than to any other continent in its first seven years, total European commitments between May of 1947, when the Bank's first loan was made, and the end of 1953, a period that bracketed the Marshall Plan, amounted to only $753 million or little more than a twentieth of Marshall aid (see table 1.3). The Bank's capitalization, agreed to in 1944 before the financial requirements of post-war reconstruction were known, proved inadequate. The formula for subscriptions was inflexible; when the US elected to devote more resources to European reconstruction, it was easier to extend aid on a bilateral basis. That the bilateral treaties signed as a condition for Marshall aid enhanced US control over the disposition of the funds was not unwelcome to American officials.

The Bank nonetheless played a useful role before the Marshall Plan.

Loans to France, the Netherlands, and Denmark (the Bank's first, second, and fourth commitments, the third being a small loan to Luxembourg) lent additional impetus to the recovery process. The thirty-year French loan contracted in May 1947 (and disbursed in January 1948) "came at a critical time for France, for its dollar resources were almost exhausted, it had fully utilized the credit it had received from the US Government and the European Recovery Program had not yet been formulated" (IBRD, 1954, p. 150). The proceeds were used to import raw materials such as copper, zinc, lead, and cotton, and fuels such as coal and oil. The coal thereby purchased amounted to two-thirds of that imported from the US during the first eleven months of 1947 and more than a tenth of all the coal available to France in the same period. The loan financed two steel mills and underwrote the purchase of 113 locomotives, eighteen tankers, thirty-six cargo vessels and some 180 smaller craft. The $195 million loan to the Netherlands, disbursed by June 1948, was spent on machinery and equipment, surplus US merchant vessels, rolling mill products, and fodder and feed grains. The August 1947 Danish loan was used to pay for agricultural and textile machinery, machine tools, trucks, steel, cotton, and other textile fibers, non-ferrous metals and chemicals. It was the equivalent of 9 percent of Danish capital expenditures in 1947–8, the period over which it was disbursed.

Efforts to impute more than marginal significance to World Bank loans, however, run up against the same objections registered against such a role for the Marshall Plan. Machinery and equipment may have been needed, but World Bank loans in 1947–8 were only a drop in the bucket of capital expenditure. Repair of road beds and rolling stock was well underway, and in some cases largely complete, by the time Bank funds became available. Imports of coal and cotton being even smaller than those made available by the Marshall Plan, attempts to attach importance to them encounter the same objections. Only in France in 1947 is it plausible that World Bank assistance played more than a marginal role.

The IMF got off to a similarly slow start. Efforts to have members declare par values and restore the convertibility of their currencies produced little of more than symbolic value. Foreign exchange rationing remained widespread. France experimented with multiple exchange rates. Devaluations were undertaken in 1949 and on other occasions without the due deliberation written into the Articles of Agreement. When the EPU was established in 1950, it operated not through the Fund but, as explained above, on the basis of existing bilateral agreements and with the assistance of the BIS. Contrary to the expectations of the Bretton Woods negotiators, who had foreseen a transitional period of not more than five years, currencies remained inconvertible even for current account transactions

Table 1.3. *Loans classified by purpose and area as of December 31, 1953 (in millions of US dollars, net of cancellations and refundings)*

Purpose	Total	Area				
		Asia and Middle East	Africa	Australia	Europe	Western Hemisphere
GRAND TOTAL	1,750	218	201	150	754	427
Reconstruction loans						
Total (France, the Netherlands, Denmark, Luxembourg)	497	—	—	—	497	—
Other loans						
Total	1,253	218	201	150	257	427
Electric power (machinery, equipment and construction materials)	492	68	88	30	35	271
Transportation	**304**	**67**	**69**	**39**	**35**	**94**
Railroads: locomotives, rolling stock, rails, shop and station equipment	193	63	61	16	3	50
Shipping: vessels and marine equipment	12	—	—	—	12	—
Airlines: planes and equipment	14	—	—	7	7	—
Roads: building machinery and equipment	64	—	7	16	—	41
Ports: docks, loading and dredging machinery, and harbor craft	21	4	1	—	13	3
Communications (telephone and telegraph equipment and supplies)	26	—	2	—	—	24

	152	**51**	—	**54**	**29**	**18**
Agriculture and Forestry						
Mechanization: general farm machinery and equipment	60	—	—	44	2	14
Irrigation and flood control: construction equipment and materials	60	41	—	5	13	1
Land improvement: machinery, construction equipment and materials	20	10	—	5	3	2
Grain storage: construction materials	5	—	—	—	4	1
Timber production: machinery and vehicles	7	—	—	—	7	—
Industry	**169**	**32**	—	**27**	**90**	**20**
Manufacturing machinery	146	32	—	20	74	20
Mining equipment	23	—	—	7	16	—
General development	**110**	—	**42**	—	**68**	—
Development banks	20	—	2	—	18	—
General development plans	90	—	40	—	50	—

Source: IBRD (1954), p. 73.

through 1958. Only thereafter were Western Europe's international monetary relations shaped by the global institutions constructed at Bretton Woods rather than the regional stop-gaps of the first five post-war years. The Bretton Woods institutions mattered, as Harold James emphasizes, mainly by providing a framework within which regional arrangements might operate. The desire to make those regional stop-gaps "Bretton Woods compatible" minimized deviations from prevailing international norms.

After 1958 the Bretton Woods System came into its brief but glorious prime. For more than a decade the system operated without suffering a major crisis (Bordo, 1993). Britain's 1967 devaluation and revaluations by Germany and the Netherlands perturbed but did not disrupt pegged-rate arrangements. Exchange rate stability encouraged the expansion of international trade. Large-scale private lending finally resumed. The $35 gold price maintained in conjunction with the pegged exchange rates declared by other countries anchored price expectations, enhancing the effectiveness of macroeconomic policy (Eichengreen, 1993b). Inflation, though accelerating in the 1960s, remained moderate by the standards of prior and subsequent decades. So long as commitments by governments to Bretton Woods' nominal anchors were credible, measures which put upward pressure on prices were regarded as temporary. If their policies drove up prices today, governments would have to take steps tomorrow to stem that rise and prevent their commitment to the prevailing exchange rates and the fixed dollar price of gold from being undermined. Obtaining wage increases when prices rose was not therefore regarded as urgent. Hence expansionary demand-management policies tended to drive up output and employment rather than labor costs, and Keynesian stabilization policy proved effective in moderating the amplitude of the business cycle.[19] Sustained high investment and buoyant growth were the result.

8 The GATT

Exchange rate stability was not the only force behind the expansion of trade. More important by any measure was the reduction in trade barriers achieved through the GATT. The GATT circumscribed the use of quotas. Tariffs protecting Europe's major export market, the United States, were reduced by a third in the Geneva Round in 1947, by an additional third in the Annecy Round in 1949, and by another third in the Torquay Round in 1951. By the conclusion of the Kennedy Round in 1967, they had fallen to a

---

[19] For evidence relevant to this argument, see Alogoskoufis and Smith (1991) and Eichengreen (1993b).

mere 10 percent of pre-Geneva levels. Trade liberalization allowed European countries to specialize in the products in which they had a comparative advantage and to exploit economies of scale and scope.

The question is whether trade fueled growth or vice versa. Throughout the quarter century that ended in 1971, industrial country exports expanded more quickly than GDP, the only exception being a short period toward the end of the 1950s. Bhagwati (1988) concludes on this basis that causality ran from trade to growth. Yet these observations are equally consistent with causality running from growth to trade so long as the income elasticity of the demand for exports exceeded unity. Douglas Irwin in his chapter on the GATT reports evidence of causality running in both directions, though he concludes that the influence of growth on trade was dominant.

The extent of liberalization was limited by exceptions and exemptions from the GATT process. From the beginning, quotas on imports of agricultural products were allowed in special circumstances. The US secured the right to exempt from GATT rules a substantial part of its agricultural imports. Restraints in Europe's agricultural trade were lineal descendants of these early initiatives. Quotas on Japanese exports of textiles and other goods making use of labor paid at sub-European rates were granted early exemptions, planting the seeds of the Short Term Agreement on Textiles in 1961 and the Multifiber Agreement. Such exclusions significantly slowed the overall pace of trade liberalization, as Irwin's account of early GATT rounds shows.

9 Implications

Ultimately, it was decisions taken at the domestic level, not just by governments but by trade unions, employers associations, households, and firms, that lay at the root of the quarter century of exceptionally rapid economic growth ignited by Western Europe's successful post-war recovery. The decisions of households to save, of firms to invest, and of workers to moderate their wage demands fueled the rapid growth of productivity and capacity in the 1950s and 1960s. In turn, stable governments, educated workers, and abundant labor supplies encouraged saving, investment, and wage moderation. They lent Europe the capacity to close the technological and income gaps *vis-à-vis* the United States.

But as the contributions to this volume make clear, domestic decisions did not occur in isolation from the international environment. The Marshall Plan helped to facilitate an accommodation between European capital and labor over the distribution of income which permitted stabilization and liberalization and encouraged saving and investment. It insured a role for the price system in the allocation of resources in post-war Europe's social market economy. Institutions such as the European Payments Union and the European Coal and Steel Community coordinated national programs of economic restructuring along export-oriented lines and lent credibility to European governments' commitment to openness. Countries were encouraged to more fully exploit their comparative advantages, enhancing the productivity and profitability of investment and thereby encouraging saving. The Bretton Woods international monetary system, the World Bank, and the GATT insured that Europe's regional initiatives would not injure the rest of the world and thereby delivered continued US support.

Thus, this volume can be thought of as "bringing international institutions back in" to the analysis of post-war Europe's growth.

References

Abelshauser, Werner (1975), *Wirtschaft in Westdeutschland 1945–1948*, Stuttgart: DMV.

(1991), "The Economic Role of the ERP in German Recovery and Growth After the War: A Macroeconomic Perspective," in Charles S. Maier and G. Bischof (eds.), *Germany and the Marshall Plan*, New York: Berg Publishers, pp. 367–407.

Abramovitz, Moses (1989), *Thinking About Growth*, Cambridge University Press.

Alogoskoufis, George and Ron Smith (1991), "The Phillips Curve, the Persistence of Inflation, and the Lucas Critique," *American Economic Review*, 81: 1254–75.

Barro, Robert J. (1991), "Economic Growth in a Cross Section of Countries," *Quarterly Journal of Economics*, 105: 407–43.

Baumol, William (1986), "Productivity Growth, Convergence and Welfare," *American Economic Review*, 76: 1072–85.

Bhagwati, Jagdish (1988), *Protectionism*, Cambridge, Mass.: MIT Press.

Bloomstrom, Magnus, Robert E. Lipsey, and Mario Zejan (1993), "Is Fixed Investment the Key to Economic Growth?" CEPR Discussion Paper no. 870.

Boltho, Andrea (1982), "Growth," in Andrea Boltho (ed.), *The European Economy: Growth and Crisis*, Oxford: Clarendon Press, pp. 9–37.

Borchardt, Knut and Christian Buchheim (1991), "The Marshall Plan and Economic Key Sectors: A Macroeconomic Perspective," in Charles S. Maier and G. Bischof (eds.), *Germany and the Marshall Plan*, New York: Berg Publishers, pp. 410–51.

Bordo, Michael (1993), "The Bretton Woods International Monetary System: An Historical Overview," in Michael Bordo and Barry Eichengreen (eds.), *A Retrospective on the Bretton Woods System*, Chicago: University of Chicago Press, pp. 3–98.

Casella, Alessandra and Barry Eichengreen (1993), "Halting Inflation in France and Italy After World War II," in Michael Bordo and Forrest Capie (eds.), *Monetary Regimes in Transition*, Cambridge University Press, 312–345.

Crafts, N.F.R. (1992), "Institutions and Economic Growth: Recent British Experience in an International Context," *Western European Politics*, 15: 16–38.

DeLong, J. Bradford (1988), "Productivity Growth, Convergence and Welfare," *American Economic Review*, 78: 1138–54.

DeLong, J. Bradford and Barry Eichengreen (1993), "The Marshall Plan: History's Most Successful Structural Adjustment Program," in Rudiger Dornbusch, Willem Nolling, and Richard Layard (eds.), *Postwar Economic Reconstruction and Lessons for the East Today*, Cambridge, Mass.: MIT Press, pp. 189–230.

Diebold, William (1959), *The Schuman Plan: A Study in Economic Cooperation*, New York: Praeger.

Dornbusch, Rudiger and Holger Wolf (1990), "Monetary Overhang and Reform in the 1940s," cEPR Discussion Paper 464 (October).

Dumke, Rolf (1990), "Reassessing the Wirtschaftswunder: Reconstruction and Postwar Growth in West Germany in an International Context," *Oxford Bulletin of Economics and Statistics*, 52: 451–91.

Eichengreen, Barry (1993a), *The European Payments Union: Historical Perspectives and Policy Implications*, Manchester: Manchester University Press.

(1993b), "Epilogue: Three Perspectives on the Bretton Woods System," in Michael Bordo and Barry Eichengreen (eds.), *A Retrospective on the Bretton Woods System*, Chicago: University of Chicago Press, pp. 621–58.

Eichengreen, Barry and Marc Uzan (1992), "The Marshall Plan: Economic Effects and Implications for Eastern Europe and the Former USSR," *Economic Policy*, 14: 13–76.

Ellis, Howard S. (1950), *The Economics of Freedom*, New York: Harper.

Glyn, Andrew, Alan Hughes, Alain Lipietz, and Ajit Singh (1990), "The Rise and Fall of the Golden Age," in Stephen Marglin and Juliet Schor (eds.), *The Golden Age of Capitalism*, Oxford: Clarendon Press, pp. 39–125.

Graham, Andrew and Anthony Seldon (1990), *Government and Economies in the Postwar World*, London: Routledge.

Grier, Kevin, B. (1993), "Governments, Unions and Economic Growth," unpublished manuscript: George Mason University.

Haas, Ernst B. (1958), *The Uniting of Europe*, Stanford: Stanford University Press.

Haberler, G. (1948), "Some Economic Problems of the European Recovery Program," *American Economic Review*, 38: 495–526.

Harrod, R.F. (1947), *Are These Hardships Necessary?* London: Hart-Davis.

Hazlitt, Henry (1947), *Will Dollars Save the World?* New York: Appleton-Century.

International Bank for Reconstruction and Development (1954), *The International Bank for Reconstruction and Development 1946–1953*, Baltimore: Johns Hopkins University Press.

International Labor Organization (various years), *Yearbook of Labor Statistics*, Geneva: ILO.

Kaplan, Jacob and Günther Schleiminger (1989), *The European Payments Union*,

Oxford: Clarendon Press.

Keohane, Robert (1984), *After Hegemony*, Princeton: Princeton University Press.

Kindleberger, Charles (1965), *Europe's Postwar Growth*, New York: Oxford University Press.

(1978), "The OECD and the Third World," in OECD, *From Marshall Plan to Global Interdependence*, Paris: OECD, pp. 105–21.

(1987), "The European Recovery Program," in Charles Kindleberger, *Marshall Plan Days*, Winchester, Mass.: Allen & Unwin, pp. 64–91.

Kornai, Janos (1990), *The Road to a Free Economy*, New York: Norton.

Krasner, Stephen D. (1982), *International Regimes*, Ithaca, NY: Cornell University Press.

Lecerf, J. (1963), *La Percée de L'Economie Française*, Paris: B. Arthaud.

Lieberman, Sima (1977), *The Growth of European Mixed Economies 1945–1970*, New York: John Wiley and Sons.

Maddison, Angus (1976), "Economic Policy and Performance in Europe, 1913–1970," in Carlo Cipolla (ed.), *The Fontana Economic History of Europe*, vol. V, pt. 2, London: Fontana, pp. 442–508.

(1982), *Phases of Capitalist Development*, New York: Oxford University Press.

Marglin, Stephen and Juliet Schor (1990), *The Economics of the Golden Age*, Oxford: Clarendon Press.

Milward, Alan S. (1984), *The Reconstruction of Western Europe, 1945–51*, Berkeley: University of California Press.

Mitchell, B.R. (1975), *European Historical Statistics, 1750–1970*, London: Macmillan.

(1983) *International Historical Statistics: The Americas 1750–1988*, London: Macmillan.

North, Douglass C. (1993), "Institutions and Credible Commitment," *Journal of Institutional and Theoretical Economics*, 149: 11–23.

Olson, Mancur (1972), *The Rise and Decline of Nations*, New Haven: Yale University Press.

Organization for European Economic Cooperation (1954), *Statistics of National Product and Expenditure*, vol. I, Paris: OEEC.

(1957), *Statistics of National Product and Expenditure*, vol. II, Paris: OEEC.

Polak, J.J. (1953), "Contribution of the September 1949 Devaluations to the Solution of Europe's Dollar Problem," *IMF Staff Papers*, 2: 1–32.

Postan, M.M. (1964), *An Economic History of Western Europe 1945–1964*, London: Methuen.

Price, Harry (1955), *The Marshall Plan*, Ithaca, NY: Cornell University Press.

Schran, Steve (1992), "France Without the Marshall Plan: Some Counterfactual Conjectures," unpublished manuscript, Harvard University.

Silberman, James M. and Charles Weiss, Jr. (1992), "Restructuring for Productivity: The Technical Assistance Program of the Marshall Plan as a Precedent for the Former Soviet Union," Industry and Energy Department Working Paper, Industry Series no. 64, Washington, DC: The World Bank.

Taylor, C. and D. Jodice (1983), *World Handbook of Political and Social Indicators*

(3rd edn), New Haven: Yale University Press.

Temin, Peter (1994), "The 'Koreaboom' in West Germany: Fact or Fiction," unpublished manuscript, MIT.

Triffin, Robert (1957), *Europe and the Money Muddle*, New Haven: Yale University Press.

Wallich, Henry (1955), *Mainsprings of the German Revival*, New Haven: Yale University Press.

Windmuller, John P. (1969), *Labor Relations in the Netherlands*, Ithaca, NY: Cornell University Press.

Wolf, Holger (1992a), "Miracle Prescriptions: Postwar Reconstruction and Transition in the 1990s," unpublished manuscript, MIT.

(1992b), "The Lucky Miracle: Germany 1945–1951," in Rudiger Dornbusch, Willem Nölling, and Richard Layard (eds.), *Postwar Economic Reconstruction and Lessons for the East Today*, Cambridge, Mass.: MIT Press, pp. 29–56.

World Bank (1993), *The East Asian Economic Miracle*, New York: Oxford University Press.

Part II

The Marshall Plan

2 The Marshall Plan reconsidered

LUCREZIA REICHLIN

1 Introduction

Since the collapse of central planning in the former Soviet bloc, the need for Western aid for the transforming economies of the East has been hotly debated. The case for assistance has been argued since the outset of Eastern Europe's transformation; Jacques Delors, President of the European Commission, advanced one of the first proposals in 1989. Five years after the fall of the Berlin Wall, debate continues to rage. Although some aid has been extended in the form of individual loans and technical assistance, the kind of coordinated package for which the advocates of aid call has yet to be agreed upon.

The obvious precedent for such a package is the Marshall Plan, the program of assistance extended by the United States to Western Europe after World War II. Between 1948 to 1951, $12.4 billion of Marshall aid was provided, the equivalent of $65 billion in 1989 prices. The analogy has not been lost on today's observers: the relevance of the Marshall Plan to the current debate has been considered by Kirman and Reichlin (1991), Eichengreen and Uzan (1992), and DeLong and Eichengreen (1993), among others.

This chapter extends that analysis. Its aim is to provide an explicit comparison of economic and political circumstances in post-World War II Western Europe and post-Cold War Eastern Europe to help weigh the case for a new Marshall Plan.

Several issues spring from the comparison. One is the relationship between growth and stabilization. Different Western European countries stabilized in different ways: some early, others late, some abruptly, others gradually. Yet in all of these countries, growth resumed quickly and proceeded vigorously. This fact challenges currently popular statements that early stabilization is needed to initiate growth. Moreover, while Western European countries stabilized in different ways, essentially all of them received American aid, calling into question the notion that there is a necessary connection between the form of stabilization and the provision of aid. A further issue is the degree to which donors should insist on joint planning of aid and trade, as did the Marshall planners, who required recipient governments to coordinate national programs of economic reconstruction and take concerted steps toward regional economic integration. And if there is a tradeoff between the global and regional integration of the transforming economies, for which alternative should today's policymakers strive?

This chapter argues that the tasks of reconstruction and recovery in Eastern Europe today are more formidable than those which confronted Western Europe after World War II. Their nature differs fundamentally. While the transition economies of the East, like the post-war economies of the West, need to decontrol prices, liberalize their trade, and restore the convertibility of their currencies – steps in whose initiation the Marshall Plan played an important role after World War II – the post-socialist economies must also solve a further set of growth-inhibiting problems associated with their lack of an adequate legal and institutional framework for supporting market activities. Necessarily, forging the relevant institutions is a time-consuming process; hence, financial assistance today is unlikely to exert effects as powerful as those of the post-World War II Marshall Plan.

2 Post-war recovery and the role of the Marshall Plan

The debate

For many years the conventional wisdom held that Marshall aid was crucial to Western Europe's post-World War II economic recovery. This view was predicated on a pessimistic assessment of the economic situation in 1947. Output was still depressed, it was believed, relative to prewar levels, and growth prospects were constrained by a combination of wartime destruction and insufficient resources to make good that devastation.[1] In contrast, recent contributions to the historical literature (Milward, 1984; Abelshauser, 1980) have suggested that the evidence of a post-war crisis is unconvincing. Growth, in this view, was already underway in 1947; hence, it could not have hinged on Marshall aid. A somewhat different point of view has been advanced by Maier (1987a, b), who claims that what mattered for European growth was the political impact of the Marshall Plan, not the financial effects narrowly defined. Recently, this argument has been elaborated by Eichengreen and Uzan (1992) and DeLong and Eichengreen (1993), who attempt to distinguish the financial and non-financial effects of Marshall aid.

[1] See for example Kindleberger (1987) and Bailey (1977).

Contemporaries stressed the severity of the post-war crisis. William Clayton, the US Undersecretary of State for Economic Affairs, described the collapse of Europe's economic fabric, with city and countryside no longer trading with each other because of chaotic monetary conditions (Clayton, 1947). Food shortages consequently set in following the disastrous 1946–7 harvest, and industrial production slumped. General George Marshall's Harvard commencement speech reflects this vision:

Machinery has fallen into disrepair or is entirely obsolete. Under the arbitrary and destructive Nazi rule, virtually every possible enterprise was geared into the German war machine. Longstanding commercial ties, private institutions, banks, insurance companies, and shipping companies disappeared, through loss of capital, absorption through nationalization, or by simple destruction.[2]

Subsequently, the belief that the European economy was in dire straits was challenged. Milward (1984) argues that evidence of stagnation or even a slowdown in 1947 is unconvincing. Apart from the special cases of Austria, Germany, and Italy, industrial production per man hour in 1948 was equal to or only slightly lower than the levels of 1938. In France, Ireland, Switzerland, Sweden, Turkey, and the UK, prewar levels had been surpassed. Overall, European industrial production already stood in 1948 at 96 percent of 1938 levels. Excluding Germany, the figure is 113 percent (table 2.1). Agricultural production, despite a poor harvest, was still 90 percent of 1938 levels in 1948. In terms of food production, no nation was really close to starvation; per-capita calorie intake actually rose relative to the 1945–6 crop year (UNRRA, 1947).

While contemporaries emphasized the destruction of capital wrought by World War II, subsequent estimates show that the loss of capital during the war was actually quite limited. Maddison (1976) estimates that while the loss of capital in the USSR was 25 percent, in West Germany it was only 13 percent, in France 8 percent, in Italy 7 percent, and in the UK 2 percent. Krengel (1958) suggests that German productive capacity was as high at the end of 1945 as it had been in 1940.

Another indicator of the state of the European economy is the level of investment, which, except in Germany, was already higher in 1947 than in 1938. There is little evidence here that post-war difficulties forced resources to be diverted away from investment. The importance attached to investment is evident in the early recovery of European shipbuilding, which

---

[2] Marshall (1947). Paul Hoffman, the first Marshall Plan administrator, made the same point: "Broken factories were operating fitfully and often slowed to a half for lack of raw materials and repair parts for equipment. Farmers raised little more than enough to feed themselves. The transport system was in too bad a state of disrepair to carry even the slight food surpluses to undernourished city dwellers" (Hoffman (1951), p. 28).

Table 2.1. *Indicators of production in Europe (1938 = 100)*

	Including Germany			Excluding Germany		
	1946	1947	1948	1946	1947	1948
Industrial production	72	83	96	98	100	113
Metals and engineering	64	75	91	94	111	128
Chemicals	71	81	99	98	113	135
Textiles	60	72	86	71	85	97
Building materials	58	68	86	67	81	96
Agricultural production	78	76	86	80	80	90
Railway transport (goods loaded)	—	—	—	95	102	115

Note: [a]Countries are: Austria, Belgium, Bulgaria, Czechoslovakia, Denmark, France, Germany (UK/US zone), Greece, Ireland, Italy, Netherlands, Norway, Poland, Sweden, United Kingdom.
Source: UN, *Economic Survey of Europe*, 1948.

was stimulated by the need for shipping capacity to import capital goods from the United States. The real problem, as we shall see below, was that the priority attached to investment, by European governments and American officials alike, resulted in balance of payments problems (table 2.2).

Nor did the progress of recovery escape contemporaries entirely. It is evident in representations by US manufacturers, who were concerned that with recovery Europe would shift its consumption from imports of American goods to domestic manufactures, and that European producers would expand their exports to the US and the rest of the world (Wexler, 1983).

The goal of the Marshall planners was to achieve cumulative growth of 30 percent in industrial production by the end of the ERP period. This goal was surpassed by a substantial margin. By 1951 the index of industrial production for the ERP area was 35 percent above 1938 levels (45 percent excluding Germany). All ERP countries except West Germany, where the lingering effects of pre-monetary-reform controls were still felt, and Greece, where civil war had disrupted growth, had surpassed the 30 percent target by 1951.

The role of the Marshall Plan

How then are we to understand the role of the Marshall Plan? Marshall aid from 1948 to 1951 amounted to about 2 percent of the GDP of the recipient countries, most of which was concentrated in the first year. The impression

Table 2.2. *The allocation of national income: France, Italy, UK (% of net national income at factor costs)*

	France				Italy				United Kingdom			
	1938	1946	1947	1948	1938	1946	1947	1948	1938	1946	1947	1948
Current expenditure												
Personal consumption	84	80	80	80	66	—	86	80	78	72	73	69
Government consumption	13	14	15	12	24	—	12	14	16	31	24	20
Capital formation												
Net	3	11	9	14	9	—	13	12	7	1	9	115
Gross	17	24	22	27	19	—	23	22	17	13	21	23
Balance of payments on current account	—	−5	−4	−6	1	—	−11	−6	−1	−4	−6	−6.5
Net national expenditure	100	100	100	100	100	—	100	100	100	100	100	100

Source: UN, *Economic Survey of Europe,* 1948.

Table 2.3. *US aid and capital formation in selected recipient countries*

	1948	1949	1950	1951
United Kingdom				
US aid	937	1,009	629	129
GDCF	10,400	9,000	6,400	6,300
%	9	11	10	2
France				
US aid	781	766	465	421
GDCF	5,600	6,400	4,460	5,380
%	14	12	10	7
West Germany				
US aid	1,130	948	470	362
GDCF	3,600	4,340	4,400	5,300
%	31	22	11	7
Italy				
US aid	399	437	257	261
NDCF	1,500	1,300	2,700	3,000
%	27	34	10	9

Notes: GDCF is Gross Domestic Capital Formation.
NDCF is Net Domestic Capital Formation.
All figures are in millions of current dollars.
Source: Drawn from Maier (1987b).

that Marshall aid was modest is reinforced when we consider its contribution to capital formation: after the first two years, this contribution was less than 10 percent (table 2.3).

Authors like Maier (1987a, b) have suggested that the Marshall Plan was more important for its role in changing European attitudes toward production than for financial capital formation. It encouraged the adoption of American-style scientific management and mass production techniques. Yet the Director of the ECA's Information Program, Robert Mullen, "was obliged to admit" in 1951 "that the attempts to change such [European] attitudes" through ECA's productivity advertising campaign in Europe had run into "quite a bit of [local] resistance."[3] Wexler (1983) argues that the $184 million spent on technical assistance under the Marshall Plan was insufficient to "change deeply rooted attitudes and practices overnight or create incentives where none were perceived to exist."

One attempt to weight the importance of the Marshall Plan's indirect

[3] Wexler (1983), p. 92.

effects is Eichengreen and Uzan (1992). On the basis of a regression analysis of the 1948–55 period, they conclude that Marshall aid had a strong effect on European growth, with countries receiving the larger allotments growing faster, but that the channels through which aid operated were not the traditional ones of financing investment, imports, and government spending. The first claim is controversial. The second opens up the issue of the political economy of the Marshall Plan.

The political economy of US aid must be understood in the context of the organizational effects of World War II. On the one hand, those effects entailed initiatives now associated with economic planning, such as strict controls over the allocation of raw materials and, in particular, imports. On the other hand, in some spheres the war economy was conducive to competition: companies continued to vie with one another in the effort to sell armaments to the government.

The planning and controls of the "war economy" were regarded favorably by most of those involved in their administration. After several successful experiences, such as the reorganization of agriculture in the UK, governments gained confidence in their ability to control the level and the composition of production; they were therefore tempted to behave in more interventionist ways. In many countries, the structure of trade and production was deliberately modified in more autarkic directions. In particular, the objective of self-sufficiency in food production prompted an increase in agricultural production in many countries. Indicative planning was used to stimulate investment. It largely achieved its goals: in the immediate post-war period, the effort to orient resources toward the reconstruction of industrial infrastructure produced an increase in the trade deficit of Europe with the US from $380 million in 1938 to $1.7 billion in 1948 (United Nations, 1949).

The legacy was a powerful one. As Eric Roll of the UK Treasury recalled of the preparation of the Paris OEEC Report, "the whole of that report was based on these micro-planning conceptions, which were then the vogue in Britain, and which fitted well with French indicative planning also."[4] The policy orientation of Western Europe was to promote reconstruction using the mechanisms elaborated during the war. Government intervention continued to be regarded with favor. Some (e.g., Chester, 1952) even complained that European governments were insufficiently dirigiste.[5]

---

[4] Roll (1984), p. 42.

[5] Unlike in the centrally planned economies of the former Soviet bloc, however, economic activity in Western Europe during the war continued to be based on private property. Where property rights were compromised, the war was considered a transitory episode. The clarity of this commitment to private property is in contrast to the current Eastern European situation, as we shall see below.

While the United States was the leading proponent of the free market, the economic philosophy of ECA administrators contained interventionist elements. Among the principles guiding the Marshall planners were coordination of financial assistance and the linkage of dollar aid to specific projects. They believed that ERP funds should be used to lever up government efforts to restructure production, not just to provide additional productive capacity. They were confident that technical assistance could be used to achieve permanent increases in productivity via the adoption of the American model of production and industrial relations.

Maier (1987a, b) has argued that US aid must be understood as the politics of productivity. "The productivist view of America's postwar mission," he writes, "arose naturally out of the domestic modes of resolving social conflict, or, rather, the difficulty of resolving conflicts cleanly."[6] The Marshall planners brought with them to Europe the idea that social conflict could be relieved by policies designed to stimulate productivity, economic growth, and rising living standards. As Romero (1988) put it:

> the ERP appeared, from its very beginning, not only as a policy best suited to reach the strategic goals of the US in the Cold War, not just as a project for international economic coordination, but – much more comprehensively – as a social philosophy addressed to European society at large, and particularly to industry and workers . . . the economic and social nature of the American proposal turned the previously abstract issues of international conflict into very practical and inescapable matters of economic policies, social alliances, political alignments and bargaining attitudes.[7]

This belief had developed out of New Deal experience in the United States, where industrial codes had been used to raise wages and restructure labor relations with the goal of stimulating productivity and minimizing labor strife, and cooperation among competing enterprises had been encouraged to rationalize capacity and stimulate investment. The question was whether these techniques could be successfully applied in Europe,

[6] Maier (1987a), p. 125.
[7] Romero (1988), pp. 6–7. Indeed, the role of the Cold War was key. It is impossible to understand Marshall aid without taking into consideration US foreign policy strategy in the period. The issue is summarized by Maier (1987a) in this way. "Originally an apolitical aid was thought to secure the broad range of American objectives. Once, however, the USSR was acknowledged as a threat, the liberals' image of a healthy political economy became strained. It was no longer clear that maximization of output adequately answered American interests. Increasingly, policy makers rejected those forms of international assistance which provided no direct political dividend, such as the UN Relief and Rehabilitation Administration (UNRRA). Harriman and others criticized this form of aid early on. On the other hand, foreign aid could not become purely subordinate to politics, for it followed from the earlier axioms that problems of political stability and capitalist recovery were resolved by efficient and neutral applications of planning and social engineering" (Maier (1987a), pp. 139–40).

where class divisions were deeper than in the United States and mass production techniques were less well developed.

Political coalitions adequate to implement the productivity policies of the Marshall Plan required the participation of European labor unions. But the political parties affiliated with the strong communist unions present in countries like Italy and France found it hard to cooperate politically with more market-oriented parties. Once the Cold War erupted, their participation was problematic from the point of view of both the Truman administration and Europe's centrist parties. Communist parties were ejected from governing coalitions in France and Italy, splitting the labor movement. Thus, the Marshall Plan sealed the division of the European labor movement between communist and other unions.

The outcome

The Marshall planners acknowledged that inflation stabilization was a necessary prerequisite for the resumption of sustained economic growth. But ECA administrators did not favor restrictive stabilization measures such as those adopted by Italy in 1947 and Germany in 1948 because they feared that such draconian measures would disrupt recovery. While the Marshall planners had more than a little sympathy for Keynesian ideas, their priority was sustaining the growth which would make it possible to moderate social conflict and, through that channel, eventually permit stabilization. The role for Marshall aid, in their view, was to defray the costs of stabilization that would have to be borne by wage earners and thereby promote the completion of a gradual stabilization process.

Not all European countries embraced the Marshall planners' strategy of gradualism. Indeed, what is most striking is the wide variety of policies pursued. Some countries opted for radical reforms entailing the confiscation of financial assets. Others permitted inflation to erode financial assets. Some opted for rapid decontrol; others liberalized much more gradually.

Each government had to solve the problem posed by excessive liquidity. Wartime shortages of consumer goods had resulted in the accumulation of financial assets by the public. These threatened to undermine policies of inflation control. The monetary overhang could be eliminated through either inflation or monetary reform. Most countries opted for the latter. Between October 1944 and May 1945 there were twenty-four monetary reforms.[8] While many reforms simply established a conversion rate between old currency and new without freezing assets, some countries, including Belgium, France, Austria, and the Netherlands, adopted policies

---

[8] For details see Kirman and Reichlin (1991) and Dornbusch and Wolf (1990).

of partial confiscation under which some portion of assets was frozen in blocked bank accounts. West Germany's reform was a combination of these two types.

These reforms should not be understood merely in terms of inflation control. To a considerable extent their ultimate objective was microeconomic: by eliminating repressed inflation and permitting price decontrol, they helped to restore the incentive to work for the market. Monetary reform in most of the places it was adopted was successful in achieving this goal. Moreover, there is no evidence that the capital levies and wealth taxes that monetary reform sometimes entailed had an adverse impact on growth. A clear illustration is Germany, where the problem of monetary overhang was even more pronounced than elsewhere.[9] There monetary reform not only cured the liquidity problem but also restored the incentive to work.

Table 2.4 provides an overview of the various national stabilization programs. Italy and Belgium opted for restrictive credit policies and substantial price liberalization, stabilizing relatively early. In France and Germany, stabilization was delayed. German monetary reform was accompanied by a restrictive fiscal program that brought a quick end to inflation. In France, in contrast, reform preceded fiscal stabilization and significant price decontrol by a period of years. The UK and the Netherlands decontrolled more gradually still. In many cases, some price controls remained in place well into the 1950s. Sometimes countries that had removed controls quickly were forced to reimpose them, following the outbreak of the Korean War, for example.

It is hard to say whether the more radical stabilization measures adopted by some countries (viz. Italy) hindered economic growth. The Marshall planners worried more about this prospect than many European governments. De Cecco (1968) and De Cecco and Giavazzi (1992) support this view, criticizing the 1947 Italian stabilization for its contractionary effects. They argue that Einaudi's program, while successful in halting inflation, had a high cost in terms of unemployment. It delivered increasing international reserves (from $70 million in September 1947 to $440 million at the end of 1948) but also a sharp recession. In France, where stabilization was more gradual, its implications for growth are less clearcut. The French economy recovered quickly in the final years of the 1940s but stagnated, by European standards, for much of the 1950s. While it is true that the Italian growth rate of the late 1940s and early 1950s was higher than the French, other determinants of growth also need to be held constant. In general, as

---

[9] Gurley (1953) estimated that the volume of liquid assets in the hands of the West German population was sufficient to buy, at current prices and conditions of rationing, the equivalent of one to two years of consumption goods.

Table 2.4. *Monetary reforms, stabilization, and economic performance*

	Confiscatory monetary reform	Stabilization program	Growth of GNP per capita (%) 1949–59	Inflation (%) 1950–9
Austria	July 1945, Nov. 1945		5.6	7.0
Belgium	Oct. 1944	Restrictive credit policy, 1945. Price decontrols 1946–47	2.4	2.2
Denmark	July 1945		2.6	3.5
France	June 1945, Jan. 1948	Price decontrols, austerity policy, 1948	3.6	6.3
Germany	June 1948	Restrictive credit policy, price decontrols, mid 1949	6.3	3.1
Italy	No reform	Restrictive credit policy, summer 1947	5.5	3.1
Netherlands	Sept. 1945	Price controls in place until 1950s. Austerity policy late 1945	3.3	5.7
United Kingdom	No reform	Price controls and rationing in place until 1950s. Austerity policy 1947	2.1	4.4

Source: Dornbusch and Wolf (1990), author's computations.

can be seen from table 2.4, there is no clear correlation between stabilization strategy, growth, and inflation.

Would stabilization have been possible without Marshall aid? It has to be argued that the Marshall Plan was important in mitigating the costs for wage earners of these stabilization programs. This is Maier's view, and it has been reinforced recently by DeLong and Eichengreen (1993) and Casella and Eichengreen (1993). Financial assistance from the United States, they suggest, helped the recipient countries resolve distributional

Table 2.5. *Balance of payments of OEEC countries (billions of $, current prices)*

| | 1947 | | | | 1948 | | | |
	Total	US	Other outside Europe	Other Europe	Total	US	Other outside Europe	Other Europe
Imports (fob)	13.9	5.6	7.3	1	15.3	4.6	9.3	1.4
Exports (fob)	6.7	0.7	5.2	0.8	9	0.9	7.1	1.0
Trade account	−7.2	−4.9	−2.1	−0.2	−6.3	−3.7	−2.2	−0.4
Current account	−7.2	−5.4	−1.7	−0.1	−5.6	−3.6	−1.7	−0.3

Source: Drawn from Kirman and Reichlin (1991).

conflicts. By increasing the size of the distributional pie, it reduced the magnitude of the burden that had to be borne by the distributional interests that agreed to shoulder the costs of stabilization policies.[10] A popular variant of this argument is that the Marshall Plan facilitated the resolution of distributional conflicts by relaxing the balance of payments constraint. Roll (1984), Kindleberger (1984), and Maier (1984) all argue that American aid limited the distributional consequences of stabilization by financing imports of consumption goods in quantities sufficient to reconcile an acceptable standard of living with the costs of reconstruction.

This thesis directs our attention to the external effects of the Marshall Plan. In the wake of World War II, European economies maintained strict exchange controls and overvalued currencies and settled their international transactions by negotiating bilateral agreements. By the end of 1947, the bilateral debts of the OEEC countries *vis-à-vis* one another had grown to $762 million (about $3.8 billion in today's dollars). OEEC countries were dependent on each other for over 50 percent of their imports and nearly 50 percent of their exports (see tables 2.5 and 2.6). This system of bilateral clearing was essentially an alliance of countries with weak currencies, all of which lacked a mechanism to equilibrate the balance of payments. Bilateralism produced a situation in which countries became permanent creditors against some trading partners and permanent debtors against others, with no possibility of using credits acquired in transactions with one trading partner to settle deficits incurred with another.

---

[10] A problem with this argument is reverse causality. One can imagine that stabilization, which permitted growth which raised national incomes, was more important in resolving distributional conflict than the distributional settlement was for facilitating stabilization. For suggestions to this effect, see De Cecco (1968).

Table 2.6. *Geographical distribution of OEEC countries' foreign trade (1938 prices, fob, as percentages of total trade)*

	Intra-OEEC	Other countries
1938		
Imports	45	55
Exports	35	65
1946		
Imports	63	37
Exports	42	58
1947		
Imports	63	37
Exports	44	56
1948		
Imports	55	45
Exports	45	55

Source: UN, *Economic Survey of Europe*, 1948.

The return to multilateralism and convertibility proved long and arduous. External convertibility was finally restored at the end of 1958. The length of the transition reflected conflicts of interest among European countries and in turn exacerbated their disputes. These conflicts were multifaceted: some countries were persistent creditors, others persistent debtors; small countries such as Belgium were more dependent on intra-European trade than their larger partners.

Early attempts at multilateralizing the pattern of intra-European settlements failed. The first such agreement was reached in November 1947. Its results were negligible because the agreement presupposed a certain degree of transferability (a country was supposed to pay another country with a third currency) and an acceptable rate of exchange. But no government was willing to accept payment in the currencies of deficit countries with overvalued exchange rates.

The creditors wished to see Marshall aid used for the establishment of a multilateral payments system. The United States, for its part, was hostile to this idea for fear of losing control of the funds and warned that it would not grant Marshall Plan dollars to finance deficits in a system of multilateral compensations. The European response was a plan for financing intra-European deficits with counterpart funds. This formula, which eliminated the distinction between loans and gifts, was opposed by both the United States and the International Monetary Fund, which feared that a

Marshall-aid-financed mechanism for multilateral clearing might delay the restoration of current account convertibility.

Over time the Cold War heightened US appreciation of the advantages of European integration, and the American attitude toward using aid to finance multilateral settlements shifted. On October 16, 1948 the Agreement for European Payments and Compensations was signed; it did not envisage assistance from the IMF but allowed the utilization of ERP funds to finance limited intra-European trade deficits. It established drawing rights for European countries, to be financed with ECA conditional aid.[11] This saved intra-European trade from collapse and stimulated its expansion in 1948 and 1949. However, the system still had a bilateral character since drawing rights were not transferable. This agreement nonetheless marked a turning point in American attitudes: from then on measures to promote intra-European trade and integration more generally were seen as stepping stones toward the restoration of free international trade and payments over a wider area.

Transferability was the main stumbling block in negotiations over the renewal and revision of the Agreement on Payments and Compensations for 1949–50. While the ECA considered transferability a precondition for the liberalization of European trade, it was opposed by certain European countries. The ECA insisted on transferability of drawing rights into dollars, which implied a prospective devaluation of European currencies *vis-à-vis* the dollar, and was opposed by European debtors and creditors alike.

Eventually, a compromise was found.[12] On September 18, 1949, as a result of a growing external deficit and rapidly shrinking UK reserves, sterling was devalued by 30 percent against the dollar. This induced the other major European countries to similarly devalue their currencies. By enhancing Europe's competitiveness against the dollar world, these devaluations facilitated trade and payments liberalization. One year later almost to the day, the European Payments Union (EPU) was created. The goal of the EPU was not only to promote intra-European trade but also to encourage economic cooperation. It was organized to provide multilateral settlements but also possessed its own resources to finance temporary payments imbalances. Unlike preceding agreements, compensation was automatic. The EPU's ultimate objective was to insure transition toward freedom of intra-European trade and payments once ECA aid was terminated.

Initially, European countries had hesitated to embrace such a radical

[11] Drawing rights covered about 40 percent of gross deficits and surpluses of participating countries.

[12] The ECA dropped its insistence on convertibility, and only 25 percent of the drawing rights to be established were made multilateral.

step. They feared that trade liberalization would exacerbate unemployment in sectors that were uncompetitive internationally and that it would hamstring stabilization policy. Moreover, the particular weakness of the pound sterling, which was still vulnerable to the liquidation of the sterling balances, was a special preoccupation. In part to entice the UK into the EPU, the Marshall Plan authorities agreed to contribute ERP funds to the payments union. In February 1950, they asked the US Congress to authorize $600 million of working capital for the EPU. In a matter of months, the EPU was established: it lasted eight and a half years. Upon its termination in 1958, all of the participating countries, aside from Iceland, Greece, and Turkey, restored non-resident current account convertibility.

To appreciate the importance of the EPU, recall that during the twenty-one months preceding its inauguration, the bilateral deficits of the OEEC countries amounted to $4.4 billion. Only a quarter of this total was successfully cancelled through the operation of the two compensation agreements that preceded the EPU. During the first twelve months of the EPU, total bilateral deficits never exceeded $3.2 billion, two thirds of which were automatically cancelled. The other third was financed as follows: $225 million was financed using gold deposited with the EPU by the participating countries, $54 million with credits, and $317 million with dollar aid.

Over the life of the EPU, total bilateral credits settled through the union reached $47 billion. The size of this figure is an indication of the EPU's success. While the degree of trade liberalization achieved over the period when the EPU was greasing the wheels of intra-European trade and finance varied across countries, overall results were impressive: after three months, 60 percent of intra-European private trade was liberalized; this figure reached 84 percent in April 1955 and 89 percent in June 1959.

While the Marshall Plan provided only a fraction of the financial resources used by the EPU to facilitate intra-European trade and payments, its contribution to the union's working capital is commonly credited with having played a catalytic role. Thus, the Marshall Plan was important not just for helping to restore domestic political and economic stability but in promoting the reconstruction of Europe's trade and encouraging European integration, factors which combined to stimulate European growth over the post-war decades.

3 Lessons for Eastern Europe?

Initial conditions

By the time the Berlin Wall fell, the Eastern bloc had already experienced a decade of slow growth. Output performance relative to the OECD countries had deteriorated steadily for more than ten years. With the radical political and economic changes of 1989, output began to fall absolutely and persistently. Only in Poland were there glimmers of improvement as early as 1991 (see table 2.7). Figures for 1992 also indicate modest improvement in Czechoslovakia. Although there is some controversy about the quality of the data, there is no question that the region is experiencing a major slump. The collapse of output has been accompanied by rising unemployment and a major acceleration of inflation. While inflation slowed in 1992 in both Poland and Czechoslovakia, in most countries it remains a chronic problem.

Table 2.8 summarizes early economic reform and stabilization programs in the countries of Eastern Europe.[13] In many countries, reforms have been guided by liberal principles and drastic stabilization measures in the IMF tradition. These aim at restricting the growth of money and credit and reducing fiscal deficits. Although there are differences across countries, reforms today are generally more market oriented and radical than after World War II. Anti-inflation programs more closely resemble post-war Italy's policy of radical retrenchment than France's gradual stabilization, for example.

Aghion and Burgess (1992) argue that Eastern Europe's most serious challenge has to do not with the pace of liberalization but with the microeconomics of reform. The transition to a market economy based on private ownership and control of the means of production creates principal–agent problems between shareholders and managers in an environment characterized by incomplete information and primitive institutional mechanisms for corporate control. These microeconomic difficulties are not unrelated to the problem of macroeconomic stabilization, of course, since inadequate corporate control is conducive to operating losses that create pressure for government bailouts of loss-making enterprises. Kornai (1984), in commenting on Hungarian reforms, made this point more than a decade ago. A similar point of view, based on the experience of Poland and Yugoslavia, has been advanced by Coricelli and Rocha (1991). Insofar as the problem of post-socialist transformation is greatly complicated by the absence of adequate legal, administrative, and social institutions (banks, courts, peak associations) to monitor management, enforce contracts, and facilitate labor–management negotiations, the post-socialist East faces an even more serious challenge than Western Europe after World War II.

---

[13] The successor states of the former Soviet Union are not included, since that region is still in a state of flux.

Table 2.7. *Macroeconomic indicators in Eastern European countries and the ex-USSR, 1989–91*

	National product, annual % change[a]			Inflation			Unemployment rate (%)			Industrial output: % change over same period of preceding year		
	1989	1990	1991	1989	1990	1991	1989	1990	1991	1989	1990	1991
Albania	11.8	−13.1	−30	—	—	—	—	—	—	8.5	−11.1	−60
Bulgaria	−0.3	−11.5	−25.7	6.2	19.3	338	—	1.7	10.7	2.2	−14.1	−27.3
Czechoslovakia	0.7	−1.1	−19.5	1.4	10.1	58	—	1	6.6	0.8	−3.7	−23.1
Hungary	0.4[b]	−3.3[b]	−10.2[b]	17	28.9	35	0.3	1.7	8.3	−2.5	−5	−19.1
Poland	0.2[b]	−11.6[b]	−7[b]	244.1	584.7	70	0.1	6.1	11.5	−0.5	−23.3	−11.9
Romania	−8	−9.9	−13.7	—	5.6	165	—	1.3	3.1	−2.1	−19.8	−18.7
Yugoslavia	0.6[c]	−8.5[c]	−15[c]	1256	588	164	12.5	13.6	19.6	0.9	−10.3	−20.7
ex-USSR	2.4	−4.0	−10	3.2	6.9	96	—	1.4	—	1.7	−1.2	−7.8

Notes: [a] Net material product unless otherwise noted.
[b] Gross domestic product.
[c] Gross material product (value added of the material sphere including depreciation).
Source: UN, *Economic Survey of Europe,* 1990–1 and 1991–2.

Table 2.8. *Eastern Europe: characteristics of stabilization–cum–reform programs*

Feature	Bulgaria	Former Soviet Union	Hungary[a]	Poland	Romania	Yugoslavia
Program start	1 Feb. 1991	1 Jan. 1991	continuous	1 Jan. 1990	1 Nov. 1990	19 Dec. 1989
Price liberalization (% of goods covered)	Instant 70%	Instant 85% (increased to 90% in July and 95% in Nov. 91)	Gradual	Instant 90% (6 month freeze on energy prices after initial 400% increase)	Gradual (80% in four stages from 1.11.1990 to 15.11.1991)	Instant 80% (6 month freeze on energy and public sector prices, after initial rises)
Monetary policy	Moderately restrictive (refinancing rate: 54% per month)	Restrictive	Moderately restrictive	Restrictive (controls on net domestic assets of the banking system; initial refinancing rate: 36% per month in real terms)	Accommodative (credit ceilings; refinancing rate of 12.5%; negotiated bank interest rates)	Temporarily restrictive (controls on net domestic assets of central bank; initial discount rate: 23% p.a. negative real)
Wage policy	Liberal (with limits on minimum wage growth)	Restrictive (excess wage taxes)	Moderately restrictive (excess wage taxes)	Restrictive (partial backward indexation with punitive taxes)	Unrestricted (periodical indexation)	Initially restrictive (6 month freeze on nominal wages)
Exchange rate policy	Sharp initial devaluation (900%), floating rate thereafter	Devaluation (fixed rate for "basket")	Gradual devaluations (crawling peg)	Sharp initial devaluation (46% against US dollar)	Devaluation and unification of rate	Initial devaluation (20% against D-mark; fixed rate abandoned subsequently)

Nominal anchors	Yes (money supply, incomes)	Yes (exchange rate, wages)	No	Yes (exchange rate, wages)	No	Yes (discount rate, wages, exchange rate)
Real anchors	No	Yes (money supply, interest rate)	Yes (money supply)	Yes (interest rate)	No	No
Internal convertibility for firms	Yes	Yes	Yes	Yes	No	Yes
Internal convertibility for households	Limited	Limited	No	Yes	No	Yes
Capital account convertibility	No	No	No	No	No	Restricted
Foreign trade liberalization	Limited	Extensive	Gradual	Extensive (no import quotas, few export quotas)	Limited	Extensive (few import and export quotas)
Foreign investment regulations	Liberal	Liberal	Liberal	Partly liberal (profit transfer restricted)	Restricted	Liberal
Small-scale privatization	Limited	Yes	Gradual	Extensive	Limited	Limited
Large-scale privatization	No	Delayed	Limited	Slow	Planned	Slow

Table 2.8. (cont.)

Feature	Bulgaria	Former Soviet Union	Hungary[a]	Poland	Romania	Yugoslavia
Property restitution	Under review	Yes	No	Selective	No	No
Banking reform	Initialized	Initialized	Advanced	Initialized	Initialized	Initialized
Stock exchange	No	No	Yes	Planned (April 1991)	No	No
External assistance	Yes (IMF stand-by credit)	Yes (IMF stand-by credit; stabilization fund)	Yes (IMF stand-by 3 years facility in 1991)	Yes (IMF stand-by credit; stabilization fund)	Yes	Yes (IMF stand-by credit)

Note: [a]Hungary was the only country which did not introduce a standard stabilization plan similar to other Eastern countries; this column has been inserted in the table for the sake of completeness. The data presented refer to economic policies followed in Hungary in 1991.
Source: Drawn from UN, *Economic Survey of Europe*, 1991–2.

The role for aid

In contemplating the role for Western aid for economies attempting to complete the transition to the market economy, it is important to distinguish the different effects with which the Marshall Plan has been credited: solving distributional conflicts, transferring to Europe the politics of productivity, and helping to rebuild intra-European trade.

The capacity of aid to moderate distributional conflicts seems less today than in Western Europe after World War II. Distributional conflict is so intense that a bit of Western aid may not suffice to paper over deep divisions between interest groups. Compared to early twentieth-century Europe, income distribution in centrally planned Eastern Europe was relatively equal; thus, the new inequality that has emerged since the advent of liberalization represents a major social and political shock.[14] Miners and other organized groups with market power vociferously express their objections to the impact of reforms on their standards of living, but other workers are in a poor position to make their objections heard. Freeman (1992) predicts that the most likely labor-relations outcome in Eastern Europe is weak and fragmented labor unions concentrated mainly in the public sector. A likely consequence is that wage earners and others who bear a disproportionate share of the costs of stabilization and transformation will be in no position to make their objections felt; insofar as they are unable to effectively resist the implementation of stabilization policies whose costs fall disproportionately on the working class, there is no need for aid to facilitate a distributional settlement and seal the process of macroeconomic stabilization.

Another scenario is that the proliferation of bickering interest groups will lead to total social breakdown. In this case, quantities of Western aid on the scale that can be realistically promised will not suffice to bridge the distributional gap.

While this perspective throws cold water on the case for Western assistance as a way of modestly increasing the size of the distributional pie, the comparison with the Marshall Plan nonetheless suggests ways in which aid might help to avert the kind of social breakdown that some observers fear. As we have seen, Marshall aid was tied to policies of

---

[14] While the evidence on income distribution in pre-1989 Eastern European societies is less than clearcut, most observers believe that income distribution there was more equal than in Western European market economies. Atkinson and Micklewright (1992), for example, claim that, in Czechoslovakia, to find the person earning twice the median wage one has to go up to the top 2.5 percent of the distribution, while in Britain more than 6 percent of the population receives more than twice median earnings. Income (as opposed to wage) inequality in both the former USSR and Central Europe was also less pronounced than in the UK.

conditionality and technical assistance aimed at transforming European labor relations in more cooperative ("corporatist") directions. One can imagine that Western aid to Eastern Europe might be tied to provisions designed to produce the institutions required for cooperative labor-market relations.

In addition to its role in helping to achieve and sustain a domestic distributional settlement, the Marshall Plan was important for its contribution to the reconstruction of Europe's trade. The countries of the former CMEA area now face trade and payments problems similar to those of post-war Western Europe. The former members of the CMEA are in fact more dependent on trade with one another than were the countries of Western Europe after World War II. This larger volume of inter-regional trade was accompanied by larger bilateral imbalances. The latter are due mostly to trade with the former USSR, however, on which the rest of the CMEA relied for energy imports. In 1989, before the transition to convertibility, the potential trade deficits of the countries of Eastern Europe with the USSR were estimated by the OECD to be approximately $5 billion. Bilateral imbalances within Eastern Europe were a relatively modest $288 million. Since 1989, the elimination of the transferable ruble and the shift to world market prices has caused a deterioration in the terms of trade of Eastern European countries with respect to the former USSR, further increasing the relative importance of imbalances *vis-à-vis* Russia.

The termination of the CMEA led to an immediate collapse of intra-Eastern European trade. Eastern European countries hoarded their foreign exchange earnings for energy imports from the former USSR and capital goods imports from the West. The share of intra-regional trade in the total trade of the former CMEA (including trade with the former Soviet Union) declined from 39 percent in 1990 to 32 percent in 1991. Trade within Eastern Europe fell more sharply still.

Developments in the former USSR have been even more dramatic and distressing. The breakdown of intra-republic payments and loss of confidence in the ruble led to a fall in intra-republican trade in 1992 of the order of 30 to 50 percent. While there has been a shift in exports (mainly of energy and raw materials) away from CMEA partners in favor of developed market economies, the trade of the former USSR with the West has been stagnant.

A key question for Eastern European policy is therefore whether to create a regional framework for trade or to encourage individual countries to move unilaterally toward current account convertibility and integrate themselves into the world economy. Should Eastern Europe create an EPU-like set of regional preferences or move directly to unilateral current account convertibility? The argument for the regional approach is that trade with the West has not and cannot expand rapidly enough to offset the decline in intra-Eastern European transactions. The countries of Western Europe, in this view, are unlikely to welcome Eastern European exports of products of sensitive sectors like steel, textiles, chemicals, and agriculture. The transition economies will be better off if they seek to develop their trade with one another.

Whether regional initiatives can be successfully completed is another matter. Unlike Western Europe after World War II, regional integration is not an independent aim of policy in Eastern Europe today. After World War II, policies promoting regional integration were motivated by strategic considerations (the desire to lock a peaceful Germany into the European economy and the need to build an economic bulwark against potential Soviet incursions). Today, there is no analog to post-war Germany (assuming that any Eastern European payments union does not include the economically troubled Russian Federation). Whereas post-World War II politics dictated regional integration, post-Cold War politics push the Eastern European region to integrate instead with other parts of the world, most notably the European Union.

In contrast, the case for a regional payments arrangement is stronger for the former Soviet Union. Regional integration there can help to prevent economic collapse, while there is little immediate prospect of integration into the global trading system.

The obvious alternative to a gradual EPU-like transition is to attempt to restore current account convertibility immediately. In those parts of the Eastern bloc where this has been attempted, the policy has not been a success. Internal convertibility has been achieved only by the Czech Republic, Hungary, Poland, and Estonia. Capital account transactions are still subject to approval everywhere. Attempts to achieve internal convertibility by Albania and by the successor states of former Yugoslavia have led to severe shortages of convertible currencies and rapid exchange rate depreciation. In Russia, an attempt to make the ruble convertible in July of 1992 and to replace the multiple exchange rate system with a unified floating rate applicable to all transactions proved a failure. The rapid depreciation of the ruble quickly led the authorities to again limit convertibility.

Could these developments have been prevented by opting for a payments union along the lines of the EPU? There are good reasons to think that the answer is no. Two prerequisites for the success of the EPU were the coordination of national stabilization policies among member countries and concerted steps toward regional integration (Kirman and Reichlin, 1991). Stabilization first had to be completed to prevent economies characterized by continued excess demand from quickly and permanently absorbing all of the credits possessed by the payments union. Other forms of regional integration helped to buttress cooperation by raising the stakes and thereby preventing countries from reneging on their commitment to behave cooperatively. Neither of these conditions is obviously present in Eastern Europe today. In the former Soviet Union, the situation is more complicated still. A payments union scheme would lack credibility until it is clear who controls the quantity of rubles in circulation, which participating republics possess an independent currency, which ones are prepared to liberalize their trade, and which ones have succeeded in stabilizing. Absent these conditions, a payments union might still work if its largest participant, Russia, agreed to underwrite its operation in return for enhanced political and diplomatic leverage in its traditional sphere of influence. In return for diplomatic and political prerogatives, Russia might agree to provide credit to finance intra-republican trade imbalances to other republics in weaker economic positions.[15]

But the experience of the EPU warns that such an arrangement is unlikely to endure in the absence of effective stabilization and policy coordination. All regional clearing systems suffer from a fundamental weakness: countries which run deficits inside the union and surpluses with the rest of the world will be tempted to use their surpluses in other ways than that of repatriating them within the union. Russia may wish to forego this option in return for diplomatic and political prerogatives, but it is hard to imagine a similar argument for the persistent surplus countries in a prospective Eastern European Payments Union.

Since the original proposal by Delors in January 1989, which advocated coordinated economic aid to Eastern Europe of $23 billion per year for a period of five years, aid has been granted in uncoordinated fashion by many countries and international organizations. Owing to the number of donor countries and institutions and the variety of programs underway, it is difficult to assemble a complete picture of financial assistance since 1990. Some have estimated that aid as a proportion of the national income of the Eastern European recipients has averaged about 2 percent, which is roughly the same as the amount allocated under the Marshall Plan (Collectif, 1992). But the question is not only volume of aid but also the mechanisms through which it is transferred and the incentives it consequently provides. Here three differences with the Marshall Plan are worthy of note.

First, the aid extended to Eastern Europe by the industrial countries of the West has not been coordinated. Indeed, it is argued that too much coordination may be counterproductive insofar as it is conducive to the

[15] For discussion, see Bofinger (1991).

creation of new bureaucracies. The European Community is supposed to coordinate assistance from the G-24, from international organizations such as the European Bank for Reconstruction and Development, the IMF and the World Bank Group, and from European entities such as the European Investment Bank and the European Coal and Steel Community. In practice, however, most of the assistance to Eastern Europe extended by G-24 countries has been organized bilaterally. There has been no effective coordinating structure to organize assistance for the former USSR.

Second, whereas more than 80 percent of Marshall aid took the form of grants, the bulk of assistance today (again, more than 80 percent) has taken the form of loans. This creates the prospect of a future debt burden that may prove difficult for the transforming economies to handle.

Third, in contrast to the Marshall Plan, under which recipient governments had to negotiate each expenditure of American funds with ECA officials, Western aid to the East has not been targeted at particular projects. Instead, aid is conditioned on the implementation of policies of reform and the achievement of macroeconomic stability. Thus, some of the decline in multilateral support for Eastern Europe in 1992 was attributable to the failure of countries to satisfy the macroeconomic conditions that had been set down. The situation with regard to early aid to the former USSR was somewhat different, since a large percentage of assistance was devoted to food purchases and related relief initiatives.

In all these respects it can be argued that early aid initiatives for post-socialist Eastern Europe have been inferior to the Marshall Plan. That aid has been inadequately coordinated across countries, threatens to create an intractable debt burden, and could have been better linked to particular investment projects.

4 Conclusion

The comparison of post-World War II Western Europe and post-socialist Eastern Europe today suggests that the case for financial assistance to the latter cannot be built on the experience of the Marshall Plan. One difference between the two contexts concerns convertibility and economic integration. The Marshall-Plan-financed European Payments Union that was the bridge between bilateralism and current account convertibility worked because Western Europe and the United States had explicitly opted for a strategy of European integration. Today, the countries of Eastern Europe, rather than integrating with one another, prefer to strengthen their links with the outside, specifically with the European Union. Thus, the case for Western aid to establish an Eastern European Payments Union is less than compelling. The argument is stronger in the case of successor states of the

USSR. But there, one country, the Russian Federation, would be a persistent creditor in a regional payments arrangement. Even if there is a case for creating a mechanism to support and encourage trade among the successor states of the Soviet Union, doing so requires creating a mechanism to provide Russia the incentive to repatriate its surpluses in the union. It requires clarifying the monetary situation in the ruble area and terminating financial chaos. Western assistance could play a limited role in these connections.

An important difference between the two episodes is that the economies of Western Europe had already embarked on the road to recovery when Marshall aid began to flow. Though financial and monetary stabilization took time, growth resumed quickly after World War II. That resumption in fact preceded the arrival of Marshall aid. The Marshall Plan may have still played some role in cementing macroeconomic stabilization in countries where there existed strong distributional and political conflicts. But insofar as it did, its role was not merely economic but also political and institutional. It increased the size of the distributional pie, helping to ameliorate distributional conflicts and encourage stabilization. At the same time, the narrow financial effects of American aid were strengthened by the effort to export to Europe the American model of cooperative labor relations and scientific management, a process designed to stimulate productivity growth and encourage interest groups to trade current austerity for higher future incomes.

In contrast to conditions in Western Europe after World War II, Eastern Europe and the former Soviet Union were in dire economic straits at the time of the 1989 revolution. Western aid could not simply solidify an ongoing process of growth and recovery. Moreover, the economic difficulties of the region are a consequence of more than conflicts over income distribution. The lack of an adequate legal framework and institutions capable of supporting market activities has been the fundamental obstacle to the resumption of sustained growth. The implication is that differences in economic and political conditions dictate that aid should be targeted differently than after World War II. Unlike the Marshall Plan, financial assistance in the amount of 2 percent of recipient-country GDP is unlikely to be adequate to bridge deep distributional cleavages and bring inflations to a halt. But insofar as the most pressing problem in Eastern Europe is the absence of the institutions needed to support market activities, linking aid to institution building, in the way that the Marshall Plan was linked to the politics of productivity, becomes all the more important.

References

Abelshauser, W. (1984), "The Economic Role of the ERP in German Recovery and Growth," paper presented at the Conference on the Marshall Plan and Germany, Washington, DC.

Aghion, P. and R. Burgess (1992), "Financing and Development in Eastern Europe and the Former Soviet Union," LSE Financial Market Group, special paper no. 46, May.

Atkinson, A.B. and J. Micklewright (1992), *Economic Transition in Eastern Europe and the Distribution of Income*, Cambridge University Press.

Bailey, T.A. (1977), *The Marshall Plan Summer*, Stanford: Hoover Institute Press.

Baudhuin, F. (1958), *Histoire Economique de la Belgique 1945–56*, Brussels: Bruyland.

Bofinger, P. (1991), "Options for a New Monetary Framework for the Area of the Soviet Union," CEPR Discussion Paper no. 604, August.

Casella, A. and B. Eichengreen (1993), "Halting Inflation in Italy and France After World War II," in Michael D. Bordo and Forrest Capie (eds.), *Monetary Regime Transformations*, Cambridge University Press, pp. 312–345.

Catinat, M. (1981), "La production industrielle sous la IV République," *Economie et statistique*, 129 (January): 17–36.

Chester, D.N. (1952), "Machinery of Government and Planning," in G.D.N. Worswick and P.H. Ady (eds.), *The British Economy 1945–50*, Oxford: Clarendon Press, pp. 336–364.

Clayton, W.L. (1947), "The European Crisis," *Foreign Relations of the United States*, May 27, vol. 3.

Cleveland, H. van B., (1984), "If There Had Been No Marshall Plan," in S. Hoffmann and C. Maier (eds.), *The Marshall Plan: a Retrospective*, London: Westview Press, pp. 59–64.

Collectif (1992), "Repenser le soutien de la communauté internationale à l'Europe de l'Est," *Observations et diagnostiques économiques*, no. 42, October.

Coricelli, F. and R. Rocha (1991), "A Comparative Analysis of the Polish and Yugoslav Programmes," in P. Marer and S. Zecchini (eds.), *The Transition to a Market Economy*, Paris: OECD, pp. 101–134.

De Cecco, M. (1968), *Saggi di politica monetaria*, Milano: Giuffre.

De Cecco, M. and F. Giavazzi (1993), "Inflation and Stabilization in Italy, 1946–1951," in Rudiger Dornbusch, Wilhelm Nolling, and Richard Layard (eds.), *Postwar Economic Reconstruction and Lessons for the East Today*, Cambridge, Mass.: MIT Press, pp. 57–82.

DeLong, J.B. and B. Eichengreen (1993), "The Marshall Plan: History's Most Successful Structural Adjustment Program," in Rudiger Dornbusch, Wilhelm Nolling, and Richard Layard (eds.), *Postwar Economic Reconstruction and Lessons for the East Today*, Cambridge, Mass.: MIT Press, pp. 189–230.

Delors, J. (1990), "Discours devant le Parlement Européen à l'occasion de la présentation du programme de travail de la Commission pour 1990," 17 January, *Official Journal of the European Communities*, Annex, Debates of the European Parliament, No. 3–385, pp. 108–117.

Dornbusch, R. and H. Wolf (1990), "Monetary Overhang and Reforms in the 1940s," CEPR Discussion Paper no. 464, October.

Dow, J.L.R. (1964), *The Management of the British Economy 1954–60*, Cambridge University Press.

Eichengreen, B. and M. Uzan (1992), "The Marshall Plan: Economic Effects and Implications for Eastern Europe and the Former USSR," *Economic Policy*, 14: 13–75.

Freeman, R.B. (1992), "What Direction for Labor Market Institutions in Eastern and Central Europe?" Harvard University, mimeo, October.

Gordon, L. (1984), "Lessons from the Marshall Plan. Successes and Limits," in S. Hoffmann and C. Maier (eds.), *The Marshall Plan: a Retrospective*, London: Westview Press, pp. 53–58.

Gurley, J.G. (1953), "Excess Liquidity and European Monetary Reforms, 1944–1952," *American Economic Review*, 43: 76–100.

Haberler, G. (1948), "Some Economic Problems of the European Recovery Program," *The American Economic Review*, 38(4): 495–525

Hardach, J. (1980), *The Political Economy of Germany in the Twentieth Century*, Los Angeles: University of California Press.

Hoffman, P.G. (1951), *Peace Can Be Won*, Garden City, NJ: Doubleday.

Hoffmann, S. (1984), "Final Remarks on the Marshall Plan," in S. Hoffmann and C. Maier (eds.), *The Marshall Plan: a Retrospective*, London: Westview Press, pp. 91–94.

Hoffmann, S. and C. Maier (1984), *The Marshall Plan: a Retrospective*, London: Westview Press.

Hogan, M.J. (1987), *The Marshall Plan: America, Britain and the Reconstruction of Western Europe, 1947–1952*, Cambridge University Press.

Kaplan, J. and G. Shlemeinger (1989), *The European Payments Union*, Oxford: Clarendon Press.

Kenen, P. (1990), "The Reconstruction of International Monetary Relations of the CMEA Countries," paper presented at the CEPR Conference East-Central European Payments Union Proposals, Rome, June.

Kindleberger, C.P. (1984), "The American Origins of the Marshall Plan: a View from the State Department," in S. Hoffmann and C. Maier (eds.), *The Marshall Plan: a Retrospective*, London: Westview Press, pp. 7–14.

(1987), *Marshall Plan Days*, Boston: Allen & Unwin.

Kirman, A.P. and L. Reichlin (1991), "L'aide aux pays de l'Est: les leçons du Plan Marshall," in J.-P. Fitoussi (ed.), *A l'Est en Europe: des économies en transition*, Presse de la Fondation Nationale des Sciences Politiques.

Kornai, J. (1984), "Adjustment to Price and Quantity Signals in a Socialist Economy," in B. Csikos-Nagy, D. Hague, and G. Hall (eds.), *The Economics of Relative Prices*, London: Macmillan, pp. 60–77

Krengel, R. (1958), *Anlaagervermogen, Produktion und Beschaftingung der Industrie im Gebiet der Bundesrepublik von 1924 bis 1956*, Berlin: Dunker Quand Humblot.

Lehoulier, J. (1948), "L'évolution des salaires," *Revue d'économie politique*, 58 (November–December): 1164–1192.

Maddison, A. (1976), "Economic Policy and Performance in Europe 1913–1970," in Carlo Cippola (ed.), *The Fontana Economic History of Europe*, vol. V, London: Fontana, p. 442–508.

Maier, Charles (1984), "Supernational Concepts and National Continuity in the Framework of the Marshall Plan," in S. Hoffmann and C. Maier (eds.), *The Marshall Plan: a Retrospective*, London: Westview Press, pp. 29–38.

(1987a), "The Politics of Productivity: Foundations of American International Economic Policy After the War," *In Search of Stability*, Cambridge University Press, pp. 121–152.

(1987b), "The Two Postwar Eras and the Conditions for Stability in Twentieth-Century Western Europe," *In Search of Stability*, Cambridge University Press, pp. 153–184.

Marshall, G.C. (1947), "Harvard Commencement Address, June 5th," *Foreign Relations of United States*, 3: 237–9.

Milward, A.S. (1979), *War, Economy and Society 1939–1945*, London: Allen Lane.

(1984), *The Reconstruction of Western Europe 1945–51*, London: Methuen.

(1988), "Was the Marshall Plan Necessary?" *Diplomatic History*, 18: 231–53.

Roe, A. and J. Roy (1988), "Trade Reform and External Adjustment: The Experience of Hungary, Poland, Portugal, Turkey and Yugoslavia," EDI Policy Seminar Report, 16, Washington: World Bank.

Roll, E. (1984), "The Marshall Plan as Anglo-American Response," in S. Hoffmann and C. Maier (eds.), *The Marshall Plan: a Retrospective*, London: Westview Press, pp. 39–46.

Romero, F. (1988), "The U.S. and Western Europe: A Comparative Discussion of Labor Movements in the Postwar Economy," EUI Working Paper no. 89/401, March.

Saint-Paul, G. (1991), "Economic Reconstruction in France, 1945–1958," DELTA Working Paper no. 91–25.

United Nations, Economic Commission for Europe (various years), *Economic Survey of Europe*, Geneva: United Nations.

UNRRA (1947), *Operational Analysis Paper*, no. 41, April.

Wexler, I. (1983), *The Marshall Plan Revisited*, London: Greenwood Press.

3 Influencing aid recipients: Marshall Plan lessons for contemporary aid donors

CHIARELLA ESPOSITO

Today, at the end of the Cold War and with the collapse of communism, the Eastern European and ex-Soviet economies find themselves in an economic quandary no less formidable than that of Western Europe after World War II. While Eastern Europe and the former Soviet Union did not undergo the large-scale physical destruction wrought by World War II, they are beset by another predicament perhaps more difficult to overcome, namely the lack of entrepreneurial skills and institutional frameworks required in a capitalist system. Moreover, Western European economic recovery and democratic stabilization, it can be argued, was greatly aided by the external funding of the Marshall Plan. No such aid package has yet been offered to the struggling Eastern economies. But it is quite important to define just what was the role played by the massive American aid package in achieving Western Europe's recovery.

As we shall see the Marshall Plan was conceived as a panacea for all of Western Europe's immediate and long-term problems. But did the Americans succeed in achieving their goals? This chapter will argue that while Marshall aid was not a success in terms of achieving specific economic goals, it did attain its political aims. These conclusions will be reached through an analysis of two key areas of Marshall Plan operations. First, we shall recount how, at the Europe-wide level, the United States sought to influence the creation of an intra-European payments system. Second, we shall examine the impact of conditional Marshall aid funding in France and Italy. In both contexts we shall see how complex, rigid, and at times conflicting American priorities defeated specific United States economic goals and how political constraints based on British, French, and Italian national priorities stood as insurmountable obstacles to the Americans. Marshall Plan experience thus suggests that donors will have greater chances of exerting a positive influence on recipients' policies if they put forth a program negotiated with the recipients, and if donors support that program itself rather than merely a particular political coalition or group.

1 Influencing the making of a European payments system

During World War II the European countries had accumulated a large balance of payments deficit, with gold and convertible currency reserves insufficient to cover debts and at the same time buy the necessary raw materials and equipment abroad. The problem was to define an international trade and payments scheme that would allow Europe to run large foreign account deficits.

European economic policymakers realized that if Europe was to invest for economic recovery while running large balance of payments deficits, they would have to support an international payments system different from the traditional gold standard. In a multilateral trade and payments system based on the gold standard, debtor countries would be forced to correct their international position through domestic deflation, i.e., by cutting domestic consumption, lowering prices, and thus making their products more competitive on foreign markets. In several Western European countries, ambitious and expensive reconstruction plans precluded that solution.

European economic experts were also aware that recovery was ultimately dependent on the acquisition of foreign raw materials and goods, as well as on international competitiveness. Neither could be achieved if Europe resorted to a system of bilateral trade that rigidly set the amounts and types of goods to be exchanged between pairs of countries. Such in fact had been the solution of the 1930s, when European countries had abandoned the gold standard system. By signing bilateral treaties of trade and payments, Europeans had forfeited their ability to maximize trade. Bilateralism guaranteed that payments would be effected regularly without resort to gold but not that prices would be competitive or that overall demand could be met.

One possibility was the injection of substantial foreign credits to finance reconstruction imports while breaking the log-jam of European payments. After the war, the only country capable of providing the necessary capital was the United States, but the new Western superpower had different plans. America preferred the establishment of a so-called gold-exchange standard. This system would be more flexible than the gold standard, because it would be based on a gold-convertible dollar, whose supply could be managed by an international institution. However, the American plan was aimed at creating a multilateral, near-free world market based on convertible currencies, ultimately leading to international equilibrium. In such a system debtor countries might yet have to curtail their domestic programs in order to reach international trade and payments equilibrium. Therefore, the American plan did not eliminate deflationary perils for the reconstructing European economies.

Until mid 1947 the Truman administration was not expected to provide the large credits necessary to finance the European countries' reconstruction plans. It was difficult to ask the American public for a substantial financial commitment so soon after the war, especially when the President's political health appeared shaky: Truman's electoral victory in the fall of 1948 was a surprise. The Republicans were expected to seize the presidency and perhaps cut short US foreign aid programs. The Western Europeans would face uncertainty about the availability of American aid until at least late 1948.

American international monetary plans were embodied in the International Monetary Fund (IMF), created in 1944. The IMF fell far short of European expectations. Above all it did not provide sufficient credits to cover deficits and for investment in reconstruction at the same time. But the Western European countries were in no position to influence the making of the IMF. Great Britain alone had leverage and managed to exact some concessions from the Americans, but these were insufficient to shelter Europe's economies.[1]

In such circumstances most European countries resorted, between 1945 and 1948, to bilateral trade and payments treaties while maintaining quantitative and other wartime trade controls. This system was no more than a sophisticated form of barter.[2]

The bilateral trade and payments network in fact could not prevent the outbreak of a major international payments crisis in 1947. European countries were running short of gold and dollars with which to import from the dollar area the raw materials and machinery needed to continue the recovery process. Western European countries had signed two successive intra-European payments agreements that sought to liberalize a portion of trade while minimizing compensation in gold or dollars. However, these European attempts failed, mainly because countries quickly reached the maximum level of exchanges authorized without payment in gold or dollars and were then unable to purchase all the foreign items needed. The system then could not foster as great an expansion of intra-European trade as markets required. This payments crisis, coupled with political instability

[1] Concerning American international monetary plans see Gardner (1980) and Horsefield (1969).

[2] Concerning Western European trade and payments after the Second World War, see Milward (1987), Diebold (1952), and Triffin (1957).

and possible communist advances in Eastern Europe, France, and Italy, led the United States to assume a far greater share of the financial burden of European reconstruction through the Marshall Plan launched in mid 1947. Marshall aid would supply those funds for recovery which the IMF proved unable to provide.

The Marshall Plan, or European Recovery Program (ERP), was one of the most ambitious initiatives of the Truman administration: through the Marshall Plan, Truman sought to achieve a wealth of interrelated political and economic objectives.[3]

The Marshall Plan was designed to help the Western European countries cover their enormous foreign debts while pouring into those war-ravaged regions large quantities of badly needed commodities. It was a mechanism to circumvent the Europeans' lack of gold and dollar reserves and put Europe in a position to fulfill American plans for world-wide free trade and multilateral payments. But the Marshall Plan was far more than a solution to payments problems. It would also inject capital for productive investments and planned modernization of the European industrial apparatus. Coordinated European national plans would lead to integration of all Western European markets in a single unit that would favor high productivity, economies of scale, and efficient regional rationalization and specialization. In the process European workers' standards of living would be raised to American levels, thus leading them toward capitalism and away from revolutionary communist schemes. West Germany could also be reintegrated peacefully within the European community of nations, as the ERP would substitute for the reparations of the interwar period. European countries would have ample capacity to reconstruct and grow without exploiting the defeated ex-enemy. Germany in fact had to be rebuilt rapidly to become an anti-Soviet bastion in central Europe solidly anchored to Western Europe and the United States and to be the main motor of European prosperity.

These United States plans were ambitious, as they sought to solve a host of problems at one stroke. In many cases American plans had been devised without prior consultation with the European allies and were destined to meet resistance once voiced in Europe. American payments schemes suffered precisely that fate and were steadfastly opposed by the British and the French.

Great Britain sought to maintain the pound sterling as a major currency in international markets, especially through a continuation of the Commonwealth trading system and Imperial Preference. Britain's overseas

---

[3] On the Marshall Plan see Milward (1987); Hogan (1987); Wexler (1983). For Franco-American relations in particular see Wall (1991).

commitments conflicted with tighter European economic and political unity. In addition the British Labour government was committed to achieving and maintaining full employment, which stood in stark contrast to American demands concerning a payments system that might force domestic deflationary measures.[4]

In particular the British opposed a European integration scheme that might lead to loss of gold or dollars when effecting intra-European payments. Such a danger was posed by a 1948–9 intra-European payments provision called "drawing rights." Drawing rights were granted by creditor countries to their debtors on a bilateral basis to help cover deficits between pairs of countries. Drawing rights in turn were matched by "conditional aid," or ERP dollars extended to creditors in exchange for the unrequited intra-European credits. With their conditional aid, dollar creditors could then purchase goods in the dollar area. The system could become a problem for the British if, as the United States proposed, drawing rights were made transferable – usable in any of the ERP countries – or even convertible into gold or dollars. Had drawing rights been made transferable among the ERP countries, each country that held sterling surpluses would seek to use them to pay its debts where most necessary, chiefly in Belgium which held a large surplus because of its intra-European trade. That would make Belgium a holder of sterling balances surpassing the amounts it accepted to hold according to Belgian–British bilateral accords, thus compelling Great Britain to exchange this excess into gold or dollars, endangering Britain's overall reserve position.

The British and the Americans were then at odds. To the Americans transferability and/or convertibility of drawing rights was a stepping stone toward multilateralism. To the British it was a system leading to reserve depletion. Accusations were made that the British compromised European integration through their full-employment programs and Commonwealth commitments. But full employment was a national political imperative at the heart of Labour's platform that could not be relinquished. Labour was equally committed to preserving the independence of the sterling area, still the largest payments bloc in the world, and that independence and position of prestige appeared threatened by American attempts to drag Britain into a European payments system. As a consequence, Britain boycotted American integration plans, insisting on a system that would allow for a continuation both of Commonwealth ties

---

[4] This section on Britain is based on Milward (1984), pp. 265–81 and chapter 10; Triffin (1957), pp. 143–60, 209–18; Diebold (1952), pp. 15–110. In the French archival files cited below there is also a large number of papers that deal with Britain's position and her controversies with Belgium and the United States.

and of unimpaired British sovereignty in domestic economic policy making.

France too objected to American international monetary plans, though for different reasons. Her policy was national in character insofar as it purported to solve not only France's economic woes but also the "German problem." At the end of World War I France had demanded German reparations while attempting a return to the gold standard and a liberal economic policy. After World War II a *dirigiste* economic policy, at home and abroad, was chosen instead to provide the framework for a lasting European settlement. The novelty consisted in the belief that an overtly *dirigiste* economic course, nationally and internationally, would help resolve the decades-old problem of creating a Europe in which Germany could be "contained." This *dirigiste* policy would in many ways become France's answer to alternative European settlement plans sponsored by the American superpower which did not provide sufficient guarantees for French national security *vis-à-vis* Germany.[5]

As a consequence, starting in the early 1940s, the provisional Free French government (CFLN) devised plans for a post-war international monetary system which would neither be regulated by a gold standard nor reduce the overall volume of trade through bilateralism.[6] Indeed the best solution for French planners was a gradual and carefully planned move away from bilateral treaties and toward a multilateral trade and payments

---

[5] See Esposito (1991), pp. 117–40. While most historians have concentrated on France's domestic programs, in this chapter I showed that France's *dirigiste* choice also influenced international economic policy making.

[6] The following section on France's international monetary plans is based on these documents: "Note sur le problème monetaire français," May 21, 1942; "Suggestions Regarding an International Monetary System," undated; Archives of the French Ministry of Foreign Affairs (MAE), Guerre 1939–45, Alger CFLN-GPRF, 725. "Problèmes économiques d'après-guerre: un point de vue français," by Hervé Alphand, July 1942; "Rapport Préliminaire sur les questions économiques financières et sociales d'après-guerre," undated; MAE, Guerre 1939–45, Londres CNF, 174. "Note," October 8, 1942; MAE, Guerre 1939–45, Alger CFLN-GPRF, 1532. "Résumé du projet anglais et du projet américain," undated; MAE, Guerre 1939–45, Londres CNF, 175. "Note – a.s.: De certains aspects des problèmes économiques de l'après-guerre," October 1, 1943; MAE, Papiers 1940, Bureau d'études Chauvel, 159. "Note sur les négociations relatives à l'établissement d'un plan monétaire international," November 15, 1943; MAE, Guerre 1939–45, Alger CFLN-GPRF, 1194. "Note," March 25, 1943; MAE, Guerre 1939–45, Alger CFLN-GPRF, 1533. "Note sur les relations financières de la France avec l'étranger," February 18, 1946; "Note sur les relations financières de la France avec l'étranger," April 20, 1946; Letter from the French Ministry of Foreign Affairs to the French Ministry of Finance, Brunet, April 5, 1946; Brunet to Alphand, May 20, 1946; "Note No. 4 sur les accords de paiement," June 1, 1948; Archives of the French Ministry of Finance (AEF), B 33854. Horsefield (1969), III, pp. 97–102.

system more flexible than one regulated by the gold standard. The French envisioned the creation of an international institution endowed with extensive resources supplied by the world's creditor countries. This institution's capital would be used to provide substantial credits to countries ravaged by war and in debt, so that these countries could sustain large volumes of trade while not restricting their domestic consumption, but indeed while promoting growth. That went hand in hand with France's own Modernization and Equipment Plan (PME), the so-called Monnet Plan, whose aim it was to modernize the French economy.[7]

The French feared above all the possibility of competing as peers with a resurgent German economy and sought a European integration system through which they could gain a competitive advantage *vis-à-vis* Germany, especially in the sectors of coal and steel. To the French, economic integration was a way to bring West Germany back into the Western family of nations on French terms, terms that would allow French economic modernization targets to be achieved. Only if the French economy was modernized, in part by acquiring access on favorable terms coal and steel from the Ruhr, could France become a viable competitor with Germany.[8]

American integration plans, however, provided no guarantee of creating a favorable competitive position for France. On the contrary, both the Americans and the British were adamant that, in order to block Soviet encroachment in Europe, West Germany should be rebuilt quickly and made into the economic pillar of Western Europe. While not disagreeing with Germany's anti-communist role, France would accept an American-sponsored intra-European payments system that heightened the level of competitive risks and the possibility of gold and dollar losses only if guarantees against German competition were provided.

Between 1945 and 1948 France protected her economy and her currency in two ways: on the one hand, it maintained strict controls over the flow of goods and capital across her borders; on the other hand, it instituted a system of multiple exchange rates for the French franc designed to strengthen the terms of trade. Both systems, however, fell short of providing a definitive solution. What plans did the French then put forth in 1949 and 1950 in order to help resolve their own and Europe's trade and payments problems?

France favored trade liberalization reached in carefully planned stages.[9]

---

[7] See especially Kuisel (1981); Bloch-Lainé and Bouvier (1986); Mioche (1987).

[8] See Gillingham (1991); Milward (1987).

[9] The following section on French integration plans is based on these documents: "Note pour le Président," July 27, 1949; "Note pour le Président," December 13, 1949; "Projet d'exposé du délégué de la France en ce qui concerne la libération des échanges," January 25, 1950;

It called for transitional protection of firms that would become uncompetitive through liberalization – above all in order to shelter employment – and for safeguards in case liberalization caused an increase in a country's intra-European debts. Intra-European trade liberalization was to be managed by committees of European experts. These would help coordinate investments in order to promote integrated Europe-wide growth and discourage purely national projects. These supra-national committees would issue rules for fair competition: countries would be discouraged from adopting excessively deflationary policies that would lead to the dumping of products on European markets. They could be prohibited from using "double prices" – one price at home and another abroad in order to favor exports.

In particular, the French accused the West Germans of operating their economy in "abnormally" depressed conditions which might lead to a flood of German goods into French markets. The Germans, French policymakers charged, operated a system of double prices and dumped goods on other European markets, creating an unfair advantage for German producers. By setting precise rules of equitable intra-European competition, a supra-national agency would forbid unfair practices, and only then, the French maintained, could West Germany be allowed into a Western European trading bloc.

In short, the French authorities resisted an international or intra-European free trade mechanism based on the American model. European integration without safeguards was considered dangerous for French growth. Above all it might seriously imperil France's capability to compete with Germany. France wanted trade and payments liberalization, because

MAE, DE/CE 1945–60, vol. 351. "Projet de création d'un office des investissements," undated; "Projet de memorandum sur les accords prives de coopération," November 25, 1949; "Rapport du groupe de travail sur les accords prives de coopération industrielle, agricole et commerciale," December 1, 1949; "Note," December 5, 1949; "Projet – Rapport du Comité Financier," December 5, 1949; "Note pour le comité interministériel," January 7, 1950; MAE, DE/CE 1945–60, vol. 363. "Projet – Note (M. Guindey)," May 9, 1949; "Projet de directives pour la délégation française aux entretiens de Washington," August 25, 1949; Secret memorandum from Ministry of Foreign Affairs, November 14, 1949; French National Archives (AN), F60 ter, 469. Minister of Agriculture to President of the Council of Ministers, December 24, 1949; "Projet d'instructions aux negociateurs français," January 16, 1950; AN, F60 ter, 384. "Note sur les conditions financières nécessaires à la libéralisation des échanges," May 31, 1949; "Note pour le Ministre," October 28, 1949; "Problèmes du relèvement européen," October 29, 1949; Dispatch from French Ministry of Foreign Affairs, November 2, 1949; "Note sur la coopération européenne," January 9, 1950; "Thèses françaises sur la libération des échanges," January 31, 1950; "Note sur les principes posés par l'OECE pour la libération des échanges," July 1950; "Note pour Monsieur Filippi," July 24, 1950; AN, F60 ter, 383. "Note pour le Ministre," June 1, 1949; AEF, B 44810. "Note pour M. Bloch-Lainé," October 25, 1949; AEF, B 18675.

it alone could resolve France's economic problems and her relationship with Germany, but it had to be carefully managed from above according to France's *dirigiste* schemes.

Both the British and the French then set out to soften American demands. Both countries ultimately succeeded. In the end the European Payments Union established in 1950 provided a system whereby intra-European trade could operate more smoothly, as member countries' intra-European debts would no longer be bilateral but could be offset against one another, with the remaining debt or surplus outstanding against the EPU itself. Marshall aid would help cover the balance.

The sterling balances problem was resolved to the satisfaction of the British. The solution was made easier because Britain's intra-European trade balance began to improve dramatically between the end of 1949 and the beginning of 1950. Britain was shifting to creditor status which greatly reduced the possibility of gold and dollar losses. Accumulated sterling balances could now be used to pay for British goods coming to the Continent in larger quantities. Moreover, the Americans conceded "to make good any losses of gold or dollars that Britain suffered as a result of the use of sterling balances to cover their owners' net deficit with EPU."[10] Finally, sterling could be used to settle intra-European and other payments, strengthening sterling's international position and preserving its traditional role as an international currency.

France obtained concessions as well. Liberalization of trade would be gradual and would initially cover 60 percent of all products, then 75 percent, and finally 100 percent. Discrimination would be allowed against countries which either obstructed further liberalization or which dumped goods on other countries' markets. The EPU contained several safeguards to cushion the effects of trade liberalization while providing the means to increase intra-European trade, as France had sought. It must also be noted, as Alan Milward has pointed out, that France signed the EPU agreement only after the European Coal and Steel Community was created. The ECSC provided France with a measure of protection in her competition with Germany in the sectors of coal and steel through the creation of a supra-national agency to regulate prices and distribution.[11]

British and French priorities were therefore substantially preserved. The Americans were unable to force on them a multilateral trade and payments scheme that might endanger the success of their national economic policies. In order to rebuild Western Europe the United States

[10] Diebold (1952), p. 106.
[11] On the making of the ECSC, see Milward (1987) and Gillingham (1991).

needed British and French cooperation. Planning for a payments scheme without them had proved self-defeating. Yet by 1950 an EPU was in place that, thanks to Marshall aid, greatly aided in the solution of European payments.

2 Conditionality of aid in France and Italy

Marshall aid funding in each European country was accomplished primarily through the mechanism of "counterpart funds." Counterpart fund operations are an excellent example of how domestic politics could render futile the American donor's efforts to influence a recipient's economic policies.

Counterpart funds were local currency sums, in our case francs and lire, that European governments earned through the sale of goods sent by the American government without the requirement of payment in dollars under the provisions of the Marshall Plan. Counterpart funds were deposited in Special Accounts and could be used only with the consent of American Marshall Plan, or Economic Cooperation Administration (ECA), officials. Since the Americans had the power to block or authorize "releases" (withdrawals) from the Special Accounts, the counterpart fund system was one of the principal means through which the Americans tried to influence the economic policies of European governments.

In fact, the Americans could not use counterpart funds to successfully influence the domestic economic policies of either the French or Italians. While the Americans sought a delicate equilibrium between investment and financial stabilization in which economic growth would occur without excessive inflation, the French and Italian governments had different priorities and managed to pursue them unhindered. Nonetheless, counterpart funds helped achieve one of the most important American objectives in Europe: centrist, pro-American forces in both countries used the counterpart funds as a tool to consolidate their positions.[12]

[12] The following sections on France and Italy are based on Esposito (1994). The book is based on: 1) the ECA files at the United States National Archives, Record Group (RG) 469; these are generally telegrams – coded ECATO, TOECA, Torep, and Repto – memoranda or letters exchanged among American Marshall Plan officials or between the ECA and European officials or ministers; 2) records at the French National Archives (F60 ter series, or the papers of the French interministerial sub-committee which handled Marshall Plan affairs) and at the French Ministries of Foreign Affairs and Finance; and finally 3) records of the Italian Archivio di Stato (Presidency of the Council of Ministers) and of the Italian Ministry of Foreign Affairs.

The French case

In France, Marshall Plan officials had to contend above all with high rates of Monnet Plan investment that helped fuel powerful inflationary pressures.[13] Counterpart funds very soon became part of national economic

[13] In the context of this chapter the most relevant documents concerning France's case are: "Note sur la situation actuelle de la Trésorerie et son évolution probable jusqu'à la fin de l'année 1948," September 1948; "Note pour le Président," September 13, 1948; "Résumé des conversations se portant au déblocage d'Octobre 1948," undated; Document without title, October 29, 1948; Queuille to Bruce, November 4, 1948; "Quatrième déblocage (45 milliards)," November 24, 1948; Boyer to Wood, November 30, 1948; Boyer to Ledoux, December 1, 1948; "Note sur les conversations concernant le déblocage d'une partie de la contrevaleur en francs de l'aide américaine au titre du mois de Décembre," December 14, 1948; AN, F60 ter, 497. Bingham to Petsche, August 8, 1949; Bingham to Petsche, August 29, 1949; "Explanation of the Second Paragraph of Mr. Petsche's Letter of August 5, 1949," undated; Bingham to Petsche, September 29, 1949; "Projet Révisé," April 1949; "Renseignements relatifs au déblocage de la fin de l'année 1949," November 17, 1949; AN, F60 ter, 498. "Résumé des conversations," undated; Bruce to Queuille, November 4, 1948; Ledoux to Lamy, July 11, 1949; Petsche to Bingham, May 23, 1949; Petsche to Bingham, August 29, 1949; Petsche to Bingham, September 27, 1949; AN, F60 ter, 357. Schweitzer to Baraduc, November 24, 1948; "Note sur la politique du crédit," end November 1948; "Note sur l'application de l'Aide Marshall à la France," December 4, 1948; AN, F60 ter, 378. "Note sur la situation de la Trésorerie et son évolution probable au cours des trois derniers mois de l'année 1948," undated; "Note sur le programme gouvernemental dans le domaine financier," September 13, 1948; AEF, B 33507. Bruce to Queuille, December 3, 1948; AEF, B 33510, 1949. Berard to Schuman, September 28, 1948; MAE, B-Amérique, 1944–52, EU, 167. TOECA 1188, September 2, 1949; RG 469, ECA/OSR, Confidential (eyes only) Cables, box 1. TOECA 340, September 7, 1948; Torep 2639, January 3, 1949; RG 469, ECA/OSR, Adm. Serv. Div.-Comm. Rec. Sec., Country Files, box 16. TOECA 356, September 13, 1948; TOECA 551, December 29, 1948; TOECA 895, May 9, 1949; RG 469, ECA/OSR, Adm. Serv. Div.-Comm. Rec. Sec., Country Files, box 17. Queuille to Hoffman (and enclosed annexes A, B, C), September 25, 1948; Bruce to Queuille, September 27, 1948; TOECA 457, November 3, 1948; Queuille to ECA, December 28, 1948; RG 469, ECA/OSR, Adm. Serv. Div.-Comm. Rec. Sec., Country Files, box 18. "French Franc Counterpart Negotiations," July 22, 1949; ECATO 785, July 27, 1949; "French Treasury Operations in 1949," TOECA/Torep Dispatch 221, November 7, 1949; TOECA 1136, August 10, 1949; ECATO 803, August 5, 1949; TOECA 1280, October 13, 1949; William Tomlinson to Victor Abramson, November 15, 1949; "Statement for Discussion," November 17, 1949; TOECA 1416, November 29, 1949; "Introduction from National Advisory Council on Proposed Exchange of Letters," undated; TOECA/Torep Dispatch 273, December 19, 1949; RG 469, ECA/OSR, Adm. Serv. Div.-Comm. Rec. Sec., Country Files, box 70. Bruce to Hoffman, September 14, 1948; Hickerson to Labouisse, October 12, 1948; Labouisse to Assistant Chief of the Division of Commercial Policy (Moore), October 16, 1948; "Memorandum of Conversation, by the Secretary of State," November 18, 1948; United States Department of State, *Foreign Relations of the United States* (FRUS), 1948, vol. III (Washington, DC: United States Government Printing Office, 1974), pp. 649–82. TOECA 949, Reed to Hoffman, May 23, 1949; Bruce to Secretary of State, June 6, 1949; TOECA 1392, Bingham to Hoffman, November 21, 1949; ECATO 1057, from Foster, December 6, 1949; FRUS, 1949, vol. IV, pp. 645–86. Auriol (1974, 1977), vols. II and III.

overhaul plans, as they were employed in large proportion to cover the government's investment drive. But high rates of investment meant a precarious budget and soaring prices. Financial stability therefore appeared a distant and uncertain goal in 1948 when the Marshall Plan was launched.

As a consequence, American officials set their eyes on financial stabilization. They spent the better part of 1948 and 1949 attempting to push the French toward sounder budgets and stringent ceilings on credit and on advances from the Bank of France to the Treasury in order to contain and eventually defeat inflation. But while French authorities generally agreed that inflation should be kept under control, they continued to produce unbalanced budgets that marred the investment–financial stabilization balance sought by the Americans.

In these circumstances the Americans considered blocking counterpart fund releases. If counterpart funds were not released at all or were used to retire Treasury debt at the Bank of France, they would exert deflationary pressure and neutralize the French government's inability to contain prices. The Americans threatened that if financial stabilization measures were not adopted, counterpart funds would stay blocked in the Special Account.

The French government, however, succeeded in overcoming such threats and in obtaining releases on a regular basis. All American threats proved in vain because the French could threaten to obtain more advances from the Bank of France if counterpart funds were not released. All the French government had to do to obtain releases was to proffer promises of financial stabilization measures while arguing that such financial stabilization would never obtain if France had to resort to more advances.

The French authorities understood the perils of inflation.[14] Some

---

[14] "Rapport presenté au nom de la Commission du Bilan National," October 26, 1948; AEF, B 16020. "Note relative aux suggestions de M. Perrin," July 4, 1949; "Note pour le Ministre," July 8, 1949; AEF, B 16021. "Note pour le groupe de travail constitué par la Commission des Investissements," October 4, 1948; "Directeur du Trésor – Cabinet – Note pour le Ministre," undated; Document without title, December 13, 1948; Memorandum without title, December 21, 1948; "Note pour le Ministre," December 5, 1948; "Réductions successives apportées aux programmes d'investissements," December 13, 1948; "Modifications successives des programmes d'investissements pour 1949," undated; "Memorandum sur le Plan de Modernisation et d'Equipement," December 18, 1948; AEF, B 33507. "Commission des Investissements, Procès-verbal du 2 décembre 1948"; AEF, B 42268. "Grandes lignes d'une réforme monétaire française," November 22, 1948; "Sur le problème français," February 1949; AN, F60 ter, 378. "Note sur la politique de crédit," end November 1948; AN, F60 ter, 497. Letter to Lamy, Inspecteur des Finances from SGCIQCEE, January 5, 1949; "Note sur les critiques adressées au programme français 1949–50," January 8, 1949; AN, F60 ter, 357. "Note pour le Ministre (Projet-Secret)," January 16, 1949; "Papier de Wormser," March 11, 1949; AN, F60 ter,

investment and other cuts were imposed and more revenue was collected. However, the Monnet Plan, one of the chief causes of the deficit, basically remained in place with United States blessing: it was precisely the sort of plan that could lead France to economic self-sufficiency by 1952. As much as 48 percent of counterpart funds went to the PME.

Generally, then, the Americans released counterpart funds both to avoid inflationary financing of deficits and to keep French modernization plans on track.

But the most important factor inducing the Americans to release counterpart funds was the fragility of France's centrist coalition. Counterpart fund blockages and monetization could lead not only to inflation but also to economic collapse that might bring about the fall of the French centrist government. Coalition alternatives would have had to include, in order to reach a parliamentary majority, either the communists or General de Gaulle's followers. The former were anathema to the Americans and the latter nearly as undesirable, given the bad relations that had always existed between de Gaulle and the United States. The French centrist cabinets of 1948–50 were the type of "middle-of-the-road" coalitions that the Americans preferred, committed as they were to good relations with Washington and to French recovery. Counterpart fund blockages then would do more harm than good from a political point of view. Indeed, the ECA released funds in order to save the government from political collapse quite regularly between 1948 and 1950. The French government, aware of the weak bargaining position of the Americans, mooted more than once the specter of a communist or Gaullist-led cabinet, and proceeded to cover budget gaps, and especially productive investment expenditures, with counterpart funds it knew it could obtain with relative ease.

The Americans were aware of the necessity of throwing their support behind the French centrist coalition, and the lack of palatable political alternatives became a widely admitted political obstacle to the effectiveness of the counterpart fund mechanism. By the end of 1949 France clearly had profited greatly from counterpart funds and the Marshall Plan in general. Spectacular production growth had started, inflation was at least temporarily under control, and the communist left was on the defensive: American aid had helped sustain tottering centrist coalitions and reinforced France's role in the Western anti-communist effort.

388. Chauvel to Bonnet, January 5, 1949; MAE, Papiers d'Agents, Henri Bonnet, vol. I. Bloch-Lainé and Bouvier (1986), pp. 156–9.

The Italian case

In Italy the economic policy situation encountered by American Marshall Plan officials was nearly opposite that of France.[15] In Italy there was no emphasis on economic modernization, but rather on the necessity of achieving financial stability. Economic overhaul and reforms were envisioned by the Christian Democratic-dominated cabinets but would take place only once financial stability was achieved. This prudent course was dictated by Italy's weak international position as an ex-fascist power allied to Nazi Germany: there was no place for ambitious modernization schemes as in France, but only for a return to international respectability, for which American friendship was fundamental. Italy's prudent economic course was also determined by resentment against fascist economic policies. Mussolini's regime had intervened extensively in the Italian economy, with meager results. At the end of the war, liberal economists and businessmen called for strict limits on government intervention.

The party of sound finance was dramatically reinforced in 1947 when the government adopted a drastic recipe to strangle an apparently uncontrollable inflation. Results were immediate. By severely curtailing bank credit and cutting budgetary expenses at the same time, widespread dumping of speculative stockpiles took place, and prices plummeted. In the space of a few months inflation was tamed, but not without suffering: the number of the unemployed soared to well above two million and would remain a major concern for years to come. In political terms the crushing of inflation in 1947 was a major victory for the Christian Democrats: middle-class savings and purchasing power had been restored. Bourgeois voters gave overwhelming support to the Christian Democrats in the elections of April 1948. Deflationary policies had become inextricably tied to middle-class support for the government, reinforcing the latter's willingness to continue its policy of financial stabilization for several more years. Counterpart funds became part of the government's deflationary efforts as soon as Marshall Plan operations started in 1948. The Italians decided to invest their counterpart funds at a slow pace, because a rapid injection of these funds in the economy might lead to a resumption of inflation.[16]

---

[15] De Cecco (1972), pp. 156–80; Bottiglieri (1984a, 1984b); Giovagnoli (1982); Harper (1986); Baget-Bozzo (1974); Possenti (1978); Einaudi and Goguel (1952); Mammarella (1964).

[16] The following section on counterpart funds in Italy is based on chapters 5–7 of Esposito (1994). The most relevant documents are: "Serious Situation Prevalent in Italy," Ozer to Shishkin, June 22, 1949; RG 469, ECA/OSR, Adm. Serv. Div.-Comm. Rec. Sec., Country Files, box 38. "Excerpts from Conversations and Aide Memoires Concerning the Use of

These circumstances created difficulties and considerable confusion among the Americans. While American officials in Washington greatly appreciated Italian efforts to achieve financial stability, Marshall Plan officials in Rome instead maintained that inflation was under control and that Italian economic policy was too cautious: higher investment rates were in order. The Americans therefore presented a divided front.

Italian Local Currency Counterpart," September 30–October 12, 1948; RG 469, ECA/OSR, Adm. Serv. Div.-Comm. Rec. Sec., Country Files, box 39. "Minutes of Meeting held at 11.30 hrs., July 12, 1948, between Mr. Zellerbach and the Hon. Campilli"; "Meeting for Discussion of the Italian program, Viminale Palace, Rome," September 11, 1948; "Meeting between Messrs. Zellerbach and Tremelloni, November 16, 1948," November 17, 1948; Zellerbach to Harriman, November 19, 1948; TOECA 385/Torep 240, November 18, 1948; Freudenthal to Hoffman, December 17, 1948; Zellerbach to Pietromarchi, December 16, 1948; Repto 177, December 29, 1948; Marget to Harriman, November 15, 1948; "Comment on Your Memo of November 10, 1948; Procedure on Release of Lire Counterpart," Harriman to Marget; Kamarck to Marget, December 4, 1948; Marget to Kamarck, December 13, 1948; TOECA 292/Torep 157, October 9, 1948; ECATO 247, October 9, 1948; ECATO 273/Torep 1719, November 2, 1948; "Memorandum of Conversation: Prime Minister Alcide De Gasperi and Minister James D. Zellerbach, Viminale Palace, November 4, 1948; 12:00 to 12:25 p.m."; "Points in Financial and Monetary Program on Which Firm Commitment Should Be Requested from the Prime Minister," "Stated Policy of Italian Government on Fiscal, Monetary and Budgetary Equilibrium and Tax Reform," and "Program of the Italian Government for the Maintenance of Financial Stabilization and Monetary Equilibrium" are all three undated and attached to memorandum, Foster to Marget, Brewer, Bonsal, Arthur, October 28, 1948; Marget to Harriman, December 21, 1948; "Statement of Program of the Italian Government for the Maintenance of Financial Stabilization and Monetary Equilibrium," undated document attached to Zellerbach to Hoffman, December 14, 1948; TOECA 474/Torep 331, December 27, 1948; Torep 2677, January 5, 1949; Brewer to Botwin, December 8, 1948; "Use of Lire Counterpart Fund in Italy," Carter de Paul to Chief of Finance Division, December 27, 1948; Repto 2148, January 4, 1949; Repto 2167, January 5, 1949; ECATO 409/Torep 2736, January 7, 1949; TOECA 499/Torep 353, January 7, 1949; Torep 303, December 16, 1948; TOECA 678/Torep 527, February 21, 1949; TOECA 645/Torep 496, February 18, 1949; Hoffman to Zellerbach, January 11, 1949; ECATO 517/Torep 3423, February 18, 1949; ECATO 519/Torep 3432, February 19, 1949; "Memorandum of Telephone Conversation between Mr. Bissel (Washington Calling Party) and Ambassador Foster (Paris)," February 19, 1949; Torep 847, May 14, 1949; Torep 197, October 27, 1948; Albert O. Hirschman, "Report on Italy: Recovery or Stagnation?," December 1948; RG 469, ECA/OSR, Adm. Serv. Div.-Comm. Rec. Sec., Country Files, box 40. US Rome Embassy Telegram 947, April 2, 1949; RG 469 ECA/OSR, Adm. Serv. Div.-Comm. Rec. Sec., Country Files, box 41. "Resume of Conversation between Mr. De Gasperi and Mr. Zellerbach, on October 12, 1948, at 12:00 hours"; RG 469, ECA/OSR, Central Secretariat, box 6. "Sull'utilizzo del Piano Marshall" and "Piano Marshall," undated memoranda attached to document dated June 12, 1948; Fanfani to De Gasperi, June 12, 1948; "Appunto per il Presidente del Consiglio – Oggetto: Colloquio Harriman Tremelloni," June 12, 1948; Italian national archives (Archivio Centrale dello Stato, ACS), Pres. Cons., Segr. Part. De Gasperi, 1945–53, b. 21, f. 162. ECA (1949); Kaplan (1949).

The Italian government received contradictory demands for several months and took advantage of American indecisiveness to pursue its own course. Since the Americans were pushing for investment one day and for financial stability the next, it was relatively easy for the government to sit on its counterpart funds and continue to enforce deflationary measures. Only in early 1949 did Washington ECA officials come to realize that their colleagues in Rome had been right: the Italian government had to be pushed forcefully in the direction of investments. But eight months of Marshall Plan operations had been wasted without a visible improvement in the Italian economy other than price containment. Hardly any counterpart funds had been invested.

Consequently in early 1949 a second phase in counterpart fund negotiations began. Now the Americans insisted upon investments. One of the principal American requests was that the Italians prepare a detailed and comprehensive investment budget with the aim of increasing production and productivity, absorbing unemployment, and raising standards of living so that the Italian economy would grow at a fast pace and become independent of United States aid by 1952. Counterpart funds would provide the financial means with which to carry out investments. But there was a problem. The Italians had no intention or ability to prepare such a plan. Counterpart fund investments continued at a lethargic pace.[17]

The situation began to change substantially only between late 1949 and

[17] Katz to Zellerbach, July 13, 1949; TOECA 1285/Torep 1054, July 16, 1949; "Procedure for Project Review of Counterpart Proposals in Italy," August 12, 1949; ECA/Washington Repto 4026/Rome Repto 422, May 4, 1949; ECATO 1069/Torep 7106, August 16, 1949; De Gasperi to Zellerbach, July 27, 1949; De Gasperi to Zellerbach, September 27, 1949; Zellerbach to De Gasperi, September 21, 1949; Dayton to Harriman, September 29, 1949; ECATO 1012/Torep 6615, July 22, 1949; ECATO 1072/Torep 7127, August 16, 1949; TOECA 1325/Torep 1092, July 29, 1949; ECATO 383/Torep 3224, April 19, 1950; RG 469, ECA/OSR, Adm. Serv. Div.-Comm. Rec. Sec., Country Files, 1948–9, box 77. "Political Repercussions of Present ECA Project Review Procedure," Dunn to Zellerbach, July 26, 1949; RG 469, ECA/OSR, Central Secretariat, Country Files, 1948–1952, box 6. Torep 830, May 11, 1949; RG 469, ECA/OSR, Adm. Serv. Div.-Comm. Rec. Sec., Country Files, box 40. "Status of the Lire Fund Program as of 30 September 1949," October 7, 1949; "Report on Progress Made from 1 January 1949 to 30 September 1949 in Carrying out Italian Government's Program for Maintenance of Financial Stabilization and Monetary Equilibrium Adopted by CIR on 23 November 1948," October 7, 1949; "Memorandum on Monetary and Financial Stability Presented by the Italian Government," document attached to "Progress by Italian Government in Its 'Program for the Maintenance of Financial and Monetary Stability'," Kamarck to Dayton, January 10, 1950; RG 469, ECA/OSR, Progr. Div.-Country Desk Sec., Country Files, box 11. Italian Washington Embassy Telegram, 3171, April 2, 1949; "Piano Marshall. Progetti industriali. Apparecchi aeronautici," May 5, 1949; Italian Ministry of Foreign Affairs, Archivio Storico (ASMAE), DGAP 1946–50, Stati Uniti, 19.

early 1950. The turning point had to do not so much with American pressures as with mounting domestic protests against the stagnating economy. In 1949 several groups had begun to mount a campaign against the government. Direct opposition was exercised by some of the smaller parties in the governmental coalition, such as the Social Democrats, and by the left wing of the Christian Democratic party. Outside high-level policy-making circles, pressure on the government was expressed in violent riots and land seizures by impoverished peasants, especially in the South. These groups demanded an end to the deflationary course, high investment for economic growth, and radical agrarian and fiscal reform. With the formation of a new cabinet in early 1950, a more expansionary course was adopted.[18]

American ECA officials, however, failed to take advantage of the new situation. They never showed sufficient political ruthlessness to support left-wing Christian Democrats who promised to push the government toward more aggressive investment plans. The Americans could not find any political force that would be as pro-American and anti-communist as the moderate Christian Democratic leadership that was committed to financial stabilization and to the middle-class support that was its reward. The Americans felt compelled to continue supporting a government whose economic policies were contrary to the Americans' own preferences because they saw no satisfactory political alternatives. In so doing the Americans virtually forfeited the possibility of exercising more forceful and direct pressure for investment.

But during the first six months of 1950, owing to domestic political pressures from the left and from southern peasants, the government began to speed up investment and reform. Counterpart funds were spent at a faster rate. The Americans were pleased that many of the counterpart funds

[18] ECATO 71/Torep 648, January 22, 1950; RG 469, ECA/OSR, Progr. Div.-Country Desk Sec., Country Subject Files, 1950–1, box 10. US Rome Embassy Telegram 267, received January 25, 1950; "Italian Monetary and Financial Review, First Quarter 1950," Report No. R-178, July 18, 1950; "Status of the Lire Fund Program as of 31 July, 1950," Memorandum 1–17, August 2, 1950; RG 469, ECA/OSR, Progr. Div.-Country Desk Sec., Country Files, box 10. TOECA 164/Torep 171, February 7, 1950; RG 469, ECA/OSR, Central Secretariat, Country Files, 1948–52, box 6. TOECA 339/Torep 367, March 15, 1950; TOECA 470/Torep 493, April 13, 1950; RG 469, ECA/OSR, Progr. Div.-Country Desk Sec., Country Subject Files, 1950–1, box 11. "Counterpart Release Level for 1950–1951 and Its Relation to Italian Internal Financial Stability," June 19, 1950; RG 469, ECA/OSR, Progr. Div.-Country Desk Sec., Country Files, box 11. "Monthly Report for February 1950, Italian Mission," No. D-43, March 15, 1950; RG 469, ECA/OSR, Labor Info. Div.-Off. Dir., Country Files, 1948–51, box 11. TOECA 470/Torep 493, April 13, 1950; Report No. R-161, May 18, 1950; RG 469, ECA/OSR, Adm. Serv. Div.-Comm. Rec. Sec., Country Files, box 78. Tamburri (1979), pp. 47–8; Kogan (1966), pp. 58–61.

invested in the South were used for public works, such as building roads and aqueducts. Still, all the investments of the first half of 1950 were made without the aid of the comprehensive investment plan requested by Marshall Plan authorities.

The progress of early 1950 was halted suddenly when the Korean War broke out in June. Prices began to soar; the threat of inflation had returned. In the emergency atmosphere of the summer, several Italian ministers argued that a return to the cautious course of 1948–9 was advisable. The Americans instead continued to push for investment, but with a twist: Italy now should invest in the military sector. All American pressures, however, continued to be in vain. The partisans of deflation pushed successfully for caution. While higher levels of economic activity later i 1951 were produced by favorable global conditions, the government continued with financial stabilization. Italy did not prepare a comprehensive plan for economic overhaul until 1953–4. As in France, the Americans proved unable to use counterpart funds as an effective tool to modify Italian economic policy.[19]

The counterpart fund weapon proved ineffective both in France and Italy. But this conclusion does not imply that the Marshall Plan was a failed policy. In both France and Italy, counterpart funds and Marshall aid in general helped achieve one major objective, the consolidation of pro-American centrist forces. In the French case the government's economic policy and very survival rested on the ability to rescue the French Treasury periodically with the injection of counterpart funds. In the Italian case, controlling inflation was necessary to maintain the support of middle-class Christian Democratic voters, and counterpart funds undoubtedly helped, as the Italian government essentially used them to exert deflationary pressures by keeping them stored in the Special Account. Later, when political protest mounted, counterpart funds became a tool for investing in public works projects and appeasing peasant and left-wing demands to relieve unemployment.

[19] *New York Times*, October 3, 1950, 1:6, 7:6, 19:5; October 5, 1950, 21:5; October 6, 1950, 2:8; October 10, 1950, 4:5; October 22, 1950, 39:3; October 23, 1950, 7:4; October 26, 1950, 20:4; October 28, 1950, 3:5. Pacciardi to De Gasperi, November 24, 1949; Pacciardi to De Gasperi, May 5, 1950; AS, Pres. Cons. Min., Segr. Part. De Gasperi, 1945–53, b. 25, f. 199. Dunn to Acheson, November 27, 1950; Acheson to US Embassy in Rome, December 2, 1950; FRUS, 1950, vol. III, pp. 1500–2. Harlan Cleveland to Leon Dayton, October 20, 1950; RG 469, ECA/OSR, Progr. Div.-Country Desk Sec., Country Files, box 10. "'Business and Industry in the Struggle against Communism,' Speech by Mr. Dayton Before the American Chamber of Commerce for Italy – Genoa Branch, October 19, 1950"; RG 469, ECA/OSR, Info. Div.-Pol. Plan. Sec., Country Files, box 7.

In terms of communist containment and the consolidation of moderate pro-American forces, American aid was key. The fact that the Americans were compelled to support French and Italian governments which shunned American economic priorities is proof not so much of overall American failure as of the overwhelming importance the Americans attached to political consolidation. This political victory, however, produced paradoxical results: the French and Italian centrist governments knew the Americans "needed" them and took full advantage to pursue policies of their own. American objectives could not be attained when the United States could not count on the recipient governments' cooperation.

3 The lessons of Marshall aid

What conclusions might we then draw in the context of the economic woes of today's Eastern Europe and former Soviet Union?

First of all, we have seen that the IMF system was inadequate to cope with the disrupted European payments situation and that an extraordinary package of aid had to be put forth by the United States. Thus, the Marshall Plan "rescued" the Western European nations from the stringent demands for financial stability made by the IMF.[20] The ERP was an American admission that, for political reasons, it was not advisable to pursue the IMF's austerity course. At the core of the Marshall Plan was the idea that "to win the peace," economic and therefore political stability in Europe were crucial. Ultimately, payments problems could only be resolved through economic growth, modernization, and a return to international competitiveness. As a consequence, carefully planned investments had to accompany financial stabilization measures.

Today, however, by its own nature as an international payments agency, the IMF again proposes austerity measures as a solution to the current problems of Eastern Europe and former Soviet Union. Moreover, some Western economic experts have encouraged "shock therapy" – the rapid introduction of market forces in an ex-communist economy – which Poland in particular adopted whole-heartedly in January 1990. But a comparison between the Polish and Czech experiences is illuminating. The Czechs, who rejected austerity and "shock therapy" and chose a slower path to capitalism, have been able to avoid hardship, while their economy is now booming. Granted, they had some historical advantages. One cannot help but wonder, however, whether Poland could not have done the same. Instead millions of Poles have been thrown into poverty owing

---

[20] The historian who has advanced this argument most forcefully is Milward (1987).

to their government's belief that introducing market mechanisms over-night would set Poland on the road to prosperity. It comes as no surprise that at the Polish elections in 1993 the winners were the former communist party.

Today the IMF austerity course is being pursued by countries which do not have the possibility of rejecting it or seeking concessions, as the British and the French could after World War II. It would seem wiser for the West to encourage the former communist economies to cooperate in the development of investment plans, drawn up with the emerging private sector and taking into account the payments' positions and established trade patterns of each partner. There are new nations, such as Ukraine, which cannot cope without cooperation from Russia. There are few plans, however, emanating from the IMF or elsewhere, to foster intra-East European economic cooperation.[21]

Moreover, the West appears to be committing the same mistakes American officials made in the late 1940s when planning for an intra-European payments system. We are substantially ignoring the *national* priorities of Eastern European and ex-Soviet Republics. This is a mistake because, above all, it can drive those countries to dangerous forms of *revanchisme*. The purpose of taking their national economic priorities into consideration is not a sort of "appeasement" but to help forge a consensus on economic programs to which aid recipients would be willing to commit themselves.

We have also seen that in Italy internal American divisions concerning what course to follow prevented the ECA from exerting effective pressure on the Italian government. Some in the Truman administration were more in favor of "planning" than others. That kind of problem is only too likely to repeat itself today and in a magnified form. Today there cannot be only one donor. Several Western countries and Japan would have to contribute together. Internal divisions will be inevitable. It would appear best to open a debate concerning a possible *collective* aid package for the Eastern European and ex-Soviet Republics. If aid recipients perceive divisions among donors, they might be tempted to exploit those disagreements politically. Though in a different context, that of civil war, the populations of the ex-Yugoslavia have demonstrated how easy it is to exploit differences of opinion among the Western powers. A *collective* Western (and Japanese) effort is essential.

Finally, both the French and Italian cases show the perils of attaching

[21] See Köves (1992), esp. pp. 108–11; Barre *et. al.* (1992), pp. 39–41; Keren and Ofer (eds.) (1992).

aid to the political support of one particular political group or set of men. It was the fear of weakening pro-American governments that compelled United States officials to act in support of those governments, even when doing so meant accepting those governments' national economic agendas. While in France it might have been quite difficult to support other groups, in Italy there were democratic forces willing to push for planning. But U.S. political squeamishness, or narrow mindedness, prevailed when those forces were judged less than wholeheartedly pro-American. Surely such a choice did not strengthen the democratic process in Italy. It would seem far wiser to thrust support behind a program than behind any political coalition or group.

Thus, the United States and its Western allies have not been well advised in lending all their support to Russian President Boris Yeltsin. Regardless of Yeltsin's merits or faults, supporting him personally does not foster a truly democratic grassroots movement or further economic recovery in Russia. If Yeltsin falls from power the West would be left without interlocutors, or with non-democratic and hostile ones.

All in all, Marshall Plan experience suggests that aid can achieve important political results, and that it can do so when the donors present a united front in support of a democratic program of economic recovery that takes into account recipient countries' national priorities and seeks to promote collegial solutions. A narrower approach like that of the IMF today has less chance of political and economic success.

References

Auriol, Vincent (1974, 1977), *Journal de septennat, 1947–1954*, unabridged edition, vols. II and III, Paris: Librairie Armand Colin.

Baget-Bozzo, Gianni (1974), *Il partito cristiano al potere: la DC di De Gasperi e di Dossetti, 1945–1954*, Florence: Vallecchi.

Barre, Raymond *et al.* (1992), *Moving Beyond Assistance*, New York, Prague: Institute for East–West Studies.

Bloch-Lainé, François and Jean Bouvier (1986), *La France restaurée, 1944–1954: dialogue sur les choix d'une modernisation*, Paris: Fayard.

(1952), *Lo sviluppo dell'economia italiana nel quadro della ricostruzione e della cooperazione europa*, Rome, Istituto Poligrafico dello Stato.

Bottiglieri, Bruno (1984a), *La politica economica dell'Italia centrista, 1948–58*, Milan: Comunità.

(1984b), "Tra Pella e Vanoni: la politica economica degli ultimi governi de Gasperi," *Storia Contemporanea*, 14(4) (August): 781–839.

De Cecco, Marcello (1972), "Economic Policy in the Reconstruction Period,

1945–51," in S.J. Wood (ed.), *The Rebirth of Italy, 1943–50*, London: Longman, pp. 156–180.

Diebold, William Jr. (1952), *Trade and Payments in Western Europe: A Study in Economic Cooperation, 1947–51*, New York: Harper & Brothers.

ECA (1949), *Italy, Country Study*, Washington, DC: United States Government Printing Office.

Einaudi, Mario and François Goguel (1952), *Christian Democracy in Italy and France*, Notre Dame, Ind.: University of Notre Dame Press.

Esposito, Chiarella (1991), "French International Monetary Policies in the Late 1940s," *French Historical Studies*, 17(1) (Spring): 117–40.

(1994), *America's Feeble Weapon: Funding the Marshall Plan in France and Italy, 1948–1950*, Westport, Conn.: Greenwood Press.

Foreign Relations of the United States (FRUS) (1948, 1949), United States Department of State, Washington DC: United States Government Printing Office.

Gardner, Richard (1980), *Sterling–Dollar Diplomacy in Current Perspective: The Origins and the Prospects of Our International Economic Order*, New York: Columbia University Press.

Gillingham, John (1991), *Coal, Steel, and the Rebirth of Europe, 1945–1955: The Germans and the French from Ruhr Conflict to Economic Community*, Cambridge University Press.

Giovagnoli, Agostino (1982), *Le premesse della ricostruzione – Tradizione e modernità nella classe dirigente cattolica del dopoquerra*, Milan: Nuovo Istituto Editoriale Italiano.

Harper, John L. (1986), *America and the Reconstruction of Italy, 1945–1948*, Cambridge University Press.

Hogan, Michael J. (1987), *The Marshall Plan: America, Britain, and the Reconstruction of Western Europe, 1947–1952*, Cambridge University Press.

Horsefield, J. Keith (1969), *The International Monetary Fund, 1945–1965: Twenty Years of International Monetary Cooperation*, Washington, DC: IMF.

Kaplan, Jacob J. (1949), *Economic Stagnation in Italy*, New Haven, Conn.: Yale Institute of International Studies.

Keren, Michael and Gur Ofer (eds.) (1992), *Trials of Transition: Economic Reform in the Former Communist Bloc*, Boulder, Colorado: Westview Press.

Kogan, Norman (1966), *A Political History of Postwar Italy*, New York: Praeger.

Köves, Andràs (1992), *Central and Eastern European Economies in Transition: The International Dimension*, Boulder, Colorado: Westview Press.

Kuisel, Richard F. (1981), *Capitalism and the State in Modern France: Renovation and Economic Management in the Twentieth Century*, Cambridge University Press.

Mammarella, Guiseppe (1964), *Italy After Fascism: A Political History, 1945–1963*, Montreal: Mario Casalini Ltd.

Milward, Alan S. (1984), *The Reconstruction of Western Europe, 1954–1951*, Berkeley: University of California Press.

Mioche, Philippe (1987), "Le Plan Monnet: genèse et élaboration, 1941–1947," Diss., Université de Paris I.

Possenti, Paolo (1978), *Storia della DC dalle origini al centrosinistra*, Rome: Ciarrapice Editore.

Tamburri, Gianni (1979), "La politica negli anni cinquanta," in Fillippo Peschiera (ed.), *Sindacato industria e stato negli anni del centrismo*, vol. II:I, Florence: Le Monnier, pp. 1–127.

Triffin, Robert (1957), *Europe and the Money Muddle: From Bilateralism to Near-Convertibility, 1947–1956*, New Haven, Conn.: Yale University Press.

Wall, Irwin M. (1991), *The United States and the Making of Postwar France, 1945–1954*, Cambridge University Press.

Wexler, Imanuel (1983), *The Marshall Plan Revisited: The European Recovery Program in Economic Perspective*, Westport, Conn.: Greenwood Press.

Part III

Other international initiatives

4 The IMF and the creation of the Bretton Woods System, 1944–58

HAROLD JAMES

Faced with a task of immense complexity, we often search for historical parallels. Currently, two contrasting approaches are offered to the problem of economic reform in East European and former Soviet republics and their integration into the world economy. On the one hand, there is full and rapid international integration (with multilateral trading practices and immediate currency convertibility), on the other, a regional approach (with regional trade preferences, and non-convertible currencies grouped in a clearing union).

In arguments against sudden "big bang" transitions to full convertibility, the example of post-war Europe is frequently cited (see the discussion of Polak, 1991; van Brabant, 1991; Williamson, 1991). European states did not return to convertibility on current account transactions until after 1958, thirteen years following the end of World War II. Yet they provided the most convincing example in all of economic history of an "economic miracle." Do they in fact give a historical argument against quick convertibility?

While advocates of the multilateral approach emphasized Bretton Woods and the Marshall Plan, the regionalist approach saw the European Payments Union as the key institution in the international restructuring of Western Europe. Alan Milward (1984) examined the development of trade policy and argued that the drive to European integration came not so much from American pressures or from the European Recovery Program (Marshall Plan) but from French, Belgian, and German calculations of national interest. DeLong and Eichengreen(1993) in reinterpreting the history of ERP have claimed that the global aspects of the post-war system (the Bretton Woods institutions) cannot really hold the key to the post-war European miracle, since this was also the time when Latin American

The research for this chapter was supported by the International Monetary Fund. The opinions presented in this paper are those of the author alone and do not represent those of the IMF.

growth lagged relatively. Kaplan and Schleiminger (1989) have written the story of liberalization of currencies in the 1950s through a narrative of the European Payments Union.

This debate between globalists and regionalists should not be allowed to obscure two important characteristics of the European post-war recovery. In the First place, not all attention should be devoted to the institutional environment. As Kindleberger (1967) and Postan (1964) in particular pointed out some time ago, there were powerful non-institutional reasons for recovery. The labor market had turned around completely from the prewar period, with the new availability of large supplies of labor from Eastern Europe (in the German case), or from the countryside, and later from North Africa (for France), or from the South of Italy. A new combination of labor and capital provided a precondition for rapid economic growth that did not depend for its primary impetus on imports of foreign capital.

Secondly, at the institutional level, there are links between regional issues and global developments. The regionalization of the 1930s and the creation of *Grosswirtschaftsräume* and Co-Prosperity Spheres had taken place in the context of a disintegrating world economy. Though, as will be discussed, there were tensions between the EPU and the global institutions, the universal framework imposed limitations on regionalism and over time altered its character and helped to make it more universalist. The most rapid progress toward liberalization only took place after the global institutions had been strengthened.

The first part of this chapter examines the tensions between regionalism and globalism and shows how at some times, as in 1947 and 1949, they impeded development; and how, at other moments, and especially between 1956 and 1958, the interplay facilitated the expansionary dynamic of the European and world economies. The decisive debates about the nature of the international financial order for the first ten years of the post-war period fundamentally took place within the Anglo-American world that had produced the Bretton Woods accord in the first place. Bretton Woods meant the attempt to reconcile a general and global conception of the functioning of international monetary institutions as advocated by the US with a British resistance to the damage that might be imposed by immediate globalism on the war-ravaged economies of Europe, and in particular on the UK. The clash between differing US and UK visions did not end with the New Hampshire conference but remained a central and thorny problem for the next decade. The preference for globalism rather than regionalism was asserted by the US but was only realized at the end of the 1950s.

Secondly, the chapter explores another problematic characteristic of the

US position at Bretton Woods: its insistence on clearly defined limits to the functions of a global financial and regulatory agency and on the obligations to adjust of surplus countries. Britain, on the other hand, seeing the evolution of the world system from the standpoint of a probable long-term debtor, had a strong interest in avoiding such limits. The conflicts of debtor and creditor, which remained a perpetual element in the design and redesign of the international financial order, were at this time largely fought out between the US and the UK; and other European states then began to develop their own criticisms of American attempts to limit the activity and liability of the new international institutions. Finding an institutional mechanism for dealing with the clash of interests – and specifically the story of the development of the principle of the IMF stand-by arrangement – was a crucial part of reconciling the fundamentally opposed philosophies of economic management held at the beginning of the post-war epoch. The world economy needed an appropriate framework for global economic management.

The third goal of the chapter is to document a change in attitude toward capital flows. At the beginning, these were regarded as inherently destabilizing, and the Bretton Woods agreement explicitly limited capital account transactions in order to preserve national policy autonomy. By the end of the 1950s, increased capital flows had emerged as a feature of the world economy and provided a powerful stimulus for national economies to liberalize; at the same time, they produced temporary imbalances and liquidity shortages which required the facilities of a global agency which could supply additional liquidity.

Finally, the chapter includes a speculation about what might have been the consequences of an earlier transition toward global convertibility.

1

The Bretton Woods conference and the negotiations that preceded it constituted the first attempt to provide a sustained analysis of the world financial order as a system. Bretton Woods created a set of institutions designed to smooth the course of financial development and a code of conduct to make possible the orderly interaction of states. Most importantly, the settlement recognized at the political level the importance of multilateral trade to world economic development (and also to the maintenance of world peace).

There is a considerable ambiguity in many discussions of the Bretton Woods System. Most economics textbooks treat it primarily as a fixed parity exchange rate regime that lasted from 1945, 1958 or 1961 until the early 1970s (until 1971 or 1973 for American writers and 1972 for some

Europeans). Political science texts treat it as a multilateral trading order that is still with us, despite increasing protectionist pressures since the late 1970s. At the same time, the most authoritative historical account of post-war financial diplomacy concludes that Bretton Woods had died by 1947: "The founders of the Bretton Woods institutions had assumed that after a short period of post-war adjustment the world would move quickly toward political as well as economic equilibrium. On both counts this assumption was finally shattered in the spring of 1947" (Gardner, 1956, p. 293).

A system with such different potential terminal points appears as less than completely systematic. It might help to see Bretton Woods rather as a vision, parts of which were realized, while other parts faded into historical oblivion. The most obvious immediate achievements of Bretton Woods, the par value system of fixed exchange rates and the principle of currency convertibility, represented a dramatic break with the economic management methods of the 1930s. The new approach would only make sense within the framework of a much more general set of principles for treating the international financial order; and the instruments designed to secure the adoption of par values and to deal with resulting balance of payments problems could (and did) evolve into an institutional framework that could handle very different problems. (This, by the way, constitutes the fundamental difference with an institution such as the EPU, which had a specific task to perform and was redundant after the completion of that mission.)

At the most fundamental level, there was a liberal economic vision of the world, but it was coupled with a need to deal with an order in which individual nation-states were major players. Some commentators recognized the problem of the tension between globalism and national sovereignty – on the one side seemed to stand the historical figure of Adam Smith, on the other side Edmund Burke. Keynes's fellow Cambridge economist, D.H. Robertson, for instance, in 1941 welcomed Keynes's thoughts as a "growing hope that the spirit of Burke and Adam Smith is on earth again" (Harrod, 1971, p. 628). Keynes himself frequently spoke of the post-war arrangements as "an attempt to use what we have learned from modern experience and modern analysis, not to defeat, but to implement the wisdom of Adam Smith" (Moggridge, 1992, p. 817).

Two quite practical elements formed a part of the original Bretton Woods vision: first, the need to integrate different national policies into a coherent global order; and, secondly, the restraint on international capital movements that would, in the eyes of the makers of Bretton Woods, be needed for that international order to function. It was agreement on certain shared beliefs that made possible the wartime negotiations between the American proponents of the Stabilization Fund (chiefly, of course, Harry

Dexter White) and the British advocates of John Maynard Keynes's scheme for an International Clearing Union.

Both of the original plans surfaced roughly simultaneously during the war: the White plan was first formulated in late 1941, and Keynes had worked on drafts in the autumn of that year.

The first common element was the working out of the reconciliation of Burke and Smith: the practical desire to see a universal system that would encompass within a general framework nation-states with widely differing interests, policies, and approaches.

In the 1930s Keynes had acquired the reputation of being an economic nationalist. He had announced his approval of the New Deal in an article entitled "National Self-Sufficiency" because it applied the correct economics and ignored a world order still locked into false dogmas. The rejection of economic nationalism only came in wartime, mostly because the politics of the wartime alliance required a new kind of approach to issues to economic cooperation.

The use of economic nationalism for political ends had come to be identified with German policy (known as "Schachtianism" after Hitler's Economics Minister). Keynes had some sympathy for the Schachtian position even in 1941. In his memorandum on "Post-War Currency Policy" he wrote: "Dr Schacht stumbled in desperation on something new which had in it the germs of a good technical idea." The world needed "not a return to the currency disorders of the epoch between the wars . . . but a refinement and improvement of the Schachtian device" (Keynes, 1980, pp. 23–4). During the war, however, the US had made its opposition to Schachtianism clear. The State Department had long been campaigning against discriminatory British trade practices and against imperial preference. Any scheme that depended on American support would have to accept multilateralism. Britain had been obliged officially to accept this approach by Article VII of the 1941 Lend-Lease Agreement which provided for the "elimination of all forms of discriminatory treatment in international commerce, and the reduction of tariffs and other trade barriers."

But Keynes, who had been appalled by the original American draft of Article VII, believed firmly that any commitment to multilateralism should not stand in the way of domestic policies.

It appeared unlikely that after the war there could be any agreement on domestic economic strategies to be pursued in the member states of the new international financial order. Central planning had appeal not only in the USSR and those areas over which the USSR had a direct influence. French economists and politicians had developed a belief in *planisme* in response to the perceived failures of the 1930s. British parties committed themselves to the full-employment goals set out in Sir William Beveridge's plan and in his book *Full Employment in a Free Society* (London, 1945). In the eyes of the founders of Bretton Woods, all these economic philosophies required inclusion in any economic order that would be truly global. One result of this approach was that the extent to which the logic of the centrally planned economy was incompatible with the idea of a liberal global order was never satisfactorily worked out.

The British draft of April 1943 produced by Keynes stated: "There should be the least possible interference with internal national policies, and the plan should not wander from the international terrain. . . . The technique of the plan must be capable of application, irrespective of the type and principles of government and economic policy existing in the prospective member states." And White's version of April 1942 similarly claimed: "No restrictions as to membership should be imposed on the grounds of the peculiar economic structure adopted by any country" (Horsefield, 1969, II, pp. 19 and 72). The USSR took part in the conference, and the eventual Bretton Woods agreements were specifically designed to encompass centrally planned economies. Keynes was pleased that White's plan offered "the same or greater" concessions to national sovereignty (Moggridge, 1992, p. 687).

The accords reflected, however, not just an abstract commitment to the idea of national sovereignty in economic affairs: the expectation was that post-war states would have as their highest priority the objective of full employment. The chief Canadian negotiator at Bretton Woods, Louis Rasminsky, put the point most succinctly:

The International Monetary Fund is a new type of international monetary standard which seeks to reconcile the desire of all countries to carry out economic policies which are aimed at high levels of income and employment, with the desire of countries to have orderly international economic and monetary arrangements so that trade can go forward and take place to the benefit of all.
(House of Commons Standing Committee on Banking and Commerce, Testimony December 1945, p. 7)

In other words, Bretton Woods allowed the pursuit of national interventionist policies, for which the participants recognized there was pent-up demand, and sought to reconcile them with international stability. The agreements tried to make the post-war national cries for domestic economic regulation and management compatible with each other and with global stability. In the 1930s the most common argument against international cooperation was that made in 1933 by Keynes, that it stood as an obstacle to healthy domestic policies. The aim of the new system was to avoid such policy conflicts. As Keynes put it in 1943, it constituted "an attempt to reduce to practical steps certain general ideas belonging to the contemporary climate of economic opinion" (Horsefield, 1969, III, p. 21).

This insistence on the preservation of national sovereignty in economic affairs meant that the operation of the institutions should be tilted as far as possible in the direction of automaticity rather than discretion. Keynes's drafts in particular emphasized the automatic operation of the Fund and the easy availability of its resources. Such an approach raised problems in dealing with the USA, where many influential voices opposed the incurring of an automatic and virtually unlimited liability. The automaticity had a symmetry which not only meant access for countries with balance of payments problems but also the obligation of surplus countries (in practice, in the post-war period, this would mean the USA) to fund deficits.

A fund operating in this way would not be very political. Keynes had attempted to make the Bretton Woods institutions as free as possible from political pressures and for this reason opposed the siting of the Fund and the Bank in Washington. At the first Fund and Bank meeting at Savannah in March 1946, when the decision about location was taken, Keynes felt defeated and humiliated by what he believed to be the new politicization of the twin institutions. His final speech included a subsequently famous passage designed to make the point forcefully to the victorious American delegation:

I hope that . . . there is no malicious fairy, no Carabosse, whom he has overlooked and forgotten to ask to the party. For if so the curses which that bad fairy will pronounce will, I feel sure, run as follows: "You two brats shall grow up politicians, your every thought and act shall have an arrière pensée; everything you determine shall not be for its own sake or on its own merits but because of something else."

(Harrod, 1971, p. 748)

Treasury Secretary F.M. Vinson rightly took Carabosse to refer to him, and later complained that Keynes had called him a "fairy."

Politicization meant the end of a principle of automatic operation and the beginning of a policy of the Fund, based on conditions. This represented a development and alteration of the original design. The British proposals originally treated large debtor and creditor positions symmetrically and envisaged that both would be penalized. There has been a lively debate as to how far the notion of conditionality was present in the original Fund Articles of Agreement (Gold, 1979; Dell, 1981; Guitian, 1981; Diz, 1984). It was a doctrine originally suggested by the American negotiators, but their position was considerably modified in the course of negotiations. The US draft preamble of July 1943 stated: "The Fund would be influential in inducing countries to pursue policies making for an orderly return to equilibrium." In the final version, Article V, Section 5 on "Ineligibility to use the Fund's resources" laid down what would happen "whenever the Fund is of the opinion that any member is using the resources of the Fund in a manner contrary to the purposes of the Fund," and dropped the original phrase "purposes and policies." The implication was that the Fund was not a policy-making body, and would not impose specific conditions as a way of implementing those policies (Diz, 1984).

Britain later claimed that Article I, Section 5, referring to balance of payments adjustment "without resorting to measures destructive of national or international prosperity," had been introduced into the Articles of Agreement by Keynes in the autumn of 1943: "With a view to supporting by a specific statement in the purpose of the Fund our contention that the Fund would fail of one of its principal objectives if Members had to submit to 'policing' every time they wanted to draw on its resources."[1] At that time, White opposed Keynes's idea that members should be allowed to borrow their quota without any restriction, but explained that: "Supervision from the start of the use by members of their quotas was quite sound as no action would be taken except in cases of too rapid withdrawal of flagrant misuse of the funds obtained."[2]

Keynes's belief in the necessity of a de-politicization of the Fund had also been reflected in an important part of the American proposal, which British negotiators treated as a major British victory. Roy Harrod movingly reports his initial reaction to the US proposals on Clause 7 (the Scarce Currency Clause):

I was transfixed. This, then was the big thing . . . Now they had come forward and offered a solution of their own, gratuitously. This was certainly a great event. For it was the first time that they had said in a document, unofficial, it was true, and non-committal, but still in a considered Treasury document, that they would come in and accept their full share of responsibility when there was a fundamental disequilibrium of trade.   (Harrod, 1971, pp. 644–5)

The eventual drafting of Article VII of the Fund Articles of Agreement in fact did not conform to Harrod's (or presumably Keynes's) initial hopes. It made (and was designed to make) almost impossible any action by the deficit states to alter the policies of a country running apparently permanent surpluses (which meant in the immediate post-war future the US). The practical incapacity of the Fund ever to apply the Scarce Currency

[1] Bank of England (BoE) OV38/21, July 31, 1936, Thompson-McCausland to Grafftey-Smith.

[2] September 17, 1943 meeting.

Clause followed from the construction of its Articles. Section 3(b) of Article VII stated: "A formal declaration under (a) above shall operate as an authorization to any member, after consultation with the Fund, temporarily to impose limitations on the freedom of exchange operations with the scarce currency." But what did this mean? The next sentence added that "subject to the provisions of Article IV, Sections 3 and 4, the member shall have complete jurisdiction in determining the nature of such limitations." These two sections, when taken together, prohibited multiple cross-rates (4(b) allows transactions "only within the limits" of Section 3, where clause (i) allows movements open percent away from parity). This is in addition to Article VIII, Section 3 ("Avoidance of discriminatory currency practices").

The practice implied in the linking of Articles VII and IV became a real political issue in 1947–8. From the summer of 1947, the "dollar shortage" was discussed as the major international exchange problem; but it arose not out of a US depression but out of a dynamic European economy sucking in imports. In early 1948, France proposed and then carried out a devaluation coupled with an exchange rate system which imposed a penalty on imports from and a premium on exports to the dollar area. Since, it was argued in the Fund, there was no US depression, the Scarce Currency Clause was not applicable, France had behaved outside the rules of the Fund, and it remained ineligible to use Fund resources (this ban was lifted only in October 1954) (Horsefield, 1969, I, pp. 202–8).

In private, many Europeans came to the conclusion that the US would rather destroy the Fund than allow the Scarce Currency Clause to be used against the dollar. The French dispute arising out of the interpretation of the "scarce currency" provision had obvious implications for other European countries. It laid the ground for the so-called ERP decision, a few months later, which removed the Fund from the operation and administration of the Marshall Plan. With regard to access to Fund resources by non-European countries, a series of principles for conditionality were evolved. In 1949, in relation to an application for a drawing by Mexico, the US executive director laid out four "conditions": (1) par value approval; (2) that the disequilibrium was temporary; (3) that the drawing was not needed for rehabilitation or development; and (4) that the member was "undertaking all steps essential to assume as soon as possible its full obligations under the Articles of Agreement of the Fund, in particular, maintenance of convertibility, avoidance of restrictions on current payments, and avoidance of discriminatory currency arrangements and multiple currency practices" (Horsefield, 1969, I, p. 245). The assertion and victory of this viewpoint marked a defeat for the automatic conception of the Fund's activity. In 1950, the Dutch banker J.W. Beyen concluded that "automaticity was a dead horse" (Horsefield, 1969, I, p. 280). Such a result appeared for the moment to end much of the attraction of the Fund to non-Americans.

"Automaticity" had implied a further important principle. Keynes described it as "anonymity":

No particular member States have to engage their own resources as such to the support of other particular States or of any of the international projects or policies adopted. They have only to agree in general that, if they find themselves with surplus reserves which for the time being they do not themselves wish to employ, these resources may go into the general pool and be put to work on approved purposes.

(Horsefield, 1969, III, p. 34)

The USA, in other words, would not help a particular country or make political decisions about the size or use of such aid. The practice of post-war relief, and then of the ERP, was completely at odds with this principle and involved very specific US decisions on the level of support. Instead of being bound by a system of international agreements and law, the US could make policy and be political. In the context of the developing Cold War, American policymakers saw such a result as a necessary condition for their participation.

The second principle of Bretton Woods, which again was very widely shared by the economists and politicians who framed the new order, was a lesson drawn from the experience of the interwar depression. The new institutions were specifically created to prevent the recurrence of that economic trauma. Though debate about the causes of the depression remained controversial, by the time of Bretton Woods a broad explanatory consensus about the international features of the Great Depression had begun to emerge. This new consensus shifted the emphasis away from the favorite villains of 1930s literature – the uneven distribution of gold and the sterilizing policies of the Banque de France and the Federal Reserve System, the allegedly excessive monetary inflation of the 1920s, and structural weaknesses in major industrial centers. Rather the new view looked at the transmission process of depression and came to the conclusion that the large short-term capital flows of the 1920s and 1930s had led to disaster. These movements had made it impossible for states to pursue stable monetary policies, threatened exchange rate stability, and made fiscal stabilization highly hazardous.

This approach to the interwar economy oriented toward capital movements had been developed by League of Nations economists in the 1930s, and its most influential academic statement was Ragnar Nurkse's *International Currency Experience* (1944). "In the absence of international reserves large enough to meet such speculative and often self-perpetuating capital movements, many countries had to resort to exchange control and to other less insidious means of correcting the balance of payments" (Nurkse, 1944, p. 220). From this historical experience, Nurkse drew the conclusion that greater international cooperation was needed: "But if, owing to anticipated exchange adjustments, political unrest or similar causes, closer control of hot money movements is inevitable, then some of its difficulties and dangers might be overcome by international understanding" (ibid., p. 222). As a consequence, when he wrote about plans for an IMF, Nurkse added: "If in addition to trade and other normal transactions, such a fund had to cover all kinds of capital flight, it might have to be endowed with enormous resources. In fact, no fund of any practicable size might be sufficient to offset mass movements of nervous flight capital" (ibid., p. 188).

The restoration of a multilateral financial system thus depended on control of capital movements for an unlimited time. This approach appealed to Keynes, who had repeatedly asserted his skepticism about the benefits of both capital exports and capital imports. Keynes fully shared the belief that capital flight had been the major international interwar problem: "There is no country which can, in the future, safely allow the flight of funds for political reasons or to evade domestic taxation or in anticipation of the owner turning refugee. Equally, there is no country that can safely receive fugitive funds, which constitute an unwanted import of capital, yet cannot safely be used for fixed investment" (Horsefield, 1969, III, p. 31; see also Moggridge, 1992, p. 673). It is true that Keynes added that the new controls, which might become a "permanent feature of the post-war system," should not bring an end to the "era of international investment": but it would need states and international agreements to define (in accordance with national priorities) what was desirable investment and what was unwanted capital movement. The British economist Sir Hubert Henderson noted: "It has been generally agreed in the UK that we must retain the right to regulate capital movements, effectively and indefinitely."[3]

In the US, the feeling that the capital exports of the 1920s had been misused was a commonplace for the New Deal. White fully agreed with Keynes that:

The theoretical bases for the belief still so widely held, that interference with trade and with capital and gold movements etc., are harmful, are hangovers from a Nineteenth Century economic creed, which held that international economic adjustments, if left alone, would work themselves out toward an "equilibrium" with a minimum of harm to world trade and prosperity . . . The task before us is not to prohibit instruments of control but to develop those measures of control, those policies of administering such control, as will be the most effective in obtaining the objectives of world-wide sustained prosperity.　　　(Horsefield, 1969, II, p. 64)

---

[3] BoE OV38/49, Sir Hubert Henderson note of August 1, 1944.

White's immediate superior, Treasury Secretary Henry Morgenthau, made the target of these controls much more explicit. The new institutions of the international order would be "instrumentalities of sovereign governments and not of private financial interests." The task that the statesmen should set themselves was to "drive the usurious money-lenders from the temple of international finance" (Gardner, 1956).

The prevention of destabilizing capital flight was the only way of permitting the operation of a fixed exchange rate system with relatively limited reserves. Payments problems, in such a world, would either reflect structural problems in trading performance (which were termed "fundamental disequilibrium" and could be corrected by parity alteration) or temporary difficulties, for which the Fund's resources were intended to provide a solution.

However, there was a problem in differentiating capital movements from current account movements, and the task of the international order required a particular approach to accounting practice. In Morgenthau's and White's opinion, the need to control capital movements in particular – an objective with which Keynes fully concurred – required abandonment of the automaticity principle:

> The Fund might wish to supply the foreign exchange when the demand arises from an outflow of private funds. Whether or not it would wish to do so depends on a number of factors, including the cause of the outflow, the rate of outflow, the countries involved, the reserve position of the capital losing country, and the rapidity with which the mechanism of adjustment in the balance of payments is operating ... What this matter boils down to is that the Fund should have authority to determine whether the transactions causing a balance to turn unfavorable include transactions which the Fund would consider "illegitimate" under the circumstances.   (Horsefield, 1969, I, pp. 49–50)

These decisions required a much larger room for maneuver, and a more sophisticated supply of information, for the Fund's staff, which would have to undertake a major responsibility in managing the new international system. Activism and discretionary application of rules, rather than their automatic application, would be the new organizational principles. White saw that the demand for flexibility meant "technical knowledge, careful examination and good judgement by the Fund's staff" (Horsefield, 1969, I, p. 52). The Fund's decisions would be made on the basis of an assessment of the position of the members' international accounts, which "would be to the Fund's research staff, what the thermometer, stethoscope, x-ray, and microscope etc. are to the diagnostician" (Horsefield, 1969, I, p. 57).

The expression of these concerns appeared in Article VI of the Articles of

Agreement. Section 1(a) stated: "A member may not make net use of the Fund's resources to meet a large or sustained outflow of capital, and the Fund may request a member to exercise controls to prevent such use of the resources of the Fund." Moreover, Article VIII, Section 2(b) provided for mutual cooperation "for the purpose of making the exchange control regulations of either member more effective." The goals of fixed exchange rates *and* convertibility *and* national economic policies aiming at full employment might and probably would conflict with each other. The Fund as originally conceived would itself carry out the short-term capital movements (rather than leaving them to a destabilizing market mechanism) that were required to harmonize these three goals.

Throughout the operation of the classical Bretton Woods System (to 1971), capital movements represented a problematic, and in the late 1960s a destructive force.

2

In practice, the Fund and the Bank evolved in a rather different direction to that envisaged by the founders at Bretton Woods.

In the first place, their actual resources were much more restricted than the figures bandied about in the wartime discussions. The Bank was much less involved in practice in the task of reconstruction, and its interests were shifted toward development issues as a way of making it less sensitive politically, removing it from the politically troubled questions that arose when the future of Europe stood under debate. The Fund's capital was much closer to the smaller US figure than to the very large sum originally proposed by Keynes. In addition, the value of this capital was reduced by the unanticipated price rises of the post-war era.

Secondly, the idea of liberalizing current account transactions but not capital movements raised problems both definitional and political. US bankers were reluctant to cooperate after 1945 with European attempts to control capital movements. They voiced their opposition powerfully during the congressional debates over the Bretton Woods agreements. Harry Carr of the First National Bank of Philadelphia for instance attacked the plan as being an outgrowth of "the same idealistic but totally impractical collectivism that has characterized so much of the New Deal thinking" (Frieden, 1987, pp. 64–5). Though Congress accepted Bretton Woods, the bankers' stance was increasingly reflected in a more *laissez-faire* attitude on the part of the administration. As a result, there were large outward movements, which hostile commentators called capital flight, less hostile observers saw as "over-investment," and others believed to be a restoration of normal relations. Some European countries, in particular Britain and

Table 4.1. *United Kingdom: investment (percentage of GNP)*

	1947	1948	1949	1950	1951	1952	1953
Gross investment at home	15.6	15.1	14.3	12.7	19.5	15.1	16.9
Foreign investment	4.0	1.8	1.8	0.8	2.4	0.8	1.4
Total investment	19.6	16.9	16.1	13.5	21.9	15.9	18.3
Gross saving	8.3	14.5	14.8	14.9	16.2	17.1	17.6
Excess investment	11.3	2.4	1.3	−1.4	5.7	−1.2	0.7

Source: IMF, September 13, 1954 Poul Host–Madsen memorandum: "Sterling Convertibility."

France, saw capital outflows to their imperial areas as essential for power political purposes. Critics pointed out that British capital exports amounted to more or less the figure for "excess investment" that in the first half of the 1950s made it impossible for Britain to liberalize her payments with the dollar area (table 4.1).

The result was that capital flight came to be seen (as it had been in the 1930s) as the major problem confronting the international economy. A *New York Times* correspondent, Michael Hoffman, later reported that the total volume of US aid to Europe was less than European capital flight (with the implication that the resources of ERP had been completely squandered).[4] (There is an odd analogy here with the claim of 1992 that capital flight from the USSR since the mid 1980s had been greater in volume than the proposed $24 billion emergency package for the successor states (*Financial Times*, June 6–7, 1992)).

Thirdly, and most obviously of all, the political element counted for much more than had been hoped by the advocates of automaticity and anonymity. For Keynes, Carabosse seemed to have won the day. He spent the voyage back from Savannah on the *Queen Mary* composing an article intended for publication and "condemning American policy with extraordinary ferocity and passionately recommending His Majesty's Government to refuse to ratify the Fund and Bank agreement" (Bolton, 1972; Kahn, 1976).[5] Only the interventions of Sir George Bolton and Sir Ernest Rowe-Dutton persuaded Keynes to destroy this draft for a second *Economic Consequences of the Peace*, and to substitute instead the much more sober language of a memorandum on the Savannah meeting. "The

[4] *New York Times*, July 25, 1953, Hoffman, "Europe feels drop in capital flight."
[5] See also Moggridge (1992), p. 834, where Bolton's account is challenged. Moggridge points out that the UK had already ratified the Fund and Bank agreements.

Americans," this version went, "were becoming increasingly conscious of the force and justice of our criticisms . . . They nearly all confessed, in private, to cold feet about the effect of what they had been doing on the daily efficiency of the young twins." The struggle, which Keynes believed he had lost, contributed to the rapid decline in his physical health. He had a severe heart attack on the train from Savannah to Washington, and within four weeks he was dead.

White came to share completely Keynes's disenchantment. As American Executive Director of the Fund, and already under a deep political cloud for alleged excessive sympathy to the USSR, he worked to restore an element of the original vision. In 1948 he prepared what he thought to be a reflationary plan, which would create additional international reserves and revitalize the Fund. In laying this out, he used the strongest language of criticism he could summon up: "I am sure that it is not necessary to point out to the Board of Governors the extent to which performance has fallen short of promise . . . As drawn up at Bretton Woods, the institutions were to have man's capacity for a man-sized job. Since then, the job has grown to giant size, while the man to handle it has, figuratively speaking, shrunk to a mere boy." He blamed the Cold War: political developments "since 1945 have, in short, thrown a monkey-wrench into the delicate machinery of world economic development and reconstruction." The only major operation by the Fund in its early years (that involving the UK), White said, had been completely futile because it had not been used to promote adjustment of British economic policies: because of "adverse and unforeseen developments due, in the last analysis, chiefly to the ramifications of growing international political tensions."[6]

White was thinking primarily about growing Soviet–American tensions and the resulting reordering of policy priorities away from the economy and toward security issues. But he was also quite correct in noting that the most obvious area where politics had spoiled the chances of constructing a new world financial order was Anglo-American relations. The dollar and sterling were the major international currencies of the post-war period. Although in modern accounts the immediate post-war period is usually described as the period of "dollar hegemony" and the central issue for economic debate in the 1950s was the existence of a "dollar shortage," until the mid 1950s the pound was the most widely used of all international currencies: in the mid 1950s half of all international transactions were conducted in sterling.[7] The post-war Labour Chancellor of the Exchequer, Sir Stafford Cripps, proudly referred to Britain as being

---

[6] White Papers, Princeton University Library, 11/27f, May 19, 1948. Rough draft of a statement that might be used to introduce proposed amendments on the agenda.

[7] IMF, July 1954, "The Convertibility of Sterling." Also Cmd 9108.

the center of "the largest multilateral trading area in the world for which it acted as banker" (Hogan, 1987, p. 276).

But Britain had emerged from the war severely strained financially and economically depleted. She had turned from a major creditor into a debtor nation. Immediately following the end of the war in the Far East, American lend-lease stopped abruptly, and a British mission went to Washington in search of some new American assistance. The outcome was a $3.75 billion loan and a favorable settlement of the lend-lease debt, but on the condition of trade liberalization and a commitment to the restoration of sterling convertibility.

The brief period of sterling convertibility in 1947, at the time stipulated in the Loan Agreement, turned into a fiasco. It lasted just six weeks and led to a massive drain of British reserves. The British position was bolstered after 1948 not by the Bretton Woods institutions but by Marshall aid. The 1947 experience of premature convertibility left a lasting bitterness and postponed British willingness to undertake stabilization. Williamson (1991, p. 352) describes Britain as a classic case of a country "that tried to implement reforms before preconditions were in place." In 1958, the incident was still used by British officials as a warning of the dangers of convertibility, and it delayed negotiations over the dissolution of the EPU. One minute ran: "We must be able to convince home and world opinion so clearly that we have moved from strength that no one will doubt that we can hold the position" (Fforde, 1992, p. 558).

It was made clear in 1947 that Britain represented an immense obstacle to global convertibility, as claims on sterling ("sterling balances") far exceeded British holdings of gold or dollars, and widespread awareness of this predicament deprived the sterling systems of the credibility needed to operate in a multilaterally convertible world. Many sterling area countries (most importantly India and Egypt) ran a deficit with the dollar bloc and wanted to use their sterling balances in London to clear this deficit. But Britain could not afford such a liquidation of sterling balances, and as a result needed to limit convertibility. It became a long-standing requirement for UK policy that "adherence to the IMF must not entail any obligations which would damage the essentials of the sterling area system."[8]

After the events of 1947 the path to liberalization appeared infinitely longer, slower, and harder. At the Fund meeting in September 1947 the Managing Director Camille Gutt stated that: "A premature attempt to force the acceptance of exchange and trade practices suited for a balanced world economy can do much harm and even endanger the achievement of these objectives" (Second Annual Meeting of the Board of Governors,

[8] BoE OV38/49, February 28, 1956, note.

1947, p. 10). In 1949 the Annual Report concluded meekly: "The difficulties of the postwar period are greater than foreseen at the time of the Bretton Woods Conference" (p. 2).

The difficulties of 1947 made it clear that a fundamental task of the Fund would be the determination of new exchange parities. But there was a general reluctance to move in this direction because in conditions of supply constraints, downward adjustment of exchange rates would not necessarily promote an increase in exports and an improvement of the trade balance.[9] The key to the continental European position lay in Britain: a British devaluation was needed to clear the way for a general European adjustment.

The Fund's ability to shape European events was severely limited by the so-called ERP decision of April 5, 1948, by which the Fund agreed not to finance countries participating in the European Recovery Program or the Marshall Plan. The Fund's virtual exclusion from European affairs greatly reduced its global function. Some of its staff members – Robert Triffin (who became Head of the Fund's Paris office in July 1948) and Maurice Parsons (the Director of the Fund Operations Department) – proposed creating a European version of the IMF that would give credit to make multilateral payments possible.

But the ERP decision did not stand in the way of some extraordinary attempts to influence British policy making. The British Executive Director of the IMF (who had been alone in voting against the resolution) reported back shortly after the Fund's discussion: "you may be aware that during the debates on the Fund Board on their relations with countries enjoying ERP facilities, we were told behind the scenes that the ban on drawing rights would not apply to the UK." He was outraged by the extent of the Fund's pressure: "If the Fund is going to become an institution which confers no benefits on Members but requires them to carry out impossible obligations besides interfering in all their complex financial arrangements, we should seriously consider suggesting to Washington that the Fund should be put into a state of suspended animation."[10] In June 1948 Gutt proposed a mission to London. Britain responded by objecting to the description of Gutt's trip as a "mission" as having a "very special meaning which might be described as derogatory."[11]

In 1948 there were no immediate balance of payments reasons to press ahead with a British devaluation. Indeed the Fund's Research Department was much more hesitant about the desirability of such a move: the British

---

[9] See Gutt's address: "The Practical Problem of Exchange Rates," February 13, 1948, Address to Littauer School of Public Administration, Harvard University.

[10] BoE OV38/19, April 26, 1948, Bolton to Siepmann.

[11] BoE OV38/19, June 15, 1948, Oliver Franks (Washington) to Foreign Office.

believed that the Director of the Research Department, Edward Bernstein, was arguing that the sterling–dollar rate should be changed only when there was "a clear cut case," and this would depend on a decision "that latent [British] inflation had diminished to an extent which made it possible to remove controls."[12]

In the second quarter of 1949 the British balance of payments deficit became a pressing problem once again as a reaction to a slowdown in US growth. The USA, and particularly the Treasury and its representatives in the IMF, pressed for a British devaluation. For them, the temporary British difficulty presented an opportunity; the liberalization of European payments depended, they believed, on a general European devaluation, yet none of the European states would be prepared to move before Britain had shown the way (Cairncross and Eichengreen, 1983, pp. 117–18; Hogan, 1987, p. 210). In May the US Executive Director of the Fund told his British colleague that "the Fund ought to be in a position where it could make positive suggestions to certain countries that their currencies were overvalued by x per cent and that exchange and other domestic action should be taken to enable them to reach reasonable equilibrium in their overall balance of payments." The British reply was quite abruptly hostile:

I also reminded [Frank] Southard [the US Executive Director] that the Fund was a negative and not a positive instrument of international exchange policy and that we were not prepared to tolerate interference by the Fund in our affairs. This exercise would therefore probably end in a stalemate, the Fund's authority diminishing throughout the period, Anglo-American relations probably continuing to diverge.[13]

Almost all British ministers opposed the American recommendation, as they interpreted the British problem primarily in terms of domestic inflationary pressures, which needed to be counteracted through fiscal economies and further price and wage controls. This view was shared by the Chancellor of the Exchequer, Sir Stafford Cripps, as well as by the Bank of England, whose Governor, C.F. Cobbold, put the issue in quite traditional terms: "the two things that would really change the atmosphere in North America would be a real attack on government expenditure and a deferment of further nationalization plans." In April 1949 Cobbold suggested that the UK "might consider leaving the IMF" if any attempt was made to put pressure on her by leaking news about the discussion of sterling exchange rates.[14] Cripps, in the meantime, attacked those of his

[12] BoE OV38/19, April 1, 1948, British Embassy Washington to Foreign Office.
[13] BoE OV35/21, May 23, 1949, Bolton note.
[14] BoE OV35/21, April 1, 1949, APGS [Grafftey-Smith] note.

economic advisers who favored devaluation as believers in a "free economy" who were closer to American than to British views (Cairncross Eichengreen, 1983, pp. 122, 133). In the end, devaluation was adopted in the absence of Cripps and at the pressing of three junior ministers (Hugh Gaitskell, Harold Wilson, and Douglas Jay).

Other countries followed the British lead, and continental devaluation led to the establishment of more realistic parities, although France felt strongly that her plans for a small European economic union had been torpedoed by the British action. The sterling area and Scandinavian countries also devalued by 30 percent, France by 22 percent, Germany by 20 percent, and Belgium and Portugal by 13 percent.

This was, however, not a triumph of the American liberalizing vision. British devaluation was accompanied by new controls on trade and exchange, and there was no relaxation of existing ones, although the IMF tried to argue that the "success" of British devaluation indicated that a relaxation of restrictions would be beneficial.[15] As Britain joined the EPU in 1950, rather than providing through the sterling area an anchor for a region that might move toward convertibility, American policymakers were appalled. The EPU conducted its transactions through the Basle-based Bank for International Settlements, an institution created in 1930 as a reparations bank, which had always been controlled by the European central banks and was almost closed down after World War II because of suspicions of undue sympathy to Germany. To the EPU managers, the BIS appeared to be a way of avoiding multilateral, and American, interference.

Though the idea of a European payments mechanism had originally been propounded by the ECA [Economic Cooperation Administration, the Washington-based coordinating agency for ERP], Washington's early response to the EPU was hostile. Structurally, the EPU resembled the original Keynes proposals for an automatic International Clearing Union, with a clearing mechanism and a symmetrical distribution of the adjustment burden between surplus and deficit countries. As a mechanism for expanding intra-European trade, it aroused American suspicions. Though the State Department was prepared to accept it on the grounds that it brought enhanced political stability to Europe, the US Treasury and the IMF at first saw the EPU as a denial of the American principles of private initiative, liberal trade policy, competition, and the belief that strength and stability are not achieved through controls, doles, and relief. In 1951 the Fund discussed with the ECA the possibility of a censure of European behavior and a firm call for the relaxation of restrictions and

---

[15] BoE OV38/27, November 14, 1950, Gutt to Bolton.

discrimination. But by 1952, there was greater optimism and a quite new language of closer collaboration between the EPU and the IMF.[16]

There was nothing inevitable in this development of the EPU away from being the American nightmare and toward becoming a means of realizing the American dream. It depended upon a series of decisions, some taken against Washington's wishes and advice, and upon the pressures exerted on the regional solution by the fact of economic growth.

(1) The initial optimistic sign came during the first major crisis to affect the EPU, the German payments problem of 1950. German imports surged as a result of a dramatic and rapid recovery (Milward, 1984; Kaplan and Schleiminger, 1989, p. 102). The High Commissioner, John McCloy, advised the suspension of the liberalization program and the imposition of trade control. But an EPU delegation composed of the Swedish economist Per Jacobsson (from the BIS) and the Briton Alec Cairncross recommended strongly against this course and in favor of using monetary policy (a discount rate rise) to deal with the German balance of payments. Jacobsson was a committed liberalizer; Cairncross took a more pragmatic stance but saw in the German situation a "straightforward liquidity crisis in an otherwise healthy economy" (Jacobsson, 1979, p. 243). Against the opposition of both the American authorities and Federal Chancellor Konrad Adenauer, the central bank (Bank deutscher Länder) eventually accepted the EPU recommendation and took the road to economic liberalism. Jacobsson wrote to Roger Auboin, the General Manager of the BIS:

I had one and a half hours with the Americans and I pointed out that there are some very favorable tendencies as regards German trade and added that if liberalization were discarded by Germany, people would say that another measure pressed on Europe by the Americans had shown itself unsuitable and impossible (as in 1947 the convertibility of sterling).   (Jacobsson, 1979, p. 239)

The Jacobsson/Cairncross course proved to be completely correct, and its success greatly strengthened the impetus to liberalization within the EPU. It proved to be a highly attractive model for future international action: the provision of resources linked to a conditionality which required liberalization. In this respect it served as a precedent for the dramatic liberalization process of the later 1950s.

(2) Once this had occurred, some scholars have argued that liberalization and the lifting of trade controls had a momentum of its own (Buchheim,

---

[16] See Hogan (1987) p. 297 for US views on EPU; IMF June 16, July 2, 1951, Irving S. Friedman: Notes on discussions with Mr. Tenenbaum (ECA).

1990). The proportion of intra-European trade liberalized rose from 66 percent in mid 1952 to 84 percent in mid 1954, and discrimination against US products also was reduced after 1954 (Kaplan and Schleiminger, 1989, pp. 158–9). But in 1952, despite the growth of production and trade, the original objectives of the IMF seemed as remote as ever. The 1952 Annual Report stated: "The attainment of a stable international equilibrium, however, still eludes large parts of the world, and there has been little secure or sustained progress toward the Fund objectives of unimpeded multilateral trade and the general convertibility of currencies" (p. 1).

(3) In 1952 the relationship between the IMF and the EPU improved dramatically, and both sides appeared willing to cooperate. Belgium was the central player in this reconciliation, as the relationship of the EPU with the rest of the world depended heavily on the Belgian position.

The IMF's work had been paralyzed after the ERP decision by an inability to agree to a policy on the use of Fund resources. Managing Director Gutt was frequently on the verge of despair: he told central bankers that if the issue were not resolved "you can, to my mind, write off the Fund."[17] The Fund's staff had devised the principle of the stand-by already in 1950 as an attempt to break out of the impasse. An agreement in advance on the supply of funds would be conditional on the adoption of a stabilization policy: "Members should be expected to have a monetary policy and such policy should consist, inter alia, in plans to cope with an expected or existing disequilibrium."

The drawback of a case-by-case discussion of particular policies lay in a potential "arbitrariness," as the Dutch central banker J.W. Beyen, a leading critic of the Fund's operations, noted. He complained that it could "easily mean the use of the Fund's policy for what happens at a given moment to be US Treasury policy." But stand-bys seemed the only way of overcoming what European central bankers believed to be the "mothball policy" of the US.[18]

In the early 1950s, Belgium built up a large surplus within the EPU but had a deficit with the dollar countries. In view of this relationship, in 1951–2 the criticisms within the IMF by Americans and Canadians concentrated on Belgium (Horsefield, 1969, I, p. 314). The EPU depended on a credit from the Belgian Treasury, and in order to cover this, the Belgians proposed to borrow from the IMF and to secure francs from the National Bank in exchange for the borrowed dollars. On February 13, 1952 the principle of the stand-by arrangement, a potential drawing over an agreed

[17] BoE OV38/27, November 14, 1950, Gutt to Bolton.
[18] BoE OV38/27, J.W. Beyen: "Will the International Monetary Fund Come to Life at Last?"

period of time, had been laid down (Gold, 1979). The proposed operation looked rather like a technical device to avoid laws on government spending and credit ceilings. The stand-by credit of $50 million agreed by the IMF was renewed until the end of the operation of EPU but was only drawn upon in April 1957. (Belgium's trade balance with the dollar area in fact improved quite quickly by itself after 1952.) In making the application for the stand-by facility, Belgium promised (in what was the first letter of intent): "Minimum use of restrictions and further progress to convertibility are permanent objectives of Belgium. Assurance from the Fund that adequate assistance will be available if needed would be very helpful in maintaining the determination of Belgium to pursue these policies."[19]

The negotiations of 1952 on how the credit could be used, the assessment of Belgium's general economic position, and the commitments as to further policy: these features became central to IMF practice and marked a definitive end of any possible practice of "automaticity."

(4) Another challenge came from a completely opposite approach to international economic relations. Instead of a fixed rate maintained under the surveillance of international regulatory agencies, relations could also proceed by an unregulated determination of prices. In the discussions preceding Bretton Woods, the fear had been that countries would repeat the experience of the 1930s and engage in competitive devaluation for price advantage in export markets. The problems that became increasingly apparent in the 1950s were rather different ones: the reluctance of countries to devalue, the persistence of official overvalued exchange rates, and consequently a need to keep exchange controls.

In the mid 1950s some European states flirted with floating exchange rates as an answer to this problem. The most important early proposal (in 1952) came from Britain, and was known as ROBOT (partly because of the names of its authors; but the title also suggested rather obviously a principle of automaticity). ROBOT would have "killed the EPU" by reopening the gold market and allowing a wide band for a sterling float, between $2.40 and $3.20 (Kaplan and Schleiminger, 1989, p. 164). Though ROBOT was abandoned (largely because Commonwealth countries feared a loss in value of their sterling balances), the scheme left a powerful memory and also an inspiration. As late as 1958, the Governor of the Bank of England while arguing on practical grounds against floating, still added: "It would probably be prudent to organize monetary policy both at home and abroad, on the probability that something like a floating rate policy is inevitable but to make no attempt to force the pace until it becomes

---

[19] IMF, March 15, 1952, Visit of Maurice Frère; June 17, 1952, Maurice Frère to Managing Director of IMF.

acceptable to the western world as a whole" (Fforde, 1992, p. 590).

In the early 1950s British economic vulnerability led to fierce opposition to the then conventional IMF wisdom of convertibility at fixed parities. One example of the difficulty was provided in 1952 with the first IMF consultations on Exchange Restrictions (Article XIV consultations). The meetings almost broke down at the beginning because of the strength of the British assertion of resistance to convertibility and the resolution to resist what was believed to be interference in national policies, and because of the IMF's similarly obdurate defense of convertibility. The Dutch central banker J.W. Beyen described the IMF's relation with Britain at this time as "the schoolmaster's desire to have at least one boy in the class who washed his hands properly."[20] But by the end of 1952 British politicians had become much more sympathetic to the notion of convertibility. The December 1952 Commonwealth Economic Committee communiqué stated: "The aim is to secure international agreement on the adoption of policies by creditor and debtor countries which . . . will by progressive stages and within reasonable time, create an effective multilateral trade and payments system covering the widest possible area."

The abandonment by Britain of the floating alternative followed from a renewed willingness to make use of the IMF. At the OEEC meeting of the Council of Ministers in March 1953, the British Chancellor of the Exchequer said that "the international institutions should be revivified . . . particularly the IMF which should come into the international picture as a practical going concern."[21] As Governor Cobbold put it in 1954, "agreement on an IMF stand-by credit would take us further along the road and make reversal of policies more difficult . . . if we did not take the further step within six months or a year it might well lead to a lack of confidence" (Kaplan and Schleiminger, 1989, p. 207). Britain initiated discussions about a stand-by, which eventually failed because of US insistence that Britain should abolish all trade discrimination if she were to be allowed to draw on the stand-by. In practice Britain went a considerable way toward meeting this demand, abolishing bilateral account status (i.e., no longer insisting that another country accept in sterling payments made from another transferable account country) and removing the distinction between capital and current account transactions. Despite major concessions on chemical and paper imports, in September 1954 only 55 percent of British imports from the dollar area were free from control (compared with 70 percent from the OEEC area).[22]

There was thus in reality still a good deal of caution. In June 1954, the

---

[20] BoE OV38/27, November 20, 1950, Beyen note.
[21] March 23, 1953 (see also *Journal of Commerce*, November 18, 1953).
[22] IMF July 1954, Memo: "Sterling convertibility."

Financial Times quoted British "official circles" as saying that "convertibility is not worth having if it is to be achieved at the expense of a contraction, or even a halt in the expansion, of world trade."[23] In 1955 the IMF's Managing Director suggested again a British drawing from the Fund to smooth the way to convertibility.[24] But in August 1955 EPU members signed the European Monetary Agreement, in which the restoration of convertibility was to be undertaken on the basis of a collective approach by continental Europeans with the British, a provision which in practice delayed implementation yet further.

Floating also found adherents in Germany because it seemed to offer a faster path to true convertibility than the par-value approach. This was the position taken by the German Economics Minister Ludwig Erhard, who in 1952 called for the complete abolition of foreign exchange control in Europe and added that "if the system of rigidly fixed rates of exchange were maintained, not only would the EPU be doomed, but European integration would fall" (*The Statist*, July 19, 1952). This was a position intellectually close to the academic criticism of fixed exchange rates and the EPU mechanism put forward in 1953 by Milton Friedman. In a more subtle form, the German central banker Otmar Emminger in an article in 1957 pointed out that a floating system was in theory compatible with the IMF agreement and that floating had been tolerated in a few cases (Canada and Peru) (Emminger, 1957).

But it was in the British case that the defeat of the notion of floating was crucial for the development of the whole international financial system. The crisis that eventually pushed Britain away from floating did not arise out of any economic situation, but rather from a crisis produced by accident.

(5) Political events intruded rather abruptly to push forward the IMF-convertibility approach. It was purely chance that a crisis with major financial implications (Kunz, 1991) erupted in 1956 in the wake of the Anglo-French attempt to use Israeli forces to seize the Suez Canal from Egypt. There was no particular economic problem in 1956 in the Anglo-American relationship. For the first ten months of 1956, the UK had a favorable balance of payments on current account, and the account was *ex post* in overall balance for the year July 1, 1956 to June 30, 1957. The UK needed a stand-by of unprecedented proportions ($738.5 million) as well as a drawing on the gold and first credit tranche because of a run on sterling, and because British politicians had convinced themselves that a major sterling crisis existed. Discussing the size of the stand-by operation, Lord Harcourt, the British Economic Secretary in Washington and Executive

---

[23] *Financial Times*, June 9, 1954.
[24] BoE OV38/48, October 30, 1955, Sir Roger Makins cable.

Director of the IMF, argued that the larger the support fund, the more successful it was likely to be and the less likely was it to be necessary to use it. When the American Executive Director asked the US Treasury Secretary (George Humphrey) about the size of the UK request, the latter replied: "You know, Frank, I have always felt that if you are going to do something you have to go all out, so what is the UK's quota?" He then agreed to the unprecedentedly large drawing and stand-by.[25]

Both the American and the British view of stand-bys was fundamentally changed by the 1956 operation. From the US perspective, larger operations became possible; from the British view, convertibility became the price for assistance. In making his arguments in Washington, Harcourt had tried to put the problem in a longer-term perspective than that of the political crisis arising out of Suez. He spoke of the enormous advances toward convertibility made by the UK and Western Europe since 1953 and claimed that the British emergency drawing was needed in order to avoid any retreat.

There was no retreat. Britain only drew $561.5 million in 1956 and made no subsequent drawings in the period of the stand-by. The stand-by, which had originated as a panic measure, became viewed instead as a way of increasing British reserves in the build-up to convertibility.

(6) The Suez operation had initiated a new phase of IMF activism, and many countries required balance of payments assistance as a consequence of faster growth. World economic recovery made more countries dependent on IMF assistance for balance of payments problems. The final moves to widespread current account convertibility occurred in 1958, after a vigorous boom in late 1956 and 1957 which created payments problems in a number of countries which then required stand-by IMF packages: Bolivia, Brazil, Chile, Colombia, Cuba, France, Honduras, India, Japan, Netherlands, Nicaragua, Peru, and South Africa. Japan in 1957 took a $125.0 million drawing, and France, which ran into acute inflationary difficulties in 1957 and 1958, $262.5 million. French monetary expansion made France as dependent on the IMF as Britain had been in the immediate aftermath of the Suez crisis (Block, 1977). France in 1957 and 1958 devised its economic and currency stabilization programs in very close consultation with the Fund.

After the strains imposed by expansion, recession provided a relief. In 1958, the US trade balance shifted adversely, and the UK ended discrimination on imports from the dollar area for a wide range of previously restricted goods. At the September 1958 IMF meetings in New Delhi, the British Chancellor of the Exchequer spoke about the removal of currency discrimination, and the IMF Managing Director, Per Jacobsson,

---

[25] Remarks by Frank Southard, *The Caravan*, January 1989, p. 9.

offered a quota increase rather than a renewal of the unneeded stand-by as the solution to Britain's problems. The general increase in quotas was a response to the now evident need for greater IMF activity.

(7) Over the course of the 1950s, the dollar shortage, which had often been treated as if it were a permanent phenomenon caused by an intrinsic superiority of American capitalism, became less acute. At first the major alleviating factor was US military spending abroad, but after the mid 1950s this was increasingly supplemented by private capital transfers (table 4.2). This development startled most observers: in the late 1940s Marshall Plan administrators had tried, but very frequently failed, to interest American business in guarantees for European investment. After 1956, however, the stream of US participations took off. US direct investment overseas and long-term capital outflows exceeded for the first time since the war official grants and capital flows.

Robert Triffin later commented in another context that "History teaches us . . . that the most crucial reforms of the international monetary systems as well as national monetary systems have already been determined, with very rare exceptions, by the private sector of the economy rather than by the governments and their bureaucracies" (Triffin, 1984, p. 151). This was the case with the private flows of the 1950s.

It is possible to detect a new attitude toward capital movements. The 1952 Annual Report stated: "Balance of payments adjustments are also made more difficult by the virtual absence of any effective private international long-term capital market" (p. 6). As capital flows developed, they became not a problem and a source of destabilization but a way of making adjustments within the framework of growth.

3

In the later 1950s, the combination of a rapid expansion in world trade, the growth of capital markets, and simultaneously the widespread emergence of balance of payments problems focused discussion on a perceived inadequacy of international reserves. The surprisingly large volume of capital movements directed attention toward the issue of reserves. One of the most famous formulations of the problem was produced by Robert Triffin (1960): the inadequacy of reserves could be made good by the increased holding of dollar reserves, but this involved the risk of a loss of confidence in the dollar and the sudden liquidation of dollar assets, a repetition for the US currency of the traumatic events of 1931. The more the world tried to stabilize its reserve position, and the larger dollar assets became relative to gold, the greater the risk of a crisis in confidence. Triffin's

Table 4.2. *United States: balance of payments, 1946–59 (millions of US $)*

Year or quarter	Balance on goods and services	Remittances and pensions	US government grants and capital, net	US private capital, net			Foreign capital, net	Errors and unrecorded transactions	Balance	
				Direct investment	Other long-term	Short-term			Liquidity basis	Changes in gold, convertible currencies, and IMF gold tranche position (increase (−))
1946	7,744	−648	−5,293	−230	127	−310	−615	218	993	−623
1947	11,529	−728	−6,121	−749	−49	−189	−432	949	4,210	−3,315
1948	6,440	−631	−4,918	−721	−69	−116	−361	1,193	817	−1,736
1949	6,149	−641	−5,649	−660	−80	187	44	786	136	−266
1950	1,779	−533	−3,640	−621	−495	−149	181	−11	−3,489	1,758
1951	3,671	−480	−3,191	−508	−437	−103	540	500	−8	−33
1952	2,226	−571	−2,380	−852	−214	−94	52	627	−1,206	−415
1953	386	−644	−2,055	−735	185	167	146	366	−2,184	1,256
1954	1,828	−633	−1,554	−667	−320	−635	249	191	−1,541	480
1955	2,009	−597	−2,211	−823	−241	−191	297	515	−1,242	182
1956	3,967	−690	−2,362	−1,951	−603	−517	615	568	−973	−869
1957	5,729	−729	−2,574	−2,442	−859	−276	545	1,184	578	−1,165
1958	2,206	−745	−2,587	−1,181	−1,444	−311	186	511	−3,365	2,292
1959	147	−815	−1,986	−1,372	−926	−77	736	423	−3,870	1,035

Source: Economic Report of the President 1969, Washington DC, 1969, pp. 324–5.

article in fact reflected a notion that had become almost commonplace in the later 1950s among those who worked with international institutions.

A discussion along very similar lines had developed in the Fund, where the Research Department under Edward Bernstein devoted a great deal of attention to the international liquidity issue. The conclusion of the first investigation of 1953 ("The Adequacy of Monetary Reserves") had reflected a rather restrained position. There was, it concluded, no immediate evidence of a shortage of liquidity, or that such a shortage hindered world development:

Major world trends of production and trade are not determined solely by liquidity. The developments of the last forty years or so have been dominated not by changing liquidity ratios but rather by two major wars, several minor wars, vast expenditures preparing for wars, and large expenditures to repair the damages of wars.

(Horsefield, 1969, III, p. 405)

Later the problem became more acute. In the discussions that took place in 1958, the IMF repeatedly raised the possibility of a Triffinesque collapse. In July 1958 Jacobsson told US Under-Secretary of State for Economic Affairs, Douglas Dillon, that "we have not got enough if there is a major crack" (Jacobsson, 1979, pp. 305–6). A staff paper warned that: "Past experiences have shown that when cracks occur, they may not be confined only to the currencies immediately affected. The consequences of allowing such cracks to widen and spread may indeed be serious" (Horsefield, 1969, III, p. 410). The September 16, 1958 paper on "International Reserves and Liquidity" stated the problem: total world reserves had risen from the end of 1948 to the end of 1957 from $53.2 billion to $62.1 billion. Reserves of countries other than the USA had risen from $22 billion to $30 billion, while world trade had risen much faster over the same period (by 110 percent). The dependence on the dollar had increased: whereas at the end of 1948, 77.5 percent of the world's currency foreign exchange assets were in sterling, and only 20.9 percent in dollars, in 1957, 51.7 percent were in dollars, 36.3 percent in sterling, and 7.9 percent in EPU credits (Horsefield, 1969, III, p. 371). Not just the shortage of reserves was alarming (the IMF staff concluded "in 1928, despite substantially higher reserves, the world economy headed for disaster"); the distribution of reserves looked like a major impediment to further expansion: "Many non-industrialized countries have decreased their reserves" (Horsefield, 1969, III, pp. 505–6).

The same issue was seen in other countries as being both a current objection to restoration of convertibility and a problem to which convertibility, in the correct institutional setting, might provide the answer. The correction demanded greater liquidity and greater activism. In Britain, the idea of a "super-central-bank" was actively pushed by Maxwell Stamp of the Bank of England (and a former Director of the IMF's European Department) and Oliver Franks, the Chairman of Lloyds Bank. "There is a serious risk that a deflationary disturbance in the US and Europe will compel a general and disastrous retreat from liberalization of trade and payments some time before any redistributional *trend* can reassert itself" (Fforde, 1992, p. 578).

In April 1958, Lucius Thompson-McCausland of the Bank of England went to Washington on a visit, described by the Governor as "very useful" (Fforde, 1992, p. 583), to discuss the liquidity problem. The figures suggested for desired increases in liquidity were 40 percent, by Jacobsson, and 50 percent, by Frank Southard, the American Executive Director (Fforde, 1992, p. 582; Jacobsson, 1979, pp. 304–5). Recognition and discussion of the liquidity issue was the final part of the preparation for convertibility.

Although the Managing Director of the Fund was in general less troubled by the issue than his staff, he saw the expansion of Fund activity as offering a way of disarming the worries of members undergoing the transition to convertibility. In 1960 he reassured Britain in the following way:

He said he had been thinking about world liquidity and thought it was adequate; the Fund however was trying to be helpful. One thing they had done was to encourage the granting of standby credits. These gave countries the confidence to use their own reserves; thus the provision of standbys was very nearly the creation of fresh international liquidity.[26]

4

The reader will notice that the story told above depends quite critically on a number of chance elements, and in particular on the consequences of the political crisis of 1956 and the subsequent large UK and French drawings. It is clear that some European countries, notably Germany, were ready for dollar convertibility much earlier, and that others, notably the UK, would find dollar convertibility difficult in any circumstances. But the victory of regionalism in the aftermath of the establishment of the European Recovery Program meant that the Europeans moved as a bloc. In the light of the European determination to maintain a coordinated exchange rate regime, and at the same time of the disparities in macroeconomic experience, it is inevitable that the timing of the movement to convertibility should have had this chance characteristic. It depended on the generation in the major

---

[26] BoE OV38/61, March 6, 1960, Talk with Mr. Per Jacobsson.

political players – France and the UK – of a political willingness to accept a convertibility that held considerable economic risks.

The fact that the timing was fortuitous prompts a reflection on the story of the European adoption of current account convertibility. This is best presented as a thought experiment.

What would have happened if the US Treasury/IMF scheme of the late 1940s had actually been realized, and convertibility had been adopted *then*, and not as it was in historical reality between 1958 and 1961? Such an operation would have required greatly reduced European dollar parities. As the European catch-up of the 1950s proceeded, the result would have been large European current account surpluses in the absence of a revaluation of the original low European parities. Yet the experience of the 1960s was that revaluations are highly difficult to achieve in the Bretton Woods system, and that in the surplus countries political coalitions built around export interests resist such revaluations. The large US deficits would have been the source of additional world liquidity, but would have brought an increased risk of a rapid 1971-style collapse. In short, the end of Bretton Woods might have come much earlier if convertibility had been achieved in the circumstances of the post-war world, and not after the catch-up was nearly complete.

But even such a reflection need not be convincing as a justification of the actual historical experience of late convertibility. It might equally be argued that it was the experience of the 1950s, in which rapid growth coincided with exchange rates held stable through controls, that made Europeans so reluctant to change parities. Without that experience, Bretton Woods might have come to mean fixed but adjustable exchange rates rather than fixed and inflexible rates. The undesirable and excessive rigidity of the classical phase of the Bretton Woods system in the 1960s might thus be seen as a consequence of the excessively delayed adoption of general convertibility.

5

The crucial shifts between 1945 and 1958 contained two features that represented a fundamental break from the world view of Bretton Woods and a move toward the creating of a functioning international monetary system. First, the principle of automaticity (which had been a linchpin of the earlier philosophy of globalism) was abandoned in favor of a discretionary approach. This was the approach that in 1952 healed the IMF–EPU rift through the Belgian stand-by agreement. It represented the major problem in French–American and French–Fund relations. France had consistently kept to the position, which was very close to the original

Keynes view, that the Fund had no right to question any drawing: the only option available to the Fund was the institution of ineligibility proceedings.[27] By the end of the 1950s, the opposite view had been formulated, defended, and implemented by the Fund:

Not only do they [discretionary programs] serve to give coherence to the financial side of the Fund's work, but the fact that they have been made fully known in an authoritative way to the members leaves no room for uncertainty as to the principles which are applied in the Fund's decisions on financial assistance.

(Horsefield, 1969, III, p. 425)

Such an approach rescued the Fund from the immobility to which it had seemed condemned after 1948.

Secondly, there was the acceptance of the substantial capital movements of the 1950s. A flow of private investment from the US had taken over when official aid (UNRRA relief or ERP) ended. This development represented a return to the major capital movements of the sort that had been characteristic of the pre-1914 world, something which had never been contemplated during wartime discussions of capital movements. The expansion of capital movements raised the liquidity issue in a more direct way than had been assumed in the wartime discussions of monetary issues. Then it was taken for granted that capital movements would be severely limited; by the 1950s private capital movements had begun to play a critical part in economic development.

It was these two steps which created the appropriate incentive structure to induce European states to agree to dismantle and dissolve the EPU. The result was a triumph of the principles of internationalism and multilateralism, though on rather different terms to those envisaged in 1944 by the founding fathers of Bretton Woods. With 1958, the idea of monetary regionalism suffered a setback – it began to be presented as nothing more than a transitory phase on the way to full global integration. As such, of course, it was completely acceptable and reconcilable, at least in retrospect, with the global perspective on international economic connectedness.

Was it the prior adoption of regional solutions that made globalism eventually acceptable? Such a transition had certainly not been a part of anyone's vision at Bretton Woods. When the "system" started to function at the end of the 1950s, it had some features that were more a legacy of the world of the 1950s than a product of the Bretton Woods debates: the inflexibility of parities and the increased size of international capital movements.

One of the historical peculiarities of the first post-war decade – the low

[27] IMF October 4, 1954, Albin Pfeifer to J.M. Stevens: "French Views Regarding Automaticity in Use of the Fund's Resources."

level of private (as opposed to official) capital flows – makes this a rather poor model on which to base recommendations for dealing with the current problems of countries making the transition between planned and market economies. The single greatest intellectual limitation of the Bretton Woods achievement was its unwillingness to contemplate the role to be played by private capital movements. If the modern transition economies are to be successful, they will require large private capital flows, and policies will be needed to encourage this development. It is precisely in this respect that global institutions have a critical role to play. In the 1950s, capital movements eventually helped to create incentives for a global liberalization; perhaps this is an encouraging precedent for the 1990s.

References

Block, Fred L. (1977), *The Origins of International Economic Disorder: A Study of United States Monetary Policy from World War II to the Present*, Berkeley: University of California Press.

Bolton, George (1972), "Where Critics Are as Wrong as Keynes Was," *The Banker*, 122: 1385–7.

Buchheim, Christoph (1990), *Die Wiedereingliederung West-deutschlands in die Weltwirtschaft 1945–1958*, Munich: Oldenburgh.

Cairncross, Alec and Barry Eichengreen (1983), *Sterling in Decline: The Devaluations of 1931, 1949, and 1967*, Oxford: Blackwell.

Dell, Sidney (1981), "On Being Grandmotherly: The Evolution of IMF Conditionality," *Essays in International Finance*, 144, International Finance Section, Department of Economics, Princeton University.

DeLong, J. Bradford and Barry Eichengreen (1993), "The Marshall Plan: History's Most Successful Structural Adjustment Program," in Rudiger Dornbusch, Willem Nölling, and Richard Layard (eds.), *Postwar Economic Reconstruction and Lessons for the East Today*, Cambridge, Mass.: MIT Press, pp. 189–230.

Diz, Adolfo C. (1984), "The Conditions Attached to Adjustment Financing: The Evolution of the IMF Practice," in *The International Monetary System: Forty Years after Bretton Woods*, Boston: Federal Reserve Bank of Boston, pp. 214–35.

Emminger, Otmar (1957), "Internationaler Währungsfonds und Weschselkurspolitik," *Zeitschrift für das gesamte Kreditwesen*, 10/18: 732–6.

Fforde, John (1992), *The Bank of England and Public Policy 1941–1958*, Cambridge University Press.

Frieden, Jeffry A. (1987), *Banking on the World: The Politics of American International Finance*, New York: Harper and Row.

Gardner, Richard N. (1956), *Sterling-Dollar Diplomacy*, New York: Columbia University Press.

Gold, Joseph (1979), *Conditionality*, Washington DC: International Monetary Fund.

Guitian, Manuel (1981), *Fund Conditionality: Evolution of Principles and Practices*, Washington DC: International Monetary Fund.

Harrod, Roy (1971), *The Life of John Maynard Keynes*, Harmondsworth: Penguin (originally London 1951).

Hogan, Michael J. (1987), *The Marshall Plan: America, Britain and the Reconstruction of Western Europe 1947–52*, Cambridge University Press.

Horsefield, J. Keith (1969), *The International Monetary Fund 1945–65*, Washington DC: International Monetary Fund.

Jacobsson, Erin E. (1979), *A Life for Sound Money: Per Jacobsson (His Biography)*, Oxford: Oxford University Press.

Kahn, Richard Lord (1976), "Historical Origins of the International Monetary Fund," in A.P. Thirlwall (ed.), *Keynes and International Monetary Relations*, London: Macmillan, pp. 3–35.

Kaplan, Jacob J. and Günther Schleiminger (1989), *The European Payments Union*, Oxford: Oxford University Press.

Kenen, Peter (1991), "Transitional Arrangements for Trade and Payments among the CMEA Countries," *International Monetary Fund Staff Papers*, 38: 235–67.

Keynes, John Maynard (1980) (ed. Donald Moggridge), *Collected Writings XXV: Activities 1940–1944, Shaping the Post-War World: The Clearing Union*, Cambridge: Macmillan and Cambridge University Press.

Kindleberger, Charles P. (1967), *Europe's Postwar Growth*, Cambridge, Mass.: Harvard University Press.

Kunz, Diane B. (1991), *The Economic Diplomacy of the Suez Crisis*, Chapel Hill: University of North Carolina Press.

Milward, Alan S. (1984), *The Reconstruction of Western Europe 1945–51*, London: Methuen.

Moggridge, Donald (1992), *Maynard Keynes: An Economist's Biography*, London: Routledge.

Nurkse, Ragnar (1944), *International Currency Experience*, Geneva: League of Nations.

Polak, J.J. (1991), "Convertibility: An Indispensable Element in the Transition Process in Eastern Europe," in John Williamson (ed.), *Currency Convertibility in Eastern Europe*, Washington DC: Institute for International Economics, pp. 21–30.

Postan, M.M. (1964), *An Economic History of Western Europe 1945–1964*, London: Methuen.

Solomon, Robert (1982), *The International Monetary System 1945–1981*, New York: Columbia University Press.

Triffin, Robert (1960), *Gold and the Dollar Crisis*, New Haven: Yale University Press.

(1984), "The European Monetary System: Tombstone or Cornerstone?" in *The International Monetary System: Forty Years after Bretton Woods*, Boston: Federal Reserve Bank of Boston, pp. 127–73.

Van Brabant, Jozef M. (1991), "Convertibility in Eastern Europe through a Payments Union," in John Williamson (ed.), *Currency Convertibility in*

Eastern Europe, Washington DC: Institute for International Economics, pp. 63–95.

Williamson, John (1991), "The Economic Opening in Eastern Europe," in John Williamson (ed.), *Currency Convertibility in Eastern Europe*, Washington DC: Institute for International Economics, pp. 361–431.

5 The GATT's contribution to economic recovery in post-war Western Europe

DOUGLAS A. IRWIN

1 Introduction

The contrast between the decade of economic instability in Western Europe after World War I and the economic recovery established in the decade following World War II is nowhere more evident than in the area of international trade relations. Economic reconstruction following World War I lacked any institutional mechanism to facilitate the reduction of trade barriers that had arisen during the war and had become entrenched thereafter. The political weakness of European countries in trade policy was evident when a proposal for "equality of trade conditions" in a draft League of Nations charter was rejected in favor of a weaker provision for "equitable treatment." The World Economic Conference in 1927 still found it necessary to call upon governments to remove wartime controls on trade, which included import quotas, licensing requirements, and foreign exchange controls. A decade after its formation, the League of Nations had yet to sponsor any negotiations on liberalizing world trade from high tariffs, and the onset of the depression vanquished any serious prospect of trade reform in Europe and elsewhere.

Yet during World War II, even in advance of official US participation in the conflict, the United States and the United Kingdom already envisioned a post-war world trading system based on reducing all trade barriers and limiting discriminatory tariff preferences. Just two years after Germany's surrender, twenty-three countries established a General Agreement on Tariffs and Trade (GATT) that set rules to restrict national trade policies and even started to decrease tariffs in binding agreements. Just five years after the end of the war, all major Western European countries had

Financial support was provided by the James S. Kemper Faculty Foundation Research Fund of the Graduate School of Business at the University of Chicago. I wish to thank the Division of International Finance at the Board of Governors of the Federal Reserve System for their hospitality during my stay as a visiting scholar when much of this paper was completed, as well as Barry Eichengreen and J. Michael Finger for helpful comments.

participated in three separate negotiating rounds that had expanded GATT membership and further reduced import tariffs.

The GATT often has been hailed, almost by virtue of its very existence, as a key factor in promoting post-war recovery in Western Europe and in preventing a return to the disasters of the interwar period. By freeing Europe's regional and international trade from government restrictions, the GATT permitted economies to take advantage of specialization along lines of comparative advantage and thereby expand more rapidly and efficiently. While it is exceedingly difficult to quantify the impact of any institution on aggregate economic activity, *prima facie* evidence of the GATT's success arises from the divergence in the behavior of European trade after World War I – when no such institution was in place – and after World War II – when the GATT facilitated the reduction of trade barriers.

Figures 5.1 and 5.2 depict the path of a GNP-weighted average of export volume and real income for five major West European countries – France, Germany, Italy, the Netherlands, and the United Kingdom – after the two wars. By 1929, a dozen years after the war, the export volume of these countries had just barely surpassed its prewar (1913) peak. After World War II, by contrast, exports surpassed their prewar level in about five years, although it is important to note that the prewar (1938) level was perhaps artificially low owing to protectionism and the depression. Still, exports expanded by a factor of eight in the decade after World War II compared with a four-fold increase after World War I. The picture for national income is similar. This favorable outcome cannot clinch the case for the GATT's positive impact in promoting economic recovery after World War II, but the correlation between the dramatic increase in post-war trade and income and the establishment and activities of the GATT negotiations has weighed heavily in the minds of economists and policymakers.

This chapter describes and assesses the contribution of the GATT in fostering economic recovery in Western Europe during the decade from 1947 to 1956. Three questions will be posed for consideration:

(1) What were the origins of the GATT and what did it aim to achieve?
(2) How successful was the GATT in liberalizing Europe's trade?
(3) Was the GATT responsible for the post-war export boom?

To anticipate the chapter's main conclusions, the formation of the GATT does not appear to have stimulated a particularly rapid liberalization of world trade in the decade after 1947. It is therefore difficult to attribute much of a role to the GATT in the dramatic economic recovery during the immediate post-war period beyond that of an effective supporting actor. The principal contribution of the GATT during its first decade of operation

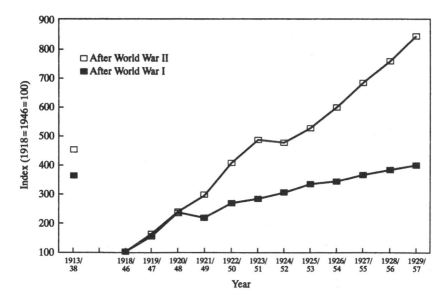

Figure 5.1   Export volume after World Wars I and II (in five West European economies)

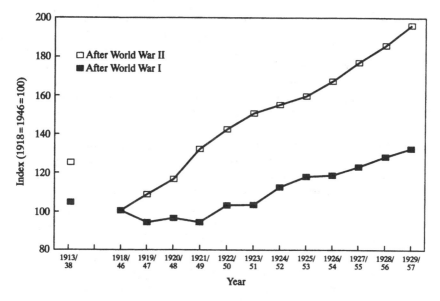

Figure 5.2   Real output after World Wars I and II (in five West European economies)

rests more in securing binding agreements on early tariff reductions, thereby preventing countries from instituting higher tariffs as import quotas and foreign exchange controls were being phased out during the 1950s under the auspices of other international institutions. Yet despite the GATT's weaknesses on several fronts, the institution succeeded in establishing among major countries a fairly credible commitment to an open and stable environment for world trade that fostered the post-war rise in trade and income.

2 The origins and purposes of the GATT

Preparations for a new world trading order began during World War II and date from the Atlantic Charter (August 1941) and the Lend-Lease (February 1942) agreements between the United States and the United Kingdom. In early discussions, both governments endorsed the principles of non-discrimination and free trade in post-war commercial policy. The British War Cabinet proposal on "Commercial Union" (drafted by James Meade) and the US State Department document "Multilateral Convention on Commercial Policy" emerged in September–October 1943 and formed the basis for ongoing bilateral discussions until 1945. In December 1945, the State Department completed a draft multilateral accord on rules for international trade that was acceptable to both governments.

The architects of the post-war international economic order were principally concerned with establishing institutions and promoting policies that would avoid the repetition of the interwar experience. To this end, their first objective was to design a stable international monetary system that would allow for domestic policies to maintain full employment. The reduction of tariffs and elimination of quantitative restrictions on international trade was an important part of the broad objective, but was not seen to be as urgent a priority as restoring monetary stability and achieving full employment. Consequently, while the Articles of Agreement of the International Monetary Fund (IMF) and the International Bank for Reconstruction and Development (IBRD) were formalized at the Bretton Woods Conference in 1944 and took effect shortly thereafter, agreements and institutions on commercial policy materialized more slowly. That trade was placed on this second track was to have important consequences for the types of agreements and institutions that later emerged.

With the completion of a draft charter in 1945, the US proposed opening international negotiations to finalize multilateral agreement on a charter for an International Trade Organization (ITO) that would take a place along side the IMF and IBRD. The ITO was to have wide scope over various aspects of international economic activity, with rules covering not just commercial policy but also employment, commodity agreements, restrictive business practices, and international investment. To hasten efforts at reducing tariff barriers, the US also invited countries to participate in tariff negotiations in concert with the ITO talks. In February 1946, the Economic and Social Council of the United Nations resolved to convene an international conference on trade and employment to negotiate an ITO charter, and eighteen countries attended a preparatory meeting in London during October–November 1946. In January–February 1947 at Lake Success, New York, negotiators drafted the technical articles of the charter along with a preliminary general agreement on commercial policy, and by August a subsequent conference in Geneva prepared an ITO draft charter for submission to the UN conference. From November 1947 to March 1948, the UN Conference on Trade and Employment in Havana (composed of fifty-six countries) finalized and ratified the ITO charter. This approval came nearly four years after the Bretton Woods Conference, over two years after the initial US proposal for an ITO, and almost half a year after the first post-war negotiations on reducing tariffs (as will be discussed shortly).

The lack of urgency with which the ITO was created portended its demise as an institution. The Havana Charter languished for an additional three years as the agreement encountered domestic controversy in the United States during efforts to obtain formal approval. Business interests that had supported bilateral tariff negotiations in the 1930s under the Reciprocal Trade Agreements Act of 1934 balked at supporting an international organization with wide-ranging regulatory authority over trade, investment, and business practices. The Executive Committee of the US Council of the International Chamber of Commerce, as quoted in Diebold (1952a, pp. 20–1), denounced the draft ITO charter as a "dangerous document because it accepts practically all of the policies of economic nationalism; because it jeopardizes the free enterprise system by giving priority to a centralized national governmental planning of foreign trade; because it leaves a wide scope to discrimination, accepts the principles of economic insulation, and in effect commits all members of the ITO to state planning for full employment."

Other pressing international concerns also prevented the Truman administration from viewing the ITO as a major priority and from marshalling business support for the agreement; the United States was preoccupied with the Marshall Plan in 1948, with the North Atlantic Treaty Organization in 1949, and with the Korean War in 1950. In the face of continued opposition to the ITO, the Truman administration announced in December 1950 that the ITO would not be submitted for Congressional approval, effectively killing the agreement.

Fortunately, the collapse of the ITO did not extinguish the only means of liberalizing world trade policies. Also at the Geneva meeting in 1947, on a parallel track with the ITO negotiations, twenty-three nations agreed to enact revised versions of the commercial policy articles in the existing ITO draft charter – called the General Agreement on Tariffs and Trade – and agreed to reduce tariffs amongst themselves. The agreement and the tariff reductions were finalized on October 30, 1947 and came into force for most countries on January 1, 1948 – and did not require Congressional approval in the case of the United States. The GATT was viewed as an intermediate measure to implement the commercial policy clauses of the ITO and accelerate the reduction of tariffs on world trade while the ITO was being finalized. The GATT was never designed to exist as an institution itself, but only to serve as a temporary agreement until it could be absorbed into the ITO structure. The GATT immediately became the forum for early trade policy discussions, however, and in the wake of the ITO's failure became the sole body for overseeing international commercial policies.

The Geneva negotiations in 1947 that produced the GATT were undertaken by twenty-three participating countries, listed in table 5.1, who became Contracting Parties. The purpose of the GATT, as stated in its preamble, was to contribute to rising standards of living and full employment by "entering into reciprocal and mutually advantageous arrangements directed to the substantial reduction of tariffs and other barriers to trade and to the elimination of discriminatory treatment in international commerce." Part I of the General Agreement contained two articles, the first mandating unconditional most-favored-nation (MFN) treatment for all Contracting Parties and the second consisting of annexed schedules of all tariff reductions that arose during negotiations. Part II of the Agreement included the main rules on commercial policy but was applied "provisionally," meaning the Contracting Parties were obligated to implement them "to the fullest extent not inconsistent" with existing national legislation. Article XI contained a general prohibition on quantitative restrictions, although Article XII made an exception in the case of balance of payments safeguards. Article XIX described conditions under which a GATT obligation could be nullified or withdrawn with compensation for trading partners. Many of the other articles dealt with mundane issues such as customs valuation, marks of origin, and other technical matters. Part III of the Agreement contained articles on the functioning of the GATT.

3 What did the GATT accomplish?

In light of the protectionist legacy of the 1930s and the deeply entrenched state regulation of economic activity bequeathed by World War II, the

Table 5.1. *Participants at GATT negotiating rounds*

Geneva, 1947

Australia, Belgium, Brazil, Burma, Canada, Ceylon, Chile, China, Cuba, Czechoslovakia, France, India, Lebanon, Luxembourg, the Netherlands, New Zealand, Norway, Pakistan, South Africa, Southern Rhodesia, Syria, the United Kingdom, the United States

Annecy, 1949

Above, plus

Colombia, Denmark, Dominican Republic, Finland, Greece, Haiti, Italy, Liberia, Nicaragua, Sweden, Uruguay

Torquay, 1950–1

Above, plus

Austria, Germany, Guatemala, Korea, Peru, Philippines, Turkey

Note: Not all participants became Contracting Parties to the GATT.
Source: Various GATT publications.

GATT's agenda of trade liberalization and constraints on national discretion in trade policy was quite ambitious. The rules set down for the conduct of commercial policy were stringent, particularly unconditional MFN treatment for GATT members and the general prohibition of quantitative restrictions. There was sufficient latitude within the Agreement, however, to accommodate state behavior at variance with a strict interpretation of GATT rules. Colonial tariff preferences in effect in 1947 were not affected by the MFN requirement, quotas for balance of payments purposes were permitted, and import restrictions on agricultural and fisheries products were sanctioned. Gaining fuller adherence to all GATT rules by members was not immediately achieved and could only come with time – indeed, it has yet to be attained even today.

But the most pressing objective of the GATT was to oversee the reduction of import tariffs, and it was here that the GATT could make an important contribution to European recovery. These reductions took place over a series of negotiating rounds, three of which were held in the crucial, early post-war period.

First round: *Geneva, Switzerland, April–October 1947*

The Geneva negotiations in advance of the ITO's formation were motivated in part by the expiry of US presidential negotiating authority in June 1948. In 1945, Congress renewed the Reciprocal Trade Agreements Act of 1934 for three additional years and permitted the president to reduce US tariffs up to 50 percent in reciprocal agreements. The pending expiration of this negotiating authority put pressure on international negotiators to conclude a preliminary agreement with the United States on reducing tariffs. Consequently, twenty-three participating countries that accounted for roughly 80 percent of world trade successfully agreed to cut and bind tariffs in negotiations held from April to October 1947, with the tariff reductions designed to enter into effect in January 1948 for most countries.

The first several GATT rounds consisted of *bilateral* tariff negotiations on a product-by-product basis under the principle of "reciprocal mutual advantage" and the principal-supplier rule. In preparation for the negotiations, countries would exchange lists of "requests" for tariff modifications on various products. Each country would consider a request for such a tariff "concession" on a given product only from the "principal supplier" of that product in exchange for a reduction in the principal supplier's tariff on another item of interest to the country. Under the "reciprocal mutual advantage" principle, no country would be forced to make any unilateral concessions. If a bilateral agreement was reached, the tariff reduction would then be "generalized," i.e., applied in an MFN fashion to all other GATT participants. Other countries would thus benefit from the tariff reduction, but it was up to the major supplier to a particular market to ensure that a given tariff in that market would be reduced. Thus, the GATT harnessed export interests in the negotiations to create the impetus for lower tariffs.

In the first Geneva round in 1947, according to the GATT (1949, p. 11), the twenty-three countries made not less than 123 agreements covering 45,000 tariff items that related to approximately one-half of world trade. The tariff reductions were certainly not across the board or applied to import-sensitive sectors, such as agriculture, but concentrated on sectors that lacked the political strength to absolve them from consideration. Unfortunately, there is no convenient data on the precise depth of the tariff cuts of the Contracting Parties. The United States, however, calculated that the average cut in its tariff from existing levels amounted to 35 percent, as discussed in Finger (1979). As it is generally acknowledged that the United States made the deepest tariff cuts, this is probably the upper bound for the overall tariff reductions of European countries. The scaling down of the US tariff was important for Western Europe because greater access to the US market enabled these countries to earn scarce dollar reserves, which could then be used to purchase US capital goods and other imports. To place an order of magnitude on the value of these tariff concessions would be a difficult exercise, but the United States deserves credit for taking the first and largest step on the road to lower tariffs and for providing the leadership that led to the GATT.

The Contracting Parties agreed that the tariff reductions negotiated at Geneva should remain in place for at least three years, until January 1, 1951. Thus the GATT provided some protection or safeguard against the nullification or impairment of these tariff "concessions" made in Geneva. This binding applied only to tariff concessions made in the Geneva negotiations, however, and other tariffs could be adjusted freely.

Second round: Annecy, France, April 1949–October 1949

The primary purpose of the Annecy negotiations was to allow the accession of eleven other countries – listed in table 5.1 – to the GATT as Contracting Parties. The original twenty-three members did not exchange tariff concessions with each other but did negotiate with the eleven new members of the GATT, and these tariff changes were generalized. This widened the geographic scope of GATT membership and provided for a marginal reduction in tariff levels.

Third round: Torquay, England, September 1950–April 1951

The third GATT round saw the original Contracting Parties again exchanging tariff concessions among themselves along with several new members acceding to the GATT, most importantly the Federal Republic of Germany. But the additional tariff reductions emerging from these negotiations were modest, and the round was not considered a success. The official communiqué, cited in Diebold (1952b, p. 229), announced that the agreements were not "of such scope and magnitude as to represent a sufficient contribution to the reduction of existing disparities in the level of European tariffs." And the GATT (1952, p. 9) later stated that "the results of Torquay were not as broad or as extensive as some had hoped," with only 144 agreements reached out of an expected 400. Adding to the impression of failure was the announcement during the negotiations by President Truman that the ITO would not be sent to the Congress, thereby effectively killing the prospective institution.

The Torquay round ran into two problems that accounted for much of this failure: a dispute between the United States and the United Kingdom, and the growing disparity of tariff levels within Europe. The continuing dollar shortage in Europe prompted the United Kingdom to request unilateral tariff cuts by the United States, which the United States rejected on the grounds of the reciprocal mutual benefit criteria. For its part the United States sought elimination or substantial reduction of tariff preferences within the British Commonwealth. After failures to find common ground, the United Kingdom agreed to reduce the preference margin only slightly so both sides could claim success in the negotiations, but neither side compromised significantly and there were no bilateral tariff cuts on US–UK trade. The failure of both countries to agree on tariff concessions meant that others would not benefit indirectly from their generalization. According to Koch (1969, p. 71), "this attitude unfavorably affected countries that would have reaped indirect benefits from such tariff cuts and made them cautious about granting concessions in their own negotiations."

Also during the Torquay negotiations, the Benelux and Scandinavian countries argued that a new negotiating approach on tariffs was needed because the bargaining power of the low-tariff countries was limited and the GATT was not proving effective in reducing the tariffs of the high-tariff countries. The GATT charter stated that "the binding against increases of low duties or of duty-free treatment shall, in principle, be recognized as a concession equivalent in value to the substantial reduction of high duties or the elimination of tariff preferences." But adherence to this statement was not enforceable in practice because of the reciprocal mutual advantage provision.

In September 1951, several countries proposed to drop the bilateral, product-by-product method of GATT in favor of a broader approach to liberalization. The "GATT Plan" – put to the Contracting Parties in 1953 with the support of Belgium, Denmark, France, West Germany, and the Netherlands – called for a 30 percent weighted-average reduction in tariffs to be phased in over three years. Tariffs were divided into product categories – raw materials, food, semi-processed goods, and industrial goods – and tariff rates were capped at mandated ceilings. The plan elicited little enthusiasm from the United States and the United Kingdom, which had both become resistant to further liberalization. The GATT plan as a multilateral approach lay dormant through the 1950s, although it became the method to eliminate tariffs within the European Economic Community and was applied with great success in the Kennedy round of the 1960s.

One positive result from Torquay was that all tariff reductions from the Geneva and Annecy rounds were renewed and extended until 1954 (and later extended again until the end of the 1950s). Before the rebinding of tariffs there was a brief window in which concessions could be moderated or withdrawn, but there were only a few minor instances of countries invoking this provision.

Widespread pessimism and frustration with the GATT process marked the end of the Torquay round. After a fruitful negotiating round in 1947 and a membership expansion in 1949, the GATT's momentum had suddenly stalled very early in the post-war recovery. After the difficulties at Torquay, more than five years elapsed before the next GATT conference, and that one (in Geneva in 1956) produced similarly meager results. GATT membership also stagnated: in January 1952, the GATT had thirty-four Contracting Parties that accounted for over 80 percent of world trade, but from 1952 to 1957, GATT membership increased by only one country on net, with the withdrawal of Liberia being balanced by the accession of Japan and Uruguay. The momentum toward lower tariffs was lost; further progress on reduced trade barriers had stalled.

Intransigence on both sides of the Atlantic accounted for the faltering of the GATT. On the one hand, "an important factor [behind the passivity during this period] was the growing protectionism in the United States . . . there was a feeling that the United States had given away concessions without any real corresponding benefit, as the European countries were slow in eliminating their discrimination against dollar goods," writes Koch (1969, pp. 82, 84). On the European side, the United Kingdom refused to dismantle colonial preferences, and the low-tariff countries were frustrated by their inability to bargain effectively with high-tariff countries.

Thus, by 1951 the GATT was at a crossroads. The multilateral effort to reduce tariffs progressively was locked in a stalemate that continued through much of the 1950s. It is doubtful that an ITO, with its multifaceted agenda, could have expedited this process; indeed, things may have proceeded more slowly under an ITO owing to the greater complexity of the issues it was designed to address. The pause in GATT activity reflected the transatlantic wrangle over the future course of trade negotiations, and a shift toward regional concerns where common objectives and interests were more readily apparent. Consequently, the GATT remained largely inactive in the 1950s while a European program of trade liberalization proceeded under the auspices of the Organization for European Economic Cooperation and the European Economic Community. Not until the Dillon and Kennedy rounds in 1961–2 and 1964–7 did the GATT return as the forum for a significant attempt at world trade liberalization. Thus, if the GATT had an impact on the immediate post-war economic recovery in Europe, it would come as a result of its accomplishments in the late 1940s.

So what were the major GATT achievements and shortcomings?

TARIFF REDUCTIONS

The major achievement of the GATT was the extensive tariff reductions in the first negotiating round in Geneva. Unfortunately, as already noted, the

Table 5.2. *Average tariff levels in select countries (in percent)*

	1913	1925	1927	1931	1952
Belgium	6	7	11	17	n.a.
France	14	9	23	38	19
Germany	12	15	24	40	16
Italy	17	16	27	48	24
Netherlands	2	4	n.a.	n.a.	n.a.
United Kingdom	n.a.	4	n.a.	17	17
United States	32	26	n.a.	n.a.	16

Note: Not all years are comparable.
Sources: Calculations for 1913 and 1925 are from the League of Nations as reported in GATT (1953), p. 62, also the source for the 1952 GATT calculation. For 1927 and 1931 tariff data, see Liepmann (1938), p. 415, and Kitson and Solomou (1990), pp. 65–6, for the United Kingdom in 1932.

extent of these tariff reductions is extremely difficult to quantify. The GATT itself refused to calculate the actual reductions for fear that they could be used by import-sensitive business interests to slow the liberalization process. Table 5.2 presents the sole official GATT calculation of tariff levels in major Western European countries for the year 1952, along with estimates from earlier years. The GATT figures did not include a calculation of tariff levels in 1947, just before the Geneva cuts went into effect, but a comparison with prewar (i.e., 1925) tariff levels suggest that tariffs were much lower in the United States and in Scandinavia by 1952 but remained higher in the United Kingdom, France, and Germany.

What the United States actually conceded in the GATT negotiating rounds is overstated by this calculation, however, because a significant amount of trade liberalization took place from 1934 to 1947 under the Reciprocal Trade Agreements Act. According to Lavergne (1983, pp. 32–3), these agreements cut tariffs by 44 percent on over 60 percent of US trade (by value), amounting to a 33.2 percent reduction in duties overall and leaving duties at 66.8 percent of their level in 1930. The first GATT round in Geneva reduced duties by 35.0 percent on just over 50 percent of all dutiable imports, making the overall tariff reduction 21.1 percent and leaving the US tariff at 52.7 percent of its 1930 level. The Annecy and Torquay rounds cut tariffs on less than 12 percent of trade and barely made a mark on US duties overall.

While questions remain about the extent of the tariff cuts among European countries, there is also considerable uncertainty about the effects of the tariff cuts on trade. Because quantitative restraints and foreign exchange restrictions remained in place, it is not clear that the tariff reductions translated into more open market access in Europe. The US market was demonstrably more open because the country never resorted to quotas on manufactured goods, but European imports from the United States were hampered by dollar restrictions. Even within the European market trade was hampered by exchange controls and other restrictions.

For this reason, the tariff cuts from the Geneva and subsequent negotiations may have had limited effect. One early study of the impact of GATT concessions by Lawrence Krause (1959, p. 555) found that "such tariff reductions as those given by the US at Torquay do not lead to a significant increase in the volume of imports." However, the initial ineffectiveness of the tariff reductions – particularly for European countries – may have diminished over time as other forms of liberalization took place over the 1950s. As the GATT (1952, p. 8, emphasis added) itself recognized, "the cumulative effect of the three post-war tariff conferences will permit an expanding volume of trade at more moderate levels of customs duties, *particularly when quantitative restrictions on imports are removed.*"

Indeed, the Geneva tariff cuts may have been larger than otherwise politically possible because they were viewed as initially neutralized by quantitative and foreign exchange restrictions. As Curzon (1965, p. 70) explains, "countries believing that quantitative restrictions would be a permanent feature of the post-war world gave sham but very substantial reductions on their tariff rates in exchange for real reductions from the only country not to apply quotas on manufactured goods, i.e., the United States." "As quotas and discriminatory use of import licensing fade, ultimately vanish, the concessions exchanged at Geneva . . . will acquire real substance," argued the *Economist* (April 23, 1949, p. 757). In this respect, the initial tariff concessions may have been larger than countries had anticipated, and with time – toward the end of the 1950s – their impact on trade may have become apparent. One could speculate that the GATT cut tariffs so significantly that it hindered efforts to eliminate quantitative and foreign exchange restrictions, but this contention lacks supporting evidence.

TARRIF BINDINGS

Each Contracting Party was bound to the terms of the GATT indefinitely, including any tariff concessions that became embodied in the annexes to Article II. While tariff concessions once given were considered fixed in perpetuity, countries retained the right to invoke Article XXVIII, which allowed them to revoke tariff concessions after negotiating an agreement with the principal supplier or after accepting the withdrawal of equivalent concessions from other countries. This article thus contained a mechanism by which the negotiated tariff cuts could be unraveled by mutual agreements.

To ensure the continuity and integrity of the Geneva cuts and provide for a measure of tariff stability that had been absent in the interwar period, the Contracting Parties at Geneva ruled out the right to invoke Article XXVIII for three years, i.e., until 1951. At the Torquay negotiations this period of "firm validity" was extended through 1954 and was later extended again through 1957. Each time the period of "firm validity" was extended, a short window was offered to countries to modify their tariffs as allowed in Article XXVIII, but only minor withdrawals and modifications were taken by a very few countries. Although reluctant to march toward further trade liberalization, countries at least recognized the gains from preventing an erosion of the early GATT successes. Freezing the right to resort to Article XXVIII ensured that the initial tariff cuts under the GATT would be preserved throughout the 1950s even if no further progress was made in lowering tariffs and even as import quotas were being phased out. This may have been one of the GATT's major contributions to promoting economic recovery in Western Europe – ruling out for an extended period reliance on tariffs to replace other trade barriers that were falling.

NON-DISCRIMINATION

Article I of the GATT makes unconditional most-favored-nation treatment a cornerstone of the Agreement. The major exception was for preferential tariff policies in effect in 1947, which included the United Kingdom (the Commonwealth), the United States (Cuba and the Philippines), and France and the Benelux countries (their colonies), although the Contracting Parties agreed not to increase or establish new preferences. Only British Commonwealth preference persisted as a major issue, and in the first Geneva GATT negotiations the United States and the United Kingdom wrangled over the preferences. The UK adamantly refused to bend to US opposition to these preferences, but a compromise in which preference margins were reduced defused the issue temporarily. The US failure to achieve its long-held goal of eliminating the Commonwealth tariff preferences was never achieved.

Indeed, it soon became clear that a host of discriminatory policies in Europe would exist outside the GATT purview, as Finger (1993) has described. The members of the Organization for European Economic Cooperation (OEEC), for example, began an effort to stimulate intra-European trade by eliminating license, quota, and exchange restrictions as they affected each other. Although this technically violated the GATT's MFN provision, the US not merely acquiesced but encouraged this program as part of its policy to strengthen Europe. Koch (1969, p. 116) notes that "the OEEC policy was tacitly accepted without any waiver being asked for" and, subsequently, the GATT has not posed as a barrier to discriminatory policies of this sort.

QUANTITATIVE RESTRICTIONS
For achievements on the tariff front to be fully realized, they needed to be matched by advances in the removal of quantitative restrictions (QRs). Article XI contains a general commitment of GATT members not to use QRs on trade. Article XIV, however, provides an exception in the case of the "post-war transition period" and Article XII permits the limited use of QRs in the context of short-term balance of payments problems. Their use for this reason came principally under the domain of the IMF and this justification remained viable into the 1950s. QRs were not even the subject of negotiation during the first three GATT rounds and indeed did not come under GATT negotiations until the Dillon round of 1961–2.

In 1950, with the stalled Torquay round in process, the major Western European countries in the Organization for European Economic Cooperation agreed to a Code of Liberalization that set a timetable for the gradual elimination of QRs on intra-European trade. Discrimination continued against hard-currency countries such as the United States, but the OEEC achieved considerable success in freeing Europe's trade from QRs. The OEEC countries originally agreed to remove all quota restrictions on 50 percent of their imports in 1949, and the formal Code established targets of 60 percent in 1950 and 75 percent in 1951. Although some backsliding occurred in Germany in 1951 and in the United Kingdom and France in 1952, owing to balance of payments difficulties and an economic downturn, respectively, table 5.3 shows that this reversal proved temporary.

The OEEC program of progressively eliminating intra-European trade barriers, described in more detail by Boyer and Sallé (1955), provided a distinct boost to European trade. Figure 5.3 illustrates the volume of OEEC exports to OEEC countries and to other countries. Intra-European trade grew in step with Europe's worldwide trade in 1947–9, but with the relaxation of quota restrictions in 1949–50, intra-European export volume jumped significantly above overall export volume. When further headway was made against QRs from 1953, intra-European trade again grew more rapidly than overall trade. The OEEC's great success paved the way for the creation of a Common Market later in the decade.

Thus, significant progress on a key aspect of liberalizing trade came not from the GATT but from other European institutions. According to Koch (1969, p. 144), "The fact cannot be denied that OEEC contributed to a substantial relaxation of controls on intra-European trade in a period when the members of the OEEC felt that there was little prospect of getting results

Table 5.3. *Liberalization of intra-OEEC trade, 1950–5 (percent, by end of year)*

	1950	1951	1952	1953	1954	1955
France	66	76	0	18	65	78
Germany	63	0	81	90	90	91
Italy	76	77	100	100	100	99
Netherlands	66	71	75	87	88	96
United Kingdom	86	61	44	75	83	85

Source: OEEC (1958).

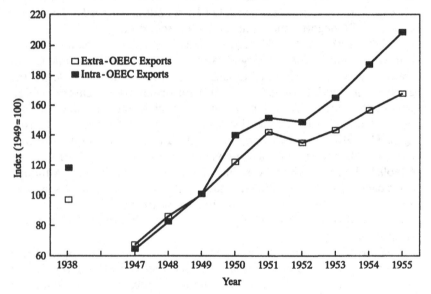

Figure 5.3   Post-war OEEC export volume
Source: OEEC (1956), p. 69.

in the GATT." Yet the GATT was not entirely moot on the QR question. As she also points out (ibid.), "the [GATT] system of consultations led to constant pressure on member countries to motivate and defend their restrictive measures. . . . Even if convertibility and economic expansion had been a contributory factor in the process of dismantling quantitative restrictions on industrial goods, there is no doubt that at a later stage GATT consultations were an important factor."

ASSESSMENT

The impression is often given that the GATT, since its formation, has made consistent and incremental progress on trade liberalization. A re-examination of its first decade illustrates that this progress came quickly in the late 1940s and then languished for some time. Indeed, the GATT experienced many shortcomings during its first decade – tariff cutting was rather limited, preferences and other discriminatory practices were not eradicated, and import quotas were not abolished and fell outside its jurisdiction. In retrospect, the initial achievements of the GATT appear somewhat modest in light of its success in the Kennedy round in the 1960s and thereafter. The GATT diminished tariffs at its founding conference in 1947, but the climate for further substantial reductions was not evident thereafter. In terms of concrete actions, the best that can be said for the GATT after 1947 is that it established non-discrimination as the presumption for the conduct of trade relations and, perhaps more importantly, that it held the line on the temptation for countries to substitute higher tariffs for liberalized quotas under the OEEC program.

The principal, initial effects of the GATT may lie in the important but nebulous areas of credibility and commitment. That is, individuals and firms may be more willing to engage in trade if they suspect that governments are committed to certain tariff rates – a stable trading environment – and the outlook promises further, if uneven, progress on trade liberalization. The GATT gained some measure of credibility by virtue of its early agreement to reduce tariffs and expand membership. In sharp contrast to the frequent government proclamations in favor of freer trade during the interwar period, proclamations that were left hanging with no concrete action whatsoever, negotiators within the GATT actually secured and implemented an agreement to reduce tariffs just two years after the end of World War II. The GATT Contracting Parties demonstrated some commitment to this outcome by not allowing tariff concessions to expire, thereby avoiding the need to renegotiate trade agreements frequently, which had created problems for pre-World War I tariff treaties, described in Irwin (1993). The interwar period was marked by the absence of any credible move toward trade liberalization or any demonstration of commitment to that objective, although the effect of these features of the GATT regime on economic performance cannot be ascertained in a precise way.

4 European trade under the GATT: a comparison with the post-World War I experience

Despite what appears to have been very limited initial achievements, especially in light of subsequent trade liberalization, the GATT did make a firm break with interwar commercial policies and set world trade policies on a new path. And the outcome of the post-World War II period, in terms of recovery in economic activity and international trade, has never been viewed as anything but a great success exactly because in the decade following the war Europe managed to avoid the interwar catastrophe. The fact that this happened under the GATT's stewardship means that the institution itself stands to credit. But a closer comparison of the behavior of European trade and income during these two periods may shed light on what the GATT (and the OEEC) helped to accomplish.

Figures 5.1 and 5.2 depict the evolution of export volume and real income (weighted by GNP) for a sample of five Western European countries – France, Germany, Italy, the Netherlands, and the United Kingdom – using data from appendices A and F of Maddison (1991). Figure 5.1 presents exports in the twelve years after the armistice (1918–29) and after Germany's surrender (1946–57). Figure 5.2 shows real income over the same period. Both figures also indicate the relevant prewar level of exports and income – 1913 before World War I and 1938 before World War II. In the dozen years after World War I, incomes doubled and exports nearly quadrupled. In the dozen years after World War II, incomes almost tripled and exports grew eight-fold. Clearly, the post-World War II expansion was significantly greater than that after World War I. While it took seven years (to 1924) for European incomes after 1918 to match their prewar level, just four years after World War II (to 1949) incomes reached their 1938 level. Exports after World War I matched their prewar peak in eleven years (to 1928), while after World War II it took just six years (to 1951) for exports to surpass their 1938 level.

Yet the tremendous increase in export volume after World War II may reflect nothing other than this more rapid increase in income – owing perhaps to favorable macroeconomic factors rather than the GATT – and the underlying relationship between trade and income could have remained similar during the two periods. But econometric evidence points to substantial differences in the relationship between trade and income in the two post-war periods. Concerns about spurious correlation because of common trends rule out any regression of the levels of export volume and real income variables alone, so consider the following error-correction model which includes the variables in both levels and differenced terms:

$$\Delta x_t = \beta_1 \Delta y_t + (\alpha - 1)\{x_{t-1} - \gamma_1 y_{t-1} - \gamma_0\} + \varepsilon_t,$$

where x_t is the log of export volume and y_t is the log of real income. This equation relates the change in exports to the change in income and a lagged deviation of the long-run association of the two variables. This reflects both the short- and long-run interaction of the variables: the differenced terms capture the short-run impact of a change in income on the change in export volume; the error-correction mechanism, expressed in levels, allows exports to return to their long-run value (because $\alpha - 1 < 0$). The long-run relationship is based on $x_t = v_0 + v_1 y_t + v_2 y_{t-1} + \alpha x_{t-1} + \xi_t$, a structure sufficient to ensure that ξ_t is white noise, and errors from the long-run solution are defined as $z_t = x_t - \gamma_1 y_t - \gamma_0$, where $\gamma_1 = (v_1 + v_2)/(1 - \alpha)$, which is the long-run elasticity of trade with respect to income, and $\gamma_0 = v_0/(1 - \alpha)$. Subtracting x_{t-1} from this equation and noting that $z_t = (1 - \alpha)x_t - (v_1 + v_2)y_t - v_0$ yields the error-correction model.

To ascertain the short- and long-run impact of an increase in income on the volume of exports, the model is estimated using OLS for the periods 1919–29 and 1947–57 with a sample of five major West European economies (France, Germany, Italy, the Netherlands, and the United Kingdom) using Maddison's (1991) data. The estimation yields the following results (standard errors in parenthesis):

1919–29

$$\Delta x_t = 1.94\Delta y_t - 0.66\{x_{t-1} - 1.53y_{t-1} + 1.52\}$$
$$\quad\ (0.73)\quad\ (0.30)\quad\quad\ (0.34)\quad\quad\ (1.59)$$
$$R^2 = 0.88 \quad F = 30.9 \quad \sigma = 6.4\% \quad DW = 3.02$$

1947–57

$$\Delta x_t = 1.40\Delta y_t - 0.63\{x_{t-1} - 2.33y_{t-1} + 5.49\}$$
$$\quad\ (0.66)\quad\ (0.10)\quad\quad\ (0.29)\quad\quad\ (1.54)$$
$$R^2 = 0.90 \quad F = 34.2 \quad \sigma = 5.2\% \quad DW = 2.60.$$

Although they must be interpreted with caution because of the short sample period, the results nonetheless provide some useful insights into the behavior of trade and income over the two post-war periods. The short-run impact of a change in real income was associated with a much larger increase in trade after World War I than after World War II – 1.94 percent as opposed to 1.40 percent. However, the long-run elasticity of trade with respect to income (γ_1) was substantially greater in the post-World War II era (2.33) than in the interwar period (1.53). These long-run relationships are sufficiently distinct from one another to suggest a much greater responsiveness of trade to rising income after World War II than after World War I. Furthermore, the long-run elasticity is greater than the short-run elasticity after World War II, indicating that the effect of income on trade grew with time instead of overshooting and reverting to a lower mean.

Unfortunately, the econometric results are incompletely informative about the underlying source of the difference in the trade and income relationship after the two wars. It could well be that the mere presence of the GATT – in stabilizing tariffs and committing countries to the path of trade liberalization – spurred a more rapid increase in trade than seen after World War I, but alternative hypotheses are also consistent with the evidence and cannot be dismissed. Other post-war institutions aiming at international monetary stability, for example, may have fostered an environment that was conducive to international exchange, or domestic economic policies that were absent after World War I may have triggered the greater trade response.

Another plausible explanation for the greater trade responsiveness to income after World War II was that a catch-up or convergence process in trade-to-GNP ratios was taking place. In the Western economies that later comprised the Organization for Economic Cooperation and Development (OECD), according to Maddison (1989, p. 143), the ratio of merchandise exports to GDP at current prices stood at 21.2 percent in 1913. This ratio fell to 18.9 percent in 1929 as a result of World War I, and fell further to 15.1 percent in 1950 as a result of the depression and wartime disruptions. Consequently, there was ample room for international trade to be restored to a higher share of economic activity as normal, peacetime patterns of trade returned. Indeed, through the 1950s and 1960s the ratio gradually moved back to over 20 percent, where it had been in 1913. In any case, the fact remains that trade grew faster after World War II than after World War I not simply because incomes grew faster, but because the underlying relationship between the two had changed. And trade liberalization under the GATT and the OEEC provides one conceivable explanation for this outcome.

These equations, which suggest that growth in trade arose from increases in real income, raise the related question of whether real income can truly be viewed as the exogenous, driving variable. An obvious alternative hypothesis, suggested by Bhagwati (1988) for example, is that expanding international trade led to higher real income after World War II. These regressions cannot even begin to address such complex, dynamic relationships between trade and income, but Irwin (1992) reports Hausman tests on similar regressions with a larger sample of countries and a longer sample period which indicate that, for econometric purposes, income is not endogenous with respect to trade and that a channel runs more distinctly from income to trade than from trade to income. This should not be interpreted as saying that trade had no effects on economic growth, but that these effects are more subtle than can be identified in annual, aggregate time-series data.

Furthermore, in a stark macroeconomic accounting sense, real net exports were a secondary contributor to rising real income in the early post-war period. Table 5.4 shows that real net exports never accounted for much more than a percentage point of economic growth in the OEEC

Table 5.4. *Sources of growth in OEEC's real national product, 1948–55*
(percentage point contribution to change in GNP)

Year	National expenditure	Net exports	Gross national product
1948	4.2	3.3	7.5
1949	6.1	1.2	7.3
1950	6.1	1.1	7.2
1951	6.2	−0.7	5.5
1952	1.9	1.0	2.9
1953	5.2	0.3	5.5
1954	4.9	−0.2	4.7
1955	6.0	0.0	6.0

Source: Calculated from the OEEC (1957), p. 39.

countries (essentially all of Western Europe) and that domestic demand was the primary source of expansion. Yet the notable exception to this pattern is in 1948, the year in which the GATT tariff cuts first took effect, when net exports amounted to 3.3 percentage points of the 7.5 percent increase in the GNP of the OEEC countries. This may have been just part of the economic recovery from 1946 to 1947, but if the GATT actually made a contribution to this figure then post-war economic growth could have been even more rapid had the movement toward lower tariffs not stalled after about 1950.

5 The GATT's contribution: a tentative assessment

One is left with tremendous uncertainty about the precise role of the GATT in promoting economic recovery in Western Europe in the first decade after the war. Its role was almost surely secondary to sound domestic macro-economic and microeconomic policies. After all, the GATT did not achieve much for an entire decade after the 1947 tariff cuts and the 1949 membership expansion. These initial tariff cuts did not fully take hold until other trade restrictions were eliminated over the course of the 1950s. And the trade liberalization of the 1950s that was of substantial importance took place outside of the GATT. The OEEC program of rolling back quantitative restrictions on intra-European trade, the Treaty of Rome and the elimination of tariffs within the European Economic Community, the unilateral liberalization by several countries – most notably West Germany, which in 1956 and 1957 cut its tariffs by 25 percent each year – all these efforts complemented the GATT's objectives but did not originate from the institution itself.

But a rather modest contribution of the GATT is probably to be found in two subtle but highly useful influences. First, the GATT set standards for state behavior, which – even if far from being met initially – at least created a reference point about the direction in which trade policies should be heading. The architects of the post-war economic system agreed that trade policy should be conducted on an open and non-discriminatory basis; by giving this objective an institutional basis they possibly prevented a drift in economic policy away from the principles embodied in the GATT. Second, while tariff cutting may have had no immediate effect in the immediate post-war environment, as the myriad of quotas and other restrictions on trade were gradually dismantled through the 1950s, the GATT ensured that countries could not substitute higher tariffs for these measures as their economies became more open to world markets.

The GATT, in other words, held the line on tariffs and did not allow them to undermine reforms elsewhere. For an *ad hoc* institution that was never designed to exist on its own, for an institution with no independent power and no financial resources or lending capability to ensure compliance to its rules, this was a notable achievement. This achievement came from a remarkably small organization which was largely dedicated to a single purpose. By concentrating its effort almost exclusively on tariffs, the GATT did not spread its scarce resources or political capital too thinly or lose sight of its main objective. One can speculate that this structure may have enabled it to be more effective than the ITO, whose multifaceted agenda and potentially sprawling bureaucracy might have proved an impediment to real action. The role of Eric Wyndham White, the first director of the GATT, in ensuring the survival of the institution during the dark days of the 1950s so that it could see another, better day, should also not be left unmentioned.

If one is looking for the proximate cause for the economic recovery in Western Europe during the decade or so after 1945, the GATT is probably not the first or even the second place to look. Taking the several decades of post-war economic growth into one's perspective, however, it is hard not to attribute some role to the GATT, conceding at the very least that it served as an effective supporting actor. By setting standards and holding the line on tariffs as other trade restrictions were lifted, the GATT was not geared or positioned to provide a quick boost to GNP but was more akin to a long-term investment with a long-term payoff. This payoff may not have been fully realized until the late 1950s when European currency convertibility had been restored and tariffs as trade barriers again mattered most.

Then the stage was set for a major advance against tariffs which came with the Kennedy round negotiations of 1964–7, when the GATT fulfilled the promise the architects of the post-war economic order had envisioned.

References

Bhagwati, Jagdish (1988), *Protectionism*, Cambridge, Mass.: MIT Press.

Boyer, F. and J.P. Sallé (1955), "The Liberalization of Intra-European Trade in the Framework of the OEEC," *Staff Papers*, 4 (February): 179–216.

Curzon, Gerard (1965), *Multilateral Commercial Diplomacy: The General Agreement on Tariffs and Trade and Its Impact on National Commercial Policies and Techniques*, London: Joseph.

Diebold, William Jr. (1952a), "The End of the ITO," *Essays in International Finance*, no. 16, International Finance Section, Department of Economics, Princeton University.

(1952b), *Trade and Payments in Western Europe: A Study in Economic Cooperation, 1947–51*, New York: Harper and Row.

Finger, J.M. (1979), "Trade Liberalization: A Public Choice Perspective," in Ryan C. Amacher, Gottfried Haberler, and Thomas D. Willett (eds.), *Challenges to a Liberal International Economic Order*, Washington: American Enterprise Institute, pp. 421–453.

(1993), "GATT's Influence on Regional Arrangements," in J. de Melo and A. Panagariya (eds.), *New Dimensions in Regional Integration*, New York: Cambridge University Press, 128–158.

General Agreement on Tariffs and Trade (1949), "The Attack on Trade Barriers," A Progress Report on the Operation of the GATT, January 1948 – August 1949, Geneva.

(1950), "Liberating World Trade," 2nd Report on the Operation of the GATT, Geneva.

(1952), "GATT in Action," 3rd Report on the Operation of the GATT, Geneva.

(1953), "International Trade, 1952," Geneva.

Irwin, Douglas A. (1992), "Long-Run Trends in World Trade and World Output," unpublished manuscript, University of Chicago.

(1993), "Multilateral and Bilateral Trade Liberalization in the World Trading System: An Historical Perspective," in J. de Melo and A. Panagariya (eds.), *New Dimensions in Regional Integration*, New York: Cambridge University Press, pp. 90–118.

Kitson, Michael and Solomos Solomou (1990), *Protectionism and Economic Revival: The British Interwar Economy*, Cambridge University Press.

Koch, Karin (1969), *International Trade Policy and the GATT, 1947–1967*, Stockholm: Almquist and Wiksell.

Krause, Lawrence B. (1959), "United States Imports and the Tariff," *American Economic Review*, 49 (May): 542–51.

Lavergne, Real P. (1983), *The Political Economy of US Tariffs: An Empirical Analysis*, New York: Academic Press.

Liepmann, Heinrich (1938), *Tariff Levels and the Economic Unity of Europe*, New York: Macmillan.

Maddison, Angus (1989), *The World Economy in the 20th Century*, Paris: OECD.
  (1991), *Dynamic Forces in Capitalist Development*, New York: Oxford University Press.

Organization for European Economic Co-operation (1956), *Statistical Bulletin*, no. 4, July, Paris.
  (1957), *Statistics of National Product and Expenditure*, no. 2, 1938 and 1947–1955, Paris.
  (1958), "A Decade of Cooperation: Achievements and Prospects," 9th Annual Report, Paris, April.

6 The European Coal and Steel Community: an object lesson?

JOHN GILLINGHAM

The creation of the European Coal and Steel Community (ECSC) in April 1951 was a watershed in the history of the twentieth century. The event marks the beginning of a long-term integration process which, in fits and starts, is transforming a continent of formerly warring states into an economic and political federation. The ECSC was based on an original idea, supra-nationality: membership required transference of sovereign powers to a new European authority. The coal/steel pool did not, however, contain a new operating mechanism that propelled integration forward, as optimistic social scientists have maintained both at the time and since. Operationally, the ECSC was a disappointment. The popular notion that it could lead to sectoral integration, in which success in one field triggered success in another, has no basis in historical fact (see discussion in Milward, 1992).

Jean Monnet, the father of the proposal for the coal/steel union, was the source of the idea that supra-nationality would give rise to some higher form of economic and political organization. It suffuses the studies of political scientists and economists of the 1950s and 1960s. Only one major author of that era, Louis Lister, expressed theoretical reservations as to the value of the institution (Lister, 1960). More characteristic was a powerfully argued book of breathtaking scope written by Ernst Haas (1968), *The Uniting of Europe: Political, Social and Economic Forces, 1950–1957*. In it he predicted that the ECSC would have a very welcome and constructive "spillover effect" in which the formation of new interest groups at the European level would generate counterparts nationally and vice versa. The reciprocating action that resulted would strengthen national power while at the same time creating a Euro federalism. Even though Haas would later express reservations about his thesis, it remains convincing to many and, for lack of a more persuasive theory of integration, has never been displaced.

Alan Milward's recently published study of the origins of the European Community, *The European Rescue of the Nation State*, does not change the picture (Milward, 1992). Milward views integration as the purposeful application of national power internationally. In his account the chief agents of change were the governments of the member states who created the European Community in an attempt to solve jointly specific economic and social problems too big to handle individually. Milward specifically denies the importance of American influence and rejects the idea that changes in the international context influenced the integration process. His analysis, though powerful, is incomplete and therefore only partly persuasive.

The European Coal and Steel Community provided a solution to the problem of the Ruhr that had plagued Europe since World War I and stood in the way of a Franco-German political reconciliation. The great achievement of the ECSC, in other words, was to have made the revival of Germany acceptable to its former victims in Western Europe. The new principle animating the coal/steel pool, integration, was supposed to allow the immediate merger of the former enemy nation into Europe as well as the future fusion of Europe around it. And this did in fact occur, though in ways unforeseen by Jean Monnet. He wanted to tame Germany politically and regulate it economically. Thanks to Adenauer, the former was unnecessary; due to forces beyond Monnet's control, the latter was frustrated. The security and prosperity of Europe would owe little to the ECSC per se. The myth surrounding the heavy industry community would prove more important than the organization itself. Integration was too potent a symbol merely to fade away. The effort to give the idea real substance would eventually lead to the formation of the European Economic Community (Gillingham, 1992).

One should pause before drawing parallels between the problems facing Western Europe after 1945 and those confronting Eastern Europe today. No one is seriously worried about a powerful revival of the Soviet economy, first of all. The industry of the former USSR, unlike that of post-war Germany, is a shambles. The question facing it is not when, or how powerfully, but whether recovery will occur. Secondly, the nations of Eastern Europe are unlike those of Western Europe after 1945 in being highly uncompetitive. Whereas the post-war recovery involved a restoration of property and trading relationships, the future one will require the creation of wholly new industrial bases. External conditions are also less propitious than after the war. No super power is willing or able to serve as benevolent hegemon, to act, in short, as the United States once did in providing massive reconstruction loans, forcing third parties to make tariff and trade concessions, and otherwise exact economic sacrifices on behalf of the less fortunate. A worldwide boom like that of the 1950s is, moreover, still not in sight. A review of the operations and impact of the European

Coal and Steel Community can therefore offer little guidance to those grappling with the economic problems of Eastern Europe. It may, however, provide at least a measure of inspiration. The ECSC changed the context of diplomacy and set in motion an intense search for constructive transnational solutions that continues even today.

1 The politics and economics of the ECSC

On May 9, 1950 the French Foreign Minister Robert Schuman announced in a speech drafted in Monnet's offices at the *Plan de Modernisation et d'Equipement* that France was ready to enter a heavy industry partnership, on the basis of equality, with West Germany and any additional European nation. His overriding purpose in making such a commitment was to prevent future wars. Coal and steel production, he proceeded, would be placed in a new European agency with the power to plan, allocate, and, in general, administer. Contracting states would be obliged to cede a measure of sovereignty to this supra-national authority. With strong American support and the addition of Italy and the Benelux nations as participants, the French and Germans began negotiations on June 20 in Paris. Monnet presided on the basis of a preliminary draft produced under his direction, the *Document de Travail*. The talks would continue, though interrupted by the outbreak of the Korean War, until the following March (Gillingham, 1992; Gerbet, 1962).

The Schuman Plan treaty, which was initialed by the foreign ministers of The Six on April 15, 1951, differed from Monnet's original blueprint in some respects, was watered down in others, and contained still further provisions that were meaningless or unenforceable. When it took effect in June of the following year, Monnet's influence had declined while that of his adversaries had increased. As President of the High Authority (HA) he would head a fractious organization with little real power. The much-heralded official openings of the common markets for coal and steel in spring 1953, supposedly the greatest achievements of the ECSC, were public relations events. Monnet resigned in November 1954 but remained in office until forced out in June of the following year (Gillingham, 1992).

The essential elements of Monnet's design first appeared in position papers prepared for the coal/steel conference. They left no doubt that the equality mentioned by Foreign Minister Schuman was, in the German case, to be earned rather than granted; the machinery set up during the occupation to limit the production and the scope of operations in steel, allocate coal, and, in general, regulate the future development of both industries would operate until reform had taken place. The latter was patterned on the trust-busting ideology of the American New Deal.[1] The High Authority was to direct the conversion of big business from cartelist vices to competitive virtues. The HA was to enlist the cooperation of the unions and other constructive elements but of course avoid contact with "the interests" themselves. Its *modus operandi* was to be precisely the opposite of that employed by cartels: productivity not profit was to be the objective, open covenants were to replace secret deals, and the public interest was to take precedence over private ones. The HA was empowered to promote competition, devise and apply a common pricing policy, steer investment, and buy and sell on behalf of the community.[2]

The HA was the most striking feature of the draft proposal, the *Document de Travail*, used as the basis for the conference negotiations. The relevant articles provide for a muscular directorate acting collectively on the majority principle but with executive power concentrated in a *primus inter pares*, the president. External restraints on its exercise of authority were minimal. They included a High Court to which governments might appeal and a parliament with power only to interpellate. Three separate committees composed of producers, consumers, and labor were to advise the new directorate upon request but lacked statutory powers of their own. Regional producer organizations, whose composition was not specified, were to transmit HA directives and provide information upon request. The HA was to act on the basis of mandates assigned it by the member states as defined in Article 19 of the *Document*. These were to include everything needed to create a "single market" (*marché unique*), "pool production," and specifically eliminate "all privileges of entry or exit, tax equivalents [or] quantitative restrictions on the circulation of coal and steel within the area of the member states." The HA was also to have special authorization to abolish "all subventions or aids to industry" and "all means of differentiation between foreign and domestic markets in transportation rates as well as all coal and steel prices" and to eliminate additional enumerated "restrictive practices."[3]

The basic German working paper prepared for the conference contained the gist of an alternative scheme which, though its recommendations were

---

[1] Archives Jean Monnet pour l'Europe, Lausanne (JM) AMG 2/3/2 Bis Note de P. Reuter, "Problèmes posés par l'institution d'une Haute Autorité internationale en regard du statut actuel de la Ruhr," May 5, 1950; AMG 2/3/3 "Note (Reuter) sur la proposition française dans ses rapports avec le statut de l'Allemagne et celui de la Ruhr" (n.d.).

[2] JM AMG 2/4/4a "Note concernant la Haute Autorité: Domaine, Objet" (n.d.).

[3] JM AMG 3/3/9 "Document de Travail," June 27, 1950; Hanns Juergen Küsters, "Die Verhandlungen über das institutionelle System zur Gründung der Europäischen Gemäinschaft für Kohle und Stahl," in Schwabe (1980), pp. 73–102; Griffiths (1980), pp. 35–72; Gillingham (1992), pp. 239–241.

not often incorporated into specific provisions of the treaty, would after numerous struggles surrounding the establishment and operations of the HA eventually carry the day. The Federal Republic wanted to shackle the HA. It therefore took up a Dutch proposal to establish a Council of Ministers with veto power over its actions and further recommended assigning the High Court broad powers of review and allowing the General Assembly to set up committees with supervisory authority. The German draft deliberately precluded the HA from exercising social responsibilities and emphasized that the promotion of efficiency should be its main task. Here, too the HA was to have its wings clipped; specifically it could *not* set prices, establish manufacturing programs, or engage in production planning. Such powers, the draft proceeds, should belong to the producer associations.[4]

The anti-Monnetist outcome of the coal/steel negotiations was due partly to the inadequacies of the *Document de Travail*, which set lofty, unattainable, and often contradictory, goals as objectives of HA policy. It was unclear, for instance, how the HA could, on the one hand, eliminate all "falsifications" of competitive conditions and on the other, equalize wages and working conditions throughout Western Europe, and simultaneously still enforce "identical delivery conditions for coal and steel at the point of departure from mine or mill."

Pricing policy (Article 25) was similarly confused. The consumer was to be protected against discrimination and producers against "disloyal practices," while being assured a steady expansion of markets and outputs as well as the creation of conditions "guaranteeing the spontaneous allocation of product at the highest level of efficiency." As for wage policy (Article 26), the HA was to prevent cuts during slumps, eliminate "exploitative competition," guarantee "coal and steel workers the highest standard of productivity compatible with economic equilibrium," and introduce "wage equality" by imposing assessments on producers. Though over many months of intense negotiation Monnet's experts defended these provisions with great tenacity and intellectual skill, the zeal of these men could not conceal their unenforceability (Gillingham, 1992).

A completely unexpected world development, the outbreak of the Korean War on June 25, 1950, undercut Monnet's original scheme and changed the course of, as well as considerably lengthened, the coal/steel talks. Monnet understood almost immediately that the war would strengthen the bargaining position of the West Germans. Who else could slow down the ninety-plus Soviet and Bloc divisions believed poised for general invasion of Western Europe? Secretary of State Dean Acheson's announcement on September 16 that the United States was prepared to

---

[4] Bundesarchiv (BA) B156/263 "Gruendsätzliches zum Schuman-Plan," August 8, 1950.

proceed with the rearmament of four divisions from the Federal Republic, which shocked public opinion in France, came as no surprise to the author of the Schuman Plan. By the end of the month he had readied a scheme to conscript West Germans as foot soldiers of a future European army. This was the famous Pleven Plan for a European Defense Community. The proposal would long outlive the purpose for which it was created, indeed move to the very forefront of integrationist aspirations until, paradoxically, the French Assembly rejected it in August 1954 (Gillingham, 1992, pp. 250–86; Schwartz, 1985, pp. 286–7).

In a further attempt to offset the increase in German power, Monnet cranked up decartelization in the Ruhr. The campaign to break up the big trusts had been pursued with varying degrees of Allied enthusiasm since the war. The then unenforced Allied High Commission Law 27 provided the legal basis for the get-tough policy. Monnet further demanded that the HA be granted the authority to act as guarantor of this law, in other words to perpetuate the organizational dismemberment of the Ruhr heavy industry complex. In December 1950 the negotiations threatened to collapse in the face of bitter opposition from German coal and steel producers. Chancellor Adenauer, who viewed the Schuman Plan talks as a mere skirmish in a much larger campaign to recover German political respectability, finally forced the Ruhr to accede to the harsh anti-cartel provisions of the treaty. Though duly concluded it resulted in only a brief truce between Monnet and his enemies. The hard line adopted in October 1950 fanned the smoldering embers of producer resentment into a white heat of opposition by the end of the year. The flames of resistance would continue to flare up long after the treaty had been initialed and ratified (Gillingham, 1980, pp. 305–36).

Winter 1950–1 witnessed an intense episode of "Ruhr bashing" that involved a gang effort led by Monnet in Paris and conducted by his US allies, locally directed by High Commissioner John J. McCloy in Bonn. Monnet hoped to make Europe safe for France, the Americans to "keep the playing field level," as a leading negotiator named Robert Bowie described US policy, so that European federation could proceed (Gillingham, 1992, pp. 266–83). Neither Monnet nor the Yankee idealists who brow-beat the Ruhr on behalf of Europe had much political support outside of the United States. Monnet in fact never brought the Paris proceedings before the French Cabinet, as this would purportedly have introduced a fatal element of divisiveness into policy. The man from *Rue de Martignac* was also as good as his word as regards distancing the "interests" from the negotiations. Neither steel nor coal representatives were included on the French delegation and scant effort was made to keep them "in the loop" (Gillingham, 1986, pp. 381–405).

The men of the *Comité des Forges* disliked Monnet's anti-trust policies as intensely as did their West German compeers, and on matters of industrial organization held generally similar views. The two business communities had been linked together since 1926 as co-founders of the International Steel Cartel. In the process of sharing world markets they had developed not only common interests but similar organizational structures and methods of doing business. The bonds of friendship and cooperation survived war and occupation. German defeat ended any formal relationship between the former partners. Monnet's attempt to decartelize the Ruhr revived it; French steelmen regarded the attack on German producers as a threat to themselves (Gillingham, 1986, pp. 381–405, 1985, pp. 83–101).

The first important French business initiative came in early November 1950 and resulted in meetings between the steel industrialist, Pierre Ricard, who directed the French employers' association, and his German counterpart, Fritz Berg. Several gatherings between key producers occurred the following month. On January 27, 1951 an "Association of the Schuman Plan Nations" was formed in order to oppose the "super-dirigism" of the proposed HA; curtail its powers to borrow, tax, lend, and underwrite investment; and demand the assignment of its remaining powers to strengthened national producer associations. They in turn, according to the signed agreement to create the proposed organization, were to assume responsibility for establishing joint production programs, common supply and marketing mechanisms, and unified reporting procedures as well as to determine what and how much the HA needed to know about firm operations. The proposed articles in the draft treaty (60 and 61) concerning cartels and concentrations were declared illegal and invalid. The signers of the document called in conclusion for convening a conference of states to determine whether, after a transitional period, the treaty should take effect of simply be dropped.[5]

The "Treaty Instituting the European Coal and Steel Community," which was initialed by the Foreign Ministers of the six contracting nations on April 18, 1951, contained an even 100 articles along with a lengthy appendix describing complicated transitional arrangements for the Belgian coal and the Italian steel industries. The treaty read much like a constitution; it defined structures and methods of operation and contained

[5] JM AMG 12/3/3 "Les Fédérations industrielles de l'Europe de l'Ouest et Plan Schuman," February 8, 1951, AMG 11/2/5 "Observations des fédérations industrielles nationales des pays intéressés par le Plan Schuman sur les clauses économiques de Projet de Traité en préparation," January 17, 1951; Klöckner Archiv/G. Henle Papers (KA) EGKS Schuman Plan, WVESI 1.1.51–31.12.51 "Die Industrieverbände Westeuropeas zum Schuman-Plan" (n.d.).

a preamble enumerating values and objectives. The outlines of Monnet's original plan were evident in the document, but it provided little guidance to the solution of practical difficulties and reflected rather than resolved many points of contention (Gillingham, 1992, pp. 281–2).

The High Authority remained the centerpiece of the organizational edifice. The Council of Ministers was to be advisory, the Common Assembly a forum for discussion, and the High Court an advocate for the HA's power *vis-à-vis* the contracting states. Anti-trust ideas pervaded the economic sections of the treaty. Modernization was to be the goal of the European Coal and Steel Community's economic policy, to which end it was to create common markets, reduce prices, increase efficiencies, and eliminate all forms of restriction and discrimination. The HA therefore had the authority to regulate prices as well as require their publication. It could also penalize a host of suspect business practices such as secret rebating and price gouging, impose quotas to limit overproduction, allocate raw materials at times of scarcity, and levy fines for a broad array of reasons. The lengthy anti-cartel and anti-concentration provisions (Articles 65 and 66 in the final version of the treaty) enumerated a long list of circumstances requiring HA intervention. The treaty did not, however, define the relationship between the HA and regional producers' associations, specify the powers of the Advisory Commissions representing the interests of producers, or describe the internal organization of the HA itself. And it gives little insight into how the ECSC would actually operate.

Something called merely the Interim Committee is what gave rise to the Eurocracy that would eventually take root and thrive at the Community's headquarters in Luxembourg. The origins of this organization are obscure. It first met, however, on May 17, 1951 and would continue to meet until June 1952, when the last of The Six finally ratified the Treaty of Paris and the HA could thus begin operations.[6] During these months Monnet was tied up with negotiations for the European Defense Community. In his absence, and apparently without benefit of official mandate, senior former Schuman Plan negotiators representing their respective national economics ministries took it upon themselves to "handle all questions preliminary to the commencement of the operations of the High Authority."[7] These included establishing procedures and making appointments.

The work was still underway when Monnet, as President designate, suddenly announced that Luxembourg would be the seat of the new

---

[6] BA B102/8603b "Kurzprotokoll über die erste Sitzung des interministeriellen Ausschusses," May 17–19, 1951.

[7] BA 102/12608 "Vermerk über eine interministerielle Besprechung zur Frage der Organisation der Hohen Behörde," September 26, 1951.

supra-national institution. What followed has been described by the head of the German Schuman Plan Desk, Dr. Ulrich Sahm in a 1984 interview. Sahm had readied "wonderful papers, full of grandiose organizational plans, personnel guidelines, compensation scales and so on," but Monnet "swept the whole thing off the table, saying that he was going to begin with a small team and work from there on an informal basis. In other words, he wanted to keep his hands on everything" Arriving with his chief, Franz Etzel, to the opening ceremony of the new organization, Sahm found that "there were French names tacked to every door. The entire High Authority was in French hands . . . They had planned the thing down to the last secretary and concierge." Etzel thereupon told every German in sight to attach his calling card to the first door available, "no matter whether he planned to work there or not." It was thus, Sahm deposed, that he found himself in the service of the HA.[8]

The HA was, structurally, a bureaucratic nightmare and Monnet could never exercise control over it, largely because he managed to bring only a handful of his loyalists on board. Apart from this hard core of dedicated supporters he could count on sympathy only from representatives of labor and a fraction of appointees from the civil service. Most key positions in the administration were filled by non-Monnet men. The German mining engineer Hermann Dehmen and a senior manager of ARBED, Tony Rollmann, were the chief figures in the Main Branch for Production. Wilhelm Salewski, who had been the business manager of the German Steel producers' association, became the director of the Main Branch for Investments. The chief statistician of the Ruhr coal cartel, Dr. Rudolf Regul, played a strong second fiddle in economic policy making to Pierre Uri, the most influential of Monnet's men. As for the rest, a French civil servant headed the department of finance; two senior railroad officials shared responsibility for the transportation sector; an Italian politician headed the labor section; and an Italian nobleman took charge of office staff. Two of the three legal counsels were German, as was the director of the statistical section, Rolf Wagenführ. The German steel industry privately admitted to being well represented in the organization. By its own estimation it held sixty-three leading positions, the French forty-one, the Belgians seventeen, the Italians nineteen, the Dutch thirteen, and the Luxembourgers (among whom support staff was recruited) sixty-four. The Ruhr producers expressed dissatisfaction with only one appointment: they wanted to replace the head of the cartel division, a Monnet man, with Ernst Wolf Mommsen, the director of the sales syndicate for rolled steel products.[9]

---

[8] JM "Interview mit Dr. Ulrich Sahm," February 27, 1984.

[9] Wirtschaftsvereinigung Eisen- und Stahlindustrien (WVESI) "Vermerk über die Vorstandssitzung am 13.1. 1953."

Monnet launched the European Coal and Steel Community with an address so imperious that a former associate later likened it to a Speech from the Throne. The treaty was, he asserted, "Europe's first antitrust law," one, he claimed, that gave him a mandate to dissolve cartels, eliminate concentrations of power, and end restrictive powers generally (Gillingham, 1992, pp. 313–14). There would be little progress in this direction, however, during his tenure as President of the HA. The body met thirty-seven times between August 1952 and January 1953, when preparations for the openings of the common markets began, often in the intense, exhausting, almost wartime atmosphere of crisis that Monnet liked to maintain. Yet it accomplished little. External relations consumed the bulk of its efforts, much of which involved a chimerical attempt to bring Great Britain into the union. Relations with OEEC, GATT, and other international organizations were also prominent features on its agendas (ibid., p. 315).

Disagreements on procedure, which are hard to avoid in any new organization, bedevilled operations at the European Coal and Steel Community. Monnet's refusal to abide by the results of majority voting, in contravention of the treaty, was a sore point with the other members of the HA. His policy toward the Advisory Committee (AC) created a running battle with the representatives of producers, whose interest it was in some unspecified manner to have represented. Monnet never admitted wanting to eliminate the body, but he waited six months before convening it for the first time and did so only after having failed in an attempt to create so-called external committees, directly responsible to the HA, to take over its functions. The AC would unofficially direct the recartelization process launched in preparation for the opening of the common markets (Gillingham, 1992, pp. 282, 283, 306, 310, 317, 318, 320, 324, 330–1).

The real significance of these well-publicized actions differed by product. Coal, the market for which officially opened on February 10, 1953, afforded the HA little scope for policy making. Community outputs were all subsidized and officially sanctioned agreements binding producers and consumers regulated prices. Any attempt to introduce market pricing would have been disruptive and inflationary. Moreover, the coal of both the Ruhr and the Saar, which together comprised about three-quarters of total community exports, remained under the authority of various occupation agencies. The Deutsche Kohlen Verkauf (DKV) set prices in agreement with the federal government and the mine operators in a relationship fundamentally unchanged since the 1920s. The Deutsche Kohlen Bergbau Leitung, a trusteeship organized by the British early in the occupation, fixed export prices. The International Authority for the Ruhr, in operation since 1948, allocated German coal exports. The HA simply lacked the power to interfere with these arrangements. In coal, where furthermore tariffs were absent, the opening of the common market was an exercise in ribbon cutting (Abelshauser, 1984, p. 71).

Steel presented more complicated problems. "The establishment of the common market for steel," Monnet announced magisterially on the eve of its May 1, 1953 opening, "signifies the suppression of restrictions on exchange and the transference to the High Authority in [this] domain of powers exercised up to now by the governments of the six member-nations."[10] Customs, quotas, and currency barriers would be eliminated and, the communiqué added, external tariffs harmonized. Prices were also to be freed. Reality fell considerably short of rhetoric. Customs and quotas had generally little influence on the intra-European steel trade. Externally, tariffs were harmonized rather than reduced. Power did not discernibly shift from the seats of government to Luxembourg. And the price-setting function, though liberated from national controls, devolved upon revived cartels (Gillingham, 1992, pp. 325–30).

In preparation for the opening of the common market, wide-ranging discussions between delegates from the steel producing industries of The Six began in January 1953. Held periodically over the following five months, they would deal with such technical matters as basing points, the organization of freight pools, the harmonization of district price structures, methods of wholesaling, and (most often) nomenclature. The resulting understandings advanced cooperation beyond anything known either before or during the war and furthered the process of institutional convergence long under way in Western European heavy industry. In the first quarter of 1953, moreover, twelve new European steel syndicates formed to regulate sales in third-country markets and another two to do likewise within the community itself. An additional four were limited in scope to France and West Germany.[11] The International Steel Export Cartel, which began operations in Brussels in March 1953, capped the new edifice. It set up price minimums for about 15 percent of total community production – a higher percentage than its forerunner of the depression years.[12]

Monnet could do little about this resurgence of business power. On April

[10] Historical Archives of the European Community (ECSC), CEAB 53/1953 174–9 "Communiqué de la Haute Autorité sur l'Etablissement du Marché Commun de l'Acier," April 30, 1953.

[11] JM AMH 323/39b "Liste des Associations formées après l'institution du Plan Schuman," May 22, 1953; AMH 23/39c "Liste des cartels conclus après l'institution du Plan Schuman," May 22, 1953.

[12] Ibid.

22, 1953 he summoned the AC for a dressing down and, in a brutal session lasting fifteen hours, instead received a savaging from its members. In sentiments expressed somewhat more politely by other steel representatives, Pierre Ricard, who directed the Comptoir Français des Produits Sidérurgiques, ridiculed the President of the HA for having called a press conference to warn that cartel formation threatened to wreck plans for the common market. Ricard accused Monnet of being unaware that market pricing could cause increases (which had in fact been sharp) as well as decreases; of ignoring that in the US "price leadership" provided a cartel ersatz; and of overlooking that price maintenance as envisaged in the new international cartel arrangement would reduce the dollar gap. He further warned Monnet that the ECSC could not survive without the discipline imposed by cartels and that the current decline for steel products internationally might very well undermine both them and the community.[13] The April 22 session brought Monnet's last real attempt to work through the AC. None of the conflicts between the two had been resolved by the time of his unexpected resignation in November 1954.

Because the HA never overcame its weaknesses, it failed to extract enough information from producers to determine how prices were set. Much confusion still surrounds the process. Lister's surmise that domestic prices were aligned, by product group, to levels prevailing on international markets is probably as good as any (Lister, 1960, pp. 226–7). Objecting to the price upswings of summer 1953, the HA imposed schedules for reductions, then, when demand collapsed in autumn, found itself vainly ordering halts to price cutting, rebating, and other illicit practices. In January 1954 producers agreed to accept a "Monnet margin" of allowable price movements which, though occasionally exceeded, generally held throughout the year thanks to the stability of world steel markets. Though the scheme broke up in 1955, it gave the HA at least the appearance of authority in the months between Monnet's official resignation in November 1954 and his actual departure from office six months later (ibid., pp. 233–4, 237–8).

Decartelization was simply farcical, like a re-run of a bad movie on a faulty projector. In the case of coal, a new organization created at the opening of the common market named GEORG (*Gemeinschaftsorganisation Ruhrkohle*) provided a nominally respectable replacement for the Deutsche Kohlen Verkauf, itself a post-war permutation of the old producer syndicate. Listless flogging of the German mining industry in fact continued until 1958, when a crisis of overproduction in the face of new

[13] JM AMH 15/13/1 "Comité Consultatif Compte-rendu in extenso séance du 22 April 1953."

competition broke out that in the end would prove fatal (Abelshauser, 1984, *passim*).

By the time Monnet was ready to step down the traditional Ruhr *Konzerne* had re-emerged. The process was relatively unproblematic. Three of the old trusts (Mannesmann, Guthoffnungshütte, and Hoesch) came back to life by means of tendered stock swaps between headquarters companies. It took a private act of the government of the Netherlands before a fourth one, Klöckner, could re-surface. It had formerly been administered by a Dutch holding company, which was subject to seizure as enemy property. Thanks to legal and financial maneuvering, two new giants, August Thyssen Hütte and Rheinstahl, would be formed from what remained of the mega-enterprise known as Vereinigte Stahlwerke, which had been fashioned as an emergency contrivance in the 1920s out of the wreckage of the Stinnes empire. The re-appearance of Krupp would be delayed for legal and political reasons relating to the special status of this firm as "armorer of the Reich," but with the exception of this trust the restoration process was complete by 1957 (Gillingham, 1992, pp. 352–7).

The history of the Schuman Plan negotiations and the ECSC under the presidency of Jean Monnet may not be particularly edifying but is possibly instructive. Monnet had clear goals, an elaborate plan, and the powerful backing of the United States. Yet he could not break a traditional pattern of producer relationships that developed against a background of what, for lack of a better term, has been called organized capitalism. Its characteristic features are the cartel, the producer association, and close ties to the state. The restoration of this way of doing business did not occur in response to any particular set of economic circumstances – ironically, the cartels formed at great political risk had little operational importance – but simply because neither producers nor their governments could imagine life without them.

Sustaining the myth that the ECSC represented a triumph of sectoral integration was the fact that the coal and steel industries of Western Europe, though not necessarily competitive, were at least functional components of advanced industrial economies. The would-be Monnet of present-day Eastern Europe would enjoy no such advantage. The coal and steel industries of the region belong to an earlier age of production. If Monnet's experience in the ECSC suggests any one single thing it is the difficulty of making a clean break. Any attempt to reform and revive existing industry must reckon with the likelihood of at least a partial restoration, no matter how implausible such an outcome would first appear.

2 The West German revival

The reappearance of the trusts manifested a tidal change in the course of events. Recovery, stimulated by the Korea boom, took hold in the early 1950s. Demand for the kind of manufactures in which Germany specialized became seemingly insatiable (Kramer, 1991, pp. 182–9). Dashed to pieces by the powerful current were punitive and reformist policies of post-war inspiration like those championed by Monnet. In a fast-changing world, they were increasingly archaic.

In the years that the ECSC began operations, Germany became, as Alan Milward puts it, the economic pivot of Europe (Milward, 1992, pp. 134–67). Its export-led growth created important new markets for the industries of the rest of "The Six" ECSC founder members, which in turn gave rise to a "virtuous spiral" that would ascend for another twenty years of increasing prosperity (ibid., pp. 167–96). Much remains to be learned about the mainsprings of German economic growth in the 1950s. Most recent explanations rest on the availability of reserve capacities in industry. Given prevailing high demand and, as we shall see, an absence of external constraints, German producers could quickly re-enter traditional markets. And so they did, except in Eastern Europe, where such outlets no longer existed. The existence of the ECSC made little difference in this respect. German exports grew most rapidly to the secondary European states, regardless of whether they belonged to "The Six" or not (ibid., p. 168). Coal and steel followed rather than led export growth. *Steel* exports increased only 100,000 tons over the 1950s. *Coal* exports to ECSC countries increased 1.6 million tons between 1952 and 1955, but as a percentage of overall exports fell from 15.2 to 7.6 between 1952 and 1959 (Gillingham, 1992, pp. 357–8).

The non-German members of "The Six" derived several specific benefits from the ECSC thanks to the Federal Republic. Some evidence of a "virtuous spiral" can be found in the movement of heavy industrial goods. Even though German steel outputs increased from 8.3 to 9.3 million tons from 1952 to 1959, domestic producers could not fill manufacturing demand. The result was an impressive increase of steel imports into the Federal Republic of 1.6 million tons annually, most of which came from France (Gillingham, 1992, p. 357). Germany furthermore continued to export coal to the rest of the ECSC at low subsidized prices, while increasing its own importation of high-cost American coal. In the field of scrap metal, another commodity in short supply, the Germans, a surplus nation, sold to the other members, who except for France were in chronic deficit, at artificially low prices. Finally, the Federal Republic partly subsidized the operation of the Belgian coal mines (ibid., pp. 248–9; Milward, 1992, pp. 83–113).

These deals do not, however, get to the heart of the ECSC's importance. Adenauer was happy to offer *pourboires* as need be to gain European respectability. The ECSC led to it, though hardly as the crow flies. In agreeing to join the coal/steel pool the German Chancellor shrewdly accepted a prolongation of occupation-type controls with the hope, and increasingly confidence, that recovery would make them irrelevant. The history of the diplomacy through which this was achieved reaches beyond the ECSC and into its ill-fated sequel, the European Defense Community. Though ending with the famous French "non" of August 1954, it led to eventual German membership in NATO. The German state treaty, which terminated the operations of the Allied High Commission, dates from May 1955 (Gillingham, 1992, pp. 342–8).

The negotiations surrounding the Schuman Plan got the process of German rehabilitation under way. As of May 8, 1950, the day before the Schuman Plan announcement, the Federal Republic lacked diplomatic representation above the consular level, belonged to no official international organization, and was morally isolated even within the Western world. Its most important production units, the *Konzerne*, were subject to decartelization, which put them legally under a cloud. Uncertainty extended to their very physical existence. The British dismantlement program, launched in November 1948, had been broken off a year later but could have been resumed at any time. In the thirteen months between the Schuman Plan announcement and the conclusion of the Treaty of Paris creating the ECSC, Adenauer had raised his nation to formal diplomatic equality with the other five signatories. Now West Germany had at least an acknowledged right to be treated like other nations.

The European Coal and Steel Community, which merged into the European Community in 1968, was something more than a German re-entry vehicle into Europe: it occasioned a *Lernprozess* in the craft of integration. The negotiations for the treaty as well as the debates that raged within the HA brought to light a number of problems with which those intent upon advancing European economic and political unification would have to contend in the future. They involved such arcana as the international standardization of freight rates, the elimination of inequities in national systems of taxation, the development of programs for industrial readaption and of policies aimed at harmonizing wages and social benefits (Fursdon, 1980). In this sense it smoothed the path to the 1957 Treaty of Rome. As an institutional model, however, it left no legacy. The EEC would have no counterpart to the HA and no socio-economic agenda: the governments of the member states collectively held the ultimate power to determine how it would develop. Economically as well, the ECSC contributed little to the subsequent integration of Europe. Those seeking the antecedents to the EEC would be better advised to examine the history of post-war trade and monetary liberalization in its many ramifications. Without the steady removal of impediments to commerce, the "virtuous spiral" would soon have petered out, and integration might have become an object of ridicule instead of a beacon of hope.

Conclusion

The principle of supra-nationality, proclaimed for the first time in the Schuman Plan announcement, was indeed something new under the sun. In lieu of traditional international agreements of limited scope, contracting states would be required to transfer a plenitude of powers to a permanent institution that was unaccountable to national governments. As a diplomatic approach, the Schuman Plan had the merits of simplicity and novelty. Monnet promised to end the historic antagonism between France and Germany at a single stroke, and though such a hope was wildly optimistic, the French initiative broke a logjam of problems stemming from the war and led to a succession of settlements, the net result of which was to re-knit Germany into the fabric of Europe in less than a decade. The Germany in question was no longer Das Reich, though it soon developed the economic strength to re-emerge as such, but a federal republic whose political revival went hand in hand with the integration of Europe and the formation of the Atlantic Alliance.

The European Coal and Steel Community never had much more than a shadow existence, however. The anti-trust ideology that animated the original French draft proposal for the pool was a poor springboard to action. Its provisions regarding wages, pricing, terms of sale, the role of producer associations, and a myriad of other specific technical matters were either contradictory, vague, or overly complicated. The Treaty of Paris, which contained an even 100 articles, looked like a constitution. Yet it never functioned as one. Apart from its inherent deficiencies, it failed because industry objected to Monnet's approach and the contracting states accepted the coal/steel settlement only because of American pressure. When it weakened, old habits re-emerged and what was to have been a reform program for European industry, in effect, restored the producers of the Ruhr to their traditional prominence within the coal/steel sector. Yet heavy industry was no longer either economically dominant or strategically critical. Nuclear warfare and consumer capitalism were the prime realities in the new age that was dawning. The Schuman Plan succeeded politically in part because history itself had relegated the problem of coal/steel mastery in Western Europe to the old curio chest.

The creation of the European Coal and Steel Community is of little relevance to the problems facing Eastern Europe today. Economic revival in Western Europe after World War II occurred, one must remember, in what traditionally had been the most industrially advanced region of the globe. As a result of the two great European wars of this century vast wealth had been squandered and economic leadership had been taken over by, and for the better part of a generation would remain firmly in the hands of, the United States. Still, German industry was intact in 1945. Politically, the post-war settlement involved overcoming the threat of super power domination that the Reich posed to Europe in the first half of the century and, economically, greasing the skids. Modernization, critical for growth over the long term, was of less immediate importance than the removal of restraints that impeded trade and economic growth generally. It was a process that involved liberalization as achieved by means of the European Payments Union, the General Agreement on Tariffs and Trade, and the Organization for European Economic Cooperation. Students of Europe's post-war recovery should examine these institutions rather than the European Coal and Steel Community, which had little economic import-ance.

Liberalization is a necessary but hardly sufficient condition for the recovery of Eastern Europe, the nations of which must either rebuild industry from scratch or find some other form of wealth-creating activity to provide employment for their citizens. Costly experiments like the ECSC, whose diplomatic success depended on highly propitious conditions, are best avoided, even though fierce determination and a commitment to change turned what might have been a short-term failure into an undoubted long-term success.

References

Abelshauser, Werner (1984), *Der Ruhrkohlenbergbau seil 1945, Wiederaufbau, Krise, Anpassung*, Munich: Verlag C. H. Beck

Fursdon, Edward (1980), *The European Defense Community*, London: Macmillan

Gerbet, Pierre (1962), *La Genèse du Plan Schuman, les origines à la declaration du 9 mai 1950*, Lausanne: Foundation Jean Monnet pour l'Europe.

Gillingham, John (1980), "Solving the Ruhr Problem: German Heavy Industry and the Schuman Plan," in Klaus Schwabe (ed.), *Die Anfaenge des Schuman-Plans*, Baden-Baden: Nomos, pp. 305–36.

(1985), "Coal and Steel Diplomacy in Interwar Europe," in Clemens Wurm (ed.), *Internationale Kartelle und Aussenpolitik*, Stuttgart: Steiner Verlag, pp. 83–101.

(1986), "Zur Vorgeschichte der Montanunion: Westeuropas Kohle une Stahl in Depression und Krieg," *Vierteljahreshefte für Zeitgeschichte*, 3: 381–405.

(1987), "Die französische Ruhrpolitif und die Ursprünge des Schuman Plans," *Vierteljahrshefte für Zeitgeschichte*, 1: 1–24.

(1992), *Coal, Steel and the Rebirth of Europe: The Germans and French from Ruhr Conflict to Economic Community, 1945–1955*, Cambridge University Press.

Griffiths, Richard (1980), "The Schuman Plan Negotiations: The Economic Changes," in Klaus Schwabe (ed.), *Die Anfänge des Schuman-Plans*, Baden-Baden: Nomos, pp. 35–72.

Haas, Ernst (1968), *The Uniting of Europe: Political, Social, and Economic Forces, 1950–1957* (2nd edn 1968), Stanford: Stanford University Press.

Kramer, Alan (1991), *The West German Economy, 1945–1955*, New York: St. Martin's Press.

Küsters, Hanns Jürgen (1980), "Die Verhandlungen ueber das institutionelle System zur Gründung der Europäischen Gemeinschaft für Kohle und Stahl," in Klaus Schwabe (ed.), *Die Anfänge des Schuman-Plans*, Baden-Baden: Nomos, pp. 73–102.

Lister, Louis (1960), *Europe's Coal and Steel Community: An Experiment in Economic Union*, New York: Twentieth Century Fund.

Milward, Alan (1992), *The European Rescue of the National State*, London/Berkeley: University of California Press.

Schwartz, Thomas (1985), "From Occupation to Alliance: John McCloy and the Allied High Commission in the Federal Republic of Germany," Ph.D. thesis, Harvard University.

7 The European Payments Union: an efficient mechanism for rebuilding Europe's trade?

BARRY EICHENGREEN

With the disintegration of the Soviet Union, the trade of its successor states has declined precipitously. Enterprises have found it difficult to obtain the imported inputs needed to produce industrial and agricultural outputs that might be exported. Confusion over the availability and acceptability of inter-republican credits has left potential exporters hesitant to sell and potential importers unable to buy. Governments have applied export controls to a variety of products. While estimates of inter-republican trade are notoriously unreliable, the figures suggest a decline in the volume of inter-republican trade of 30–50 percent in 1992 alone, a drop in excess even of the dramatic decline in production.[1]

The problem resembles to a remarkable extent conditions in Western Europe after World War II. Intra-European trade had fallen to negligible levels in the aftermath of the war. It was rebuilt in the second half of the 1940s on the basis of bilateral agreements. The most important step was the European Payments Union inaugurated in 1950. Member countries agreed to accept the currency of any other participant in payment for exports, unsnarling the suffocating tangle of bilateral agreements. Credits were provided to deficit countries, eliminating the need to balance exports and imports by reducing demand and, potentially, employment and growth. Intra-European commerce expanded vigorously, as shown in figure 7.1, permitting the convertibility of currencies for current account transactions to be restored by the end of the 1950s.

The EPU's successful operation renders it an obvious model for a payments union scheme for reconstructing trade among the successor states of the Soviet Union.[2] Yet a payments union also has potential costs. It can distort the pattern of trade by subsidizing intra-union transactions relative

I thank Luisa Lambertini and Graham Schindler for research assistance.
[1] See for example Gros (1993) and Michalopoulos and Tarr (1993).
[2] Recent studies that invoke the comparison with the EPU include Bofinger and Gros (1992), Kenen (1991), and Dornbusch (1992).

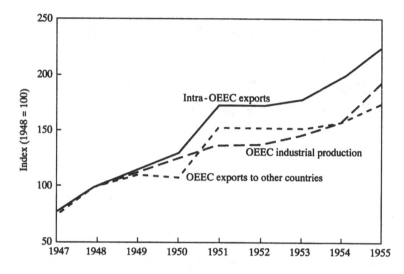

Figure 7.1   OEEC production and trade, 1947–55 (1948 = 100)

to those with the rest of the world. In the case of the former Soviet republics, which under central planning traded excessively with one another and inadequately with the West, this might only reinforce existing inefficiencies. Moreover, a payments union can distort relative prices by insulating producers from the chill winds of foreign competition. In republics dominated by large industrial enterprises possessing considerable market power, this is a worrisome prospect. And a payments union which hinders the repatriation of principal and profits can be an obstacle to foreign borrowing. This is especially troubling in the case of former Soviet republics whose need for capital is so pressing. Current account convertibility, while more expensive than a payments union scheme, avoids these drawbacks.[3]

The goal of this chapter is to understand how these pitfalls were avoided under the EPU. The analysis comes in six parts. Section 1 reviews the structure and operation of the EPU. Sections 2 through 4 search for trade distortions, price distortions, and capital-market distortions. Section 5 assesses the factors that allowed the EPU to function with a minimum of distortionary effects. Section 6 evaluates its contribution to Europe's post-war recovery and growth. The conclusion returns to the implications for the former Soviet republics.

---

[3] An advantage of a payments union is that it allows the pooling of the international reserves of the participating countries (since, at a point in time, some participants will be in surplus with the union and gaining reserves, while others will be in deficit and losing reserves). Thus, an added cost of convertibility will be the resource cost of additional reserves.

Table 7.1. *Initial schedule of settlements in the EPU (percent of current deficit or surplus)*

Cumulative surplus or deficit (percentage of EPU quota)	Country with cumulative deficit		Country with cumulative surplus	
	Gold	Credit	Gold	Credit
From 0 to 20 percent	0	100	0	100
From 20 to 40 percent	20	80	50	50
From 40 to 60 percent	40	60	50	50
From 60 to 80 percent	60	40	50	50
From 80 to 100 percent	80	20	50	50
Overall percentage	40	60	40	60

Source: Kenen (1991), p. 256.

1 The operation of the EPU

The EPU was a mechanism for multilateralizing the bilateral agreements upon which intra-European trade had been restarted following World War II. At the end of each month, each EPU country's net balances with each other country were reported to the Bank for International Settlements (BIS), the EPU's financial agent, which cancelled offsetting claims. Remaining balances were consolidated, leaving each country with claims on or liabilities to not individual countries but the union as a whole. From the perspective of any one country's assets and liabilities in foreign currencies, it thus made no difference with which other European country it traded. Only the overall balance in European currencies mattered at the end of the day.

Net debts could be financed initially with credits, but eventually these liabilities had to be settled in dollars and gold. Each country received a quota equal to 15 percent of its total trade with the EPU area in 1949. So long as its liability to the EPU remained less than 20 percent of its quota, it was financed entirely by credit. The net position was carried on the books of the EPU without requiring any payment. After the liability reached 20 percent of the quota, settlement had to be 20 percent in gold. Debts in the amount of 40, 60, and 80 percent of quota required settlement in 40, 60, and 80 percent gold. (Here, as in the remainder of the discussion, settlement in gold is shorthand for settlement in gold or dollars.) Cumulative surpluses were settled in similar fashion, as table 7.1 shows. Once the quota was exceeded, settlement with the union had to be made entirely in gold, although under exceptional circumstances additional credits were extended by the EPU's Managing Board. Not only was trade multilateralized but its volume was stimulated by the availability of EPU credit lines.

Accumulated claims could be converted into commodities or hard currency only partially and with delay. Until its quota was exceeded, a surplus country would receive gold amounting to only 40 percent of its cumulative net exports to other EPU countries. For debtor countries securing loans and relieved of the need to settle bilaterally, the attraction of this system was obvious. But what was the attraction to a creditor like Belgium in persistent surplus with the union?

The answer comes in three parts.[4] First, a lower proportion of gold payments was initially required of debtors than was extended to creditors. This increased the likelihood that surplus countries, which would otherwise be trading their exports for inconvertible claims, would wish to participate. Giving creditor countries more gold than was contributed by debtors required working capital: this the US contributed in the form of a grant of $350 million of Marshall Plan money to the EPU.

Second, membership came with conditionality minimizing the scope for exploitation of creditors by debtors. When a member exhausted its quota, the EPU Managing Board, comprised of independent financial experts reporting to the Council of the OEEC, met to advise it and compel the adoption of corrective policies. Thus, the creditors had reason to anticipate that the debtors would be forced to adjust.

Third, EPU membership required the liberalization of trade. Countries, when joining, pledged to eliminate discrimination against other participants based on balance of payment considerations. An instrument entitled the Code of Liberalization formalized this commitment. By February 1951, less than a year after the EPU came into operation, all existing trade measures were to be applied equally to imports from all member countries.[5] Participants were required to reduce trade barriers by a given percentage of their pre-existing level, initially one half and then escalating to 60 and 75 percent. The most internationally competitive European countries, such as Belgium, stood to gain disproportionately from such liberalization.

The value of intra-European trade expanded vigorously under the EPU, from $10 billion in 1950 to $23 billion in 1959. Imports from North America grew more slowly, from $4 billion to $6 billion. Although both intra-European trade and trade with the rest of the world expanded more quickly than European production over the EPU years, the spurt in European trade occurred in 1950–1, coincident with the inauguration of the EPU. All

[4] I return to this question of the appeal of the EPU to the participating countries in section 6 below.

[5] Diebold (1952), p. 172.

this suggests that its liberalizing effect was considerable.[6] Despite the relatively slow expansion of trade with the United States, Europe's strengthening dollar balance more than doubled its dollar holdings between the end of 1949 and mid 1956. As dollars grew less scarce, the need to discriminate against the US became less pressing. The terms of EPU settlements were hardened, and the removal of quantitative controls on intra-European trade accelerated.

To what extent did EPU credit fuel this trade? Participating countries had $46 billion of surpluses and deficits against one another during the EPU years. Nearly half ($20 billion) was cancelled multilaterally. Another quarter ($12.6 billion) was cancelled intertemporally, as countries ran deficits in one month, financing them wholly or partially with credit, and ran offsetting surpluses in subsequent months, cancelling their previous position. Settlement in gold and dollars was limited to most of the remaining quarter ($10.7 billion).[7] Thus, the EPU agreement reduced settlement in gold and dollars by more than 75 percent compared to what would have been required under strict bilateralism.

2 Trade distortions

Even EPU enthusiasts like Robert Triffin admitted that the system "entailed a certain degree of discrimination against non-EPU members."[8] EPU members could use import licensing and foreign exchange rationing to discourage purchases from non-member countries. The liberalization provisions committed the participants to free their trade with other EPU members but allowed them to continue restricting imports from other countries. The governments of non-member countries, notably the United States, were aware of the arrangement's discriminatory nature.[9] The IMF similarly disapproved of the discriminatory aspects of the EPU. But the Americans, for the same motives that lay behind the Marshall Plan,

---

[6] The spurt in intra-European trade in 1950–1 also coincides with the initiation of the German *Wirtschaftswunder*, suggesting that it may have been monetary reform, price liberalization, and economic recovery in Germany rather than the EPU per se that lay behind the surge in trade depicted in figure 7.1. Below I present evidence showing that the increase in trade in this period was in fact in considerable part a product of the EPU.

[7] The balance to be settled in credit reflected the positions outstanding when the EPU was terminated in 1958.

[8] Triffin (1957), p. 203. Circa 1954, Triffin himself estimated that the discriminatory provisions of the EPU led to a $650 million reduction in the demand for dollar imports. Cairncross and Watts (1989), p. 310. These authors cite a number of other contemporary estimates, by experts such as Scott and Maton, also based on the perception of significant discriminatory effects.

[9] See Rees (1963), p. 101 and *passim* for details.

hesitated to object. As one commentator put it, "so long as such a pronounced bias of world trade in our favor persists, we ought not to stand in the way of measures which may help to correct it."[10]

In addition, credit was extended through the provision of EPU quotas to help countries finance their intra-union deficits, while deficits with the dollar area had to be settled in gold. Repayments of accumulated EPU debts under the amortization schedules negotiated starting in 1954 could be used to finance intra-European trade but not trade with the hard-currency world. Thus, even after import licensing and foreign exchange rationing were relaxed in the EPU's final years, the payments union still could have had discriminatory effects through the differential availability of credit.

One might question whether the EPU's discriminatory measures had teeth. Efforts to liberalize intra-European trade in the EPU's early years were less than wholly successful. Governments reneged on these commitments when confronted with balance of payments difficulties. Countries running persistent surpluses within the EPU were permitted to adopt discriminatory policies to limit their exports to other member countries.

Moreover, even if the EPU was discriminatory, its effects may have merely offset those of other trade distortions. European importers could obtain trade credit from the US market but not from the financial markets of their European trading partners, which remained disorganized and controlled. The US Export-Import Bank, the Marshall Plan, and US aid under the provisions of the Mutual Security Act subsidized purchases from the dollar area.[11] In addition, some of the bilateral agreements under which Europe organized its trade with the rest of the world included credit ceilings even more liberal than those of the EPU agreement. The discriminatory provisions of the EPU may have merely offset these effects, neutralizing rather than spawning trade distortions.

One might go further and argue that the EPU was itself a force for trade expansion with the rest of the world. Stimulus to extra-EPU trade could have operated through two channels. First, the commitment to trade liberalization embodied in the EPU agreement could have impelled European countries to liberalize their trade both within Europe and with the rest of the world more quickly than they would have otherwise, and more quickly than countries elsewhere freed their own foreign transactions. Second, by economizing on the use of reserves for settlement between EPU members, the arrangement could have freed up reserves to finance additional trade with the rest of the world.

To analyze whether the EPU had trade creating or diverting effects, I

---

[10] Williams (1949).

[11] Aside from specific exceptions, the procurement authorization requirements associated with its extension effectively barred the recipients from using Marshall aid to finance imports from other EPU countries.

estimate gravity equations predicting the volume of bilateral trade flows for the first EPU year (1950), the system's mid year (1954), and its final year (1958). The level of trade (exports plus imports), in log form, between country pairs is regressed on country size (the log of the product of the trading partners' GNPs), a measure of personal income (the log of the product of the trading partners' per-capita GNPs), the log of the distance between the trading partners, and a dummy variable for contiguous countries.[12]

The basic arguments of the model, estimated by ordinary least squares, display their expected signs, as shown in table 7.2. The coefficient on the product of per-capita incomes, for example, ranges from 0.4 to 0.5, suggesting that trade increases with income per capita. Compared to the coefficient on this variable of 0.3 in Frankel's (1992) study of the 1980s, this suggests that the effect was stronger in the 1950s. The coefficient on the product of national incomes ranges from 0.8 to 0.85, suggesting that trade increases less than proportionately with size. This compares with a coefficient of 0.75 in the Frankel study.

I first test the impact of the EPU on intra-European trade. This involves adding a dummy variable (denoted "EPU") for when both European trade partners were members of the payments union.[13] The coefficients on this variable suggest a very considerable impact on the level of intra-European trade. The coefficient on EPU declines slightly between 1950 and 1954 and

[12] The basic specification follows Frankel (1992). Entering incomes in product form is suggested by modern theories of trade under imperfect competition (Helpman and Krugman, 1985), which suggest that countries of similar incomes will trade more than pairs of very poor and very rich countries. For information on the construction of the distance measure, see Hamilton and Winters (1992). Population and national income data are drawn from the Heston–Summers International Comparisons Project data base, trade data from the UN's *Yearbook of International Trade Statistics*. The trade figures, expressed in domestic currency, are converted to dollars using Heston and Summers' purchasing power parity exchange rates so as to insure compatibility with the national income statistics. Where UN trade data were expressed in dollars, it was necessary to first convert them back to domestic currency values using the market exchange rate. Since purchasing power parity exchange rates are not provided for Chile, market exchange rates are used instead. A sample of thirty-six countries provides data on 620 bilateral trade flows. The sample size does not equal 36 factorial because of missing observations. The countries in question are Morocco, Nigeria, South Africa, Canada, Mexico, the US, Argentina, Brazil, Chile, Colombia, Peru, Uruguay, Venezuela, India, Japan, Pakistan, Philippines, Austria, Belgium-Luxembourg, Denmark, Finland, France, West Germany, Greece, Ireland, Italy, the Netherlands, Norway, Portugal, Spain, Sweden, Switzerland, Turkey, the UK, Australia, and New Zealand.

[13] An alternative specification would include Australia, New Zealand, Pakistan, South Africa, and possibly Canada as EPU countries on the grounds that the system covered all European transactions of the sterling area. Estimates of this variant of the model were virtually identical to those reported in the text.

Table 7.2. *Determinants of trade in the 1950s*

Variable	1950	1954	1958	1950	1954	1958
Constant	−27.47	−30.54	−30.93	−27.48	−30.57	−30.95
	(21.98)	(22.81)	(21.02)	(21.96)	(22.83)	(21.06)
National incomes	0.79	0.85	0.83	0.79	0.85	0.84
	(21.25)	(22.27)	(20.06)	(21.24)	(22.27)	(20.13)
Per-capita incomes	0.40	0.47	0.50	0.39	0.47	0.49
	(6.86)	(7.50)	(7.21)	(6.61)	(7.35)	(6.89)
Distance	−0.10	−0.11	−0.13	−0.09	−0.11	−0.13
	(2.18)	(2.45)	(2.57)	(2.04)	(2.24)	(2.45)
Contiguous	0.91	0.86	0.83	0.89	0.96	0.92
	(3.38)	(3.12)	(2.70)	(3.15)	(3.32)	(2.87)
EPU	1.70	1.47	1.46	1.58	1.34	1.18
	(10.01)	(8.37)	(7.39)	(6.55)	(5.42)	(4.28)
Europe	—	—	—	0.17	0.11	0.31
				(0.74)	(0.46)	(1.16)
Western Hemisphere	—	—	—	0.02	−0.32	−0.36
				(0.07)	(1.34)	(1.36)
n	630	630	630	630	630	630
S.E.	1.414	1.453	1.615	1.416	1.453	1.613

Note: *t*-statistics in parentheses.
Source: See text.

again between 1954 and 1958, as if the hardening of EPU settlement terms and progressive removal of controls under the provisions of the Code of Liberalization diminished its effect, consistent with the views of those like Rees (1963, p. 253) and Kenen (1991, p. 258) who suggest that the effects of the EPU were most important in its early years. Discrimination intensified in the early years, they suggest, as European countries liberalized their trade with other European countries more quickly than they liberalized trade with the dollar area. In the final EPU years, in contrast, trade with the US was liberalized relatively rapidly, and the terms of settlements were hardened, in effect requiring the same payment for intra-EPU trade as for US trade.

One worries that "EPU" is picking up the tendency for European countries to trade disproportionately with one another for reasons, such as history and geography, unrelated to the payments union.[14] Geographical factors should be captured to some extent by distance and contiguity. To be doubly certain that the EPU dummy was not picking up other continent-specific factors, I added dummy variables for European countries and for those in the Western Hemisphere.[15] In no year did the coefficient on either of these regional dummies differ significantly from zero at standard confidence levels. Nor did their inclusion alter the signs, magnitudes, and statistical significance of the EPU variable.

To test whether observations for Germany, whose trade expanded enormously after 1949, dominated the results, I excluded the German observations from the sample. This reduced the size of the EPU coefficient only slightly, suggesting that the liberalizing effect of the EPU, and not just the German *Wirtschaftswunder*, contributed to the recovery of intra-European trade.

As a test for trade discrimination, I added a second dummy variable ("EPU-NON") for when only one of the two trade partners was a member of the payments union. If the EPU was discriminatory, then the magnitude of "EPU" should be significantly larger than that of "EPU-NON." The results for this variant of the model are shown in table 7.3. "EPU" is consistently larger than "EPU-NON," and one can reject at the 99 percent confidence level the hypothesis that the two are equal to one another. In other words, EPU countries traded significantly less with non-members than with fellow members, even after adjusting for the other standard determinants of trade.

[14] It might be thought that the positive coefficient on the EPU variable reflects the unusually rapid growth of the trade of the EPU countries in the 1950s due to the collapse of trade links during the war. But while this explanation is likely to hold if the dependent variable was the rate of growth of trade, there is no obvious reason why it should find reflection in the level.

[15] The EPU dummy differs from the European dummy by the exclusion of Spain and Finland and the inclusion of Turkey.

Table 7.3. *Further determinants of trade in the 1950s*

Variable	[Excluding regional controls]			[Including regional controls]		
	1950	1954	1958	1950	1954	1958
Constant	−27.55	−30.52	−30.76	−27.51	−30.49	−30.74
	(22.46)	(23.51)	(21.34)	(22.48)	(23.47)	(21.30)
National incomes	0.80	0.86	0.85	0.80	0.86	0.85
	(21.87)	(23.29)	(20.78)	(21.92)	(23.25)	(20.77)
Per-capita incomes	0.35	0.39	0.41	0.33	0.38	0.40
	(6.02)	(6.31)	(5.90)	(5.34)	(5.98)	(5.51)
Distance	−0.09	−0.10	−0.12	−0.08	−0.10	−0.11
	(2.04)	(2.29)	(2.43)	(1.81)	(2.18)	(2.23)
Contiguous	1.06	1.06	1.02	0.91	0.99	0.95
	(3.99)	(3.94)	(3.37)	(3.30)	(3.53)	(3.10)
EPU	2.11	2.01	1.97	2.21	2.10	1.86
	(11.34)	(10.57)	(9.10)	(8.38)	(7.83)	(6.14)
EPU-NON	0.63	0.83	0.76	0.74	0.89	0.79
	(4.98)	(6.40)	(5.23)	(5.36)	(6.32)	(4.95)
Europe	—	—	—	0.06	−0.02	−0.21
				(0.24)	(0.07)	(0.79)
Western Hemisphere	—	—	—	0.52	−0.28	−0.17
				(2.09)	(1.11)	(0.61)
n	630	630	630	630	630	630
S.E.	1.388	1.410	1.582	1.386	1.410	1.583

Notes: Dependent variable is imports plus exports. All trade and income variables are expressed in US dollars, using a conversion factor described in text. *t*-statistics in parentheses.
Source: See text.

How should the positive coefficient on "EPU-NON" be interpreted?[16] In part, extra-EPU trade was stimulated, as explained above, by the ability of the payments union to free up reserves to finance trade with the rest of the world. In addition, the positive coefficient on "EPU-NON" reflects the fact that the 1950s was an era of import substitution in Latin America and much of the developing world. Following the collapse of trade in the 1930s, many developing countries adopted strategies of promoting domestic industrialization by restricting access for imported manufactures. The prevalence of tariffs and quotas sheltering infant industries continued to limit the level of trade. The countries of Western Europe, in contrast, moved more quickly to restore access for imported goods, although, as described above, they liberalized intra-European trade significantly faster than trade with the rest of the world. Just why European countries liberalized trade more quickly than other economies is discussed in section 6 below.

3 Price distortions

The possibility that inconvertibility distorted relative prices has been emphasized by previous authors (for example Haberler, 1954). One reason that the EPU could have fostered price distortions, they suggest, was the tendency for governments, enjoying the insulation afforded by currency conversion costs, to manipulate relative prices through the use of taxes and subsidies on domestic production. Equally important was the tendency for producers with market power to manipulate prices themselves. In France, for example, industrial agreements were formed in industries producing gasoline, building materials, paper and cardboard, and nuts and bolts. In Italy, a commission set up to examine monopoly control and cartelization reported that concentration and inadequate competition existed in artificial silk, chemicals, engineering products, electric power, cement, and rubber. In the UK, retail price maintenance agreements limited competition in the provision of glassware and dental goods. Cartels were prevalent in Swedish electrical goods, foundry products, and paper, Swiss cement, chocolate, fats, and oils.[17]

Studying the deviation of relative prices across countries before and after the EPU requires disaggregated price indices that are comparable across countries. The World Bank's International Comparisons Project provides disaggregated price indices for matched sets of more than thirty categories of goods and services for the US and the major European countries, but 1970 is the first year for which these data were assembled (see Kravis,

---

[16] Note that this coefficient remains positive and statistically significant when the observations for Germany are excluded.

[17] United Nations (1950), p. 103; Diebold (1952), pp. 284–5.

Heston, and Summers, 1978). Fortunately, Gilbert and Associates (1958), in an OEEC pilot study that preceded the World Bank project, provide similar indices for 1950.[18] In table 7.4 I compute a measure of the distance between relative prices in the US (which is taken as an indicator of undistorted world prices) and the corresponding price structure in each of the major European countries in 1950 and 1970. If that distance is larger in 1950 than in 1970, this confirms that exchange controls on merchandise transactions in the preconvertibility period were associated with relative price distortions.[19]

Table 7.4 does not indicate that the EPU distorted relative prices significantly. As with any international comparison, how one deals with the index number problem has consequences for the results. When one uses European expenditure shares to weight the components of GNP, one finds that for two countries (the UK and Belgium) relative prices diverged from those of the US by more in 1950 than in 1970. For three countries (France, Italy, and the Netherlands) they diverged by less in 1950, while for one country (Germany) there was essentially no difference across years. When US expenditure shares are used, Belgium's prices are no longer more distant from US prices in 1950 than in 1970, but otherwise the results are the same. That the UK is the one country whose relative prices consistently differed more from US prices in 1950 than in 1970 is consistent with the fact that price controls were pervasive there. But there is little evidence here that the EPU was a source of significant price distortions.

To understand why these results obtained, I computed the distance measure separately for three sub-categories of national expenditure: consumption, investment, and government spending. It turns out that the results for countries whose relative price structures are closer to US prices in 1950 than in 1970 are driven by public-sector spending. The government-spending category distinguishes compensation of public employees from expenditure on goods and services. Public-sector compensation is relatively low throughout much of Europe in 1950 and relatively high in 1970. Thus, the tendency for public-sector pay to rise relative to other prices in Europe over the two post-war decades contributed to the growing distance between the structures of US and European prices.

[18] In a few instances the definition of expenditure categories differed across the two studies. In these cases it was necessary to combine adjoining categories to render the 1950 and 1970 data comparable.

[19] Comparing 1950 with 1970 is likely to bias the results toward finding EPU-related price distortions. The trade equations just discussed suggest that the EPU was most restrictive in its early years. Similarly, trade liberalization proceeded throughout the 1950s under the aegis of the GATT, continuing to moderate price distortions as the decade progressed. Comparing 1958, the last EPU year, with 1959, the first year of convertibility, would presumably yield less evidence of distorting effects.

Table 7.4. *Divergence of domestic price structures*

	Belgium	France	Germany	Italy	Netherlands	UK
Overall						
European 1950	3.71	0.97	1.08	5.74	0.87	1.49
Weights 1970	3.53	1.45	1.12	6.05	1.00	1.31
US 1950	3.61	1.09	1.24	5.93	0.99	1.37
Weights 1970	3.77	1.56	1.22	6.14	1.14	1.20
Consumption goods						
European 1950	3.24	0.85	0.91	5.05	0.74	1.33
Weights 1970	2.90	1.19	0.93	5.07	0.80	1.09
US 1950	3.17	0.96	1.11	5.17	0.86	1.16
Weights 1970	3.13	1.32	1.04	5.10	0.95	0.96
Investment goods						
European 1950	1.69	0.43	0.52	2.47	0.44	0.51
Weights 1970	1.76	0.70	0.53	2.78	0.52	0.59
US 1950	1.59	0.62	0.47	2.53	0.47	0.50
Weights 1970	1.60	0.49	0.52	2.70	0.47	0.62
Government spending						
European 1950	0.63	0.18	0.21	1.17	0.09	0.42
Weights 1970	0.99	0.42	0.32	1.78	0.31	0.44
US 1950	0.66	0.15	0.17	1.05	0.12	0.39
Weights 1970	1.36	0.55	0.44	2.29	0.41	0.51

Note: Distance indicator calculated as $\left(\sum_i [P_i - P_i^{US}]^2 S_i\right)^{\frac{1}{2}}$ where P is the log of the European price, P^{US} is the log of the US price, and S_i is the expenditure share of commodity i.
Source: See text.

For the UK, the distance of relative consumption goods prices from US prices is greater in 1950 than in 1970 regardless of the weighting scheme, while it is greater for investment goods so long as US weights are applied. The large difference in the relative prices of consumption goods in 1950 reflects heavy taxes on items such as tobacco imported from the dollar area. The difference in the structure of investment goods prices reflects relatively high prices for producer durables and low prices for residential construction, a pattern consistent with the hypothesis that trade restrictions drove the relative price distortions. The tendency for Belgium's relative prices to differ more from US prices in 1950 than in 1970 (when European weights are used) reflects the behavior of the relative prices of consumption goods rather than investment goods. To cite two expenditure categories, fuel and transport services were heavily taxed, while the prices of bread and other essential foodstuffs were subsidized and controlled.

For most other countries the direction of the change between 1950 and 1970 remains sensitive to the weights employed. For them, even excluding the public sector there is no evidence of a systematic decline in the extent of relative price distortions between 1950 and 1970.

Thus, there is some evidence that inconvertibility and the associated import controls distorted the relative prices of consumption and investment goods in Britain (where extensive control was retained the longest) and, depending on the weighting scheme used, in Belgium. Overall it is hard to argue, however, that inconvertibility significantly aggravated price distortions.[20]

4 Distortions of capital flows

A third possible cost of inconvertible currencies was to discourage international capital flows. Unable to repatriate their principal and earnings so long as European currencies remained inconvertible, foreign investors would have remained unwilling to lend. As the United Nations (1954) explained in a report on post-war lending, many countries limited remittances of earnings, usually to a specified percentage of invested

---

[20] A possible objection to this conclusion is that the price data used in these international comparisons are not sufficiently disaggregated to pick up distortions to relative prices *within* expenditure categories. Unfortunately, more disaggregated data for 1950 do not exist. But to test whether higher levels of aggregation automatically bias the results in the direction of fewer price distortions in earlier years. I aggregated the thirty categories of expenditure available for both years into fifteen more encompassing "super-categories." Doing so had little effect on the relative size of the distance measures in the two years.

capital. Limitations on the outward transfer of principal were even more restrictive. The UN concluded that:

Foreign enterprises are bound to feel the impact of such control in connexion [*sic*] with both the remittance of income (and the repatriation of capital, if desired) and the payment for imports required for operations. Exchange control is usually a symptom of balance of payments pressure; should the pressure increase, control may be tightened or the currency devalued. Either alternative, but particularly the former, may represent a powerful deterrent . . .

Leffingwell (1949/50, p. 209) described the implications for one country, the United Kingdom:

There is not much reason to expect any great flow of money toward sterling now, such as occurred after 1919 and again after 1931 . . . As soon as the world became convinced after 1919, and again after 1931, that the free pound was undervalued, sterling attracted flight money, the money of speculators and investors all over the world, who brought the free pound cheap for a profit . . . Now, however, the pound is not free, but is an inconvertible pegged currency, and foreign investors who hold sterling and sterling securities have had their investments frozen for years, and now devalued, and still can't get their money out.

Giersch *et al.* (1992, p. 115) similarly suggest that an earlier restoration of convertibility would have attracted larger capital inflows into Europe, shortening the time needed for "reconstruction and the partial catching up with the US."

Testing this hypothesis requires data on capital flows that are consistent over time and across countries. The IMF provides such data in its *Balance of Payments Statistics Yearbook*. These were gathered for all countries but the US, the principal international lender of the period, for which information was also available in *International Financial Statistics* on the economic determinants of capital flows.[21] The final sample included twenty-seven countries.

The format of the IMF data changes in 1959, although three years of retrospective data using the new format were also provided at that time. Given the difficulty of consistently comparing borrowing behavior across the change in format, two samples were constructed. The first covers seven EPU years (1952–8), when only Canada and Mexico of the countries in the sample had convertible currencies. The second covers six years (1956–61) spanning the resumption of convertibility.[22]

[21] Regressions including the US yielded essentially identical results.

[22] Colombia and Venezuela are borderline cases with relatively modest programs of import licensing and otherwise convertible currencies. I replicated the analysis including them among the convertible-currency countries for all years and found that this did not alter the results. Convertibility was restored as of the beginning of 1959 in most of Western Europe and in Australia and New Zealand, in Greece in 1960, and in Japan in 1961.

The specification follows previous work on the determinants of borrowing by a cross section of countries (e.g., Riedel 1983). The dependent variable is the value of private capital flows in units of domestic currency.[23] A positive number denotes a capital inflow. Explanatory variables are nominal GNP, inflation, real economic growth, exports, and export variability (the standard deviation of exports over three years centered on the current one). A vector of dummy variables for years and for whether the currency was convertible are included as well.

The results, in table 7.5, are consistent across periods and definitions of capital imports. External borrowing is related negatively to exports, negatively to export variability and, after 1955, negatively to country size as proxied by nominal GDP. The dummy variable for convertibility is positive, as if convertible-currency countries had greater access to foreign capital markets, but it differs insignificantly from zero at standard confidence levels.[24]

This analysis yields no evidence, then, that the failure to restore convertibility before the end of 1958 had a significant impact on the ability to borrow.

5 Minimizing distortions

What was it about the design of the European Payments Union that minimized distortions? The obvious explanation for why the EPU did not depress Europe's trade with the rest of the world more dramatically is that the US made liberalization a condition for providing $350 million of working capital for the system and for the continued provision of Marshall aid. The preamble to the EPU agreement committed the participating countries to "the maintenance of desirable forms of specialization . . . while facilitating a return to full multilateral trade . . ."[25] At the end of 1949, with US encouragement, the OEEC Council of Ministers agreed to abolish quantitative restrictions on 50 percent of intra-OEEC trade within six weeks. (It is relevant that the OEEC had been founded in response to US demands that Europe create an international body to coordinate the dispersement of Marshall aid.) It was agreed to precommit to a schedule of

---

[23] The manner in which public borrowing is reported for some countries makes it difficult to distinguish foreign aid from commercial loans; this is one reason I concentrate on private borrowing. In addition, the IMF's pre-1958 format lumps together public and commercial bank borrowing; hence the precise definition of the dependent variable in this period is private non-bank borrowing.

[24] As a further test, I related the *absolute value* of capital flows to these same variables. The results (not reported here) indicate that variable to be significantly related to exports and export variability but insignificantly affected by convertibility.

[25] Cited in Rees (1963), p. 123.

Table 7.5. *Effects of convertibility on private external borrowing, 1952–61*

	1952–8 Private non-bank borrowing	1956–61 Private non-bank borrowing	1956–61 Private borrowing
Nominal GDP	0.01	−0.01	−0.01
	(0.57)	(4.31)	(5.10)
Exports	−0.10	−0.25	−0.27
	(3.49)	(7.75)	(8.89)
Export variability	−0.21	−0.16	−0.11
	(2.22)	(1.33)	(1.02)
Inflation	37.65	59.70	52.60
	(0.39)	(0.41)	(0.39)
Real growth	162.71	91.40	112.94
	(0.93)	(0.61)	(0.81)
Convertibility	2.38	0.92	3.64
	(0.09)	(0.03)	(0.13)
R^2	0.26	0.47	0.54
Numbers of obs.	162	162	162

Notes: *t*-statistics in parentheses. Dummy variables for years are included in all regressions but not reported. The inclusion of the vector of year dummy variables accounts for the absence of a constant term.
Source: See text.

subsequent liberalizations that raised the share of quota-free intra-European trade to 90 percent by early 1955. Various of these liberalization measures were extended to Europe's trade with other continents, especially after 1953.[26]

Less important but working in the same direction, the Marshall Plan and subsequent aid stimulated both intra-European trade and Europe's imports from the rest of the world. Marshall aid was only loosely tied: except for shipping services and certain agricultural goods, the ECA did not require aid recipients to use the funds to import from the US rather than other countries. American administrators expressed concern that Marshall Plan-financed exports of goods in short supply domestically might hinder the expansion of the US economy and encouraged aid recipients to import such goods from other sources.[27]

[26] See Wexler (1983), pp. 198–9 and *passim*.
[27] For clarity, it may be useful to mention three factors that do not appear to explain the positive coefficient on EPU-NON. First, US credit markets may have provided private finance for European trade. But there is no obvious reason that they would have provided

Trade liberalization and credits also help to explain the lack of price distortions. Marshall Plan-financed imports limited the market power of European producers, while the liberalization of intra-EPU trade further diminished price distortions. If one European country freely imported a product line from the United States, forcing domestic prices to world levels, the freedom of intra-European trade tended to force prices elsewhere in Europe down to the same level. "Intra-European trade liberalization often weakened, through transit trade and triangular transactions, the effectiveness of dollar discrimination itself."[28] Even where imports from the US remained blockaded, the US was not always the lowest cost producer. As noted by Triffin (1957, p. 207), "for many categories of goods, the lowest European prices which [domestic producers] had to meet – Swiss prices for some goods, Belgian or German prices for others, etc. – were probably as competitive as those of any third country, including the United States."

Thus, the fact that European countries traded extensively with one another allowed efficiency-enhancing arbitrage to operate, minimizing price distortions. And the fact that Europe, notwithstanding its troubles, possessed a number of efficient industries allowed intra-EPU trade to drive prices down to the levels established by the least-cost producer.

The absence of a visible impact on foreign borrowing is attributable in part to US policies designed to neutralize the special risks posed by inconvertibility. The US adopted a program to guarantee American foreign investments against the risk of the inability to transfer funds. Pursuant to the Mutual Security Act of 1951 (the successor to the Marshall Plan), the government insured US investments against the risk of currency inconvertibility and loss through confiscation or expropriation. Individuals and companies investing in countries for which aid was authorized by the act (essentially, the former Marshall Plan recipients plus Taiwan, Haiti, Israel, and the Philippines) were eligible to participate. Through the middle of 1954, sixty-seven industrial investment guarantees totaling $47.6 million

more such credit for Europe than for other parts of the world, thereby stimulating trade between EPU and non-EPU countries relative to trade between pairs of non-EPU countries. Second, the US Export-Import Bank and kindred programs could have stimulated trade with the US relative to trade with other countries. I therefore added to the gravity equations a dummy variable for bilateral US trade flows but found that it displayed a small coefficient and a *t*-statistic of one or less. (None of the other coefficients or significance levels were noticeably affected.) Third, the Marshall Plan and post-Marshall Plan military aid could have stimulated imports by EPU countries. To test whether US aid stimulated imports by the recipient countries from the United States, I added a dummy variable for trade flows between EPU countries and the US but found that it too displayed a coefficient of zero.

[28] See Triffin (1957), p. 207.

had been issued to cover private investments. Of the total, $45.0 million insured against inconvertibility of foreign currency assets.[29]

But the fact that the EPU failed to penalize participating countries by significantly reducing their capital imports was not attributable primarily to the structure of the payments union or to accompanying policies. The legacy of interwar experience left no country, whether its currency was convertible or not, in a position to attract significant amounts of foreign capital in the 1950s.[30] Two-thirds of the US foreign loans extended in the 1920s lapsed into default in the 1930s. Default even infected markets where debts continued to be serviced. Defaults in one country depressed the bond prices of its neighbors and interrupted their access to international capital markets, as they underscored the special risks associated with international lending.

In the wake of World War II, private lenders remained demoralized, and little such lending took place. As Feis (1950, p. 1) summarized the lenders' perspective:

The great depression that began in 1929 brought our first great venture in foreign lending to a sick end. . . . It was gone, and seemingly for all time. . . . A general sigh of resolve was heard over the United States: Never again should we lend or invest our money in foreign lands.

In this climate, it mattered little for capital market access whether or not countries restored currency convertibility.

6 The role of the EPU in Europe's post-war growth

For all these reasons the EPU functioned in a relatively non-distortionary way. But was it necessary to go to these lengths to prevent distortions from arising from the operation of a payments union scheme? Were there viable alternatives like current account convertibility, in other words?

For political more than economic reasons, there are reasons to think not.[31] As argued in Maier (1987), post-World War II Western European growth was based on a distinctive social pact. A repeat of the debilitating struggle over income distribution that had characterized the post-World War I period was successfully averted. Workers agreed to moderate wage demands if management agreed to reinvest the profits they thereby accrued in productivity-enhancing plant and equipment. Each side agreed to trade short-term gains for long-term benefits so long as the other side agreed to do the same.

[29] See US Congress (1953, 1954).
[30] For details, see Eichengreen (1989).
[31] This section draws on Eichengreen (1993b).

In the Netherlands, for example, labor unions explicitly agreed that the fruits of all productivity increases in the first half of the 1950s should be used to finance investment. In Germany, they observed significant wage restraint throughout the 1950s. In Austria, German-style wage moderation and investment were secured through consultation between representatives of labor, management, and government. Even in Britain, not renowned for labor–management harmony, the Trades Union Congress cooperated with management and with the Conservative governments that ruled from 1951 by moderating wage demands.[32]

Management, for its part, raised investment rates to nearly twice the levels that prevailed before the war and to higher levels than after 1972 when the post-war settlement began to unravel. In Britain, not one of Europe's high investment countries, management agreed to restrain the payout of dividends and to reinvest profits instead. British economic growth is subject to criticism, but growth rates in the 1950s were impressive compared to preceding and subsequent periods.[33]

Reaching this settlement required minimizing the ratio of short-term sacrifices to long-term gains, especially since discount rates were high in the post-war years.[34] By strengthening Europe's terms of trade, the EPU moderated the requisite sacrifices. Devaluation implied a worsening of the terms of trade, reducing the size of the pie to be shared out among competing interest groups. For devaluation followed by convertibility to balance the external accounts, residents of other continents had to be coaxed into purchasing more European exports and Europeans had to be induced to purchase fewer imports. A decline in the relative price of European goods would have been needed to bring this about.

In contrast, a payments union which restricted imports from extra-European sources relative to how they would have been treated under convertibility had the same effect as a tariff. Europe maintained payments equilibrium *vis-à-vis* the rest of the world not by altering relative prices so as to export more but by limiting purchases of non-European goods through the use of import licensing, foreign exchange rationing, and the other

---

[32] For details, see Katzenstein (1984), Abert (1969), and Flanagan *et al.* (1983).

[33] Only in the case of Norway, for reasons discussed in Eichengreen and Uzan (1992), can it be convincingly argued that investment was pushed beyond the point of profitability. The argument here is that the point of profitability was raised by the social compact.

[34] With incomes and living standards depressed in the immediate aftermath of the war, the marginal utility of consumption was high. Reaching an agreement that involved deferring consumption was exceptionally difficult. Indeed, as Alessandra Casella and I (1993) have argued, it was only with the help of Marshall Plan transfers, which increased the size of the pie to be shared out among capital and labor, that it proved possible to strike this bargain at all.

administrative devices associated with inconvertible currencies. By reducing the European demand for US goods, this shifted relative prices in Europe's favor. Stronger terms of trade meant that fewer exports could command more imports from countries like the United States. As an implicit tax on imported goods, inconvertibility raised the level of European incomes consistent with payments equilibrium *vis-à-vis* the rest of the world.

Pursuing convertibility rather than the EPU would have shrunk European incomes by 1 to 2 percent, an effect comparable to that of eliminating the Marshall Plan.[35] This could have threatened the fragile agreements between labor and capital over distribution in post-war Europe.[36] Opting for the EPU averted this danger.

The post-war settlement, once struck, still had to be enforced. Workers had to be convinced to trade lower current compensation for higher future living standards, despite uncertainty over whether management would keep its part of the bargain to reinvest the profits that accrued tomorrow as a result of labor's sacrifices today. Awareness of this problem rendered labor hesitant to agree. Governments reassured it by adopting policies and programs that acted as "bonds" which would be lost in the event of reneging. They agreed to limit rates of profit taxation in return for capitalists plowing back earnings into investment. They provided limited forms of industrial support (selective investment subsidies, price-maintenance schemes, orderly marketing agreements) to sectors that would have otherwise experienced competitive difficulties. Workers were extended public programs of maintenance for the unemployed, the ill, and the elderly. This web of interlocking agreements – what might be called the mixed economy for short – functioned as an institutional exit barrier. It increased the cost of reneging on the sequence of concessions and positive actions that comprised the post-war settlement.

The EPU was a concomitant of these arrangements. Without import licensing and foreign exchange rationing, which provided limited insulation from international markets, intervention in the operation of domestic

---

[35] Imports were 25 percent of GNP in the participating countries. The standard formula (5% × 0.25) implies a 1.25 percent fall in real incomes.

[36] Contemporaries emphasized these terms of trade effects. Smithies (1950) stressed that removing the quantitative restrictions associated with inconvertibility would require further devaluation and that devaluation would entail terms of trade deterioration. The problem was summed up as follows by the OEEC in 1950 (p. 217): with European productivity growth lagging the American, "the competitive position [terms of trade] of Western Europe would deteriorate . . . " Attempting to rely on relative prices under convertibility, rather than the discriminatory measures permitted by a clearing mechanism, would lead to "continuous pressure on the exchanges; a fall in the standard of living would be inevitable."

markets would have been more difficult. More intense trade competition would have increased the budgetary cost of selective industrial subsidies. It would have made the wage compression across sectors sought by solidaristic trade unions more costly to achieve. Social programs would have been threatened by pressure to minimize labor costs. The web of arrangements that provided the institutional barrier to exit would have been that much more difficult to spin. In the worst-case scenario, the domestic settlement might have broken down.

The other element of the post-war growth recipe was trade expansion in the context of European integration. Rather than reverting to the pattern of the 1930s, post-World War II Europe exploited trade as an engine of growth. National economies were allowed to pursue their comparative advantages and to exploit economies of scale and scope.

This was accomplished, in the first instance, through the liberalization of intra-European trade. Quantitative restrictions on intra-European trade were removed more rapidly than those affecting transactions with other continents. European nations were natural trading partners for reasons of proximity and history. To say that Germany was a traditional exporter of capital goods and other European countries of consumer goods is to generalize excessively but to convey the essential point. Without a rapid expansion of trade to permit this pattern of comparative advantage to be exploited, it is doubtful that productivity and incomes could have risen as they did. And, for reasons described above, slower growth emanating from the international sector would have increased the sacrifices in living standards entailed in the domestic settlement, threatening stability there as well.

Restructuring along export-oriented lines was costly. Before undertaking it, policymakers had to be convinced that Europe's commitment to free trade was permanent. Reallocating resources along lines of comparative advantage entailed sunk costs; sinking them would be a costly mistake if any of the major European trading nations reneged on its commitment to free trade.

With memories of trade conflict in the 1930s still fresh, European policymakers had to be convinced that the countries concerned – especially Germany – would make benign use of their productive capacity. Two wars had heightened skepticism about whether Germany could be trusted to use its industrial power benevolently. But permanently dismantling German industry, as advocated by some in the US government, would have left a hole at the center of the European economy. A depressed Germany would drag down the demand for the exports of other European countries. Eliminating the Continent's principal supplier of capital goods would raise the cost of investment, worsen the dollar shortage, and force other countries to divert resources toward the production of capital goods.

For Germany, recovery required consent on the part of the occupying powers that controls on the level of production should be removed. In return, the Allies required that Germany be integrated into the European economy and that mechanisms be developed to prevent that commitment from being reversed.[37] Germany, for its part, needed reassurance that its access to raw materials, industrial intermediates, and foodstuffs produced abroad was guaranteed, given the prominence the Nazis had lent to Germany's dependence on foreign supplies.

For those concerned to construct institutional barriers to exit, the EPU and the arrangements in which it was embedded were preferable to unilateral convertibility. A payments union required a set of institutions capable of monitoring compliance and imposing sanctions. Furthermore, EPU membership was linked to trade liberalization. Member countries committed under the terms of the agreement to "the maintenance of desirable forms of specialization . . . while facilitating a return to full multilateral trade . . ."[38] They adopted a Code of Liberalization mandating a schedule of subsequent liberalizations. Countries failing to comply with this code or employing policies to manipulate the terms or volume of trade in undesirable ways could expect to be denied access to EPU credits.

The Economic Cooperation Administration, which administered the Marshall Plan, supported the EPU. Hence, the leverage the US enjoyed as a result of the Marshall Plan buttressed the credibility of European countries' commitment to trade. Countries which failed to adhere to the international settlement risked losing their American aid.

7 Implications for Eastern Europe

The European Payments Union was critical to the post-World War II reconstruction of the Western European economy. By greasing the wheels of intra-European trade, it allowed the participating nations to specialize in the production of goods in which they had a comparative advantage, enhancing the efficiency of resource allocation. By strengthening Europe's terms of trade and reconciling the mixed economy with expanding international trade, it helped to solidify the accommodation between capital and labor upon which the post-war generation of rapid economic growth was based.

The EPU succeeded because its design minimized the distortions otherwise created by payments union schemes. Trade distortions were

---

[37] See the chapter by Berger and Ritschl in this volume.
[38] Rees (1963), p. 123.

minimized by the program of multilateral trade liberalization to which the European participants committed themselves as a condition for the receipt of the $350 million of American credits which provided working capital for the payments union's operation (not to mention other forms of American aid). The fact that US aid under the Marshall Plan was not tied to US exports further multilateralized the pattern of trade. Price distortions were minimized by intra-European trade, especially since some European industries were already competitive on world markets, and by Marshall-Plan-financed imports, which limited the market power of European producers. Finally, obstacles to borrowing from the United States were attenuated by a US program to guarantee American foreign investments against the risk of inability to transfer funds.

It seems unlikely that these conditions can be replicated in the former Soviet Union today. A disproportionate share of the republics' trade has traditionally taken place with one another. Extensive liberalization *vis-à-vis* the rest of the world would be required to offset this pattern, especially if it was reinforced by a payments union scheme. Yet trade taxes are one of the few reliable revenue sources available to governments in the early stages of the transition to a market economy; their desperate need for revenues is likely to slow the removal of tariff barriers against the rest of the world. Moreover, to minimize trade distortions, the credit lines available for inter-republican trade would have to be matched by credits provided by Western sources for trade with the rest of the world. The $24 billion of credits promised by the G-7 in April 1992 has been slow to materialize. Western governments have not yet put their money where their mouths are. The ongoing dispute over outstanding debts incurred by the Soviet Union has been partly responsible for the delay. Thus, Spain froze a line of credit because Russia is $200 million behind on its debts. The European Community postponed the release of a $460 million food loan because it did not receive a $13 million interest payment (Bradsher, 1992). The volume of aid delivered to date is small in comparison with the Marshall Plan – too small to finance imports adequate to discipline domestic producers and minimize price distortions. The scale and concentration of Soviet industry have bequeathed enterprises possessing considerable market power but working at a level of efficiency that hardly approaches world levels. And the G-7 has offered no program of loan guarantees comparable to that extended by the US in the 1950s.

The most important difference between Western Europe after World War II and the successor states of the Soviet Union today lies in the desirability of close regional ties. Whereas the nations of Western Europe were seeking to draw together after World War II into an economic community, an effort to which a payments union could contribute, the successor states of the Soviet Union today are seeking to loosen their regional links in favor of stronger ties with the rest of the world. This they wish to do both to escape the economic straitjacket of the Soviet system and to improve their relations with other countries. For these reasons, as well as because of the more narrowly economic arguments emphasized above, it hardly seems likely that the potential participants would regard a payments union scheme as attractive.

References

Abert, J.G. (1969), *Economic Policy and Planning in the Netherlands*, New Haven: Yale University Press.

Bofinger, Peter and Daniel Gros (1992), "A Multilateral Payments Union for the Commonwealth of Independent States: Why and How?" CEPR Discussion Paper no. 654 (May).

Bradsher, Keith (1992), "Anxiety Slows Borrowing By Russia," *New York Times* (September 28), p. A4.

Cairncross, Alec and Nina Watts (1989), *The Economic Section 1939–1961*, London: Routledge.

Casella, Alessandra and Barry Eichengreen (1993), "Halting Inflation in Italy and France After World War II," in Michael D. Bordo and Forrest Capie (eds.), *Monetary Regimes in Transition*, Cambridge University Press, pp. 312–45.

DeLong, J. Bradford, and Barry Eichengreen (1993), "The Marshall Plan: History's Most Successful Structural Adjustment Program," in Rudiger Dornbusch, Wilhelm Nölling, and Richard Layard (eds.), *Postwar Economic Reconstruction and Lessons for the East Today*, Cambridge, Mass.: MIT Press, pp. 189–230.

Diebold, William (1952), *Trade and Payments in Western Europe: A Study in Economic Cooperation, 1947–51*, New York: Harper and Row.

Dornbusch, Rudiger (1992), "A Payments Mechanism for the Soviet Union and Eastern Europe," in Daniel Gros, Jean Pisani-Ferry, and Andreé Sapir (eds.), *Interstate Economic Relations in the Former Soviet Union*, Brussels: Centre for European Policy Studies, pp. 31–40.

Eichengreen, Barry (1989), "The US Capital Market and Foreign Lending, 1920–55," in Jeffrey Sachs (ed.), *Developing Country Debt and Economic Performance, Vol. 1: The International Financial System*, Chicago: University of Chicago Press, pp. 107–55.

(1993a), *Reconstructing Europe's Trade and Payments: The European Payments Union*, Manchester: Manchester University Press.

(1993b), "A Payments Mechanism for the Former Soviet Union: Is the EPU a Relevant Precedent?" *Economic Policy*, 17: 309–53.

Eichengreen, Barry and Marc Uzan (1992), "The Marshall Plan: Economic Effects and Implications for Eastern Europe and the Former USSR," *Economic Policy*, 14: 13–76.

Feis, Herbert (1950), *The Diplomacy of the Dollar: First Era, 1919–1932*, Baltimore: Johns Hopkins University Press.

Flanagan, Robert J., David Soskice, and Lloyd Ulman (1983), *Unions, Economic Stabilization and Incomes Policy*, Washington, DC: The Brookings Institution.

Frankel, Jeffrey A. (1992), "Is Japan Creating a Yen Bloc in East Asia and the Pacific?" NBER Working Paper no. 4050.

Giersch, Herbert, Karl-Heinz Paque, and Holger Schmieding (1992), *The Fading Miracle: Four Decades of Market Economy in Germany*, Cambridge University Press.

Gilbert, Milton and Associates (1958), *Comparative National Products and Price Levels*, Paris: OEEC.

Gros, Daniel (1993), "The Interstate Bank: An End to Monetary Disintegration in the Former Soviet Union?" unpublished manuscript: CEPS.

Haberler, G. (1954), "Konvertibilitat der Währungen," in G. Haberler *et al.*, *Die Konvertibilitat der Europäischen Währungen*, Zurich: Eugen Rentsch Verlag, pp. 15–59.

Hamilton, Carl and Alan Winters (1992), "Opening Up International Trade with Eastern Europe," *Economic Policy*, 14: 77–117.

Helpman, Elhanan and Paul Krugman (1985), *Market Structure and Foreign Trade*, Cambridge, Mass.: MIT Press.

Katzenstein, Peter (1984), *Corporatism and Change*, Ithaca, NY: Cornell University Press.

Kenen, Peter B. (1991), "Transitional Arrangements for Trade and Payments Among CMEA Countries," *Staff Papers*, 38: 235–67.

Kravis, Irving B., Alan Heston, and Robert Summers (1978), *International Comparisons of Real Product and Purchasing Power*, Baltimore: Johns Hopkins Press.

Leffingwell, R.C. (1949/50), "Devaluation and European Recovery," *Foreign Affairs*, 37: 203–14.

Maier, Charles (1987), "The Two Post-War Eras and the Conditions for Stability in Twentieth-Century Western Europe," in Charles Maier, *In Search of Stability*, Cambridge University Press, pp. 153–84.

Michalopoulos, Constantine and David Tarr (1993), "Trade and Payments Among the Successor States of the USSR," unpublished manuscript: The World Bank.

Organization for European Economic Cooperation (1950), *European Recovery Program: Second Report of the OEEC*, Paris: OEEC.

Rees, Graham L. (1963), *Britain and the Postwar European Payments System*, Cardiff: University of Wales Press.

Riedel, James (1983), "Determinants of LDC Borrowing in International Financial Markets: Theory and Empirical Evidence," unpublished manuscript: The World Bank and Johns Hopkins University.

Smithies, Arthur (1950), "European Unification and the Dollar Problem," *Quarterly Journal of Economics*, 44: 159–82.

Triffin, Robert (1957), *Europe and the Money Muddle*, New Haven: Yale University Press.

United Nations (1950), *Economic Survey of Europe in 1949*, Geneva: United Nations.

(1954), *The International Flow of Private Capital 1946–1952*, New York: United Nations.

US Congress (1953), *Report to Congress on the Mutual Security Program for the Six Months Ended June 30, 1953*, Washington, DC: GPO.

(1954), *Report to Congress on the Mutual Security Program for the Six Months Ended June 30, 1954*, Washington, DC: GPO.

Wexler, Immanuel (1983), *The Marshall Plan Revisited*, Westport, Conn.: Greenwood Press.

Williams, John H. (1949), "Europe After 1952," *Foreign Affairs*, 27: 426–48.

Part IV

Country studies

8 Germany and the political economy of the Marshall Plan, 1947–52: a re-revisionist view

HELGE BERGER and ALBRECHT RITSCHL

1 Introduction

The effects of the Marshall Plan on Germany's economic miracle are still controversial. On the one hand, public opinion and traditional economic history in Germany have it that the Marshall Plan marked the beginning of Germany's fabulous post-war recovery. On the other hand, an influential school among German economic historians maintains that post-war reconstruction both in Germany and throughout Europe was largely independent of the Marshall Plan; see Jánossy (1966), Manz (1968), Abelshauser (1975, 1981). In this view, both the late beginning and small magnitude of ERP deliveries to Germany provide evidence of the Marshall Plan having been irrelevant for Germany's post-war growth. Rather, the multitude of catching-up possibilities open to Germany and all other countries of continental Europe is held to have accounted for the golden fifties. The fact that supergrowth prevailed almost everywhere in Europe is taken as evidence against a major role for economic policies or even the choice between central planning and more liberal economic systems.

Defenders of the Marshall Plan have found it difficult to cope with this phenomenon of uniform growth. Most typically, the Marshall Plan is viewed as a series of nationwide aid and recovery schemes that can be analyzed independently. Thus, case studies are often presented which seek to pinpoint examples of Marshall aid having helped to overcome strategic bottlenecks in a given national economy.

Yet political historians have long adopted a radically different position.

Helpful comments by Knut Borchardt, Christoph Buchheim, Barry Eichengreen, Gerd Hardach, John Komlos, Axel Lindner, and Hans Möller are gratefully acknowledged. Sir Alec Cairncross and Alan Milward kindly provided information on specific points. The second author acknowledges financial support from the International Finance Section, Princeton University, during 1991/92. The usual disclaimer applies. A previous version of this paper was circulated as Discussion Paper No. 92-27, Dept. of Economics, University of Munich. A German version of this paper was published in *Vierteljahreshefte fuer Zeitgeschichte*, 43 (July 1995).

In their view, the Marshall Plan is to be regarded as a long-term unifying political strategy of the US for European reconstruction along free market lines that centered around reintegrating West Germany's economy into the European division of labor (Gimbel, 1976; Knapp, 1977, 1981; Daniel, 1982). In order not to be locked into providing US assistance to Europe indefinitely, it would re-establish the West German economy as the prime supplier of capital goods to Western Europe, thus rendering Marshall aid unnecessary in the medium term and closing the dollar gap in European trade with the US.

This chapter is intended to elaborate on this perspective and trace its economic implications further. We shall argue that the aim of the Marshall Plan was to create credible political commitments to Europe's economic integration both within Germany and abroad, whereas US resource transfers to Germany and other countries of Western Europe were mostly an initial pump primer and did not form the economic centerpiece of the plan.

We propose that post-war reconstruction in Western Europe can most gainfully be interpreted, not as a series of parallel national recoveries, but rather as the politically managed reconstruction of the intra-European division of labor with West Germany as its locational and industrial center. Then, the observed uniformness of growth across Europe follows almost naturally and is no longer irritating.

In the light of Germany's uncooperative trade and debt policies of the interwar period and, above all, of the horrible occupation and exploitation policies of the Nazis, political action to reinstitute economic cooperation in Europe was doubtlessly necessary. Seen in an international context, such policies would have to reassure America's allies that Germany's revived economic strength would only be used benignly and for mutual economic benefit. For Germany, they would have to signal that the Allies would irreversibly and credibly commit themselves to removing restraints on economic recovery and to reopening their markets to West German exports. It is in the perspective of this broader political agenda – including constitutional and currency reform in Germany as well as membership in the European Payments Union (EPU) – that the political success of the Marshall Plan is to be seen. Therefore, the common practice of restricting economic analysis of the Marshall Plan to the incidence of ERP transfers appears to us as missing the central point of the plan.

Our discussion is organized as follows. Section 2 briefly reviews the debate about the Marshall Plan and its effects on the West German economy. Section 3 analyzes US intentions regarding Germany's revitalization as an "ersatz" supplier for the reconstruction of Western Europe and, thus, as a device to overcome the dollar gap. Section 4 turns to international controversies in connection with this plan, arguing that the decision to revitalize Germany's industry jeopardized French plans at establishing industrial hegemony over Western Europe. Cooperation with Western Germany on almost equal terms was therefore hard to accept for French decisionmakers, and it will be shown that, far from taking the initiative, France initially opposed German reconstruction very strongly. Section 5 argues for easy credibility effects of US policies within Germany. Section 6 reviews the early history of payments settlements in post-war Europe. It argues that in the light of the multitude of Allied claims on Germany, instituting the EPU as a system of mutual free trade and credit commitments was superior to continuing protectionism under bilateral trade agreements. As it helped Germany to credibly commit itself to a regime change in its foreign trade politics, the EPU had the effect of reintegrating European trade and payments, irrespective of the bad record of clearing arrangements under the Nazi New Order. Section 7 examines how the EPU worked in practice when Germany's prewar balance of trade deficits began to reappear in the wake of the Korean crisis. In contrast to some of the recent literature, we argue that the German balance of payments crisis was overcome not so much because of monetary or fiscal sanctions imposed by the EPU, but rather because of import restrictions levied by the Organization for European Economic Cooperation (OEEC) in cooperation with the Germans themselves. In our view, this temporary violation of West Germany's fresh commitment to free trade was only tolerated by the Allies because of the credibility effects that the Marshall Plan institutions had created both within and outside of Germany.

The quick success of this European crisis management and the subsequent turn of the tide in the German balance of payments provided the cornerstone of Germany's later financial reputation. In turn, this helped to establish its position as the main powerhouse of Europe's reconstruction and thus eventually turned the Marshall Plan's broader political agenda into a success.

2 German discussions of Marshall Plan efficiency

The traditional story of the Marshall Plan may be paraphrased as follows. According to it, the complete failure of the Nazi economic system became apparent as soon as the secret police were gone. Continuing price regulation under the Four Powers and the monetary overhang made the work effort unattractive. Living standards worsened steadily, and the morale of the population declined day by day. Then came the deregulation programs of Ludwig Erhard, the deutschmark, and the Marshall Plan –

and Germany became an economic wonderland overnight. Views like this have long dominated, both in Germany and abroad.[1]

A – doubtlessly necessary – revision of this position was first advanced by Jánossy (1966) and subsequently elaborated by Abelshauser (1975, 1981). Jánossy's argument, that the uniformity of rapid post-war growth all over Europe was caused by the scope for catching-up to historical trends, is closely related to that advanced by Abramovitz (1979, 1986).[2] Dumke (1990) finds econometric evidence in support of this hypothesis.[3]

Applying this concept to Germany in the early post-war years, Manz (1968) and Abelshauser (1975) suggest that recovery was well under way at the time of the currency reform of June 1948 and even more pronounced by the end of the year when the first Marshall aid deliveries arrived. According to this view, post-war economic reconstruction in Germany was mostly an exogenous process, driven by the speed at which bottlenecks in the war-hit transportation system were eliminated. The transformation to a free market system and the Marshall Plan itself are seen to have been of only minor importance. This new approach, seemingly making a case for leftist attacks on the alleged superiority of free market systems, remained undisputed for a decade. During this time, it soon became a leading doctrine in German economic history. Only in the mid eighties did counter revisions develop (see Borchardt, 1981; Ritschl, 1985; Klump, 1985; Klemm and Trittel, 1987; Buchheim, 1988).

Industrial output figures for West Germany indeed indicate that there was substantial growth even before the currency reform (figure 8.1).

In figure 8.1, output indices are given for the Anglo-American Bizone (YBZ) and the French zone of occupation (YFZ) separately. The date of the currency reform is indicated by the vertical line marked (CR). There is one bit of evidence in these data which seems to contradict the revisionist interpretation: around the time of the currency reform, there appears to be an upward jump in the bizonal data at (CR). Anticipating this point, Manz (1968) and Abelshauser (1975) argue that it is a mere artifact created by underreporting of output to the planning authorities prior to reform. To

---

[1] See, however, Wallich (1955) and Stolper, Häuser, and Borchardt (1967) for more cautious views.

[2] It should be made clear, however, that Jánossy's political intentions were radically different. Being staff economist at Hungary's planning board, Jánossy sought to defend his country's reformist approach to communism against the seemingly more impressive growth records of both Western Europe and Soviet Russia. Employing a labor theory of value framework, he assumes long-term growth trends to be given by population and education and explains cross-country divergences of post-war growth by the severity of wartime disruptions and subsequent catching-up. His book is still interesting reading today as it rightly predicts the subsequent productivity slowdown.

[3] Compare, however, Eichengreen and Uzan (1992).

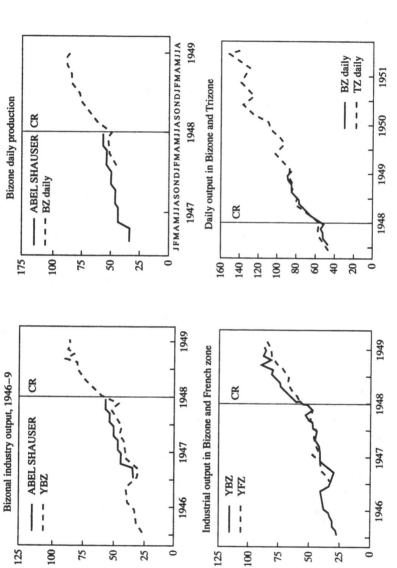

Figure 8.1 Industrial output in Western Germany *Source*: Ritschl (1985).

substantiate this hypothesis, Abelshauser (1975) considers also the output of power plants, which can be argued not to have been subject to underreporting.[4] Assuming constant average productivity of electricity output, he extrapolates aggregate industrial production backward by means of the electricity output series. The result is given in the two upper charts of figure 8.1 above. The output estimates he obtains for the pre-reform period substantially exceed the official figures. Moreover, they neatly fit post-reform data, such that the upward structural break in output in mid 1948 almost disappears.

Abelshauser's rationale for this exercise is again to be found in Jánossy's reconstruction hypothesis. In Abelshauser's interpretation, not only did the forces of recovery operate irrespective of the particular institutional setup, but they also continued to dominate economic activity during the process of system transformation. According to his view, recovery began in mid 1947 as the result of the successful attempts of the Allied authorities in the Bizone to widen bottlenecks in the transport system. As his estimates seem to imply, the currency reform and the economic liberalization acts of mid 1948 had only a minor impact, and so did Marshall aid that arrived only by the end of 1948 when an adaption crisis was underway.

Replicating Abelshauser's assumptions, Ritschl (1985) finds it possible to reject the underreporting hypothesis in various ways. Summarizing the results, there seems to be a structural break, not only in aggregate output but also in electricity output itself, whereas the null hypothesis of no effects of the economic reforms on economic performance would predict no such break in the latter series. Moreover, no significant break shows up in the input–output ratio between electric current and industrial production (a structural break would be the null under the underreporting hypothesis) if trend growth of productivity is allowed for.

The results of this have not prevented scholars from using Abelshauser's series further, as there seems to be a general consensus among historians that the underreporting hypothesis is convincing on a priori grounds (e.g., Klemm and Trittel, 1987). However, the theory of the socialist firm predicts that a planning system, in which entitlements to deliveries of scarce inputs are linked to reported output levels, provides as many incentives to overreporting as to understating output (see Kornai, 1981).

In fact, much of the discrepancy between Abelshauser's estimates and the official figures disappears when the latter are adjusted to an average daily base, correcting for various public holidays (see the series "BZ daily" in figure 8.1). But even using this adjusted series (and making similar adjustments for electric power generation), Ritschl (1985) finds structural

---

[4] The underlying reasoning for this is that coal production and electric power generation, being under close Allied control, could be better observed than aggregate industrial production, implying little or no underreporting in their respective series.

breaks that accompany the currency reform. Thus it is clear that counter to the revisionist position, the currency reform and the deregulation acts of June 1948 did have an immediate impact on industrial output.

Interestingly, different results obtain for the French zone. Here a break in the input–output ratio of electrical power supply to industrial production can be observed, although there is no break in the aggregate output series (whereas a break in the latter and no break in the former would be the null hypothesis). Moreover, during early 1949 the French zone does not experience stagnating output whereas the Bizone does (see Giersch, Paqué, and Schmieding (1992) for a short review of the debate). One of the reasons for the differential performance of the two zones seems to lie precisely in the timing of the transformation process that accompanied the currency reform. While the deutschmark was introduced in all parts of Western Germany, the deregulation acts were not, as the competence of Ludwig Erhard's administration was still limited to the Anglo-American Bizone at the time. In the French zone, transition to a market system was slower. Only in mid 1949, which is precisely the time when the French zone caught up with Bizonia, were similar levels of deregulation attained. Both the bizonal and the French zone indices of production end in the third quarter of 1949. A trizonal index of industrial production that covers most of the territory of later West Germany, given in figure 8.1 as "TZ daily," exhibits a return to normal growth in late 1949.

Two things stand out from this debate. First, evidence does seem to support the traditional idea that the currency reform did have an impact. Second, however, there remains the question of why recovery apparently began already in mid-1947, why performance during the year after the reform was so disappointing, and what the Marshall Plan had to do with all that. The issue of the timing of Marshall aid has triggered off a debate of its own. Table 8.1 summarizes key data on foreign assistance to Germany.

As regards timing, it is first worthwhile to look at earlier aid programs. Most of assistance to Germany came from the earlier GARIOA program (row 2) and related British schemes (row 5). Apparently, the combined annual levels of previous US and British assistance (sum of rows II and 5) were at no time exceeded or even reached by later ERP deliveries. This is not surprising, as the latter were designed to substitute for the former (Daniel, 1982). Total aid to Germany was largest from 1947 to 1949 and provided for the majority of imports during that period.

Borchardt and Buchheim (1991) focus attention on this transition period. They suggest that Marshall aid had its impact mainly in eliminating bottlenecks to industry and in creating announcement effects on output.[5]

---

[5] This is at slight variance with Borchardt's contribution in Stolper, Häuser, and Borchardt (1976), which gives a broader interpretation of the Marshall Plan, stressing the role of institutional change.

Table 8.1. *US aid to West Germany, 1945–52 (millions US $)*

	1945/6	1947	1948	1949	1950	1951	1952	Total 1945–62
1 Civilian supplies	195							195
2 GARIOA, etc.	75	237	788	503	177.8	11.9	0.4	1,793
3 ERP, etc.			142	420	302.6	415.8	114.1	1,678
4 Others	3							206
I US aid total	273	237	930	923	480.4	427.7	114.5	3,872
5 UK contribution	264	363	90	32	1			
II Foreign aid total	537	600	1,020	955	481	428	114	4,640
6 Current account surplus	18	103	60	−262	−323	592	649	
7 Imports (cif)			785	867	2,237	2,703	3,503	
8 Counterpart funds as percentage of aggregate fixed investment				5.8	7.8	4.1	2.1	3,854
9 GNP (billion DM)			37.5ᵃ	83.8	89.7	113.6	126.0	

Note: ᵃSecond half of 1948 only.

Sources:

1, 3, 4	Deutsche Bundesbank (1976, pp. 323, 341).
2	1945–8: adapted from Buchheim (1990, p. 72).
	1949–52 and total: Bundesminister für den Marshallplan (1953, pp. 23 f.).
5	Buchheim (1990, p. 72).
6	Buchheim (1990, pp. 184 f.).
7	1947–8: Buchheim (1990, p. 186).
	1949–52: Bundesminister für den Marshallplan (1953, p. 24).
8	Baumgart (1961, p. 47).
9	Statistisches Jahrbuch für die Bundesrepublik Deutschland (1950–4).

Comparing output of cotton textiles and imports of raw cotton with one another, they conclude that cotton stocks must have been reduced to almost zero during the fall of 1948, which would hardly have taken place without the information that large ERP deliveries were due soon. To further substantiate their hypothesis, they cite contemporary press articles speculating about an imminent breakdown of German textile production due to cotton shortages when the announced ERP deliveries underwent an unforeseen delay in November 1948. The textile industry in Germany, processing imported cotton, wool, and some synthetics, still had significant shares in value added at the time. Cotton imports thus provide an example of a significant bottleneck in German industry that was eliminated by ERP deliveries, a point which Abelshauser (1991) has acknowledged.[6]

Another argument of Borchardt and Buchheim relates to the use of the so-called counterpart funds, a deutschmark capital stock created by payments of private-sector recipients of ERP deliveries (see, e.g., Milward, 1984, pp. 108 ff.). These funds, administered first by American ECA officials, later by a newly created bank named *Kreditanstalt für Wiederaufbau* (KfW), were channeled into investment in bottleneck sectors, primarily into expanding electric power supply. The importance of these KfW investments has long been part of conventional wisdom. Table 8.1 above shows that counterpart funds attained some significance for capital formation during 1949 and 1950. Focusing on long-term capital formation and on certain sectors, the effects of counterpart funds become even more pronounced (table 8.2). However, some caveats must be made. As Borchardt and Buchheim themselves mention, both the capital market and the energy sector were still regulated: price deregulations during the reforms of 1948 had been confined to consumer goods and other downstream industries, whereas heavy industry and the energy sector still had to sell their output at regulated prewar prices. With the general price increase that took place after the currency reform, this resulted in operating losses for the public utility companies. As market interest rates were still pegged below 5 percent, initial attempts by the ECA to float public utility bonds on the market were unsuccessful (see Abelshauser, 1984b). Hence it is certainly true that, given all these regulations, counterpart funds were important for investment activity in the energy sector. However, what one is talking about here are investment subsidies to a regulated industry, and arguing that this was a

---

[6] For similar reasoning see DeLong and Eichengreen (1993), who evaluate the importance of ERP coal deliveries to Italy using a small input–output table. According to their estimates, Italian GNP in 1947 would have been around 3 percent lower without such deliveries.

Table 8.2. *Percentage share of ERP credits in gross fixed investment*

	Industry		Energy		Transport		
	Long-term capital formation	Total	Mining	Total	Total	State railways	Merchant fleet
1949	21.8	7.1	35.0	14.0	20.0	32.0	—
1950	14.5	13.3	32.0	24.0	7.1	—	35.4
1951	7.0	4.6	8.6	21.0	3.3	—	12.4
1952	4.8	2.3	4.2	5.5	2.2	3.1	4.7

Source: Baumgart (1961).

particularly efficient way of using the ERP counterpart funds is clearly problematic.[7]

But even if it is accepted that the reforms of mid 1948 boosted recovery and that this was helped by announcement effects of the Marshall Plan, some puzzles do remain, and it might be argued that they support the revisionists' cause.

First, industrial output data for 1947 and 1948 exhibit a very unusual common pattern. In both years, the typical seasonal decline in output toward the end of the year is missing entirely, while it is very marked during 1946/7 and reappears in 1949/50. This points to some common underlying cause which cannot be explained either by Marshall aid or by the economic reforms of 1948, as both came too late to be anticipated in late 1947. It is precisely this spurt in late 1947 which has been identified by Abelshauser (1975) as a "breakthrough" to accelerated reconstruction, taking place long before the advent of currency reform.

A second disturbing fact is that during the heyday of the Marshall Plan, West Germany's economic performance was far from satisfactory. Mounting difficulties developed into a full-fledged balance of payments crisis, and it was only after its resolution that confidence in Erhard's free market approach built up. Being less enthusiastic about Erhard, revisionists have pointed to the German export surge in the wake of an international rearmament boom that the Korean crisis is held to have caused, again dismissing the Marshall Plan as an explanation.

Apparently, this puzzle cannot be solved entirely by looking at macroeconomic flow data alone. A different approach is needed that provides a perspective of the process of German recovery, including the effects of policy credibility on the behavior of decisionmakers. We shall advance the hypothesis that the Marshall Plan, viewed in a broader context, was indispensable for Germany's reconstruction, and would have

---

[7] There is little work that examines the motivations behind continued regulations in industry and on the capital market in Germany after the currency reform of 1948. One possible answer is to be found in the anti-trust commitments of Ludwig Erhard, then West Germany's economic minister and the main architect of the *Wirtschaftswunder*. Himself a disciple of the socialist Franz Oppenheimer, Erhard seems to have adhered to a revisionist interpretation of the Marxist model of economic development. As such, the alleged tendency of upstream industries to overaccumulate capital, implying heavily unbalanced growth, appeared to Erhard as a real threat. Indeed, cartelization of heavy industry during the Weimar period seemed to confirm this view. Price controls during the Great Depression and the Nazi period had sought to improve relative prices of downstream producers, while capital market regulation drove heavy industry out of the market for finance. For evidence on Erhard's beliefs see Laitenberger (1986). The removal of these controls after the Korea crisis has been interpreted by Abelshauser (1984b, pp. 73–5) as a victory of heavy industry and a *de facto* return to the prewar system of organized capitalism.

remained so even if effective transfers had been zero. To see this it is necessary to go back to the earlier commitments made by the Allies – and even further to the economic record of Nazi Germany.

Dialogue of the Marshall planners:

> c: Where have you been? I haven't seen you lately.
> k: I am not working on German matters any more. I have moved over and now work on the European recovery program.
> c: Oh, that's the program which developed out of the Secretary's speech at Princeton.
> k: Phil, where did you go to college?
> c: Princeton, why?
> k: That's what I thought.[8]

3 An agenda for reconstruction

Immediately after the occupation, Allied authorities in the Western zones ordered most German businesses to close down. In September 1945, only some sawmills operated to cover the needs of the US army (OMGUS, January 1946). Gradually, shops and factories were permitted to reopen, often only after a lengthy licensing process. Industry is said to have returned to normal by the turn of 1946, as far as employment and the number of businesses in operation were concerned. But still, severe restrictions applied to politically sensitive sectors, and much of Germany's heavy industry remained idle, either for economic or political reasons. In addition, the Nazi system of economic planning was maintained in principle, with the central planning boards having been dissolved and the whole structure re-erected on a zone-by-zone base. Economic cooperation between the four zones of occupation developed only slowly, as mutual deliveries had to be negotiated between the Four Powers and as the Allied Control Council failed to reach agreement on the implementation of the economic principles laid out in the Potsdam Treaty.

Thus, no attempt was made to remove the huge monetary overhang left by the suppressed inflation of Nazi Germany. As a result, industrial output stagnated at extremely low levels (see figure 8.1), and farmers withheld their products from urban markets. Nutritional allowances often barely reached the subsistence level.[9] In the British and American zones, difficulties were aggravated by a huge inflow of refugees and expellees from former German

---

[8] From: *Foreign Records of the United States* (henceforth: FRUS) (1947, III, p. 245) (memo by Charles Kindleberger). Marshall's speech was given at Harvard on June 5, 1947.

[9] This breakdown of exchange between agriculture and industry and its adverse consequences for nutrition also figured prominently in Marshall's Harvard speech. See FRUS (1947, III, p. 238).

territories lost to Poland and of ethnic Germans from all over Eastern Europe. Their share in West Germany's population reached 16 percent by the end of 1946 and increased to about 20 percent as of December, 1952 (Bundesminister für den Marshallplan, 1953, p. 185).[10]

At the same time, productive capital stock was in much better shape than had been anticipated by the victors. Total capacity loss due to bombing has been estimated at a mere 18 percent of existing stock (Krengel, 1958), whereas urban housing was hit much more severely. As net investment in industry during the war had been considerable, Germany's industrial capacity, although partially paralyzed by bombings of bottleneck suppliers and the transport system, was actually far higher at the time of the surrender than before the war. Hence, potentially good prospects for recovery were thwarted by restrictive policies on the part of the occupying powers and a highly inefficient allocative system.

In the face of this crisis and of mounting occupation costs, Britain and the US agreed in December 1946 on merging their zones. It was understood that in order to achieve financial self-sufficiency of this so-called Bizone, living conditions would have to be improved and production incentives created. The idea at this point was not so much to beef up performance with additional aid but rather to use the country's idle capacities more efficiently, thus helping to reduce the burden on US and British resources.

The first drafts of the Marshall Plan, however, originated in a different context. In early 1947, the Truman administration felt the need to gain Congressional support for additional aid to Greece and Turkey, then threatened by internal turmoil and communist infiltration. Study groups were installed to assess the various existing foreign aid programs, evaluate them in the light of America's national and security interest, and to present these and additional ones to Congress as a package.[11] The first report, dated April 17, included lists of possible recipients of future US aid, formulated tentative policy goals such as prevention of infiltration by hostile powers, and sketched what was plainly an export promotion

---

[10] Most of the burden actually fell on the Bizonal area, as France accepted almost no refugees in its occupation zone.

[11] *Foreign Records of the United States* (FRUS), 1947, III, pp. 197 f. Under Secretary of State Acheson to Secretary of War Patterson (March 5, 1947) points out that aid to Greece and Turkey against internal turmoil and communist infiltration was only part of a much wider problem growing out of the change in Great Britain's position. A group to undertake study of this wider agenda was proposed. On March 17 (ibid., pp. 198 f.) this group came up with a provisional list of questions to be studied. See also a memo of April 7, sent by the director of the budget to Acheson, pressing for a unifying concept, as Congress "wants to see the whole picture at once," and asking that clear priorities must be set, "otherwise, legislative and budgetary 'credit' may be exhausted by the President before the highest priorities are met" (ibid., p. 200).

program (see FRUS, 1947, III, p. 204–19, for more on this). Apparently written in a Keynesian mood, the report was based on a scenario of long-term unemployment in the US and stressed the beneficial demand effects of having additional exports. The scheme proposed by this report was plainly an export promotion program along New Deal lines. Consequently, it avoided discussion of how to sustain abnormally high export-to-income ratios should domestic employment and capacity utilization take a more favorable course.

This, however, seems to have been the concern of Under Secretary of State, Acheson, in a public address on May 8. There he mentioned the dollar shortage in Europe, the pressing needs of Europe's countries for critical commodities, and the check to American export possibilities presented by capacity constraints. He wondered about the implications of all this for US foreign policies (ibid., p. 219). Similar concerns were expressed in a radio address by Marshall on April 28 in which he first deplored the sluggish recovery in Europe and then emphasized that Germany and Austria were "an area of large and skilled population, of great resources and industrial plants" (FRUS, 1947, III, p. 219).

Both lines of thought were brought together in a series of memoranda by George Kennan, then director of the State Department's Policy Planning Staff. Kennan advanced a short-term strategy for creating confidence in Europe and a long-term strategy for introducing close economic and political cooperation among European countries. As to the first, he proposed to "select some suitable bottleneck or bottlenecks in the Western European economy and institute immediate action . . .," emphasizing that "only by means of some such action can we gain time to deal with the long-term problem in an orderly manner" (FRUS, 1947, III, p. 224). With respect to the long-term problem he suggested moving toward creating close political and economic ties in Europe, although the formal initiative for this should come from Europe itself. His suggestions included gearing occupation policies in Germany toward a maximum contribution of its Western zones to European reconstruction and emphasizing that both the support and the cooperation program ought to be embedded in a paramount long-term strategy (ibid., p. 221).

Economic historians appear to have interpreted the Marshall Plan mostly as an export promotion program along the lines of the first report mentioned above. Kennan's own memoranda tell a very different story. According to them, the Marshall Plan as a transfer scheme was no more than a sideshow to the true, less visible agenda behind it. Highly visible, public-relations oriented action was needed to produce some immediate effects and to distract public attention from the long-term program it concealed. This also makes it clear that economic analysis of the Marshall

Plan as a transfer scheme has mostly focused on its visible component, which was apparently peripheral to the true intentions. In contrast, political historians have realized the far-reaching implications of these concepts much more clearly. However, exaggerated emphasis has sometimes been placed on the differences between the various programs, which were interpreted as a struggle between the military administration and the State Department (see, e.g., Gimbel, 1976; Hogan, 1987).

According to this literature, the focus of these debates was not so much on the need to reconstruct Germany but rather on how this idea could be sold to the smaller allies (on this, see Hogan, 1991). The basic conflict, in this view, was between the State Department's strategy of pursuing a "balanced" strategy of recovery in both Germany and Western Europe and the War Department's preference for the Hoover Plan which emphasized reconstruction in Germany as a locomotive for recovery in Europe.

Two main motives are attributed to the State Department. First, there was the beginning of containment policy in the light of the mounting tensions with the USSR.[12] In order to prevent Western Europe from falling into communist hands, decisive action was needed which both documented US commitment to the region and provided better living conditions. A second concern was Western Europe's widening dollar trade gap with the US. Driven by ambitious national economic policies, most Western European countries had reached full employment during the spring of 1947. Import demands were considerable, whereas export performance, hampered by modernization gaps, was relatively poor. In the absence of substantial real resource transfers from abroad, the countries of Western Europe would be forced to curb activity through deflationary pressure. In the light of the communist threat, the implications of this for political stabilization appeared gloomy.

According to conventional interpretation, the Marshall Plan solved the State Department's problems and rescued Europe's young democracies from this dilemma by providing transfers, thus deepening American influence in Western Europe and setting the stage for the Cold War of the 1950s. However, revisionists have pointed out that Marshall aid was far too small to provide much leverage. Milward (1984, pp. 90–125) argues that deliveries were often allocated according to the recipient countries' preferences rather than according to American guidelines.

---

[12] Several passages in Kennan's memo (FRUS, 1947, III, p. 229) stress that the ERP ought *not* to be viewed just as an implication of the Truman doctrine. Nevertheless, reference to US national security and to the threat of communist infiltration is made frequently in all of these documents. Citing these passages as evidence, Gimbel (1976) explicitly denies any link between the Marshall Plan and containment policies. For criticism of this, see Knapp (1977, 1981) and the insightful study of Daniel (1982).

Our own reading of the evidence is still different. From the published State Department records it emerges that two main elements of the Marshall Plan existed right from the beginning of the planning process. First, there is a sharp distinction to be made between Marshall aid itself and the wider political agenda behind it. The aim of Marshall aid was not to provide the means for European reconstruction but to restructure and advertise existing aid schemes and to set clear political priorities for the short run. Second, both Kennan's plan and the aforementioned statements of Acheson and Marshall make it clear that, in the longer run, minimizing the dollar drain and substituting West Germany for the US as the main supplier of the capital goods needed for recovery was a critical element of the program. Thus, as far as top officials were concerned, we conclude that the State Department was fully aware of the opportunities for Germany's reconstruction.[13]

The presence of idle capacity in West German industry provided a clue to the problems of both the State and the War Departments. By setting Germany's economy into motion again, its potential could be utilized to both reduce the cost of occupation and provide transfers to Western Europe without imposing an unsustainable drain on US resources. Moreover, if some intra-European payment system was introduced to foster trade and secure input deliveries to Germany, Western Europe's import and export problems might be solved simultaneously: West Germany would absorb imports from other European countries that were difficult to sell elsewhere and deliver the desired capital goods in exchange. In this way, a self-sustained recovery process would be triggered without imposing unpredictable burdens on US taxpayers.[14]

If this interpretation, derived from the debate between Gimbel (1976), Knapp (1977, 1981), and Hogan (1987),[15] is correct, the success of the

---

[13] This notwithstanding, the precise balance between reconstruction of Germany and of other European countries remained the subject matter of bitter infighting between the US military administration in Germany and the ECA. On this see Milward (1984, p. 155) and Abelshauser (1989).

[14] For a more complete analysis, it would be interesting to contrast these views with those of the Treasury. Some of these are referred to in the contribution of Harold James to this volume.

[15] According to Gimbel's hypothesis the Marshall Plan was connected neither with a long-term strategy nor with the Truman doctrine and containment policy against communism. Accordingly, Gimbel makes some effort to de-emphasize the importance of Kennan's first memorandum. Although this memo repeatedly stresses the tentative nature of its conclusions, we feel that Gimbel underestimates its impact on shaping US policies in the subsequent period. As to the economic interpretation of the plan, Gimbel establishes a link between reparations and Marshall aid, to the effect that the latter substituted for the former, which America's allies had expected to get out of Germany. At least with regard to long-run considerations, this is at variance with our own way of reading the evidence. In

Marshall Plan as a broader political agenda is not so much to be measured by the size of Marshall aid but rather by the degree to which the US authorities managed to install West Germany as a source of permanent export surpluses *vis-à-vis* Western Europe. Therefore, US Marshall aid to Western Europe does not provide the core of the program but rather an initial pump-primer and political palliative for the former victims of Nazi Germany.

Thus, several different "Marshall Plans" have to be distinguished: first, the well-known Marshall aid scheme that provided US transfers; second, another Marshall Plan that provided for German deliveries to Western Europe; and, finally, yet another Marshall Plan that aimed at providing a proper institutional framework and paved the way for political acceptance of Germany's economic resurrection among America's European Allies.[16]

4 American strategies and French objections

This agenda for reconstruction was not uncontroversial in Europe. British policies aimed at a socialization of heavy industry in the Ruhr district, Germany's industrial heartland east of the Rhine. French reconstruction programs, as laid out in the Monnet Plan, sought to secure the prime position in European heavy industry for France, assigning to the Ruhr only the minor role of France's main coal supplier. Soviet interests were apparently divided between extracting reparations from Germany and keeping its industrial potential low. What all these plans had in common was to give priority to a dismantling of German industrial capacity. Only Belgium, the Netherlands and Luxemburg adopted a different perspective. As these countries were strongly dependent on trade with Germany, they sought to revive trade of some sort. For this reason they objected to the so-called dollar clause which the US dominated Joint Import Export Agency (JEIA) had imposed on trade with the American and British zones to prevent them from accumulating deficits. The immediate effect of this was that trade could only be exerted on a cash-in-advance basis, which worked against the interests of Belgian and Dutch exporters.

our view, Germany's economy was to be revitalized in order to substitute for US aid. Gimbel's view is possibly a consequence of mixing up reparations from current production (which the Americans opposed) with real resource transfers (which they endorsed).

[16] Abelshauser (1989) introduces a related distinction. Daniel (1982) also emphasizes the need to distinguish between Marshall aid and German reconstruction. However, in both studies the two programs seem unrelated to one another. In Daniel's case this is caused by her insistence on export promotion as the basic principle of US foreign trade policy at the time, which appears quite debatable.

But there was also another common interest which ultimately gave American decisionmakers strong bargaining power: the coal question. Coal from the Ruhr had traditionally been a prime export item in German trade with the Benelux countries and France. In almost all countries of Western Europe, the ambitious recovery programs depended to a considerable degree on sufficiently large inflows of coal. Given the conditions of the early post-war period, such imports could only come from two sources, West Germany or the US. This way, the Americans found themselves to be in a key position. Neither France nor the Benelux countries could have made available sufficient foreign exchange for imports without US assistance. Access to Germany's coal reserves depended on US consent as well. When during the critical winter of 1946/7, coal had become a limiting factor, it became apparent that a formidable policy weapon had fallen into US hands.

The summer of 1947 witnessed a stormy conference in Moscow on a peace treaty with Germany. During this conference US officials succeeded for the first time in establishing agreement between the Western occupation powers which indexed Germany's coal export obligations to coal output (Milward, 1984, p. 140). Ideology ran counter to efficiency: in order to obtain more coal, France had to accept the logic that Ruhr coal exports were a function of output. But in turn, coal output was a function of investment in the mines (which had been badly run down during the war), which in turn depended on a reconstruction of other bottleneck sectors of West Germany's economy.

The US could also use a second lever. Most of West Germany's heavy industry and along with it most of its urban population were concentrated in the British zone of occupation. This soon left British occupation authorities with the choice between allowing for self-sustained economic recovery beyond envisaged levels or having to provide financial support. Given Britain's weakened economic potential, the implied transfer payments threatened to be large. Therefore, Britain soon adopted the less restrictive doctrines of the Truman administration toward German reconstruction and agreed to merge its occupation zone with the American one. This led to the creation of "Bizonia," the kernel of the later German Federal Republic, and to a common economic policy under US leadership (see Gillingham, 1991, pp. 121–37, for an account of US/UK quibbles).

French resistance was harder to overcome. In his outstanding review of Western Europe's reconstruction, Milward (1984) has advanced the hypothesis that the process of European integration in the 1950s is the story of a series of defeats of American concepts and of the ultimate victory of an entirely different agenda put together under French leadership. Certainly

US policy did suffer blows and setbacks.[17] However, this is not always the central issue. The perspective is often reversed if one recognizes the central importance of Germany for US policies toward Europe.[18] What is amazing in this regard is the bluntness with which US policies often confronted those of its allies. They soon interfered with France's interests in a field which was the main concern of all French economic planning after the war, the economic aspect of national security against a revived German state.[19]

Creating a *fait accompli* and then negotiating the technical details with the Allies was a strategy that the Americans employed several times. On the eve of the first session of the Paris conference in 1947, it was announced to the Allies that the Level of Industry Plan of 1946 would no longer be regarded as binding (see, e.g., Milward, 1984, p. 73). This was especially alarming to the French, as West Germany's industrial output at the time was still far below the levels set out in that scheme. Announcing that even higher levels were now envisaged clearly indicated a major change in US policy toward Germany.[20]

In a short memorandom of July 18 (see on this FRUS, 1947, III, p. 332), Kennan had put the objectives quite succinctly: "There is a serious gap between what is required of Germany for European recovery and what is being produced there today. Unless this gap can be overcome no European recovery program will be realistic." After proposing to have talks on this with France, he continues: "In this way we could place squarely before the French the choice between a rise in German production or no European recovery financed by the US."

Given the scarcity of coal in continental Europe, this policy meant

---

[17] Milward's (1984) account of US policy goals appears to follow largely the records of the ECA Marshall Plan administration, thus reflecting the views of its director, Paul Hoffman. There is little doubt that the far-reaching agenda of Hoffman was frustrated repeatedly. However, his policy stance was not quite representative of US policies toward Western Europe in general.

[18] We read chapter 4 of Milward's (1992) recent book, especially pp. 155f., as remarkable evidence of convergence toward such a view.

[19] Compare Eichengreen and Uzan (1992) for an interesting discussion of Marshall aid conditionality in France which, however, centers around domestic macroeconomic policies alone. This has prompted comments by Hellwig (1992) who points to the need for an analysis of France's broader agenda in the context of Marshall aid.

[20] In a protest note to Marshall (FRUS, 1947, II, p. 991), the French Foreign Minister Bidault first mentions that in accepting the Marshall Plan at the Paris Council of Foreign Ministers in 1947, "France had burned its bridges." Mentioning that both France's communists and the Soviets had predicted that the first result of the Marshall Plan would be the reconstruction of Germany, he warned against weakening his position in the French public and even threatened to resign should the revised level of industry plan be implemented. See Gimbel (1976, pp. 220–54) for an account of the bitter infighting in the American administration that followed.

jeopardizing the most important element of the Monnet Plan for France's reconstruction, the idea of channeling Ruhr coal away from Germany's to France's heavy industry (see FRUS, 1947, II, p. 995, for an intervention of Bidault in this regard).[21]

American action followed suit. Increased efforts were made to reconstruct the German railroad system, one of the few sectors that had been badly hit during the war. Study groups were installed to improve the planning system, and bank notes for a new currency were secretly printed in the US. Reconstruction of the transport system and the subsequent "breakthrough" of the West German economy in late 1947, which is such a dominant theme in Abelshauser's (1975) early work (and which is also reflected in the output figures; see section 2 above), was thus not independent of the Marshall Plan. Rather, it appears as a direct consequence – provided only that US policies for German revitalization are given their proper weight in the plan.

Of course, certain concessions had to be made in exchange. In order to prevent the French from walking out of the Paris conference of 1947, the US agreed to establish an international Ruhr coal authority, but only as part of a peace settlement in Germany, which was still far out of reach at the time.[22]

The decisive blow to French ambitions came with the London conference on Germany of early 1948, which had been called to decide both on Germany's future shape and on the economic control of Ruhr industry.

[21] During the negotiations, Secretary of State Marshall dispatched a telegram to the embassy in London which very clearly states the ultimate goals behind the ERP program and the role envisaged for the German economy. Referring to initial British opposition to discussing revised production targets for West German Bizonia, he states: "The essence of Secretary's [i.e., Marshall's, HB/AR] proposals was preparation of a program based on maximum European self-help and mutual aid and that such a program could only be prepared if the separate national programs and requirement statements were examined and coordinated such as to produce the greatest European contribution to recovery at the earliest moment. . . . Dept's impression . . . is that element of mutual aid and subordination of separate aims to a cooperative approach has been generally lacking. The force of US pressure to achieve this cooperative approach is seriously weakened in that one European area in which the US has direct responsibility abstains. . . . If British position prevails and we withhold discussion of bizonal area, we can hardly be successful in opposing a French desire to protect the Monnet Plan, Scandinavian tendencies to withdraw from full participation and other centrifugal forces working against a coordinated area approach." This is followed by instructions to the ambassador authorizing him to cast doubt on the acceptability of the ERP program to the US should British opposition on German output targets persist (FRUS, 1947, II, pp. 418 f., telegram of September 8, 1947).

[22] Milward (1984) appears to regard this as a decisive setback for US policies in Europe. However, the French were successfully prevented from raising this issue at an important juncture of the London Council of Foreign Ministers in November 1947. Evidence even suggests that the decision to break off this conference was influenced by American and British desires not to make differences on the Ruhr question visible to the Russians. See FRUS (1947, II, pp. 769 f.).

Again, the US and Britain had created a *fait accompli* prior to the start of a conference, this time by installing the nucleus of the constitutional structures of the later Federal Republic. France was once again left with the choice of pulling out or avoiding the worst through continued cooperation.[23] In the end, France had to agree to a heavily curtailed dismantling program for German industry and to resume talks on merging its zone of occupation with the Bizone on American terms. This was also an instance when the US successfully threatened to withdraw Marshall aid from France if it refused to go along.[24] Once again creating a *fait accompli* before negotiating technical details, the Bizonal Law No. 75, issued in November 1948, included a commitment to reprivatize Ruhr industry, thus jeopardizing French attempts to assume managerial control of heavy industry trusts in that region. Clearly this provoked bitter protests in France. Press reports at the time quoted General de Gaulle referring to Law No. 75 as the "gravest decision yet taken in the 20th century" (Milward, 1984, p. 153). Such were the conditions, created by American pressure, from which the Schuman Plan for Franco-German cooperation finally emerged.[25]

---

[23] See FRUS (1948, II, pp. 26 f.) where Bidault is reported to have charged the US and Great Britain with having created a *fait accompli*. After the London Council of Foreign Ministers in late 1947, France had been informally invited to join talks on the future shape of the Western zones (see, e.g., FRUS, 1947, II, pp. 811 ff.). Although failure to consult the French was officially deplored by British officials as a technical mistake, the French were told confidentially that one had "to get on with matters and could not hold up things while the French ruminated on the other side of the fence" (FRUS, 1948, II, p. 22).

[24] Before and during the London conference the French repeatedly attempted to establish a link between their approval of trizonal fusion and international control of the Ruhr and a weakening of central government powers in a future West German state. At one point this was flatly refused by the US, which pointed out that its desire in Trizonia (including the French zone of occupation) was not unlimited (FRUS, 1948, II, p. 70). Instructions by the State Department to its embassy in France reiterated the principal position that Germany's economy should be rehabilitated such as to make the maximum contribution to European recovery. In these documents, the French position of regarding Germany as a continuing threat was termed outmoded and unrealistic.

[25] Interestingly, French authors have long adopted similar interpretations of the genesis of the Schuman Plan. See, e.g., Lacroix-Riz (1986), Poidevin (1986). In contrast, German authors have emphasized elements of autonomy in shaping French policy toward Western Germany, see, e.g., Schwabe (1988). Goschler, Buchheim, and Bührer (1989) even argue that the Schuman Plan was rational from an economic point of view, as its idea of creating a European common market for steel was based on the idea of creating a comparative advantage of the French over the German steel industry. On this see also Lynch (1993). In any case it is sure that the US side pressed very hard for more French initiative, again following the guidelines laid out in Kennan's memoranda. In this spirit, a message from Acheson to Schuman of October 30, 1949 states: "Now is the time for French initiative and leadership of the type required to integrate the German Federal Republic promptly and decisively into Western Europe. Delay will seriously weaken the possibilities of success" (see FRUS, 1949, III, pp. 622 f.).

5 US policies and the German public

The aforementioned quibbles over Germany's future position already make it clear why the German public liked the Marshall Plan. As Germany's military defeat had been so complete, and as the US was clearly the dominant power, no one in Germany doubted the capacity of the US to rebuild the German economy. However, much would depend on the credibility of an American commitment to do so. Neither the original Morgenthau plan for reconverting Germany into an agrarian state nor US stop-and-go policies during 1946 were strongly conducive to creating such confidence. What did create confidence was the announcement of the Marshall Plan and the immediate removal of the limits on industrial production that the Level of Industry Plan of 1946 had envisaged. Incentives were created for workers in bottleneck sectors, increased efforts were made to repair the transport system, and all talk of nationalization of heavy industry under Allied control was suddenly over. Thus, it is precisely because of the Marshall Plan and not so much because of events before it that the improvement in the Bizone, which plays such a prominent role for Abelshauser's (1975) hypothesis, took place.

The commitment of the US to bailing the country out of its import impasse by announcing real resource transfers had a special meaning in Germany. Nazi ideology had interpreted the war in Malthusian and Social Darwinist fashion as a struggle for scarce habitat and resources (Ritschl, 1991). The prediction of this doctrine was that, after a military defeat, Germany would be exposed to losses of territory, destruction of its industrial potential, and mass starvation. Shortages and famine in Germany during the first two post-war years seemed to confirm this interpretation. Moreover, one of the central doctrines of Nazi ideology had been that both World War I and the struggle over reparations and debt obligations had served to curb Germany's international trade relations and narrow its economic *Lebensraum*, or habitat, as Nazi socio-biological language termed it. Indeed, most of Germany's autarky policies in the 1930s focused on substituting for imports from Germany's main creditors in the Anglo-Saxon world (Ritschl, 1992). Therefore, promising to supply inputs of vital importance to the German economy did not only open bottlenecks but also indicated a fundamental regime change, disproving Nazi propaganda among its own people.

However, there was one case in point where aid was indeed essential for survival, namely, the Soviet blockade of Berlin during the years 1948/9, when all supplies to the Western sectors of the city had to be brought in by air. The impressive pictures of the "raisin bombers," as the Berliners called them, provided ample evidence to the Germans that the US and its allies were serious about their commitment and that aid to the former enemy was not just an empty phrase.

6 Reconstructing intra-European trade

Reconstructing Germany and rebuilding the European division of labor heavily depended on one another. In retrospect, this task was a particularly difficult one, as the 1930s had witnessed a general disintegration of trade relations and Nazi Germany rebuilt its economy on a platform of autarky. Moreover, Nazi Germany had defaulted on its foreign debt and channeled its financial relations into a host of bilateral trade and clearing agreements, which served to increase the degree of self-sufficiency and prepare for the economic and military aggression against Eastern Europe (see Hirschman, 1945; Petzina, 1968; Teichert, 1984).

Post-war trade policies, it is commonly argued, were still faced with the disruption of trade created by beggar-thy-neighbor and autarky policies, especially on the part of Nazi Germany. However, upon closer examination this position seems questionable. Despite the political commitment to economic self-sufficiency, most of the reduction of Germany's imports in the 1930s can be explained by terms-of-trade-effects, with the remaining real stagnation a consequence of foreign exchange shortage. The most prominent effect of Nazi trade policies in the prewar years is on German trade deficits with its main creditors in the West (Ritschl, 1992).[26] But despite its autarky policies, around 1937/8 Germany still came in first on the list of the main trading partners for almost all countries of Continental Europe.[27]

Under the New Order imposed on Continental Europe after the military victories of 1940, Nazi Germany had already begun to introduce multilateral clearing, creating the nucleus of a centralized payments union with the *Deutsche Verrechnungskasse* in Berlin, a subsidiary of the *Reichsbank*, as its

---

[26] Both the terms-of-trade effect and the elimination of trade deficits with Germany's Western creditors helped to reduce the vulnerability to retaliation and seizure of German exports, just as predicted by the literature on sovereign debt (Bulow and Rogoff, 1989).

[27] See the tables in Mitchell (1975). The main exceptions are Scandinavia and Switzerland, where trade with Germany and Britain was almost equally high. The other big exceptions are Belgium, where Germany ranks second behind France, and France itself. In spite of a marked reduction of Franco-German trade during the Nazi years, in French foreign trade of 1937/38 Germany still held the third position behind Algeria (then a French colony) and Belgium.

central clearinghouse.[28] Indeed, the creation of a unified economic trade zone in Europe (the Nazi *Grosswirtschaftsraum*, or Greater Economic Sphere, as political euphemism had it) played a considerable role in contemporary German writings, being advertised to Germany's involuntary allies as a Pareto improvement.[29]

However, in practice the system worked in a markedly different direction, providing the accounting facility of the economic exploitation of Western Europe under Nazi rule.[30] Looking at the records of the *Deutsche Verrechnungskasse*, it can be seen that despite all ideological commitment to an eastward orientation of Germany's economy, most of the resources transferred to Germany under the clearing system indeed came from Western Europe, or more precisely from the countries that would eventually join West Germany in the EEC. In table 8.3, Germany's cumulative deficits on the clearing account by the end of 1944 are ordered by country groups. As can be seen, indebtedness *vis-à-vis* Western Europe was far higher than with Eastern Europe. Using the clearing debt as a measure of integration, the resource drain from the Benelux countries was by far the greatest, given the comparatively small size of their respective national economies.

Germany's wartime trade statistics include only commodities that physically crossed German borders, whereas most of the clearing debt, reflecting part of the transfers to German military units abroad, was booked on capital account. Table 8.4 summarizes key data on German and West German trade balances between 1928 and 1960.

As can be seen, commodity structures did not change dramatically, compared to either 1928 or 1950. One might expect that the Nazis simply used the occupied countries as a natural resource base. Indeed, in 1940 there is a certain shift in imports toward raw materials. However, this tendency is soon reversed, and imports of finished goods become dominant in 1943. This "de-specialization" of Germany's import structure during the war seems to us as a remarkable phenomenon which has hitherto been neglected. Even under the horrible auspices of Nazi dominance over

[28] This was based on an order by Göring of June 22, 1940. See German Federal Archives/ Bundesarchiv (BA) Koblenz, R 2/230, fols. 115 ff., for the minutes of a meeting attended by almost all cabinet members concerned, which fixed the aims of a clearing union as part of controlling the German dominated trading bloc of Continental Europe.

[29] See, e.g., Sarow (1940), von Mickwitz (1942), Ringel (1942), and Schiller (1942). An assessment of the political context is Volkmann (1977).

[30] On this see the report on clearing procedures for the end of 1941 in BA Koblenz, R 7/3283, fols. 135–9, which states that multilateral clearing was practiced only with the occupied countries, while its introduction *vis-à-vis* the "outer circle of self-governed countries" like Italy would have to be postponed to the post-war period.

Table 8.3. *Germany's cumulative clearing accounts as of end of 1944 (million reichsmarks)*

Group I ("EEC")		Group II (Scandinavia)		Group III (Southeast Europe)		Group IV (Eastern Europe)	
F	− 8,532.2	N	+ 21.5	YU	− 10.5	Poland	−4,712.7
NL	− 5,989.6	DK	− 1,421.2	Serb.	− 553.1	Estonia	+ 0.0
I	− 147.3	SF	+ 31.9	Croat.	−1,051.6	Lithuania	− 2.3
B/Lx	− 4,976.2	S	−	Alban.	− 2.3	Ukraine	+ 292.8
				H	− 803.7	Russia	+ 204.0
				RO	−1,126.4	Protectorate	− 3.6
						Slovakia	− 631.7
	− 19,645.3		−1,367.8		−3,547.6		−4,853.5

Total "EEC" (F, NL, B/Lx, I): − 19,645.3
Total "East" (Groups III, IV): − 8,401.1

Source: German Federal Archives Koblenz, R 7/3636, fol. 41.

Table 8.4. *The structure of German foreign trade (1928, 1938, 1943 in current reichsmarks, 1950 and 1960 in billions of deutschmarks)*

| | Commodity structure: share of | | | | | | | | Country structure: share of "EEC" | | | | Total |
| | Agriculture | | Raw materials | | Semi-finished goods | | Finished goods | | European trade | | Total trade | | $100*\dfrac{(X-M)}{X+M}$ |
	M	X	M	X	M	X	M	X	M	X	M	X	
1928	40.9	6.4	28.3	12.2	17.9	12.2	12.9	69.2	34.1	32.5	17.3	24.4	−7.4
1938	39.5	1.2	32.9	9.5	18.8	8.4	7.9	80.0	26.4	32.7	14.4	22.8	−1.8
1940	47.2	2.5	21.0	14.8	21.2	9.3	9.7	73.4	29.6	28.3	27.6	26.9	−1.5
1943	40.0	6.8	13.5	13.1	13.1	13.0	32.4	66.9					
1950	44.1	2.3	29.6	14.0	13.7	18.8	12.6	64.9	47.0	48.3	25.5	36.4	−13.6
1960	26.3	2.3	21.7	4.6	18.9	10.4	32.2	82.4	55.9	48.9	32.4	32.9	

Note: Saar district excluded from 1928 and 1950 totals. M denotes imports, X exports.
Source: Länderrat (1949), Statistisches Jahrbuch (1952).

Europe there appears to be an anticipation of the later tendency toward intensified intra-industrial trade, which reappears in West Germany's import accounts only during the mid 1950s. Not until 1960 did the share of finished commodities in German imports recover to its significance of 1943. This indicates the magnitude of the potential for reconstruction which lay in revitalizing West German imports after the war.[31] Hence it is also debatable whether joining the EPU really meant a reorientation of German trade, as Milward (1984) has claimed,[32] or whether it was something of a return to a previous pattern that had emerged during the war.

In contrast, the structure of wartime exports from Germany does not seem to be an anticipation of future trends. Rather, it is an obvious deviation from a long-term pattern that had existed before the war and that re-emerged afterwards. However, surprising tendencies show up even in the export balance. Apparently the export structure of 1950 is quite similar to that of 1928. But there exist striking similarities between the commodity structure of German exports in 1960 and 1938. It is tempting to interpret this as a similar reconstruction gap, with the balance of 1950 as a sign of export structures having fallen back to the outmoded patterns of the interwar years and indicating the potential for future reconstruction.

Examination of regional trade structures during the war is hampered by lack of data. Still it is apparent that despite Germany's eastward expansion, Western Europe's share in trade across German borders increased after 1938. However, as referred to above, the trade statistics underlying table 8.4 reflect real resource transfers only indirectly. If clearing account balances are considered instead of trade statistics, the share of Western Europe is far higher than indicated by trade figures even in 1940.[33]

The short-term economic record of Western Europe at the time of the Allied victory was thus not one of disintegration and national autarky but rather of forced integration in the war machinery of Nazi Germany. Apparently, the economies of occupied Western Europe did not so much supply raw material inputs for German industry as produce finished goods. In turn, they were provided with inputs and capital equipment from Germany, using the traditional input–output web of the Western European coal and steel region that extends from the Ruhr to Belgium and Lorraine (on this, see also Gillingham, 1991). Creating a continental trading bloc in Western Europe was thus by no means new, nor were the financial techniques employed. The legacy of Hitler's Reichsbank president Hjalmar

---

[31] See Milward (1992, pp. 134 f.) for an appraisal of Germany's contribution as an export market to post-war recovery of Western Europe.

[32] See also Milward (1992, p. 143) for an interesting modification of his earlier hypothesis.

[33] In table 8.3, the cumulative share of "EEC" countries in the sample total would be 65.2 percent in 1940 as compared to 65.7 percent in 1944.

Schacht was apparent, as policymakers were fully aware (see the contribution of James to this volume for an account of early post-war debates).

In any case, the problem faced by the late 1940s seemed to be the disruption not so much of trade in general but rather of trade with Germany. Outweighing most national economies of Western Europe and being centrally located, Germany had traditionally played a role as a supplier of capital goods that was hard to assume by any other country except the US. However, the economies of Western Europe lacked an established dollar-based market for their own products to pay for US supplies, which makes the emergence of the dollar gap in Europe easier to understand (Buchheim, 1990, p. 174). Hence, reactivating the German economy was an obvious way to overcome the dollar shortage.

But still, this does not explain the need for another payments union, all the more so as the record of the Nazi *Verrechnungskasse* system was so appalling. Conceptually it would have seemed more straightforward to close the post-war dollar gap by massive currency devaluation all over Europe and by implementing convertibility under the Bretton Woods system. Eichengreen (1993) finds evidence in support of this view. However, such an approach would not necessarily have solved the German problem. As we have seen, reconstructing European trade without Germany's participation had proven to be an illusion as early as 1947. But including Germany in post-war trade presented a number of problems beyond convertibility that seemed almost insurmountable in the beginning. As we shall discuss at some length, the main *raison d'être* of the EPU was precisely Germany's smooth reintegration into Europe's division of labor, something that could hardly have been accomplished merely through convertibility and exchange rate realignment.

Despite their particularly bad experience with clearing arrangements under the Nazi New Order, it was the delegates from the Benelux countries who proposed to make the transition from bilateral to multilateral clearing again and who pressed for a quick reintegration of Germany into such a scheme. The reasons for this are easy to understand. The first Belgian and Dutch plans for resumption of trade with Germany proposed that Germany should be compelled this way to service its wartime clearing debt (Buchheim, 1990, p. 10). Somehow the idea of setting Schacht's financial machinery into motion again seemed intriguing, as it could equally well supply the needs for reconstruction as it had provided guns and butter for Hitler's war.

Recipients of deliveries from Germany during 1945/6 were accordingly shocked when the Americans insisted on dollar payment and refused any linkage with claims against Germany on the wartime clearing account. In doing so, the US administration certainly blocked the way to increasing intra-European trade. However, as Buchheim (1990) has argued, this so-called dollar clause, which remained in effect until late 1949, may have actually served German interest, as it effectively prevented an untimely resource drain from Germany caused by reparation claims.

The American motivations for introducing the dollar clause become more apparent in the light of the theory of debt overhangs (Bulow and Rogoff, 1989). American and British officials were horrified by the current account deficits of Weimar Germany and its reparation payments on credit (Gimbel, 1976). Soon it had proven impossible to extract both reparation payments and accumulated debt service from the Germans. Schacht's debt default of 1933 and his subsequent autarky policies had left Germany's creditors with very little room for retaliation, a fact well explained by the Bulow/Rogoff model. Hence, US administrators sought to avoid running into similar traps again. In order to protect its own financial position in West Germany, the US had to give protection to Germany against its creditors on wartime debt and against reparation demands as well. In the absence of such measures, German foreign exchange revenues from trade would have been exposed to the risk of seizure by the authorities of the recipient countries. Therefore, the dollar clause's primary goal was to secure the solvency of their zones of occupation.

However, in 1946 it turned out that financial independence could not be attained without more pump-priming aid. To be able to secure assistance without indirectly financing future reparations, a link between claims on Germany and Marshall aid was established: future US help to Germany would be given only under a seniority clause giving US credits priority over all other claims. Indeed the London Council of Foreign Ministers agreed on this seniority clause, thus paving the way for both Marshall aid and a removal of the dollar clause in trade with West Germany. As ERP aid to Germany was shaped as a credit, it constituted a claim on Germany which had priority over all other existing debt and reparation claims. In the American administration it was understood that the main "value of this claim [is] in treaty negotiations as [a] basis for keeping other claims down."[34]

As long as the US accepted a standstill on the service of its claim, all other claims on Germany would be blocked automatically. This way it was guaranteed that future German foreign exchange receipts would be protected against seizure by Germany's wartime creditors. However, despite this device the continuing existence of claims on Germany would make it impossible for Germany to obtain commercial credit, as claims of exporters into Germany would lie at the bottom of the list, their marginal

[34] FRUS (1947, III, pp. 758 ff.).

value being zero. Hence, convertibility was not a solution, and some device was needed to reinstitute commercial credit irrespective of the debt overhang. The solution was found in the European Payments Union which provided fresh money and new credibility to West Germany, making it possible to deal with the restoration of credit and the settlement of debts and reparations separately.

The EPU, established in 1950, strongly resembled the original proposals of the Benelux states, save that the US dollar became the backing currency of the system and that any connection with Germany's war debts had been removed. Under US pressure, the settlement of German debt was delegated to a separate conference which reached an agreement in 1953 (on the latter see Buchheim, 1990).

Milward (1984) has pointed out that the protectionist bias of EPU agreements marked yet another defeat of US planners in their struggle with their French counterparts. Again, our perspective is slightly different. Germany's reintegration into the economy of Western Europe was a main concern of US officials. Also, the dollar shortage in Europe and the bad record of the gold standard in the 1920s gave clear hints of what the currency system of the future should not look like.

In this situation, devising a clearing scheme like the EPU and backing it with the dollar and Marshall aid was like killing two birds with one stone. First, including Germany provided an incentive for the other members to cooperate, although this meant getting access to German resources on American terms only. However, without an EPU-type system, trade with Germany would have exposed each country to the risks of dealing with Germany's debt overhang independently. As German foreign exchange receipts would have been liable to seizure, it would have been a dominant strategy for any single German trading partner to avoid financing a bilateral surplus by additional credits. On the other hand, it was collectively rational for the Europeans to provide such credits because without them Germany could not rebuild its factor stocks and eventually earn its debts by establishing an export surplus on its own. Therefore, in order to get out of this formidable Prisoner's Dilemma, Western Europe needed a centralized institution like the EPU that would establish rules and sanctions to secure a cooperative solution. Compared to the EPU, a scenario like in the 1930s, when trade relations were characterized by a bilateral standstill and clearing arrangements, was clearly inferior. This, however, was the historical alternative, as immediate transition to free convertibility under the Bretton Woods standard would have created cooperation problems that were even more difficult to solve.

As for the US, it played the double part of the creator and a guarantor of the system, enforcing cooperation through its economic levers and transferring much of its direct influence on German economic policy to the now European collective. That is, it provided the EPU as a collective with leverage against the revival of unsound financial and monetary practices in Germany.

Second, the prospect of getting access to the European marketplace again created complementary incentives in Germany itself. America's role as a benevolent hegemon, e.g., its aforementioned pressure on France, lent credibility within Germany to the soundness of the European approach to free trade, which made the Germans wholeheartedly embrace a strict policy of trade liberalization. The dollar gap, US influence, and the credibility of US politics in West Germany thus worked together to provide the leverage by which economic cooperation, not reverse exploitation, was enforced in Western Europe.

7 The EPU as a commitment technology: a new perspective on the German crisis of 1950/1

Our hypothesis, which links German and European reconstruction to one another in a framework of institutions imposed in Western Europe by a benevolent hegemon, is still to be confronted with empirical evidence on just how these institutions worked. This section will focus on Germany's performance within the OEEC and EPU between 1949 and 1951. It will be argued that these institutions helped to reintegrate West Germany into the traditional European division of labor, thus strengthening Europe's reconstruction and helping to close the dollar gap in the long run (on the latter see Buchheim, 1990). The OEEC and EPU both caused and solved a major adaption crisis which occurred during this process. The crisis, known as the German EPU crisis of 1950/1, will be shown to have been more or less a consequence of the need to restock Germany's economy before it could deliver the commodities wanted. It was not, as some have it, merely the result of a political gamble on the part of German decisionmakers. Not having access to any significant commercial credit other than EPU drawing rights, Germany lacked a sufficiently strong fall-back position and was thus left without sensible alternatives. In our view, the EPU as a European collective enabled Germany to commit itself to free trade and to stick to this commitment at least in principle.

This last proposition is non-trivial, for in its early phase, the EPU faced rather stern circumstances (see figure 8.2).

Figure 8.2 shows a substantial accumulation of German trade deficits

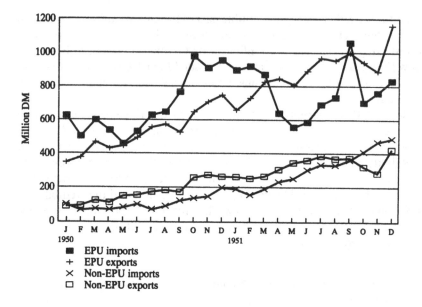

Figure 8.2   German import and export values, 1950–1

Notes: EPU-IM and EPU-EX: German exports and imports to/from the EPU.

Non-EPU-IM and Non-EPU-EX: German exports and imports (i) to/from countries covered by non-EPU clearing agreements, and (ii) exports and imports paid for in dollars (total dollar imports have been corrected by subtracting imports financed by dollar aid).

Import values are regionally differentiated on the basis of the country of purchase, that is, the numbers include transfers of non-EPU goods via countries within the EPU.

Sources: BdL, Aussenwirtschaft (II/10, II/12), and BdL, Monatsberichte.

with EPU countries,[35] which is amazing in the light of the disastrous record of the Nazi *Verrechnungskasse* system and the huge transfers it set into motion. But Germany's deficit did not build up steadily. Three stages can be discerned. The first ranges from early 1949 to May 1950, when a German trade deficit mounted but then disappeared, all within the span of the second OEEC payment agreement. The second, critical phase extends from July 1950 to March 1951, revealing a sharp and continuous increase of German deficits, whereas the last phase from April 1951 on shows a reversal of this trend.

[35] The terms "EPU-imports" or "EPU-exports" refer to West German imports from and exports to the countries that joined the EPU in 1950.

It is noteworthy that in contrast to this development, German import and export values from non-EPU countries (net of imports financed by dollar aid) stay neatly balanced, not showing a significant deficit before mid 1951. To a large extent this is explained by the constraints imposed on trade by bilateral clearing agreements. The former phenomenon, however, requires further analysis.

In 1949, German imports from the future EPU area increased significantly due to two factors. First, liberalization within the OEEC successively freed about 50 percent of import restrictions existing in 1948. Second, the asymmetric devaluations of the EPU currencies against the dollar in September 1949 amounted to a relative appreciation of the deutschmark *vis-à-vis* most other European currencies. Although the allocation of drawing rights and conditional aid (Abelshauser, 1984a, pp. 215 ff.) had been based on anticipated German surpluses, the so-called second multilateral payment agreement under the auspices of the OEEC granted coverage of Germany's deficits. Germany could also draw on some $70 million of accumulated surpluses from trade under the JIEA dollar clause system in 1948/9.

After March 1950, however, the value of imports declined again. This was predominantly caused by domestic conditions. After the first rush on imported primary products that had long been in shortage, growing orders for raw materials and intermediate products had fuelled the surge in imports from future EPU countries in 1949. Then, until May 1950, growth of industrial production exceeded raw material imports, as producers appear to have decided against investing further in expensive input stocks (BdL Monatsberichte, May 1950, pp. 30 ff., August 1950, pp. 17 ff.).

The EPU was founded on August 18, 1950, to go into effect retroactively from July 1. It substituted for the second payment agreement and also secured the bilateral consolidation of German debts accumulated under that agreement. But, more important, the provisions agreed upon included a commitment to further trade liberalization (60 percent of 1948 regulations until December, 75 percent until the end of 1951) and the introduction of multilateral clearing and credit. The EPU granted Germany multilateral clearing of its balance of payments and a quota of $320 million. Accumulation of deficits up to this sum was possible, of which $128 million had to be paid in gold or dollars immediately, while the remaining $192 million would be credited by the EPU. As we will see, it was the utilization of these credits that allowed liberalization to have a significant effect on German imports. Unexpectedly, German EPU imports began to surge right away. This tendency, which was to last up until the end of the year, was to a great extent caused by orders of primary goods and inputs, particularly of raw materials (see figure 8.3 below). Non-EPU imports of raw materials rose rather more steadily during the period in question, the pattern being, as figure 8.2 already suggested, quite different from those from EPU countries. Adding to surging import values was speculation about a possible sterling devaluation and price increases in the wake of the Korean War.[36] The rise in the prices of raw materials accounted for increased imports worth DM 75.5 million in the third, and DM 271.8 million in the fourth quarter of 1950, as compared to prices in the fourth quarter of 1949 (BdL Monatsbericht, March 1951, p. 36).

As early as September 1950, Germany had exhausted the first three tranches of its quota with the EPU and was obliged to pay back part of its debt ($31 million) in hard currency. Lacking any sizeable foreign exchange reserves, the new German republic was thus at the brink of a payments crisis. Doubtlessly political action was needed. However, in order to examine the scope of policy reactions we should point out what in our eyes was at the heart of this crisis and therefore the key to its solution. As mentioned above, the EPU much more than its predecessors provided Germany with financial and reputational credit.[37] Together with trade liberalization this allowed for a reorientation in the regional structure of German imports. Besides rearranging the regional pattern of German imports, the EPU framework also changed the commodity structure of imports.

Agricultural imports from EPU countries started to rise, as they had done after the second payments agreement of 1949/50. What was distinctive about imports after July 1950 was the widening of the share of raw materials (figure 8.3). This was helped by imports from the sterling area and, above all, by commodity transfers via EPU countries, primarily Great Britain, which underlines the importance of the EPU as a financial creditor. Changing the import structure toward inputs was complementary to the expanding share of manufactures, especially of machines, in exports. With this return of German trade to the specialization pattern of the 1930s, the integration of West Germany into the US-initiated Western European payments system restored precisely the division of labor that the Marshall planners had envisaged. In turn, this freed the US from the need to provide food to Germany, capital goods to Western Europe, and dollars to all of them.

This process did not work smoothly at the start. As early as October 1950 the German government faced the imminent exhaustion of its entire EPU

---

[36] See the letter BdL's Vocke sent to Adenauer, October 14, H. Ludwig-Erhard-Stiftung (1986, pp. 193 ff.)).

[37] The term "reputational credit" refers to the provision (through an institution) of the possibility for some economic agent to commit itself credibly, e.g., to free trade. In the absence of binding rules, i.e., time consistency of commitments, this means the possibility to accumulate a reputation of sticking to one's commitment.

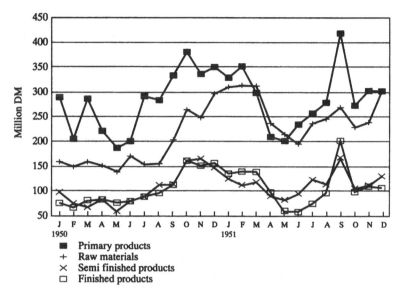

Figure 8.3   Structure of German EPU imports, 1950–1
Note: Import values are regionally differentiated on the basis of the country of purchase, that is, the numbers include transfers of non-EPU goods via countries within the EPU.
Source: see Figure 8.2.

quota, which by the rules of the game meant cancellation of its EPU membership. What was to be done?

We have already argued that the dynamics of German foreign trade after July 1950 had their roots in the institutional framework created by the Marshall Plan. One could deduce that the German balance of payments crisis was thus a problem of the EPU and that the EPU was intrinsically needed to overcome it. Besides trade policy, however, there were two other instruments available to solve the crisis, monetary and fiscal policy. During late 1950, it was yet an open question to decisionmakers which of these would be the choice.

Monetary policy was assigned to the autonomous central bank by Allied law. The *Bank deutscher Länder* (BdL) was already trying to promote exports and curb demand. Restrictive action was taken in September and again in October (Kaplan and Schleiminger, 1989, p. 102), the latter step being fiercely opposed by Germany's chancellor, Konrad Adenauer.[38] But

---

[38] Jacobsson and Erhard encouraged the BdL. See the report by Cairncross on the events prior to his arrival in Germany on October 27, 1950 (Ludwig, Erhard, and Stiftung, 1986, pp. 207 ff.). On Adenauer see Emminger (1986, pp. 53 ff.).

monetary policy was not, as is sometimes argued, profoundly restrictive.[39] This becomes visible by looking at the dynamics of West German imports in figure 8.2 above. EPU and non-EPU import values do not follow one another closely, which points against the influence of monetary policy, as it should have affected both categories equally. Whereas imports from EPU countries reached their peak in October 1950 (DM 971.7 million), non-EPU import values from countries with other clearing agreements and hard currency areas (net of dollar aid) steadily increased through October and peaked in December at DM 196.9 million. If restrictive monetary policy had an influence on EPU imports in October, it is difficult to explain these obvious asymmetries.

As far as fiscal policy is concerned, the government was confronted with the same dilemma as the BdL. A restrictive policy might have helped ease payment problems but it would also have increased unemployment. And the Adenauer government had been under political pressure to do something about employment and production since late 1949, when unemployment reached nearly 2 million, while employment still stagnated around 13.5 million as it had done since September 1948. Rejecting the Keynesian analysis of the problem by some economists, parts of the press, and especially a series of memoranda of the Bipartite Control Office and later the ECA (see, e.g., Schwartz, 1991, pp. 192 ff.), Erhard was reluctant to take expansionist measures. He was strongly supported in his views by the majority of his advisory board (Wissenschaftlicher Beirat, 1950, pp. 65 ff.), which pointed to the huge inflow of refugees and to structural inertia as the main reasons for unemployment. But when the question of unemployment overtook housing in public polls as the most urgent problem (Schenkluhn, 1985, p. 72), and the opposition produced Keynesian employment proposals that found a majority in parliament. A job creation program was launched in February 1950.[40] Having a supply-side orientation and being badly handled, it hardly had any short-term results. As political pressure continued, the department of commerce prepared a second program to be implemented if unemployment should again increase in the winter.[41] But, possibly to Erhard's relief, planning came to an end

[39] See, e.g., Kaplan and Schleiminger (1989, p. 116). It is worth noting that these were not the views held by Germany's central bank itself (Monatsbericht (May 1951, p. 44)). German advisors to the Economic Ministry also denied major effects of the monetary policy taken by the BdL, see Beirat (1951, pp. 115–19).

[40] It is interesting that these measures already included the provision of DM 300 million of credit for export promotion – explicitly as a means to enhance imports of raw materials for consumer industries (*Regierungsprogramm* February 18, 1950 (Federal Archives (B102/12593), Hagemann, 1984, pp. 93 ff.)).

[41] See the minutes of a cross-department conference on the matter July 6, 1950 (Federal Archives (B102/12593)).

when the EPU called for a more restrictive policy to stop the surge in imports after October 1950.

Fiscal policy, it seemed, would have to change gear, as did monetary policy when confronted with the EPU crisis. The EPU wanted the German government to enforce a package of restrictive fiscal measures: taxes on sales and income were to be raised, depreciation allowances to be lowered, and a tax on luxury goods to be introduced. At least on paper, Adenauer and Erhard took the advice. A German memorandum to the EPU in November promised a fiscal policy along these lines that, if implemented, would have created an extra annual revenue of approximately DM 2.3 billion.[42] The appropriate legal steps were taken mostly in early 1951. But when the OEEC evaluated proposals and efforts in May 1951 not a single fiscal measure intended to overcome the balance of payments crisis had as yet really come into effect.[43] Confidentially, it was noted in Paris that German efforts to speed up the budgetary process had been weak and disappointing.[44] As we will show below, however, the problem had already been solved otherwise.

As a matter of fact, tax revenues had increased during the first quarter of 1951 by DM 835.2 million (BdL Monatsbericht, March 1951, pp. 14 ff.). But this was due to the built-in flexibility of the tax system and not to policy action. The only tax rates which increased during that period were the "Notopfer Berlin" and the "Mineralölausgleichsteuer" (a special support scheme for Berlin and a gas tax). Both were of minor importance and accompanied by complementary expenditure programs. Without any budget cuts or significant tax increases, fiscal policy thus underwent no change during the EPU crisis. One could even argue that the announcement of tax increases probably increased demand, making the situation worse.

Given the German commitment to a more restrictive overall policy in late 1950, this course of events calls for an explanation. Besides domestic political pressure, the reason why restrictive policy was confined to the BdL, i.e. to monetary policy, was that both European and US officials did

---

[42] DM 1.3 billion would have been allocated to the "Bund," DM 1.0 billion to the "Länder" (BdL Monatsbericht (December 1950, pp. 17 ff.)). For the memorandum (November 27, 1950) and discussion of its effects see the documents of Erhard's department of commerce (Federal Archives (B102/12783 Heft 1)).

[43] The measures planned mostly became effective during summer. For the detailed OEEC analysis see OEEC Document MBC(51)48, May 19, 1951 (Federal Archives (B102/12783 Heft 1)).

[44] OEEC Document MBC(51)48, May 18, 1951, BA Koblenz B102/12783. The Central Bank Council had received a report from Paris raising similar charges against the Federal Government (Central Bundesbank Archives/Hauptarchiv der Deutschen Bundesbank B330–9, pp. 6 f.).

not press too hard. As Kaplan and Schleiminger (1989) have already stated, both the EPU and the OEEC expected monetary rather than fiscal policy to have an effect on the problem, as the federal structure of the West German republic made short-term changes in public budgets difficult. In Paris officials even signalled their willingness to permit German deficit spending, should economic stabilization and the need for rearmament call for it.[45]

Thus, there was a gradual adaptation of fiscal policy, but not a complete and in-time change toward outright contraction that could have had an influence on the EPU deficit. That deflationary monetary policies were at least employed to solve the balance of payments crisis was indeed a distinctive feature of Germany's political efforts as compared to practice in other countries (Triffin, 1957, p. 181; Kaplan and Schleiminger, 1989, p. 116). But considering their effects, both monetary and fiscal policies merely provided signals of goodwill, not a solution. Trade policy thus held the key to the crisis, and it was here that the EPU took center stage.

On October 10, 1950, the German government and the BdL faced a stock of $1.15 billion of already approved applications for both liberalized and regulated imports, which was approximately six times the monthly value of overall imports at this point (BdL Monatsbericht, December 1951, p. 23). On the advice of the central bank, the government cancelled about half of these allowances, aiming especially at those which had been applied for with no immediate urgency since the outbreak of the Korean War. In addition a 50 percent cash deposit on most import applications was introduced (lowered to 25 percent in December), and the BdL restricted credit for imports. The results of these measures are visible in figure 8.2 above, which shows that EPU imports indeed stagnated from October 1950 on. However, the liberalized sector was not really affected, as every action to restrict imports here would have violated the rules of the game under EPU regulations. Moreover, industrial production and along with it, German exports, lost momentum due to shortages of coal (see, e.g., Abelshauser, 1984b). In sum, the German handling of trade policy at this stage definitely failed to put an end to the deficits.

It is appropriate at this point to discuss two closely related arguments.

[45] See the report on ECA's Hubert F. Havlik's remarks in the Joint Trade and Intra-Europe Payments Committee on November 8, 1950, in German documents (Federal Archives (B102/12783 Heft 2)). There also was a series of informal meetings in Paris during November 14–15, 1950 (ibid. (B102/12783 Heft 1)), between German officials and ECA figures US Ambassador Wood, Triffin, and Cairncross. The latter called the Cairncross/Jacobsson report optimistic in its assumptions. If necessary, restrictive monetary policy should be lifted. He still said that deficit spending was to be avoided. But he did so pointing to anticipated occupation costs, not to the existing EPU deficit. Wood stressed the importance of stabilizing production and employment in the light of coming defense efforts.

Schwartz (1991, p. 206) calls the German policy a "calculated gamble" to acquire more credit from the ECA or the EPU. In fact, the German government signalled similar intentions as early as August 1950, and Erhard seemed to ignore the severity of the problem (Schwartz, 1991, pp. 202 ff.; Hentschel, 1989, pp. 738 ff.). But was the German government really taking a calculated risk for the chance of collective action on its behalf? Probably not. The ECA had left few doubts that any kind of "gambling" (Hentschel 1989, pp. 738 ff.) would be thoroughly rejected. Lacking alternatives, Germany simply wished to avoid the necessity of interrupting imports for as long as possible. First of all it needed further imports to sustain production and future exports.[46] Moreover, Erhard had tied himself vigorously to a commitment to free enterprise that definitely included free trade and even utilized imports as an instrument to strengthen domestic competition. He had every reason not to risk the results achieved so far and, along with them, his political career. This is all the more true as it was quite unclear in October that import restrictions could proceed on terms as favorable as those finally obtained from the EPU in February 1951. Therefore, that Germany avoided a unilateral act of protectionism for as long as possible had its rationale and was not just another try of a notorious gambler (Kaplan and Schleiminger, 1989, pp. 102 ff.).

Before returning to October 1950 we should briefly discuss a related point. Undoubtedly the crisis was mainly of a "short-term" nature (Milward, 1984, p. 429). Exports were rising, making a balanced trade account an eventual possibility. But to doubt the severity of the crisis by pointing to that smooth upward trend of exports (Giersch, Paqué, and Schmieding, 1992, pp. 103 ff.) ignores the time dimension. Before balanced trade with the EPU could be achieved, the accumulation of debt *vis-à-vis* the EPU emerged as a reality that had to be tackled within the given institutional setting. This setting included a credit ceiling and thus a time constraint. Confronted with this dilemma, one might think of trade restrictions on the part of Germany as the proper shortcut to reduce the trade deficit. Yet such a policy, if imposed unilaterally without the consent of the other EPU members, would have presented long-term difficulties, and provoked retaliation. This is also what the Germans themselves appear to have believed at the time: the BdL considered "strong countermeasures" to be "highly possible" in the case of unilateral import cuts.[47]

---

[46] Erhard's department found that the volume of deliveries of raw materials and semi-manufactures ceased to increase in October – so if there was a gamble, it was played rather conservatively. See the report of January 25, 1951 (Federal Archives (B102/12783 Heft 1)).

[47] It said so even though it was bearing most of the policy burden alone and had therefore to gain most by a deliberalization (BdL Monatsbericht (October 1950, p. 27)). See Kaplan and Schleiminger (1989, p. 117) for a quotation of Vocke stressing the same argument.

This eventuality was at least postponed when the optimistic and liberal-minded reports of Jacobsson and Cairncross induced EPU members to extend an additional credit of $120 million to Germany (Kaplan and Schleiminger, 1989, pp. 104 ff.). This implied an extra quota of $180 million that increased the total to $500 million.[48] Although these credits were to be repaid after May 1951 and were granted only in exchange for a commitment to more restrictive fiscal policies, the German government happily endorsed the inflow of fresh money. However, as we have shown above, the German pledge of more restrictive policies had no visible short-term effects.

In an internal report on the credit extension in November 1950, the department of commerce pointed to an anticipated renegotiation of the EPU quotas in July 1951, should repayment prove difficult.[49] However, during the first two months of 1951, accumulation of debt accelerated again, and the crisis escalated faster than anticipated. By the end of February, Germany's utilization of its extended quota had risen to $457 million, not including $611 million of outstanding import allowances. As $425 million of these licenses referred to liberalized imports, the government, facing the imminent exhaustion of Germany's credit lines, could no longer wait for the import surge to subside. Referring to article 3 of the OEEC liberalization code it therefore decided to suspend liberalized imports and to stop issuing new licenses for regulated imports. The new restrictions were to be reviewed in March and to be interpreted not as "default on the principle of liberalization" but as a short-term "technical measure" to save the very principle.[50]

There can be little doubt that this forced import reversal was unavoidable at this point. The trade policy measures taken in October 1950 had only postponed the necessary steps, and the credit extension merely bought the needed time. Another credit was out of question. German exports to OEEC countries being the *conditio sine qua non* for the Marshall Plan framework to function, intervention had to be on the import side. That was the basic rationale for the manner in which the EPU handled the crisis in February/March 1951.

[48] The proposal was not accepted without criticism. At least the Danish and Turkish delegations opted for general German import restrictions, arguing that this would allow for a different allocation of the incidence of the necessary cuts. But deliberalization was found to be too strong a solution to the problem and turned down for the time being. See the committee report mentioned above (Federal Archives (B102/12783 Heft 2), also Kaplan and Schleiminger (1989, pp. 96 ff.), and Hentschel (1989, pp. 740 ff.)).

[49] Report to Erhard, November 7, 1950 (Federal Archives (B102/12783 Heft 2)).

[50] BdL Monatsberichte (January/February 1951, pp. 19 ff.) and (March 1951, pp. 35 ff.). For the quotes see Hentschel (1989, p. 751, note 10).

Confronted *ex post* with Germany's unilateral import restrictions, the EPU approved of them. It decided to handle the import procedure itself, substituting retaliation against German exports with a cooperative strategy toward allocating Germany's reduced import allowances among its member countries. In addition to not enacting any counter measures, EPU members obliged themselves to promote German exports in their own national economies. The protectionist move was regarded as temporary and would be reversed as soon as possible (Hentschel, 1989, pp. 751 ff.).[51]

With regard to the voices pointing at the similarities to the 1930s and accusing Germany of playing a "gamble" again, this was certainly an exceptional reaction. The EPU enabled the German government to maintain its free trade commitment in principle while violating it in the short run. Avoiding retaliation, it solved Germany's long-term problem by promoting German exports and its short-run problem by cutting imports. In doing so the EPU actually ended a prolonged period of real resource transfers to Germany. But the decision to restrict imports came late enough not to endanger the process already set in motion. With its stocks rebuilt, Germany was now able to both supply Europe with the capital goods needed and earn the money to pay back its debt.

As import regulation was now handled by the EPU, the German government was only left with the task of promoting exports and avoiding further bottlenecks in coal and steel. To signal its willingness to overcome the need for import regulations, the Adenauer administration pointedly encouraged the BdL to push ahead with strong restrictions on short-term credits. The measures were aimed toward exports rather than toward hard currency imports: manufacturers would be restricted in domestic sales and therefore be encouraged to turn to exports.[52] The "*Wirtschaftssicherungs-gesetz*" act made intervention in resource allocation legally possible and added to the commitment to end the crisis at this time (Schwarz, 1991, pp. 208 ff.).

As far as the EPU was concerned, the policies did work out well. Import values fell to pre-EPU levels as early as April 1951. This was, first of all, due to the strictly handled regulations. Restrictions on outstanding licenses were only gradually lifted. But adding to this was, secondly, a credibility effect. When the BdL announced it would again accept import applications in May 1951, excess demand was much lower than expected (BdL

---

[51] It is noteworthy that exchange rate realignment was apparently not even considered.

[52] The BdL had the banks reduce their short-term credits by DM 1.0 billion. Given a stock of only DM 14.3 billion of commercial short-term lending this amounted to a significant reduction to about the level of October 1950 (BdL Monatsberichte (January/February 1951, pp. 7 ff.)).

Monatsbericht, May 1951, pp. 43 ff.).[53] German importers obviously had little doubt that the EPU policies would solve the problem successfully and secure the inflow of essential inputs.[54] Since exports continued to increase as anticipated, Germany's trade balance with the EPU turned positive in April. Because of additional BdL measures to influence the terms of payment, the clearing balance *vis-à-vis* the EPU became positive even sooner. The continuing surpluses that Germany earned in EPU trading after this crisis eventually turned the EPU's first major debtor into a net creditor. The continuous rise of exports eventually allowed EPU imports to expand, albeit below exports, and to substitute for falling imports out of dollar aid.

8 Conclusion

Our analysis intended to bring out four points. First, historians and political scientists have argued that the Marshall Plan entailed a broad agenda for European economic cooperation, and that this, in turn, had significance for the economics of the Plan as well. The Plan envisioned Germany's reconstruction as a workshop for European recovery. It would also take into account the security needs and fears of Germany's former victims in Western Europe. Interpreting the Marshall Plan this way, the common practice of evaluating its effects on the basis of the real resource transfers it set into motion is likely to be misleading. The main idea of the Plan lay in utilizing German rather than US capacities to provide for Europe's reconstruction. From this it is also obvious that the Marshall Plan as a political agenda operated mainly to the detriment of schemes to restore French predominance in Europe at Germany's cost, as laid out in the Monnet Plan.

Second, we view the Marshall Plan and its concomitant institutions as a device to lend credibility to German policy. On the one hand, US policies deliberately protected West Germany from its wartime creditors and thus prevented them from retaliating against the wartime exploitation policies of Nazi Germany. On the other, the institutions created by the Americans or

---

[53] Considering the time lag, there might have been an additional effect on import applications (not imports carried out) by the credit rationing measures in February.

[54] The restriction of import values at this time was aided by a fall in prices. The sudden rise in September 1951 is due to an anticipated introduction of *ad valorem* tariffs in October: 80 percent of the 31 percent rise in total import values came out of EPU countries (BdL Monatsbericht, September 1951, pp. 44 ff.). The slump of exports in the fourth quarter of 1951 was caused in part by the previous restrictions imposed upon imports, which caused input shortages. This fact emphasizes again that during the crisis Germany did not act as a gambler but out of necessity (BdL Monatsbericht, December 1951, pp. 28 ff.).

through US pressure assured the former victims of Nazi Germany that rebuilding the German economy and its complex web of trade with Europe would not endanger their national security again.

Our third point concerns the credibility effects of the Marshall Plan within Germany. It is argued that, in light of Germany's previous record of Nazi "New Order" policies, the main task of US policy was to establish international cooperation as a credible alternative within Germany. Events such as the currency reform and the Berlin airlift helped convince the German leadership of the credibility of the commitments made by the US administration.

The fourth argument is that the Marshall Plan and the creation of the EPU, both being part of a broader strategy of US policies, cannot be separated from one another. Given the dollar gap, and particularly Germany's total lack of credit and of reserves, trade had to be implemented on a cashless basis. Installing the EPU provided the means for a stable system of financial cooperation and free trade within Europe that encompassed West Germany. The Marshall Plan thus enabled Germany to credibly commit itself to free trade, which it could hardly have done on its own, and to cast its balance of payments crisis as an "EPU crisis" within the European institutional framework. With German monetary and especially fiscal policy merely providing signals of good will, it was indeed the EPU that allowed trade policy to put an end to the problem without endangering European cooperation. The crisis overcome, Germany's EPU exports continued to rise throughout the 1950s. With exports leading growth and given the history of the "German crisis" in 1950–1, it is safe to say that the Marshall Plan-born institutions contributed significantly to the ultimate success of Germany's *Wirtschaftswunder*.

Viewed this way, the common analysis of the early Marshall Plan years as the period of greatest impact on Europe needs to be modified. The Marshall Plan as a long-term agenda gained significance after 1951. From this year on, the regime change brought about by the EPU restrictions induced Germany to assume the position of a net exporter. This way, it began supplying capital goods for Europe's reconstruction in just the way the Marshall planners had anticipated.

References

Abelshauser, W. (1975), *Wirtschaft in Westdeutschland 1945–1948. Rekonstruktion und Wachstumsbedingungen in der amerikanischen und britischen Zone*, Stuttgart: Deutsche Verlagsaustalt.

(1981), "Wiederaufbau vor dem Marshall-Plan. Westeuropas Wachstumschancen und die Wirtschaftsordnungspolitik in der zweiten Hälfte der vierziger Jahre," *Vierteljahreshefte für Zeitgeschichte*, 29: 545–78.

(1984a), "Der Kleine Marshallplan. Handelsintegration durch innereuropäische Wirtschaftshilfe 1948–1950," in H. Berding (ed.), *Wirtschaftliche und politische Integration in Europa im 19. und 20. Jahrhundert*, Göttingen: Vandenhoeck & Ruprecht, pp. 212–24.

(1984b), *Der Ruhrkohlenbergbau seit 1945*, Munich: Beck.

(1989), "Hilfe und Selbsthilfe. Zur Funktion des Marshallplans beim westdeutschen Wiederaufbau," *Vierteljahreshefte für Zeitgeschichte*, 37: 85–113.

(1991), "American Aid and West German Recovery: A Macroeconomic Perspective," in Maier and Bischof (eds.), pp. 367–409.

Abramovitz, M. (1979), "Rapid Growth Potential and Its Realization: The Experience of the Capitalist Economies in the Postwar Period," in E. Malinvaud (ed.), *Economic Growth and Resources*, Proceedings of the Fifth World Congress of the International Economic Association, vol. I, London.

(1986), "Catching Up, Forging Ahead, and Falling Behind," *Journal of Economic History*, 46: 385–406.

Bank deutscher Länder (1948), *Geschäftsberichte* (annual reports), various issues.

(1951), *Monatsberichte* (monthly reports), various issues.

(1955), *Statistisches Handbuch der Bank deutscher Länder*.

Aussenwirtschaft: 1933, 1945, and 1953 (Personal Files Hans Möller).

Baumgart, E.R. (1961), *Investitionen und ERP-Finanzierung*, Berlin: Duncker & Humblot (DIW *Sonderhefte* (N.F.), 56).

Borchardt, K. (1981), "Die Konzeption der sozialen Marktwirtschaft in heutiger Sicht," in O. Issing (ed.), *Zukunftsprobleme der sozialen Marktwirtschaft*, Berlin: Duncker & Humblot (*Schriften des Vereins für Socialpolitik* (N.F.), 116).

Borchardt, K. and C. Buchheim (1991), "The Marshall Plan and Key Economic Sectors: A Microeconomic Perspective," in Maier and Bischof (eds.), pp. 410–51.

Buchheim, C. (1988), "Die Währungsreform 1948 in Westdeutschland," *Vierteljahreshefte für Zeitgeschichte*, 36: 189–231.

(1990), *Die Wiedereingliederung Westdeutschlands in die Weltwirtschaft 1945–1958* (Quellen und Darstellungen zur Zeitgeschichte Bd.31), Munich: Oldenbourg.

Bulow, J. and K. Rogoff (1989), "A Constant Recontracting Model of Sovereign Debt," *Journal of Political Economy*, 97: 155–78.

Bundesminister für den Marshallplan (1953), *Wiederaufbau im Zeichen des Marshallplans 1948–1952*, Bonn.

Daniel, Ute (1982), *Dollardiplomatie in Europa, kalter Krieg und US-Außenwirtschaftspolitik 1945–52*, Düsseldorf: Droste.

DeLong, J.B. and Eichengreen, B. (1993), "The Marshall Plan: History's Most Successful Structural Adjustment Program," in Rudiger Dornbusch, Willem Nölling and Richard Layard (eds.), *Postwar Economic Reconstruction and Lessons for the East Today*, Cambridge, Mass.: MIT Press, pp. 189–230.

Deutsche Bundesbank (ed.) (1976), *Deutsches Geld- und Bankwesen in Zahlen*

1876–1975, Frankfurt/M.: Lang.

Dumke, R. (1990), "Reassessing the Wirtschaftswunder: Reconstruction and Postwar Growth in West Germany in an International Context," *Oxford Bulletin of Economics and Statistics*, 52: 451–91.

Eichengreen, B. (1993), *Reconstructing Europe's Trade and Payments: The European Payments Union*, Manchester: Manchester University Press.

Eichengreen, B. and M. Uzan (1992), "The Marshall Plan: Economic Effects and Implications for Eastern Europe and the Former USSR," *Economic Policy*, 14: 14–75.

Emminger, O. (1986), *D-Mark, Dollar, Währungskrisen. Erinnerungen eines ehemaligen Bundesbankpräsidenten*, Stuttgart: DVA.

Forstmeier, F. and H.E. Volkmann (eds.) (1977), *Kriegswirtschaft und Rüstung 1939–1945*, Düsseldorf: Droste.

Giersch, H., K.H. Paqué, and H. Schmieding (1992), *The fading miracle. Four Decades of Market Economy in Germany*, Cambridge University Press.

Gillingham, J. (1991), *Coal, Steel, and the Rebirth of Europe, 1945–1955*, Cambridge University Press.

Gimbel, J. (1976), *The Origins of the Marshall Plan*, Stanford: Stanford University Press.

Goschler, C., C. Buchheim, and W. Bührer (1989), "Der Schumanplan als Instrument französischer Stahlpolitik. Zur historischen Wirkung eines falschen Kalküls," *Vierteljahreshefte für Zeitgeschichte*, 37: 171–206.

Hagemann, W. (1984), *Von der Ordnungs- zur Konjunkturpolitik. Zur Funktionsentwicklung staatlicher Wirtschaftspolitik in Westdeutschland von 1948–1967* (Politikwissenschaft 2), Essen: Eule.

Hardach, G. (1991), "Le Plan Marshall et l'intégration internationale de l'économie allemande," in *Comité pour l'histoire économique et financière*, CHEFF, Extrait du colloque "Le Plan Marshall et le relèvement économique de l'Europe," Paris, pp. 467–86.

(1993), "Die Rückkehr zum Weltmarkt 1948–1958," in A. Schildt und A. Sywottele (Hrsg.), *Modernisierung im Wiederaufbau*, Bonn, pp. 80–104.

Hellwig, M. (1992), *Comments*, in Eichengreen and Uzan.

Hentschel, V. (1989), "Die europäische Zahlungsunion und die deutschen Devisenkrisen 1950/51," *Vierteljahreshefte für Zeitgeschichte*, 37: 715–58.

Hirschman, A.O. (1945), *National Power and the Structure of Foreign Trade*, Berkeley: University of California Press.

Hogan, M.J. (1987), *The Marshall Plan. America, Britain, and the Reconstruction of Western Europe, 1947–52*, Cambridge University Press.

(1991), "European Integration and German Reintegration: Marshall Planners and the Search for Recovery and Security in Western Europe," in Maier and Bischof (eds.), pp. 115–70.

James, H. (1995) "The IMF and the Creation of the Bretton Woods System, 1944–58," this volume.

Jánossy, F. (1966), *Das Ende der Wirtschaftswunder*, Frankfurt/M.: Neue Kritik.

Kaplan, J.J. and G. Schleiminger (1989), *The European Payments Union*, Oxford: Clarendon.

Klemm, B. and G.J. Trittel (1987), "Vor dem 'Wirtschaftswunder': Durchbruch zum Wachstum oder Lähmungskrise?" *Vierteljahreshefte für Zeitgeschichte*, 35: 571–624.

Klump, R. (1985), *Wirtschaftsgeschichte der Bundesrepublik Deutschland*, Wiesbaden: Steiner.

Knapp, M. (1977), "Deutschland und der Marshallplan: Zum Verhältnis zwischen politischer und ökonomischer Stabilisierung in der amerikanischen Deutschlandpolitik nach 1945," in M. Knapp (ed.), *Politische und ökonomische Stabilisierung Westdeutschlands 1945–1949*, Wiesbaden: Steiner.

(1981), "Reconstruction and West-Integration: The Impact of the Marshall Plan on Germany," *Zeitschrift für die gesamte Staatswissenschaft*, 137: 415–33.

Kornai, J. (1981), *The Economics of Shortage*, Amsterdam: North-Holland.

Krengel, R. (1958), *Anlagevermögen, Produktion und Beschäftigung der Industrie im Gebiet der Bundesrepublik von 1924 bis 1956*, Berlin: Duncker & Humblot (DIW, *Sonderhefte* (N.F.), 42).

Länderrat des Amerikanischen Besatzungsgebiets (ed.) (1949), *Statistisches Handbuch von Deutschland 1928–1944*, Munich: Ehrenwirth.

Lacroix-Riz, A. (1986), *Le choix de Marianne*, Paris: Ed. Soc.

Laitenberger, V. (1986), *Ludwig Erhard. Der Nationalökonom als Politiker*, Göttingen: Muster-Schmidt.

Ludwig–Erhard–Stiftung (eds.) (1986), *Die Korea-Krise als ordnungspolitische Herausforderung der deutschen Wirtschaftspolitik, Texte und Dokumente*, Stuttgart: DVA.

Lynch, F. (1993), "Restoring France: the Road to Integration," in A. Milward *et al.* (eds.), *The Frontier of National Sovereignty. History and Theory, 1945–1982*, London/New York: Routledge.

Maier, C.S. and G. Bischof (eds.) (1991), *The Marshall Plan and Germany*, Oxford: Berg.

Manz, M. (1968), "Stagnation und Aufschwung in der französischen Besatzungszone 1945–1948," Dissertation, University of Mannheim. Repr. (1985) Ostfildern: Scripta Mercaturae.

Mickwitz, E. von (1942), *Verrechnung über Berlin*, Hamburg: Verlag "Aussenwirtschaft unter Zwang."

Milward, A.S. (1984), *The Reconstruction of Western Europe, 1945–51*, London: Methuen.

(1991), *The Marshall Plan and German Foreign Trade*, in Maier and Bischof (eds.), pp. 452–87.

(1992), *The European Rescue of the Nation-State*, Berkeley: University of California Press.

Mitchell, B.R. (1975), *European Historical Statistics, 1750–1970*, London: Macmillan.

Möller, H. (1952), "Handelspolitik zwischen Bilateralismus und Multilateralismus," *Weltwirtschaftliches Archiv*, 69: 203–61.

OMGUS (1946), *Monthly Report of the Military Governor*, January 1946.

Petzina, D. (1968), *Autarkiepolitik im Dritten Reich. Der nationalsozialistische Vierjahresplan*, Stuttgart: Deutsche Verlagsanstalt.

Poidevin, R. (1986), *Robert Schuman, homme d'Etat*, Paris: Imprimerie Nationale.

Ringel, K. (1942), "Währungspolitik und zwischenstaatlicher Zahlungsverkehr in der Großraumwirtschaft," *Weltwirtschaftliches Archiv*, 56: 490–508.

Ritschl, A. (1985), "Die Währungsreform von 1948 und der Wiederaufstieg der westdeutschen Industrie," *Vierteljahreshefte für Zeitgeschichte*, 33: 136–65.

   (1991), "Die NS-Wirtschaftsideologie: Modernisierungsprogramm oder reaktionäre Utopie?" in M. Prinz and R. Zitelmann (eds.), *Nationalsozialismus und Modernisierung*, Darmstadt: Wissenschaftliche Buchgesellschaft.

   (1992), "Nazi Economic Imperialism and the Exploitation of the Small: Evidence from Germany's Foreign Exchange Balances, 1938–40," mimeo, University of Munich.

Sarow, F. (1940), "Verrechnungszentrum Berlin," *Die Wirtschaftskurve*, 19: 181–90.

Schenkluhn, B. (1985), *Konjunkturpolitik und Wahlen: eine fallanalytische Untersuchung der konjunkturpolitischen Regierungsentscheidungen in 7 Wahlperioden (von 1949–1976)*, Bergisch-Gladbach: Eule.

Schiller, K. (1942), "Meistbegünstigung, Multilateralität und Gegenseitigkeit in der zukünftigen Handelspolitik," *Weltwirtschaftliches Archiv*, 53: 370–406.

Schwabe, K. (1988), "Ein Akt konstruktiver Staatskunst – die USA und die Anfänge des Schuman-Plans," in K. Schwabe (ed.), *Die Anfänge des Schuman-Plans*, Baden-Baden: Nomos.

Schwartz, T. (1991), *European Integration and the 'Special Relationship': Implementing the Marshall Plan in the Federal Republic*, in Maier and Bischof (eds.), pp. 171–215.

Statistisches Bundesamt (1949 ff.), *Der Außenhandel der Bundesrepublik Deutschland*, Teile 1–3, 1949–52.

   (1950 ff.), *Statistisches Jahrbuch für die Bundesrepublik Deutschland*.

Stolper, G., K. Häuser, and K. Borchardt (1967), *The German Economy, from 1870 to the Present*, New York: Harcourt, Brace & World.

Teichert, E. (1984), *Autarkie und Groß raumwirtschaft in Deutschland 1930–1939*, Munich: Oldenbourg.

Triffin, R. (1957), *Europe and the Monetary Muddle: From Bilateralism to Near-Convertibility, 1947–1956*, New Haven: Yale University Press.

Volkmann, H.E. (1977), "*NS-Außenhandel im geschlossenen 'Kriegswirtschaftsraum' (1939–41)*," in F. Forstmeier and H.E. Volkmann, pp. 92–163.

Wallich, H.C. (1955), *The Mainsprings of the German Revival*, New Haven: Yale University Press.

Wexler, I. (1983), *The Marshall Plan Revisited*, Westport: Greenwood.

Wissenschaftlicher Beirat beim Bundesministerium für Wirtschaft (1950), "Kapitalmangel und Arbeitslosigkeit in der sozialen Marktwirtschaft" (Gutachten vom 26.2.50), in Bundesministerium für Wirtschaft (ed.) (1973), *Sammelband der Gutachten von 1948 bis 1972*, Göttingen: Schwartz.

   (1951), *Wirtschaftspolitische Möglichkeiten zur Begrenzung der direkten lenkenden Eingriffe* (Gutachten vom 25.2.51), in Bundesministerium für Wirtschaft (ed.) (1973), *Sammelband der Gutachten von 1948 bis 1972*, Göttingen: Schwartz.

9 "You've never had it so good?": British economic policy and performance, 1945–60

N.F.R. CRAFTS

1 Introduction

The early 1990s provides an interesting vantage point from which to view Britain's post-war economic recovery. Both the events and the historiography of the recent past have led to revisions of earlier accounts of the period and there is a much richer literature to survey than was true ten years or so ago. Although the electorate was informed by the Prime Minister, Harold Macmillan, in 1959 that they had never had it so good and duly returned the Conservatives with a large majority, the predominant theme of this chapter is the continuing relative economic decline of the UK in the early post-war period. The performance of the British economy during the years 1945–60 was very respectable in terms of inflation and unemployment but disappointing with regard to productivity and output growth.

Several distinctive features of the UK post-war position shaped the context of economic performance and should be kept in mind.

i) The prevailing imperatives of post-war macroeconomic policy were to cope with an horrendous balance of payments position (Cairncross, 1985) and a formidable monetary overhang (Eichengreen, 1993).

ii) The Labour Party was elected in 1945, having "won the war at home" (Addison, 1975) on a program of much expanded social welfare provision and nationalization of the commanding heights of the economy. The Conservatives on returning to power in 1951 deemed it electorally prudent not to reverse these policies.

iii) The legacy of 1930s cartelization, wartime controls, and soft imperial markets was an economy in which domestic firms, on average, enjoyed substantial market power.

iv) British industrial relations were not, as in Germany, reformed as a result of the war. Traditions of voluntarism and multi-unionism continued and both parties sought implicit "social contracts" with the Trades Union Congress, in which legislation to reform industrial relations was foresworn and the welfare state was secured in return for wage restraint (Flanagan *et al.*, 1983; Tomlinson, 1991a).

v) American leverage on British policy was relatively weak but not entirely absent. Thus, the UK joined the European Payments Union but did not sign the Treaty of Rome and accepted the Anglo-American Productivity Council but was relatively immune to the conditionality of Marshall Plan funding (Eichengreen and Uzan, 1992).

vi) The scope for rapid growth from "catch-up and reconstruction" was clearly less than in most OECD economies which in the late 1940s had a larger productivity gap with the US.

Against this background, the main arguments of the chapter center around Abramovitz's well-known account of catch-up growth and, in particular, his propositions that catch-up is not automatic and that realization of its potential is based on social capability which "depends on more than the content of education and the organization of firms . . . it is a question of the obstacles to change raised by vested interests, established positions and customary relations among firms and between employers and employees" (1986, p. 389). These ideas are explored in the context of a model of productivity as an outcome of bargaining. The main hypothesis is that the post-war settlement in the UK was helpful in the short term in achieving a better inflation–unemployment performance but in the long term inhibited productivity growth.

The chapter accepts that corporatist institutions were an important conditioning factor influencing growth in the 1950s. In contrast to recent literature on post-war Europe, I argue that in the UK case the "social contract" impeded growth. This came about because of the inheritance from the interwar economy of craft trade unionism combined with monopolistic product markets and because the deal effectively precluded necessary reforms of industrial relations structures, vocational training, anti-trust policy, and locked the economy into a high degree of nationalization even when the Conservatives returned to power.

Finally, two particularly interesting issues are taken up at the end of the chapter.

i) Do recent developments in the theory of economic growth shed any new light on the reasons for relatively slow British growth and thus suggest revised assessments of policy?

ii) Are there any lessons for today's Eastern European countries from the British experience?

Table 9.1. *The short-term UK macroeconomic position (1938 = 100)*

	GDP	IP	C	I	G	X	M
1948	111.9	120	100.3	100.8	129.1	113.3	85.3
1951	123.4	145	103.6	116.6	147.2	142.2	99.3

Sources: Feinstein (1972) except for industrial production (IP) taken from Eichengreen and Uzan (1992).

2 A brief review of macroeconomic outcomes

This section seeks to sketch some of the most important dimensions of economic performance in the early post-war UK. The short-term position in terms of expenditure and output over the years of the Labour governments is reported in table 9.1.

The outstanding features of this period are readily apparent. The UK experienced a revival of industrial output at about the average rate of Western Europe excluding Germany (Eichengreen and Uzan, 1992, table 7) while the policy priority in a tightly controlled economy given to increases in exports and, to a lesser extent, investment over consumption is clearly reflected. Restraints on consumption during this period of post-war austerity were severe.

The much weaker external position of the UK post-war relative to prewar emerges in the relatively low volume of imports which were held down by policies of import control and devaluation designed to cope with the balance of payments problem. The current account deficit at its peak in 1947 was £381 million but this had moved to a surplus of £307 million in 1950 prior to the Korean War shock. Perhaps surprisingly, in these circumstances, the late 1940s were characterized by moderate inflation (an average of about 5 percent for 1946–51) and very low unemployment rates (around 1.5 percent as measured at the time).

By comparison with the interwar period, the 1950s was an era of much more satisfactory macroeconomic performance, as table 9.2 demonstrates. This was the time of what *The Economist* famously dubbed "Butskellism," featuring Keynesian attempts to fine tune demand and continued pursuit of "social contracts" between government and trade unions. Unemployment was much lower than in 1923–38 and, indeed, appreciably lower than even optimists like Beveridge had anticipated at the end of the war. This was generally regarded as the crowning achievement of the post-war world and departures from full employment were seen as electorally disastrous. Inflation at a modest rate was tolerated as preferable to the downward price

Table 9.2. *The UK macroeconomy: the 1950s compared with the interwar years*

	1923–38	1950–9
Growth of real GDP/hour worked (% per annum)	1.9	2.3
Standardized unemployment rate (%)	13.1	2.5
GDP deflator inflation rate (% per annum)	−0.9	4.2
Misery Index (%)	12.2	6.7

Sources: Derived from Feinstein (1972), Maddison (1982). Misery Index is the sum of the inflation and unemployment rates. The 1950s unemployment rate is the OECD standardized figure quoted by Maddison; interwar unemployment has been adjusted to be comparable with this using the formula proposed by Metcalf *et al.* (1982).

shocks of the 1920s and early 1930s. Growth by the standards of the previous 100 years or so was very respectable.

Table 9.3 puts this same 1950s performance into a different context, which, by the 1960s but not in the early 1950s, replaced the 1930s as the reference point of British policymakers. International comparisons show British performance on unemployment and inflation to be pretty typical of Western Europe at the time. Productivity growth was, however, distinctly lower than elsewhere. While initially this could be put down to the after effects of the war, by the end of the 1950s it was becoming accepted that persistently lower UK growth required policy reform particularly in terms of the supply side (Kirby, 1991).

Relative economic decline is indeed confirmed by table 9.4. This shows France and Germany by 1960 well on the way to overtaking British levels of overall labor productivity and that Britain failed to reduce the American lead in GDP/person employed between 1950 and 1960. Relatively weak UK performance in manufacturing productivity is also confirmed in table 9.4.

It is generally accepted that post-war OECD growth performance has been influenced by initial productivity gaps with the US, i.e., differential opportunities to catchup (Dowrick and Nguyen, 1989; Englander and Mittelstadt, 1988). Formal tests of a model which include this explanatory variable together with measures of factor accumulation confirm that British growth was disappointing. Normalizing for the initial productivity gap, UK productivity growth appears to have been 0.8 percent per year lower

Table 9.3. *UK macroeconomic performance in the 1950s*

	UK	12 country median
Growth of real GDP/hours worked (% per annum)	2.3	4.0
Standardized unemployment rate (%)	2.5	2.6
CPI inflation rate (% per annum)	4.1	3.6
Misery Index (%)	6.6	6.7

Source: Derived from Maddison (1982). The Misery Index is the sum of the inflation and unemployment rates; the twelve countries are the European economies in Maddison's advanced countries data base.

Table 9.4. *Comparative UK productivity levels (UK = 100)*

	USA/UK	France/UK	Germany/UK
a) GDP per person employed			
1938	143.0	70.0	74.9
1950	167.4	69.7	63.3
1960	167.5	88.6	90.2
1973	151.6	110.2	104.7
b) Manufacturing output per person employed			
1938	191.6	76.3	107.1
1950	262.6	83.9	96.0
1958	250.0	91.1	111.1
1968	242.6	109.1	120.0

Sources: GDP per person employed based on Maddison (1991) and manufacturing output per person employed based on Broadberry (1992); the comparisons are purchasing power parity adjusted.

than might have been expected (Crafts, 1992). This is in fact very much what might be expected, given Denison's classic growth accounting exercise. Table 9.5 rearranges Denison's own presentation of his results to emphasize this point.

The main difference between the UK and her rivals is seen to lie in total factor productivity growth, rather than capital inputs growth. A large part

Table 9.5. *Differences in the sources of growth, 1950–62*

| | Excess over the UK | |
	France	Germany
Labor input	−0.15	0.77
Capital input	0.28	0.90
Total factor productivity	2.50	3.30
"Backwardness"	1.47	2.14
Other specific	0.31	0.35
Residual efficiency	0.72	0.81
Total	2.63	4.97

Source: Derived from Denison (1968, table 6.4); "Backwardness" is the sum of rows 20 and 24 in Denison's table, other specific is row 14, and residual efficiency is row 29.

of this came from the greater initial backwardness of France and Germany, associated particularly with their greater scope to redeploy resources away from low productivity agriculture. Nevertheless, a deficiency of 0.7 percent and 0.8 percent per year respectively is attributed to lesser British success in eradicating inefficiency. Indeed, a major theme of Denison's chapter was the substantial shortfall in UK productivity levels in 1960 coming from differences in work effort, restrictive labor practices, and management quality; he estimated that this amounted to a shortfall of 14.3 percent relative to France and 13.2 percent relative to Germany (1968, p. 274).

3 Domestic policy and institutions

The context of post-war policy was described in section 1. This section begins by filling out some of the implications of the post-war settlement before proceeding to consider separately macroeconomic stabilization and supply-side policy.

Some implications of the post-war settlement

The most obvious feature of post-war Britain was the expanded size of the government budget and taxation relative to GDP and the priority given to welfare state expenditures while at the same time maintaining relatively large defense expenditures. The changed political climate reflected the wartime Beveridge Report (Cmd. 6404, 1942), perhaps the most famous

Table 9.6. *Taxation, government spending, housing and defense*

	UK	12 country median
Total tax receipts, 1955 (% of GDP)	29.8	26.6
Total government outlays, 1960 (% of GDP)	32.2	30.6
Social transfers, 1960 (% of GDP)	6.2	9.3
Defense expenditure, 1950–9 (% of GDP)	7.5	3.6
Residential construction, 1950–9 (% of GDP)	3.0	4.7

Sources: OECD (1970), (1981), (1992) and Kohl (1981).

and popular inquiry into social security ever published, which had argued the need to double benefit expenditures. Barnett (1986), in a celebrated polemic, placed much of the blame for subsequent post-war decline on this "New Jerusalemism."

Comparison of 1938 with 1951 shows that in the latter year government outlays were about 7.6 percent more of GDP, about 4.8 percent of which was accounted for by social services (Peacock and Wiseman, 1961). Table 9.6 confirms that the UK was a little more heavily taxed than the median European country and also reveals that as the 1950s wore on the exceptionally large category of UK government expenditure was defense rather than social transfers. Despite the attention given to housebuilding in the 1950s, the UK had relatively low investment in this category.

Bacon and Eltis (1976) put forward a similar thesis to that of Barnett, although they focussed on the 1960s and 1970s, and placed it in an accounting framework. They split the economy into a marketed and a non-marketed sector and argued that a good growth performance required a high level of investment in the marketed sector. Their key accounting identity is:

$$Y_m - C_m = I_n + C_n + NX_m + I_m$$

where the subscripts m and n refer to the marketed and non-marketed sectors respectively. They suggested that expansion of state employment and welfare spending (rises in C_n) came in practice at the expense of I_m since in the heavily unionized British economy workers would succeed in passing on taxes aimed at restraining their consumption to profits.

Table 9.7. *The long-run relationship of the marketed and non-marketed sectors (% of marketed output)*

	1924	1937	1955	1965	1979
Marketed sector consumption	81.4	76.4	56.7	53.0	47.0
Marketed sector investment	6.5	9.4	14.0	17.3	19.7
Government financed consumption	9.3	9.8	20.3	18.8	21.8
Government purchases of materials and investment	5.8	9.5	10.7	11.7	11.3
Balance of trade	−3.0	−5.0	−1.8	−0.9	0.2

Source: Crafts (1991, table 6).

Table 9.7 shows clearly, however, that this is a misleading account of British experience whether applied to the rise in state spending post-war compared with prewar or in the 1970s. In the long run the rise of government financed consumption comes at the expense of marketed sector consumption, not marketed sector investment. Indeed, this aspect of table 9.7 seems to run quite counter to Barnett's (1986) stress on the damage done by welfarism to post-war growth prospects. Taking tables 9.6 and 9.7 together, it seems unlikely that the major reason for relative economic decline in post-war Britain was the expansion of state spending per se.

Table 9.2 reported that British unemployment was very low in the early post-war years, while inflation was modest. In terms of conventional models, this seems to suggest a period when the non-accelerating inflation rate of unemployment (NAIRU) was low. Yet in terms of the well-known models of Layard and Nickell (1985) or Dimsdale *et al.* (1989) which consider separately the post-war and interwar economies respectively, one would have expected a significantly higher NAIRU in the 1950s than in the 1930s. Broadberry (1991) points this out noting accelerated structural change, a rise from 1937 to 1951 in trade union density from 29.6 percent to 45 percent and in taxation from 16 percent of GDP in 1937 to 29.7 percent, adverse terms of trade and similar replacement ratios.

Econometric analysis of the wage-setting equation of the NAIRU model for 1923–38 and 1951–73 confirms that there was a structural break between the two periods such that the NAIRU was much lower. The long-run solutions to Broadberry's equations are:

1923–38

$$\ln(W/P) = -1.28 + 0.048\ln TU + 0.28\ln(B/W) - 0.26\ln(PM/P)$$

1951–73

$$\ln(W/P) = -9.59 + 2.19\ln TU + 0.37\ln(B/W) - 0.27\ln(PM/P).$$

Broadberry (1991) attributes the difference to the post-war settlement, in particular the policy of wage restraint pursued by the TUC in return for welfarism and a commitment to full employment.

In effect, the UK became for a while an economy which resembled the corporatist case, which in the Calmfors–Driffill (1989) model is one of the two ways – very weak unions is the other – to real wage moderation and a low NAIRU. By the later 1950s this attempt at a social contract was self-destructing by promoting the advance of aggressive, new trade union leaders such as Frank Cousins of the TGWU and the growth of decentralized, shop-floor bargaining (Flanagan *et al.*, 1983) which seem to be reflected in the much larger coefficient on $\ln TU$ in 1951–73.

Although the post-war settlement was conducive to a low NAIRU, together with the weakness of competitive forces it had adverse effects on productivity. The most obvious way in which this happened was that it implied an effective veto on trade union reform. Even the Conservatives on returning to office in 1951 pursued a policy amounting to appeasement of the trade unions headed by Monckton, the Minister of Labour nicknamed "the oil-can," and authorized personally by Churchill (Smith, 1990).

Straightforward implications of the post-war economic and policy environment can be obtained from models which see productivity as an outcome of a bargain between firms and unions over wages and work effort (Machin and Wadhwani, 1989). In this analysis, higher unemployment and/or a more competitive product market reduce restrictive practices and raise productivity; the former reduces workers' bargaining power while the latter reduces rents and raises the cost of X-inefficiency to the firm. Separate bargaining by small subsets of a firm's labor force intensifies the tendency to overmanning (Bean and Symons, 1989). Seen in these terms the post-war settlement would be expected to have slowed down productivity growth.

The reports of the Anglo-American Council on Productivity, which are discussed in more detail in section 4, give ample evidence of a bargaining environment which resulted in an overmanning (low effort) equilibrium. Both firms' and workers' representatives argued strongly in the early post-war period against strong anti-trust policy directed against the collusive agreements which had proliferated in the 1930s and 1940s, covered perhaps 60 percent of manufacturing output, and seem frequently to have allowed survival of inefficient firms (Gribbin, 1978). In this context, fear of disruption to the post-war export drive precluded effective anti-trust legislation until 1956 (Mercer, 1991). Given the success of the "social contract" in preserving low unemployment, this implied that local shop stewards would generally continue successfully to defend restrictive practices.

Broadberry and Crafts (1992) estimated a bargaining model of productivity change in a cross-section of British industry for 1924–35, showed that it fits the data fairly well, and concluded that the move away from competition inhibited productivity advance. Table 9.8 repeats these results and adds to them some further estimates for 1954–63, which is the earliest post-war sample for which reasonable data are available. Again the bargaining model is not rejected by the data, and it seems reasonable to conclude that a price in terms of foregone productivity improvement was paid for the post-war settlement.

Macroeconomic stabilization

The approach of successive governments to their dealings with organized labor was, of course, closely linked to the continuing danger of wage inflation, which was the chief fear of prominent Keynesians like Meade (Jones, 1987). The post-war situation was precarious and the avoidance of substantial inflation was in one sense a major achievement, although not without its costs in terms of efficiency.

Some key aspects of macroeconomic policy were maintained virtually throughout. First, a nominal anchor was accepted in the form of a fixed exchange rate, which was devalued only once in September 1949, by about 9 percent against a trade weighted currency basket (30 percent against the dollar) (Cairncross and Eichengreen, 1983). Second, substantial budget deficits were eschewed and the ratio of the stock of national debt to GDP fell from an average of 244 percent in 1946–50 to 133 percent in 1956–60 (Hatton and Chrystal, 1991, p. 75). Third, convertibility of the pound sterling was not restored until 1958, with the exception of a shortlived, disastrous experiment in 1947.

At the outset, policy relied heavily on direct controls. Thus, Dow (1964, pp. 174–6) estimated that controls existed on 91 percent of imports and 49 percent of consumer prices until 1949. By 1953 these percentages had fallen to 48 and 21 respectively while by 1958 only 10 percent of both imports and consumer prices were controlled. As controls were relaxed and capital mobility increased, an initial policy of cheap money gave way to one in which interest rates responded to pressure on the pound and were appreciably higher. Toward the end of Labour's administration and clearly under the Conservatives' primitive attempts at planning, the growth of demand through controls gave way to the fine-tuning of Keynesian demand management, notably through tax changes which reacted especially to unemployment and the balance of payments, inaugurating an era of fiscal

Table 9.8. *Cross-section regressions of bargaining models of productivity growth in UK manufacturing*

1924–35					
Constant	0.800	(1.848)	NEW	1.409	(2.874)
CAPLABGR	0.134	(2.030)	TUDUM	−1.386	(−1.888)
EMPFALL	0.040	(2.222)	PCMDOWN	1.732	(2.092)
R² 0.244					
N 79					

1954–63				
Constant	2.746	(4.210)	2.508	(4.527)
CAPLABGR	0.272	(3.312)	0.216	(2.735)
EMPSHOCK	0.540	(1.218)	0.746	(1.709)
OUTPUTGR	0.490	(7.404)	0.465	(7.319)
LOCALAGT	−0.038	(−3.724)	−0.033	(−3.728)
DELTACR5	−0.036	(−1.616)	−0.039	(−1.513)
AACP			0.486	(1.165)
R²	0.548		0.541	
N	57		57	

Notes and Sources: In each regression the dependent variable is the rate of growth of labor productivity, *t*-statistics are in parentheses, and all signs are as predicted by the bargaining model.

For 1924–35 the basic source is the Census of Production, EMPFALL from Beck (1951) is the percentage decline in employment over 1929–32, NEW is a dummy variable taking the value 1 for sectors frequently referred to in the literature as "new industries," TUDUM is a dummy variable taking the value 1 for heavily unionized industries as in Crafts and Thomas (1986), PCMDOWN is a dummy variable taking the value 1 for industries whose price–cost margin fell by more than 25 percent.

For 1954–63, the dependent variable and the rate of growth of output (OUTPUTGR) are from Wragg and Robertson (1978), EMPSHOCK is a dummy variable based on the Census of Production taking the value 1 if employment declined in the sector between 1949 and 1954, the rate of growth of the capital to labor ratio (CAPLABGR) is based on NIESR estimates supplied privately by Mary O'Mahony, LOCALAGT is the percentage of workers in the sector covered by local collective bargaining agreements from Department of Employment (1974), DELTACR5 is the change in the five-firm concentration ratio between 1958 and 1963 from Hart and Clarke (1980), and AACP is a dummy variable taking the value 1 if there was a report on the industry from the Anglo-American Council on Productivity based on the list provided in Hutton (1953, pp. 243–4).

Table 9.9. *Macroeconomic management, 1950–9*

	Budget balance (%GDP)		Growth of M3 (%)	T-bill rate (%)	Current account (£mn)	Unemploy-ment rate (%)
	Actual	FES				
1950	1.4	0.5	3.1	0.52	307	1.4
1951	− 3.2	− 5.1	− 1.0	0.56	− 369	1.3
1952	− 4.9	− 5.6	1.8	2.20	163	2.2
1953	− 5.6	− 6.8	4.2	2.30	145	1.8
1954	− 3.7	− 4.7	3.9	1.79	117	1.4
1955	− 3.2	− 4.9	− 2.9	3.75	− 155	1.2
1956	− 3.7	− 5.1	1.4	4.95	208	1.3
1957	− 3.4	− 4.7	3.5	4.81	233	1.6
1958	− 2.9	− 3.2	3.5	4.56	346	2.2
1959	− 3.4	− 3.9	4.4	3.37	158	2.3

Sources: Budget balances from Ward and Neild (1978), FES (full employment surplus) is estimated at 2.5 percent unemployment, monetary figures from Dimsdale (1991), balance of payments figures from Thirlwall (1986) and unemployment from Economic Trends (1989).

policy later dubbed "stop-go" (Mosley, 1984). Some key indicators of policy stance and the variables to which policy responded are shown in table 9.9.

The devaluation of 1949 has generally been heralded as successful and a depreciation of the real exchange rate seen as necessary for combining internal and external balance (Cairncross and Eichengreen, 1983). Through the 1950s interest rates were generally a little above American levels, enough to indicate slight doubts about the credibility of the commitment to $2.80, but the competitiveness gain was not completely eroded until the late 1950s (Obstfeld, 1992).

In many respects macroeconomic policy appears to conform to the current IMF textbook approach. There are, however, some obvious departures. These include the clumsy attempts at demand management of the 1950s, the long delay before resuming convertibility, and the persistence of a serious monetary overhang for about ten years after the war. (Between 1938 and 1947 the money supply had tripled while current price GDP had risen by only 86 percent and forced saving in sterling denominated assets had been very substantial.) The first of these has had the most attention from economists and historians hitherto but from the point of view of this volume the second and third are probably more interesting.

Dow (1964) delivered a damning indictment of fine-tuning by the Keynesian governments of the 1950s when he argued that the results had been to exacerbate rather than to smooth economic fluctuations. This verdict has subsequently been disputed but the econometric evidence does not suggest any great contribution to stabilizing demand growth (Hatton and Chrystal, 1991). At the same time there is evidence that the UK experienced milder fluctuations than most other OECD economies (NEDO, 1976) and any damage done may have mostly resulted from distracting the Treasury from potentially more fruitful policy initiatives.

Eichengreen (1993) provides quantitative evidence on the existence of excess real money balances relative to what would have willingly been held during the period 1945–55. At the midpoint of this period he estimates that actual balances were excessive by about 50 percent, although economic growth was gradually reducing this monetary overhang, thus requiring a huge adjustment of both the price level and the exchange rate if it were to be eliminated that way and convertibility restored.

In these circumstances of disequilibrium, an attempt to return to convertibility at a fixed exchange rate was bound to lead to rapid exhaustion of Britain's foreign exchange reserves, as, of course, 1947 showed only too clearly. Given the attempts at social contract with the trade unions, the alternative of convertibility and decontrol with further substantial depreciation of the pound was unattractive to the government in view of its possible terms of trade effects, as the debate over the so-called ROBOT scheme proved in 1952.

The implications of this strategy (continued use of controls, non-convertibility, pegging the exchange rate, appeasement of the TUC), understandable as it was for coping with the inflationary threat, were that serious restraints were placed on the policies which might be used to promote faster growth.

Supply-side policies for growth

The macroeconomic problems described above precluded what may have been one of the most effective supply-side policies to raise productivity growth, namely increasing competition in the product market. Anti-trust policy was completely toothless until the Restrictive Practices Act of 1956 and the threat of import competition was relatively remote for most manufacturers – the share of imports in home demand was only 4.7 percent in 1955 (Scott, 1963, p. 41).

Competition was further restricted by the 1940s policy of widespread nationalization, which was strongly supported by the TUC. Nationalized industries which included airlines, coal-mining, railways, gas, and electricity accounted for nearly 10 percent of GDP and about 19 percent of fixed investment during the 1950s (Dunkerley and Hare, 1991). Principal–agent problems seem to have led to very mediocre labor productivity growth (1.5 percent per year, 1948–58, Pryke, 1971) in this sector which was characterized by public ownership but not control. For example, Hannah (1982) catalogues a tale of spectacular inefficiency and poor investment decisions in the electricity industry.

By contrast, the strength of competitive forces bearing on management through the capital market was substantially strengthened as a result of the 1948 Companies Act. This brought to Britain for the first time the hostile takeover bid (Hannah, 1974) and by the late 1950s a merger boom was well on the way. In one sense this was a very positive development seen against the background of sleepy and self-perpetuating, amateurish management revealed in studies like those of the Acton Society Trust (1956). On the other hand, in retrospect, it appears at best a mixed blessing. Studies of the merger and takeover boom which began in the mid 1950s have found little evidence that, in practice, it resulted in better productivity performance or selectively eliminated bad managers (Cowling *et al.*, 1980; Meeks, 1977; Singh, 1975) and, relative to German-style capital markets, it seems to have risked short-termism in managerial investment decisions (Franks and Mayer, 1990).

The main thrust of pro-growth policies was intervention to subsidize various forms of investment. This was a significant shift from interwar industrial policies which had focussed heavily on the problems of declining industries. Here, with the exception of policy on training, there were less constraints from industry or the unions but there seem to have been serious deficiencies in the approach adopted.

Initial allowances on industrial investment were introduced in 1945 and Morris and Stout (1985) characterized the period from then until 1972 as one where policy stressed "investment-led growth," much as might be advocated by some new growth theorists. Investment allowances were added in 1954. Tax savings on investment were £17 million (2.5%) in 1953 rising to £165 million (9.5%) by 1960 (Musgrave and Musgrave, 1968, p. 59). It is generally accepted that these incentives had rather little effect on the volume of investment, one important reason being the frequency with which the rules changed as a consequence of their being used primarily as an instrument of demand management (Kirby, 1991, pp. 241–2).

Research and development (R & D) was a major area of policy intervention. Whereas in the 1930s the UK had spent less than 0.3 percent of GDP on R & D (Sanderson, 1972), by 1955 this had risen to 1.7 percent and by 1960 to 2.5 percent, second only to the United States in the OECD (United Nations, 1964). Much of this was state funded – state expenditure of £114 million in 1950–1 rose to £196 million in 1955–6 and £289 million in 1961–2 compared with private industry spending of £24 million, £77 million, and £248 million in the same years (Edgerton, 1991). A great deal of this funding went to defense-related activities and it is widely agreed that this offered little in the way of externalities to the rest of the economy.

Overall, given the building up of an apparently much stronger technological capability, the performance of the UK looks a bit disappointing, as the patenting data of table 9.10 suggest. Normalizing for population size the UK ranks only fifth of the eleven countries listed. Saul summarized the situation as "not that the British research effort after 1945 was weak, but that British firms, for the most part, did not possess the resources or the flair to exploit what had been discovered" (1979, p. 131).

Moreover, attempts by government enterprises and agencies to sponsor British technology in sectors like nuclear power (Cowan, 1990) and computers (Hendry, 1989) in which Britain had demonstrated early technological prowess and where learning effects and network externalities provide a strong case for government intervention were unsuccessful in the face of the greater muscle of American defense budgets and subsidies.

From the standpoint of the early 1990s the scant attention paid by the government to the reform of educational syllabuses and, especially, to training seems quite astonishing. Relatively early school-leaving continued to prevail, as table 9.10 reports. Reliance was still placed on the traditional systems of apprenticeship and on-the-job training, although shrewd observers recognized that in countries like Germany more workers were trained to obtain higher, examined qualifications (Barnett, 1986) and that the British system of apprenticeship was more a method of restricting entry to skilled occupations than a reliable method of assuring quality training (Liepmann, 1960).

Here there probably were serious problems arising from the "social contract." Intervention to reform training would have involved a serious breach of the sacred principle of voluntarism in industrial relations. The difficulties were revealed when, in 1964, an Industrial Training Act was passed involving a compulsory levy system on employers to establish training boards. This was designed to meet trade union concerns but as such failed to meet the need for establishing a much higher stock of flexible, transferable skills (Vickerstaff, 1985).

4 The American influence on British recovery

This section considers three forms of American influence on the British economy after 1945, namely, the direct impact of Marshall aid, the indirect effects of the moves toward trade liberalization stemming from the

Table 9.10. *Patenting and teenage school enrollment, 1958 (%)*

	Share of foreign patents in USA (%)	School enrolment of 15–19 years olds (%)
Austria	1.12	13
Belgium	1.14	32
Denmark	0.74	19
France	10.36	31
Germany	25.60	18
Italy	3.02	16
Netherlands	5.71	33
Norway	0.61	36
Sweden	4.64	32
Switzerland	8.80	23
UK	23.45	18

Sources: Pavitt and Soete (1982) and United Nations (1964).

conditionality of the European Recovery Program (ERP), and the impact of the Anglo-American Council on Productivity, itself established in response to British perceptions of pressures emanating from the ECA.

The direct impact of Marshall aid

The general tendency of late has been to downplay the impact of the ERP on post-war recovery and, indeed, to stress that the ultimate shape of European economic arrangements ended up rather different from the original American designs (Milward, 1984). Very much the same themes have surfaced in the recent literature on Britain in particular, notably in the work of Burnham (1990). '

Eichengreen and Uzan (1992) provide both a framework and the key data to consider the short-term effects of the Marshall Plan on Britain. Aid to Britain in 1948–51 amounted to about 1.8 percent of GDP. Their regression which takes account of effects on growth working through investment, trade, government spending, and interactions predicts an impact effect sufficient to raise GDP by about 1 percent in 1948–9, far below the predicted effects for countries like Austria (7 percent) and the Netherlands (5 percent). The leverage of Marshall Plan funds was particularly low in the UK because counterpart funds were used almost entirely (about 97 percent) to retire government debt.

Looking at the wider European scene, Eichengreen and Uzan put forward the interesting hypothesis that, by raising national income at a crucial point in post-war stabilization efforts, the Marshall Plan facilitated the negotiation of the social contract upon which the Golden Age of rapid economic growth was based. This does not, however, seem to be an interpretation which is well suited to the British case.

First, the social contract in Britain was already in place as a result of the 1945 election. Burnham (1990, p. 111) explicitly rejects the notion that the extra imports paid for by the ERP made any significant difference in this respect. Second, the British post-war settlement had serious negative implications for future growth performance, as has already been stressed in section 3. Third, this social contract was undermined long before the end of the Golden Age by the switch in the locus of bargaining power from the centralized, union boss level to the shop stewards at the local plant level. It seems likely then that the ERP had little impact on British growth in any direct way.

Indirect effects of American policy

Burnham (1990) provides a detailed, archivally researched account of UK policymakers' response to American pressures on British economic policy from the conditionality of the 1946 loan through the ERP years. He concludes that Britain realized that it mattered to the US in a wider political and military sphere, that it could frequently evade apparent conditions, and that it exercised considerable influence in practice on the detailed implementation of the ERP. The main impact of American pressure was to promote trade liberalization. This matches American research; for example, Arkes concluded that "The threat to cut off assistance was abandoned very early as a practical weapon . . . In place of the continuous testing of the ERP countries for cooperative behavior, the ECA put all its hopes in the long run and was content to accept formal commitments to supranational institutions" (1972, p. 326).

Although after 1947 Britain successfully resisted American pressure to restore full convertibility of the pound, eventually the means of doing this was to concede on trade liberalization and to accept membership of the new arrangements of European payments, eventually the European Payments Union (EPU). This liberalization would not have occurred, under the Labour government at least, without the muscle of the US (Burnham, 1990, pp. 106–7).

Eichengreen (1993) concludes that the EPU was largely unnecessary as full convertibility was a viable alternative for most participants by 1950. This does not, however, include the UK which, as noted in section 3, still had a large monetary overhang and could use the EPU as a means of continuing the social contract while to a considerable extent liberalizing trade. The EPU permitted the continuation of a distorted price structure in Britain but perhaps more importantly represented a step toward increasing the competitive pressures on British firms and reducing the ability of unions to perpetuate restrictive practices and was surely a positive development in the circumstances. It was, of course, an imperfect substitute for a serious attempt to dismantle British cartels which had to await the Restrictive Practices Act of 1956.

The Anglo-American Council on Productivity

Recent research for the World Bank has stressed the large contribution to productivity growth made by the American Technical Assistance programs established during the Marshall Plan which sought to expedite the process of technology transfer to and skill formation in Western Europe (Silberman and Weiss, 1992). Although this may be generally true, it seems most unlikely that it applies to the UK and, if this verdict is correct, it may be useful to understand why.

The Anglo-American Council on Productivity (AACP) was set up in 1948. It organized numerous visits by British industrialists and trade unionists to the United States to study American production methods, published much-read reports on the findings of these study teams, and organized meetings to consider their implications. The government supported this endeavor and subsequently in 1952 established the British Productivity Council to carry on similar work after the Marshall Plan had ended.

The unanimous view in the recent historical literature is that the AACP was established to appease American opinion rather than from a genuine, widespread belief in its likely efficacy and that there is little or no evidence of any impact on British productivity performance (Carew, 1987, p. 223; Middlemas, 1986, pp. 158–62; Tomlinson, 1991b, p. 46). This would appear unsurprising in the light of the data on comparative productivity in table 9.4 but is worth a further look. A crude test is possible by re-estimating the bargaining model of table 9.8 and adding a dummy variable to represent an AACP report. The result is reported in table 9.8; although the coefficient on AACP is positive, it is not significant nor is it nearly as large as readers of Silberman and Weiss might imagine.

The reports of the AACP provide fascinating insights into British industrial productivity in the early post-war period. The picture that they paint would not be surprising to readers of section 3 above. There is a repeated stress on weaknesses in the technical training of workers and inflexible apprenticeships (for example, the report on Heavy Chemicals (AACP, 1953)), and on low effort levels and restrictive practices (e.g.,

Rayon Weaving (AACP, 1949b)). It is true, as critics such as Carew (1987, p. 134) have often said, that there is a great deal of propaganda for the American way of life but it is noticeable that references of this kind are often made together with statements about vested interests, incentives, and a more competitive environment (e.g., Steel Founding (AACP, 1949a)) which are precisely the sort of factors highlighted by the bargaining model of productivity discussed earlier.

This should alert us to the most likely reason for the apparently negligible impact of the AACP on British productivity. What was required were policy interventions which would change the bargaining equilibria across industries toward higher productivity outcomes, not simply technical information. Such moves were inhibited by the exigencies of the export drive, the persistence of controls, the desire for a social contract, etc., that is, by the bargaining power of interest groups hostile to the implementation of the changes which the AACP reports indicated were desirable.

In sum, the sources of relative economic decline in post-war Britain should be sought in domestic policy and institutions. The American influence on performance was quite slight and leverage on policy much more limited than Washington had anticipated at the end of the war. On balance, it might have been better for Britain had American bargaining power been rather stronger with, as a result, the UK doing less nationalization and joining the EC at the outset. Both these impacts would have been helpful to productivity growth by strengthening the competitiveness of product markets. Reform of key British institutions was, however, never a feasible outcome of conditionality.

5 Some implications and directions for further work

The revival of interest in growth theory has provided a richer menu of effects of government policy on long-run growth and also can explain why growth rates persistently diverge without relying on unexplained and exogenous total factor productivity growth differences.

The process of investigating post-war British economic growth using the insights of these new models is only just beginning, but some early results are worth noting. First, econometric investigation at the NIESR of a cross-section of British manufacturing for 1954–86 rejects the hypothesis of externalities to physical capital investment postulated in Romer (1986) and concludes that there are strongly diminishing returns to fixed capital formation, as in traditional growth accounting (Oulton, 1992). This seems to rule out permanent growth rate effects from any shocks from Marshall aid to the savings rate or the capital–output ratio.

Second, further econometric work by the NIESR finds evidence of significant externalities in British manufacturing coming from human capital, as suggested by Lucas (1988), and to research and development expenditures (O'Mahony, 1992). This suggests that the crucial policy mistakes and/or institutional failures may have lay in this direction rather than in inappropriate subsidies to physical investment, and that further research should concentrate on these aspects of the British supply side.

Third, the focus of new growth theory has tended to be on factor accumulation. The British experience suggests that this needs to be complemented by attention to the efficiency with which factors of production are used. Crafts (1993) reviews UK experience in the 1980s and concludes that its productivity surge was due to experiencing a delayed catch-up in which earlier inefficiencies, noted for example in Denison's work, were largely eliminated by the new Thatcher policy stance and cannot be explained using new growth theory. This implies foregone growth and productivity improvement earlier. Both the 1980s and the 1950s can be understood using the bargaining model of productivity discussed above which seems to offer useful additional insights into poor British growth in the post-war recovery.

Turning to today's Eastern European countries, the UK experience suggests a few cautionary points. First and foremost is that institutions matter both for economic growth and for the effectiveness of policy interventions: catch-up is not automatic (Crafts, 1992). In particular, British economic history throws considerable doubt on the advantages of Anglo-American as opposed to German style capital markets and suggests that it is important for the government to be able to commit itself to structures which will limit the bargaining power of groups resisting productivity improvement.

Second, the UK's conduct of macrostabilization was in many ways both understandable and sensible. Nevertheless, the post-war settlement in which this stabilization was embedded involved arrangements which improved the short-run Misery Index at the expense of damaging long-run productivity performance. There is clearly a risk of a similar outcome in eastern Germany today.

Third, the failure of the AACP underlines the importance of understanding and trying to act on the factors, in particular the ability of producer groups to resist or subvert change, which will shape productivity bargains rather than simply pouring trillions of dollars into technical assistance.

References

Abramovitz, M. (1986), "Catching Up, Forging Ahead and Falling Behind," *Journal of Economic History*, 46: 385–406.

Acton Society Trust (1956), *Management Succession*, London: Acton Society Trust.

Addison, P. (1975), *The Road to 1945: British Politics and the Second World War*, London: Jonathan Cape.

Anglo-American Council on Productivity (1949a), *Steel Founding*, London: AACP.

(1949b), *Rayon Weaving*, London: AACP.

(1953), *Heavy Chemicals*, London: AACP.

Arkes, H. (1972), *Bureaucracy, the Marshall Plan and the National Interest*, Princeton, NJ: Princeton University Press.

Bacon, R.W. and W.A. Eltis (1976), *Britain's Economic Problem: Too Few Producers*, London: Macmillan.

Barnett, C. (1986), *The Audit of War*, London: Macmillan.

Bean, C. and J. Symons (1989), "Ten Years of Mrs T.," CEPR Discussion Paper no. 316.

Beck, G.M. (1951), *A Survey of British Employment and Unemployment*, Oxford: Institute of Economics and Statistics.

Beveridge, W.H. (1942), "Social Insurance and Allied Services," Cmd. 6404, London: HMSO.

Broadberry, S.N. (1991), "Why Was Unemployment in Postwar Britain So Low?", CEPR Discussion Paper no. 541.

(1992), "Comparative Productivity Performance in Manufacturing since the Early Nineteenth Century: Europe and the United States," mimeo, University of Warwick.

Broadberry, S.N. and N.F.R. Crafts (1992), "Britain's Productivity Gap in the 1930s: Some Neglected Factors," *Journal of Economic History*, 52: 531–58.

Burnham, P. (1990), *The Political Economy of Postwar Reconstruction*, London: Macmillan.

Cairncross, A. (1985), *Years of Recovery*, London: Methuen.

Cairncross, A. and B. Eichengreen (1983), *Sterling in Decline*, Oxford: Blackwell.

Calmfors, L. and J. Driffill (1989), "Bargaining Structure, Corporatism and Macroeconomic Performance," *Economic Policy*, 6: 13–61.

Carew, A. (1987), *Labour Under the Marshall Plan*, Manchester: Manchester University Press.

Central Statistical Office (1989), *Economic Trends Annual Supplement*, London: HMSO.

Cowan, R. (1990), "Nuclear Power Reactors: A Study in Technological Lock-In," *Journal of Economic History*, 50: 541–67.

Cowling, K., P. Stoneman, J. Cubbin, J. Cable, G. Hall, S. Domberger, and P. Dutton (1980), *Mergers and Economic Performance*, Cambridge University Press.

Crafts, N.F.R. (1991), "Economic Growth," in N.F.R. Crafts and N.W.C. Woodward (eds.), *The British Economy Since 1945*, Oxford: Clarendon Press, pp. 261–90.

(1992), "Productivity Growth Reconsidered," *Economic Policy*, 15: 387–426.

(1993), "Was the Thatcher Experiment Worth It? British Economic Growth in a

European Context," in E. Szirmai, B. Van Ark, and D. Pilat (eds.), *Explaining Economic Growth*, Amsterdam: Elsevier, pp. 327–352.

Crafts, N.F.R. and M. Thomas (1986), "Comparative Advantage in UK Manufacturing Trade, 1910–1935," *Economic Journal*, 96: 629–45.

Denison, E.F. (1968), "Economic Growth," in R.E. Caves (ed.), *Britain's Economic Prospects*, London: Allen & Unwin, pp. 231–78.

Department of Employment (1974), *New Earnings Survey*, London: HMSO.

Dimsdale, N.H. (1991), "British Monetary Policy since 1945," in N.F.R. Crafts and N.W.C. Woodward (eds.), *The British Economy Since 1945*, Oxford: Clarendon Press, pp. 89–140.

Dimsdale, N.H., S.J. Nickell, and N. Horsewood (1989), "Real Wages and Unemployment in Britain during the 1930s," *Economic Journal*, 99: 271–92.

Dow, J.C.R. (1964), *The Management of the British Economy 1945–60*, Cambridge University Press.

Dowrick, S. and D-T. Nguyen (1989), "OECD Comparative Economic Growth 1950–85: Catch-Up and Convergence," *American Economic Review*, 79: 1010–30.

Dunkerley, J. and P. Hare (1991), "Nationalized Industries," in N.F.R. Crafts and N.W.C. Woodward (eds.), *The British Economy Since 1945*, Oxford: Clarendon Press, pp. 381–416.

Edgerton, D. (1991), *England and the Aeroplane*, London: Macmillan.

Eichengreen, B. (1993), *Reconstructing Europe's Trade and Payments: The European Payments Union*, Manchester: Manchester University Press.

Eichengreen, B. and M. Uzan (1992), "The Marshall Plan: Economic Effects and Implications for Eastern Europe and the Former USSR," *Economic Policy*, 14: 13–75.

Englander, A.S. and A. Mittelstadt (1988), "Total Factor Productivity: Macroeconomic and Structural Aspects of the Slowdown," *OECD Economic Studies*, 10: 7–56.

Feinstein, C.H. (1972), *National Income, Expenditure and Output of the United Kingdom, 1855–1965*, Cambridge University Press.

Flanagan, R.J., D.W. Soskice, and L. Ulman (1983), *Unionism, Economic Stabilization and Incomes Policies: The European Experience*, Washington, DC: Brookings Institution.

Franks, J. and C. Mayer (1990), "Capital Markets and Corporate Control: A Study of France, Germany and the UK," *Economic Policy*, 10: 191–231.

Gribbin, J.D. (1978), "The Postwar Revival of Competition as Industrial Policy," Government Economic Service Working Paper no. 19.

Hannah, L. (1974), "Takeover Bids in Britain before 1950: An Exercise in Business Pre-History," *Business History*, 16: 65–77.

(1982), *Engineers, Managers and Politicians: The First Fifteen Years of Nationalised Electricity Supply in Britain*, London: Macmillan.

Hart, P.E. and R. Clarke (1980), *Concentration in British Industry, 1935–1975*, Cambridge University Press.

Hatton, T.J. and K.A. Chrystal (1991), "The Budget and Fiscal Policy," in N.F.R. Crafts and N.W.C. Woodward (eds.), *The British Economy since 1945*, Oxford: Clarendon Press, pp. 52–88.

Hendry, J. (1989), *Innovating for Failure: Government Policy and the Early British Computer Industry*, London: MIT Press.

Hutton, G. (1953), *We Too Can Prosper*, London: Allen & Unwin.

Jones, R. (1987), *Wages and Employment Policy, 1936–1985*, London: Allen & Unwin.

Kirby, M.W. (1991), "Supply-Side Management," in N.F.R. Crafts and N.W.C. Woodward (eds.), *The British Economy Since 1945*, Oxford: Clarendon Press, pp. 236–60.

Kohl, J. (1981), "Trends and Problems in Postwar Public Expenditure Development in Western Europe and North America," in P. Flora and A.J. Heidenhemmer (eds.), *The Development of Welfare States in Europe and America*, London: Transaction Books, pp. 307–44.

Layard, R. and S.J. Nickell (1985), "The Causes of British Unemployment," *National Institute Economic Review*, 111: 62–85.

Liepmann, K. (1960), *Apprenticeship: An Enquiry into Its Adequacy Under Modern Conditions*, London: Routledge & Kegan Paul.

Lucas, R.E. (1988), "On the Mechanics of Economic Development," *Journal of Monetary Economics*, 22: 3–42.

Machin, S. and S. Wadhwani (1989), "The Effects of Unions on Organizational Change, Investment and Employment: Evidence from WIRS," Centre for Labour Economics, LSE, Discussion Paper no. 355.

Maddison, A. (1982), *Phases of Capitalist Development*, Oxford: Oxford University Press.

(1991), *Dynamic Forces in Capitalist Development*, Oxford: Oxford University Press.

Meeks, G. (1977), *Disappointing Marriage*, Cambridge University Press.

Mercer, H. (1991), "The Monopolies and Restrictive Practices Commission, 1949–56: A Study in Regulatory Failure," in G. Jones and M.W. Kirby (eds.), *Competitiveness and the State: Government and Business in Twentieth Century Britain*, Manchester: Manchester University Press, pp. 78–99.

Metcalf, D., S.J. Nickell, and N. Floros (1982), "Still Searching for an Explanation of Unemployment in Interwar Britain," *Journal of Political Economy*, 90: 386–99.

Middlemas, K. (1986), *Power, Competition and the State*, vol. I, London: Macmillan.

Milward, A. (1984), *The Reconstruction of Western Europe, 1945–51*, London: Methuen.

Morris, D.J. and D.K. Stout (1985), "Industrial Policy," in D.J. Morris (ed.), *The Economic System in the UK*, Oxford: Oxford University Press, pp. 851–94.

Mosley, P. (1984), *The Making of Economic Policy*, Brighton: Wheatsheaf.

Musgrave, R.A. and P.B. Musgrave (1968), "Fiscal Policy," in R.E. Caves (ed.), *Britain's Economic Prospects*, London: Allen & Unwin, pp. 21–67.

National Economic Development Office (1976), *Cyclical Fluctuations in the UK Economy*, London: NEDO.

Obstfeld, M. (1992), "The Adjustment Mechanism," CEPR Discussion Paper no. 648.

OECD (1970), *National Accounts, 1950–1968*, Paris: OECD.

   (1981), *Long Term Trends in Tax Revenues of OECD Member Countries, 1955–1980*, Paris: OECD.

   (1992), *Historical Statistics, 1960–1990*, Paris: OECD.

O'Mahony, M. (1992), "Productivity and Human Capital Formation in UK and German Manufacturing," National Institute of Economic and Social Research Discussion Paper no. 28.

Oulton, N. (1992), "Investment, Increasing Returns and the Pattern of Productivity Growth in UK Manufacturing, 1954–86," National Institute of Economic and Social Research Discussion Paper no. 5.

Pavitt, K. and L. Soete (1982), "International Dynamics of Innovation," in H. Giersch (ed.), *Emerging Technologies*, Tübingen: Mohr, pp. 105–33.

Peacock, A. and J. Wiseman (1961), *The Growth of Public Expenditure in the UK*, Princeton, NJ: Princeton University Press.

Pryke, R. (1971), *Public Enterprise in Practice*, London: MacGibbon and Kee.

Romer, P.M. (1986), "Increasing Returns and Long-Run Growth," *Journal of Political Economy*, 94: 1002–37.

Sanderson, M. (1972), "Research and the Firm in British Industry, 1919–39," *Science Studies*, 3: 107–51.

Saul, S.B. (1979), "Research and Development in British Industry from the End of the Nineteenth Century to the 1960s," in T.C. Smout (ed.), *The Search for Wealth and Stability*, London: Macmillan, pp. 114–38.

Scott, M. (1963), *A Study of UK Imports*, Cambridge University Press.

Silberman, J.M. and C. Weiss (1992), "Restructuring for Productivity," World Bank Industry and Energy Department Working Paper no. 64.

Singh, A. (1975), "Takeovers, Natural Selection and the Theory of the Firm: Evidence from the Postwar UK Experience," *Economic Journal*, 85: 497–515.

Smith, J.D. (1990), *The Attlee and Churchill Administrations and Industrial Unrest, 1945–55: A Study in Consensus*, London: Pinter.

Thirlwall, A.P. (1986), *Balance of Payments Theory and the United Kingdom Experience*, 3rd edn, London: Macmillan.

Tomlinson, J. (1991a), "The Labour Government and the Trade Unions, 1945–51," in N. Tiratsoo (ed.), *The Attlee Years*, London: Pinter, pp. 90–105.

   (1991b), "A Missed Opportunity?: Labour and the Productivity Problem, 1945–51," in G. Jones and M.W. Kirby (eds.), *Competitiveness and the State: Government and Business in Twentieth Century Britain*, Manchester: Manchester University Press, pp. 40–59.

United Nations (1964), *Some Factors in the Economic Growth of Europe during the 1950s*, Geneva: United Nations.

Vickerstaff, S. (1985), "Industrial Training in Britain: The Dilemmas of a Neo-Corporatist Policy," in A. Cawson (ed.), *Organised Interests and the*

State, London: SAGE Publications, pp. 45–64.

Ward, T.S. and R.R. Neild (1978), *The Measurement and Reform of Budgetary Policy*, London: Heinemann.

Wragg, R. and J. Robertson (1978), "Postwar Trends in Employment, Output, Labour Costs and Prices by Industry in the UK," Department of Employment Research Paper no.3.

10 "Belgian Miracle" to slow growth: the impact of the Marshall Plan and the European Payments Union

ISABELLE CASSIERS

The economic reconstruction of Belgium after the Second World War took place under conditions largely different from those in neighboring countries. A particular configuration of favorable circumstances permitted a very rapid economic recovery, subsequently known as the "*Belgian Miracle.*" But this miracle was shortlived. From the mid 1950s the Belgian economy was already showing signs of weakness that put it at a disadvantage relative to its competitors: relatively slow growth, insufficient investment, little advance in productivity. The legacy of this period may still be a burden forty years later.

This chapter reviews the characteristic features of Belgian growth after the war and examines the way in which they were influenced by the Marshall Plan and the European Payments Union. The relative prosperity of the Belgian economy in 1948 is first considered. Then the structural weaknesses which had appeared by the late 1950s and their principal causes are discussed. Finally, some hypotheses about the role of the Marshall Plan and the European Payments Union in the relative weakness of the Belgian economy are proposed.

It is argued here that: 1) the resumption of growth in Belgium was particularly rapid after the war thanks to the limited character of wartime destruction, to the specialization of Belgian industry in producer goods in strong demand, and to a timely and effective monetary reform itself reinforced by social reform. 2) The relatively slow growth in Belgium during the 1950s can be explained by its aging industrial structure, by the defensive nature of investment, and by the loss of competitiveness arising from a combination of high wages and a high exchange rate. 3) The

The author would like to acknowledge her gratitude to Philippe De Villé and Barry Eichengreen for helpful comments and Carine Deridder and Carine Stordeur for their help in assembling the documentation and processing the data. Special thanks go to Peter Solar for translating the text into English.

Marshall Plan and the European Payments Union contributed to the relative weakening of the Belgian economy by encouraging investment to be defensive and by reinforcing the traditional industrial structure.

1 The "Belgian Miracle" and the immediate post-war period

Of all European countries involved directly in the war, Belgium was the first to restore its economy, thanks to the union of several favorable factors. The causes of rapid reconstruction fall into three groups: those originating in Belgium's wartime experience, those arising from its economic structure, and those resulting from economic policy choices.

1.1 The heritage of the war

Having capitulated at the beginning of the war (May 28, 1940), Belgium suffered much less destruction than did its neighbors. Production could thus be relaunched after the war faster and more easily than elsewhere. The liberation of the port of Antwerp (September 4, 1944), the only major European port still largely intact, was a major stimulus to economic activity. The concentration of Allied troops in Belgian territory in 1945 gave rise to large expenditures, for the most part in dollars. This helped increase exchange reserves, which were already high thanks to a large stock of gold maintained intact during the war. Unlike the situation in neighboring countries, the reprovisioning of Belgium was not held back by insufficient foreign exchange.[1]

1.2 The economic structure of Belgium

Belgian industry was a major beneficiary of the structure of demand in immediate post-war Europe. Any reconstruction period is particularly favorable to an economy specializing in such basic products as coal, semi-finished metals, and cement (table 10.1).[2] The growth of industrial production was thus highly stimulated by apparently limitless markets, both at home and abroad.

1.3 Economic policy choices

The war led everywhere to an increase in government control of economic activity which was only progressively relaxed as reconstruction took place. In maintaining diverse controls on consumption, production, prices, and

[1] For more details, see Baudhuin (1958) and Van Audenhove (1990). Kindleberger (1987) lays stress on this point.

[2] A similar phenomenon occurred after World War I. See Cassiers (1989), pp. 127–40.

Table 10.1. *Sectoral distribution of industrial production, 1956 (percentage)*

	Belgium	OEEC
Mining and quarrying	15.3	6.6
Food processing	6.9	12.2
Textiles	13.3	8.4
Metal production	15.0	8.1
Metal fabrication	32.3	29.3
Chemicals	5.6	10.3
Gas, water, and electricity	2.5	5.2
Other industries	8.7	19.9
TOTAL	100.0	100.0

Source: A. Lamfalussy (1961), from OEEC.

wages until 1950, Belgian public authorities participated in this general trend.[3] But from 1944 two major decisions distinguished Belgium from other countries and shaped its subsequent growth: one was a major social reform; the other was monetary reform.

I.3.I SOCIAL REFORM AND THE RISE IN WAGES

In the same way that the First World War led throughout Europe to urgent demands for social reform, the need to maintain social cohesion during the liberation of 1944 favored the blossoming of a new series of reforms. The first measures were taken in Belgium.[4] The groundwork was laid while the country was still under German occupation as representatives of trade unions and employers organizations put together a draft agreement on social solidarity, the Social Pact. This agreement consisted of a coherent set of measures dealing with wages and social policy that were intended to protect workers, guarantee their purchasing power, and, more generally, provide a context for economic growth.[5] Most of the measures in this

---

[3] A detailed list of regulations may be found in Van Audenhove (1990), vol. I, pp. 324 f.

[4] Léon (1977), p. 527. For more details about Belgium, see Scholliers (1993).

[5] After a declaration of principle engaging the representatives of employers and employees to work together loyally, the text of the agreement foresees a series of measures for maintaining the purchasing power of wages, re-establishing immediately after the war legislation and agreements relating to the duration of work, creating a fund for re-equipping households, establishing a comprehensive system of social security, increasing family allowances, establishing worker representatives in factories, reinforcing the role of the *commissions paritaires*. (For the complete text, see Fuss, Goldschmidt-Clermont, and Watillon (1958), pp. 828–42.) The program was fully carried out, in steps, after the liberation. For detail on the measures taken, see Chlepner (1956) or Van Audenhove (1990), vol. I, pp. 326–34.

Table 10.2. *Indices of wages* in Belgian francs (Belgium = 100)*

	1938	1950
Belgium	100.0	100.0
Netherlands	142.3	65.0
Great Britain	168.4	88.6
Germany	210.5	76.9

Note: *Including social security charges; average for all workers, except miners.
Source: Masoin (1951).

agreement were enacted in the months that followed the liberation. From September 16, 1944 the *Conférence Nationale du Travail* – the official body for social negotiations at the national level – decided on an increase in nominal wages of 60 percent over the level in May 1940; a further increase of 20 percent was granted on July 30, 1945. The *Office National de Securité Sociale*, created on December 28, 1944 from scattered institutions developed before the war, was the crowning glory of post-war social legislation.[6] A decisive step was taken toward institutionalizing social negotiations at the sectoral level by granting legal status to the existing *commissions paritaires* on June 9, 1945.

These social reforms had several consequences. The first was the creation of a social peace which would guarantee that wage demands were moderate in the following years. The social reform led to what contemporaries called a *"changement de régime"* in the Belgian economy:[7] the rise in wages in 1944–5 pushed Belgium up among the high-wage countries of Europe, whereas it had always been known previously for its cheap labor (table 10.2).

The increase in wages and social security charges led to a substantial rise in firms' costs, the consequences of which will be examined later. This radical measure ensured simultaneously the increase in the purchasing power of wages and the rapid growth of consumer demand: the index of retail sales in department stores passed its post-war level by 1947.[8]

Given the already prevalent practice of indexing wages to the cost of living, such a large jump in incomes could have given rise to a vicious inflationary spiral. It did not because the draft agreement on social solidarity conceived of the rise in direct and indirect labor costs as part of a larger and more coherent set of economic policies:

---

[6] See Cassiers (1989), pp. 68–72, 195–8, and 201–3.
[7] Notably Dupriez (1951); Snoy et d'Oppuers (1953); van der Rest (1961).
[8] Banque Nationale de Belgique, *Statistiques économiques belges, 1950–1960*, vol. I, p. 18: general index of sales in large, multi-product shops deflated by the retail price index.

The problem of wages is directly linked to that of prices and money. In effect, from the economic point of view, the three elements are interdependent and the adoption of consistent measures concerning the stabilization of the domestic money supply, the adaptation of prices and the readjustment of wages will be the first conditions of the country's economic and financial recovery. . . . In the interests of the workers themselves, the concern to give the Belgian currency after the war as high a value as possible must thus be predominant. In the case where devaluation becomes inevitable, it must be kept to a minimum.[9]

This declaration follows in a direct line from the innovative policies attempted in Belgium in the late 1930s, when the Van Zeeland government successfully combined what started as independent proposals by the socialist party for a *Plan du Travail* and by Professeur Léon Dupriez for management of the exchange rate.[10] Dupriez continued his work during the war and furnished the Pierlot government constituted on September 26, 1944 with calculations that permitted an immediate and rigorous monetary stabilization.

I.3.2 THE MONETARY STABILIZATION OF 1944, OR "OPERATION GUTT"

Camille Gutt, the Minister of Finance in the first Belgian post-war government, immediately applied (October 6, 1944) an anti-inflation plan that had been prepared in London during the occupation. Notes were withdrawn from circulation and bank accounts blocked. Each citizen received, in exchange for old notes issued by the National Bank, 2,000 francs in new notes printed for the government in exile. Notes over and above this amount were transformed into "blocked assets," either temporary (42 billion francs, 24.5 percent of monetary circulation) or permanent (63 billion francs, 36.7 percent of monetary circulation).[11] As the economy recovered from 1944 to 1949, temporarily blocked assets were reimbursed progressively in such a way as to control rigorously the growth of the money supply and to maintain the parity of the Belgian franc with sterling. The franc joined the International Monetary Fund on September 17, 1946 at the rate fixed during the monetary reform: 176.5 francs to the pound. This rate was maintained until the devaluation of the pound in 1949. "The essential role of the monetary reform was to hold the franc firm amidst the monetary disorders of the world."[12]

Historians have seen the Belgian monetary stabilization of 1944 as "a

[9] Fuss, Goldschmidt-Clermont, and Watillon (1958), p. 829. Own translation.
[10] See Cassiers (1989), pp. 175–203.
[11] For more details, see Bismans (1992); Dupriez (1978); Janssens (1976); or Van Audenhove (1990).
[12] Dupriez (1978), p. 173.

good example of a successful deflation," in the same way that they have picked out the precosity and audacity of Belgian social reforms.[13] But the close connections between these two reforms have not received the attention they merit, in light of the originality of associating monetary deflation and large wage rises.[14] The draft agreement on social solidarity, as well as the comments of L.H. Dupriez, confirm that the conjunction of these two reforms was deliberate.[15] In guaranteeing a fixed exchange rate based on purchasing power parity with the sterling zone, that is, with Belgium's principal trading partners, the monetary stabilization assured at the same time strict control of inflation and stable price expectations for export industries. The health of these industries in the early days of recovery was sufficiently good – at least relatively – for a large rise in wage costs to be conceded at one go. The improvement in the living standards of the population was not seen only as a social demand: it was also perceived as a means of enhancing the qualifications and productivity of labor and as the sharp stimulus required to transform industrial structures. In the short run the role of the institutions freshly created was to prevent any uncontrolled wage rises; in the longer run they were to assure the growth of wages and the stability of the franc.

The results of this strategy seem to have been very positive in the short run and much more qualified in the long run.

1.4 The state of affairs on the eve of the Marshall Plan

By 1948 Belgium had recovered to its prewar level of economic activity (table 10.3).

Contemporary observers and historians are agreed that reconstruction, more rapid in Belgium than elsewhere (table 10.4), was achieved by 1947.[16] Agreement is also widespread that reconstruction put old structures back into place without renewing them.[17] This would hamper later growth.

2 The disquieting state of affairs at the end of the 1950s

Within ten years after the Marshall Plan was launched in Europe, Belgium

[13] Léon (1977), p. 517.

[14] The Belgian case appears to be the exact opposite of the Italian and French cases, in which post-war inflation is interpreted by Casella and Eichengreen (1993) in terms of distributional conflicts. This comparison, which is outside the brief of this paper, deserves study.

[15] Notably the pages devoted to the rise in wages in his work on the monetary reforms (1978).

[16] It is worth, however, remembering Camu's (1960) observation that all comparisons to 1938 are particularly favorable to Belgium and France since they were hit harder by the recession of 1938 than other countries.

[17] Beuthe (1964); Camu (1961); Lamfalussy (1959, 1961).

Table 10.3. *Selected indicators of economic activity (1936–8 = 100)*

	1946	1947	1948	1949
National income[a]	—	99	100	106
Industrial production[b]	80	102	109	110
Electricity production	120	140	151	157
Industrial employment[c]	—	118	—	—
Export volume	—	—	91	101
Import volume	—	—	112	110
Consumption volume[d]	84	97	94	108

Notes:
a Nominal income deflated by an average of wholesale and retail prices.
b IRES (Institut de Recherches Economiques et Sociales) index.
c 1937 = 100. Based on 1937 and 1947 census.
d Consumption index deflated by retail prices.
Source: Banque Nationale de Belgique, *Statistiques économiques belges*.

Table 10.4. *Production and foreign trade*

	1948 (1938 = 100)		1959 (1948 = 100)	
	Belgium*	OEEC	Belgium*	OEEC
Industrial production	121	97	140	209
Metal production	141	88	158	224
Import volume	116	81	179	214
Export volume	95	79	223	289

Note: *Belgian–Luxemburg Economic Union for foreign trade.
Source: OEEC, Statistical Bulletins, 1956 and 1962.

would seem to have lost its advantageous position. The slowdown in Belgian growth during the 1950s – at least in relative terms – is evident (table 10.4 and figures 10.1 and 10.2).

From the late 1950s several Belgian economists took up the question of why the economy had lost its dynamism.[18] The different arguments invoked during the 1960s are well summarized by Van Rijckeghem (1982). Only the main lines will be recalled here.

[18] The most interesting contributions are by Beuthe (1964); Camu (1960, 1961); Lamfalussy (1959, 1961); Waelbroeck and Rosselle (1961).

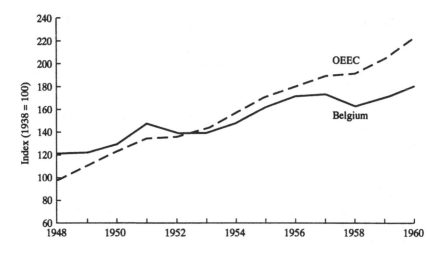

Figure 10.1   Industrial production (1938 = 100)
Source: OEEC, Statistical Bulletins.

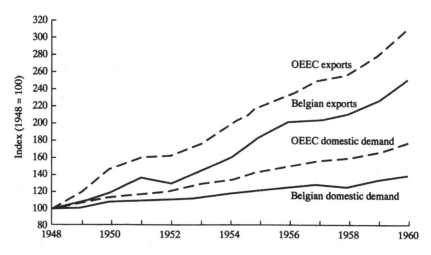

Figure 10.2   Exports (X) and domestic demand (DD) (1948 = 100); 1954
prices and exchange rates.
Source: OEEC, Statistical Bulletins

2.1 The structures of production and exports

If the particularities of Belgium's industrial structure explain in part its
rapid post-war reconstruction, could they not also have been responsible
for its slow growth in the 1950s? Did not the demand for the basic products
in which Belgium specialized have to fall off as reconstruction took place

Table 10.5. *Industrial structure and export growth, 1958 compared to 1951–3*

Index of exports for major industrial countries (1951/3 = 100)	140.7
Index of exports for Belgium* (1951/3 = 100)	121.3
Difference: [(Belgium/industrial countries) − 1]	−13.8%
of which: composition of exports	−3.9%
change of market share	−10.3%

Note: *Belgian–Luxemburg Economic Union.
Source: Own calculation from Waelbroeck and Rosselle (1961).

elsewhere? These questions were carefully examined by Waelbroeck and Rosselle (1961) who found that structural effects seem to have played only a small role. Of the 14 percent fall in Belgium's exports relative to those of major industrialized countries, only at most 4 percent could be explained by their composition. The rest of the fall (10 percent) resulted from loss of market share (table 10.5).

Before examining the possible causes of these falling market shares, it should be observed that the structure of the Belgian economy, rather than adapting to changes in the structure of world demand, appears to have become more out of kilter over the period. As Camu (1960) remarked, "Belgium continues to concentrate its efforts on sectors which once made it great, but which, today, are declining in importance in world trade." A detailed study of changes in production between 1948 and 1960 confirms this judgment: it was above all the sectors producing mainly semi-finished products that had the highest growth rates.[19]

In sum, if the initial structure of Belgian exports cannot by itself explain the slow growth of the 1950s, increasing concentration on products for which world demand was stagnant or declining seems to have exacerbated the problem.

2.2 Defensive investment

The nature of investment undertaken in Belgium during the 1950s was one important cause of slow growth. It helps explain two phenomena already cited: the accentuation of traditional specialization and the loss of competitiveness in these declining markets. In effect, according to the interpretation advanced by Lamfalussy (1961) and shared by several others,[20] two traits characterized Belgian investment in this period: (1) its

[19] Carbonnelle (1962), p. 195.
[20] Notably Camu (1960), p. 418; Beuthe (1964), p. 99.

Table 10.6. *Wage costs, productivity and unit labor costs in manufacturing in 1957 (1948 = 100)*

	Productivity	[Wage costs]		[Unit labor costs]	
		in domestic currency	in dollars	in domestic currency	in dollars
Belgium	142	164	144	115	102
Netherlands	144	169	118	117	83
Germany	223	196	155	88	68
France	164	250	135	152	83
Italy	217	153	141	77	65
United Kingdom	121	175	123	145	101
United States	128	157	157	123	123

Source: Lamfalussy (1959) from OEEC and own calculation from author's data.

concentration in stagnant industries (coal, steel, railroads, textiles) and (2) the priority accorded to rationalization as against innovation. This type of investment, described as defensive, took place on the margin of existing equipment and at relatively low cost. It was a response by industrialists to intense pressure from foreign competition under conditions of high wages and low profits.[21] It assured – at least in the medium term – reasonable gains in productivity for investment expenditures well below the average (figure 10.3).

This interpretation is consistent with international comparisons of productivity and labor costs in manufacturing (table 10.6). Belgium's productivity growth was modest but not exceptionally weak (col. 1). But Belgian manufacturing industry did become significantly less competitive relative to its Dutch, German, French, and Italian rivals (col. 5).[22] The reasons lie in the weakness of domestic demand and in exchange rate policy.

2.3 Weak domestic demand and exchange rate policy

Unit labor costs expressed in a common currency condense the three principal determinants of competitiveness: productivity, wage costs, and the exchange rate. The decomposition in table 10.6 suggests that Belgium

---

[21] The relationship between the growth of wages and that of productivity are discussed in Cassiers and Solar (1990).

[22] For a broader international comparison of unit labor costs, see Eichengreen (1993).

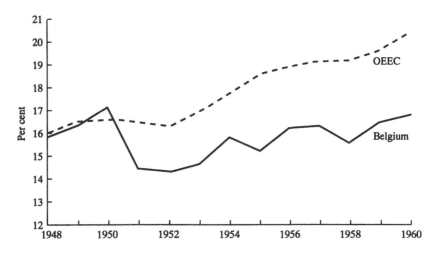

Figure 10.3   Investment as a share of GNP; gross domestic fixed capital formation, 1954 prices and exchange rates.
Source: OEEC, Statistical Bulletins

had modest productivity growth, a relatively slow growth in wage costs, and an ambitious exchange rate policy.

Faithful to the declarations in the Social Pact, Belgium made clear in 1949 its determination to give the franc "*a value as high as possible.*" While sterling devalued by 30.5 percent, followed by all of the sterling area, Scandinavia, and the Netherlands, the devaluation of the Belgian franc was limited to 12.3 percent, which meant that the Belgian currency had *appreciated* by 26.2 percent against the currencies of its major trading partners.[23]

Figure 10.4 suggests that the deterioration of Belgian competitiveness, so noticeable at the end of the 1950s, was intimately connected to the decision in 1949 to devalue the Belgian franc by less than the currencies of its principal European trading partners were devalued. This choice, painful for exporting firms, apparently contributed to slowing the growth in nominal wages. In effect, from 1950 to 1955, all of the countries in table 10.6 recorded faster growth in wages than did Belgium.

This observation can be pushed further back to the double reform – social and monetary – undertaken immediately after the war. In 1944 wages were abruptly raised but any hint of inflation was snuffed out by monetary deflation. Firms were able to tolerate this conjunction of a strong franc and

[23]   L.H. Dupriez (1978), pp. 196–204.

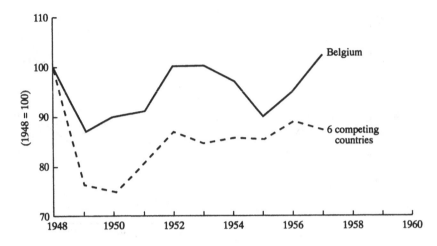

Figure 10.4 Unit labor costs in dollars (1948 = 100), relative to competing countries: unweighted average.
Source: See table 10.6.

high wages because general economic conditions were very favorable to the Belgian economy. By 1949 the overvaluation of the franc had impaired the competitiveness of Belgian enterprises. This choice of economic policy contributed to the defensive character of investment as well as to the slowing of growth in nominal wages.

The policy of the strong franc was nonetheless pursued without deviation and was encouraged by persistent surpluses on the balance of trade and services (figure 10.5). These surpluses resulted from domestic demand which was even less dynamic than exports. The more rapid growth of exports than of domestic demand was by no means unique to Belgium (figure 10.2) but it was more marked than elsewhere (table 10.7).

Lamfalussy (1959, 1961) attributed the slow growth of domestic demand to two sorts of behavior: a strong propensity to save by households (figure 10.6 and table 10.8) and a weak propensity to invest by Belgian firms (figure 10.3).[24]

To summarize, Belgian economic growth during the 1950s was slowed by weak domestic demand and by relatively weak export demand (figure 10.2). That the slowdown was not absolute but only relative to neighboring countries should be remembered, if for no other reason than to explain why it passed unnoticed until the end of the decade. The remarkable expansion of the European economy offered Belgian exporters a rapidly growing

[24] See as well Lamfalussy (1959), p. 60 and Camu (1960), p. 411.

Table 10.7. *Share of domestic demand in GNP* (percentage)*

	Belgium	OEEC
1948	81.8	87.0
1960	71.3	79.3
Percentage change	−12.9	−8.9

Note: *$(C + I + G)/(C + I + G + X)$ in constant (1954) prices, from the national accounts.
Source: OEEC, Statistical Bulletins.

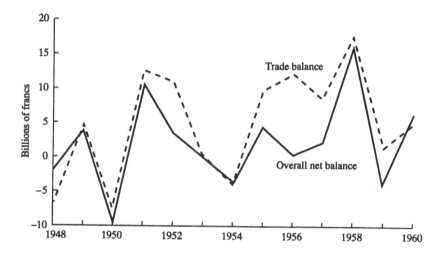

Figure 10.5   Belgian balance of payments (billions of francs)
Sources: Banque Nationale de Belgique and Lamfalussy (1959).

market, which they could exploit despite the weaknesses which would only later be identified.

The expansion of intra-European trade from which Belgium benefitted was stimulated by the Marshall Plan. But did the Marshall Plan and the European Payments Union have any role to play in the structural weaknesses or the feeble domestic demand that afflicted the Belgian economy?

Table 10.8. *Average savings rates, 1950–60 (percentage)*

Germany	12.2
Belgium	12.3
France	5.7
Netherlands*	10.1
Great Britain*	2.3
United States*	7.6

Note: *1950–9.
Source: Frank (1962) from EEC and UNO.

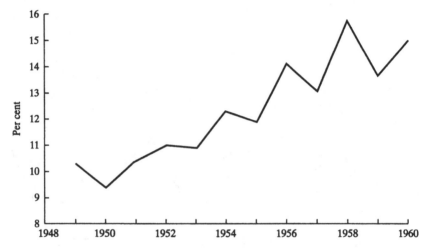

Figure 10.6   Household savings rate in Belgium (% of GNP)
Source: Frank (1962).

3 The impact of the Marshall Plan and the European Payments Union

3.1 The principles of intervention

By the time the United States offered to help accelerate European reconstruction by means of the Marshall Plan, the reconstruction of the Belgian economy had already been largely achieved.[25] This explains why the direct assistance received by Belgium was very small. Among the sixteen

[25] It was impossible to integrate the information contained in a book published after the present chapter had been written: *Le Plan Marshall et le relèvement économique de l'Europe*. Colloque tenu à Bercy sous la direction de René Girault et Maurice Lévy-Leboyer. Paris, Imprimerie Nationale, 1993.

Table 10.9. *Foreign trade by monetary zone*

		Exports as % of total exports	Imports as % of total imports	Trade balance as % of total imports
Dollar	1937	10.5	12.3	−3.6
zone	1949	8.4	23.2	−15.0
	1951	12.7	23.1	−9.8
	1953	15.0	15.9	−1.9
EPU	1937	70.4	59.1	+5.3
zone	1949	69.8	57.4	+10.8
	1951	70.9	59.9	+14.0
	1953	68.4	67.5	−4.1

Source: Ministère des Affaires Économiques (1955).

countries that signed the European Cooperation Act,[26] Belgium was the exception: thanks to the very rapid rebuilding of its industrial base, it was generally a creditor with respect to its European trading partners (table 10.9). It did not lack the means to pay for its imports; rather Belgium was beginning to feel the effects of other countries' payments difficulties.[27] As a result, Belgium benefitted above all from conditional assistance.[28] This second form of Marshall Plan intervention required that Belgium provide its European debtors with drawing rights in Belgian francs in compensation for the credits in dollars that it received. These dollar credits were to help it pay for imports from the United States, which had become very large immediately after the war because of the problems faced by its traditional suppliers (table 10.9).

[26] The Economic Cooperation Act – the official name of the plan conceived by General Marshall – was signed on April 3, 1948. American assistance to signatories of the act began on July 1, 1948. The sixteen countries concerned (Austria, Belgium, Denmark, France, Germany, Greece, Iceland, Ireland, Italy, Luxemburg, the Netherlands, Norway, Portugal, Sweden, Switzerland, the United Kingdom) were brought together in the Organization for European Economic Cooperation (OEEC), which was charged with putting together a detailed program for economic recovery and the liberalization of exchange. After enlargement the OEEC became, in 1961, the Organization for Economic Cooperation and Development (OECD).

[27] Milward (1984), p. 274; Van Audenhove (1990), vol. I, pp. 330–1.

[28] Altogether, over the period 1948–51, direct aid amounted to $68 million and conditional aid to $446 million, Baudhuin (1958), p. 93. Also see Kurgan-Van Hentenryk (1993) and Bossuat (1992).

In a Europe of inconvertible currencies[29] the direct injection of dollars and the system of drawing rights accompanying the Marshall Plan permitted a vigorous recovery of intra-European trade. This was further stimulated by the multilateral payments mechanism organized among OEEC countries in the context of the European Payments Union (EPU) from July 1950.[30]

This system did not suit Belgium well at all.[31] With its chronic surplus relative to its EPU partners and its chronic deficit relative to the United States, Belgium was continually frustrated by the inconvertibility of European currencies *relative to the dollar*, that is, by the absence of a return to full convertibility. While its reserves in gold and dollars fell, those in inconvertible European currencies rose considerably, jeopardizing domestic monetary stability.[32] Concerned since 1944 to control the expansion of the money supply, Belgium took, from 1951, a series of measures to limit its surplus relative to the EPU zone. In an article surveying these measures, the National Bank of Belgium observed that it was somewhat paradoxical to see a country taking restrictive measures to limit its balance of trade surplus, above all when the country lived to a great extent on the resources obtained through trade, but stated that the weaknesses inherent in the EPU had forced it to act.[33] Triffin described the discriminatory measures taken by creditor countries as falling into three sorts:

The incentive to discrimination by the creditors was not so much the result of inadequate gold reserves or settlements as of their reluctance to pile up an indefinite amount of EPU credits. Three methods were simultaneously used by them to reduce their intra-European surpluses. The first was to encourage capital exports and repayments to other EPU countries and to step up their rate of intra-European liberalization far beyond the formal requirements of the Code of Liberalization. The second was to restrict imports from non-EPU sources in an effort to force traders to seek substitute sources of supply within the EPU area. The third – and the most absurd from a collective point of view – was to impose restrictions on their exports to other EPU members.[34]

[29] Some since the war, others since the 1930s. The dollar, for its part, had explicitly become the official currency for international settlements in the Bretton Woods agreements of 1944.

[30] For a description of how the system functioned, see Triffin (1957) or Eichengreen (1993).

[31] Belgian representatives sought in vain, throughout the negotiations, to obtain other arrangements. See Triffin (1957); Hogan (1987); Godts Peters (1987); Milward (1987).

[32] From 6.1 to 19.6 billion francs between June 1950 and December 1951; Banque Nationale de Belgique (1952), p. 99.

[33] Banque Nationale de Belgique (1952), pp. 98 and 101.

[34] Triffin (1957), p. 204.

3.2 Impact on the orientation of Belgian growth

The confrontation of the characteristic features of Belgian growth with the principles of intervention of the Marshall Plan and the European Payments Union suggests a series of hypotheses concerning the impact of these institutions on Belgian economic development.

The Marshall Plan intervened in Belgium principally by conditional assistance, which could be considered a subsidy to those importing Belgian goods. In this respect it favored greater openness: it encouraged exporters without offering any assistance to firms producing for the domestic market.

Grants and direct loans by the United States to Belgium were negligible since the relatively good health of the Belgian economy did not justify them. Belgian industry was reconstructed largely on a traditional basis. It thus did not benefit, as did other OEEC countries, from the incentive to modernization and innovation that was a feature of direct assistance.[35]

Belgium's surplus with respect to the OEEC put it on par with the United States as a giver of aid but "American aid was given by virtue of political decisions, which took a certain time; Belgian aid resulted directly from the execution of the bilateral payments agreements."[36] It thus came more quickly and as such was appreciated. This institutional element must have endowed Belgian producers with an advantage over their competitors in obtaining sales contracts and thus permitted them perhaps to go easy on improving productivity.

The European Payments Union pushed Belgium into reacting in the three ways described by Triffin. Measures intended to restrict exports to the EPU zone must inevitably have affected the growth of exports since the OEEC countries were by far Belgium's leading trading partners (table 10.9). This may have contributed to the relatively slow growth of Belgian exports noted above.

The restrictions on imports payable in dollars that were put into effect from 1951 must have slowed the purchase of investment goods from the United States and hence the diffusion of modern production techniques. This may have played a role in the lack of innovation mentioned above, itself partially responsible for slow growth. The same restrictions, which limited imports from the United States during the period when consumers had become fascinated by the *American way of life*, may also help explain the high household savings rate noted above.

Finally, the measures which encouraged capital exports to EPU

[35] See Kurgan-Van Hentenryk (1993). The little direct aid that Belgium received went into the bottomless coal pit. On this point see Milward (1992).
[36] Dupriez (1978), p. 172.

countries – without the reverse being true – could not have favored investment in Belgium.

4 Conclusions

This chapter reviews the characteristic features of Belgian growth after the war and examines the ways in which they were influenced by the Marshall Plan and the European Payments Union. The Belgian miracle of the years 1944–8 was followed by relatively slow growth in the 1950s. The immediate post-war "miracle" was founded on the conjunction of fortuitous elements inherited from the war, of structural elements such as favorable industrial specialization for a reconstruction period, and of institutional elements establishing from 1944 the framework of labor relations and of monetary and exchange rate policies. The strong links between social and monetary reforms are worth emphasizing: the Social Pact demonstrated the complementarity between the rise in wages from before the war – pushing Belgium up among the high wage countries – and the maintenance of monetary stability.

On the eve of the Marshall Plan, Belgium's situation was so enviable that American funding hardly seemed justified. Ten years later, however, Belgium's relative position had deteriorated seriously. The search for an explanation for this deterioration has highlighted the interactions of structures, behavior, and economic policy. The relatively slow growth of the Belgian economy in the 1950s was due to problems with both export and domestic demand. The poor performance in export markets can be explained by the combination of an aging industrial structure and a deterioration in cost competitiveness. The defensive nature of investments froze the industrial structure at the same time as neighboring countries were renewing their productive capacity. The choice of a relative revaluation of the Belgian franc in 1949, just when the country's prosperity seemed established, hindered competitiveness and may have led to a vicious circle: the profit squeeze put pressure on wages and slowed investments, doubly depressing domestic demand, which in turn dimmed the prospects for profits. In such a deflationist climate the slow growth of imports gave way to a current account surplus which confirmed the central bank in its persistent choice of a strong franc.

Neither the Marshall Plan nor the European Payments Union, which responded mainly to the needs of large nations, could help Belgium to find a way out. By subsidizing Belgium's trading partners the Marshall Plan boosted Belgian growth in the short term but retarded much needed structural adjustment. Where a push toward industrial reconversion would have helped, Belgium received encouragement to develop its traditional exports. In the meantime other European countries – Belgium's competitors – could reconstruct and modernize with the benefit of direct aid of which Belgium received practically none. The European Payments Union did not suit it any better: whereas Belgium had the means for a rigorous and ambitious management of its exchange rate, it was tripped up by partial convertibility. Paradoxically, Belgium may have suffered from having achieved too early what the rest of Europe needed the Marshall Plan and EPU for: the restoration of a market economy and achievement of social stability. In other words, given the international context of the late 1940s, Belgium would have benefitted from an active industrial policy to complement social stability and exchange rate management. Only at the end of the fifties did the government take this path with the introduction of the Expansion Laws. These measures, combined with a return to the full convertibility of currencies and the integration of the European market, would contribute to the exceptionally strong Belgian economic growth of the 'sixties.

References

Banque Nationale de Belgique (1952), "L'Union Economique Belgo-Luxembourgeoise et l'Union Européenne des Paiements," *Bulletin d'information et de documentation de la BNB*, 2 (February): 85–103.
  (n.d.), *Statistiques économiques belges, 1941–1950*, Bruxelles.
  (n.d.) *Statistiques économiques belges, 1950–1960*, Bruxelles.
Baudhuin, F. (1958), *Histoire économique et sociale de la Belgique 1945–56*, Bruxelles: Bruylant.
Beuthe, M. (1964), *Economie en croissance lente. Le cas de la Belgique*, Bruxelles et Louvain: OBAP et IRES.
Bismans, F. (1992), *Croissance et régulation. La Belgique 1944–1974*, Bruxelles: Académie Royale de Belgique.
Bossuat, G. (1992), *L'Europe occidentale à l'heure américaine: le Plan Marshall et l'unité européenne 1945–1953*, Bruxelles: Complexe.
Camu, A. (1960), "Essai sur l'évolution économique de la Belgique," *La Revue nouvelle*, 11 (November): 397–418.
  (1961), "Essai sur la croissance économique de la Belgique (11)," *La Revue nouvelle*, 5 (May): 481–500.
Carbonnelle, C. (1962), "L'évolution de la production en Belgique de 1948 à 1960," *Cahiers économiques de Bruxelles*, 14 (April): 193–208.
Casella, A. and B. Eichengreen (1993), "Halting Inflation in Italy and France after World War II," in M. Bordo and F. Capie (eds.), *Monetary Regimes in Transition*, Cambridge University Press, pp. 312–345.
Cassiers, I. (1989), *Croissance, crise et régulation en économie ouverte: la Belgique entre les deux guerres*, Bruxelles: De Boeck.
Cassiers, I. and P. Solar (1990), "Wages and Productivity in Belgium, 1910–1960,"

Oxford Bulletin of Economics and Statistics, 52(4): 437–49.

Chlepner, B.S. (1956), *Cent ans d'histoire sociale en Belgique*, Brussels: Solvay Institut de Sociologie.

DeLong, J.B. and B. Eichengreen (1993), "The Marshall Plan: History's Most Successful Structural Adjustment Program," in R. Dornbush, W. Nolling, and R. Layard (eds.), *Postwar Economic Reconstruction and Lessons for the East Today*. Cambridge, Mass.: MIT, pp. 189–230.

Dupriez, L.H. (1951), "Pourquoi de hauts niveaux de rémunération en Belgique," *Comptes rendus des travaux de la Société Royale d'Economie Politique de Belgique*, February: 5–23.

—— (1978), *Les réformes monétaires en Belgique*, Bruxelles: Office International de Librairie.

Eichengreen, B. (1993), *Reconstructing Europe's Trade and Payments: The European Payments Union*, Manchester: Manchester University Press.

Eichengreen, B. and M. Uzan (1992), "The Marshall Plan: Economic Effects and Implications for Eastern Europe and the Soviet Union," *Economic Policy*, 14 (April): 13–75.

Frank, M. (1962), "L'évolution des revenus en Belgique de 1948 à 1960," *Cahiers économiques de Bruxelles*, 16 (October), pp. 483–521.

Fuss, H., P. Goldschmidt-Clermont, and L. Watillon (1958), "La genèse du projet d'accord de solidarité sociale belge," *Revue du Travail*, July–August, pp. 827–60, and October, pp. 1159–74.

Godts-Peters, S. (1987), "Le rôle des belges dans l'élaboration d'un système de paiements en Europe, de 1947 à l'Union Européenne de Paiements," in M. Dumoulin (ed.), *La Belgique et les débuts de la construction européenne. De la guerre aux traités de Rome*. Louvain-la-Neuve: Ciaco, pp. 87–102.

Groupe d'Etudes de la Comptabilité Nationale (1961), "La comptabilité nationale de la Belgique, 1948–1960," *Cahiers économiques de Bruxelles*, 12 (October), pp. 549–586.

Hogan, M.J. (1987), *The Marshall Plan: America, Britain and the Reconstruction of Western Europe, 1947–1952*, Cambridge University Press.

Janssens, V. (1976), *Le franc belge. Un siècle et demi d'histoire monétaire*. Bruxelles.

Kindleberger, C. (1987), *Marshall Plan Days*, Boston: Allen & Unwin.

Kurgan-Van Hentenryk, G. (1993), "Le Plan Marshall et le développement économique de la Belgique," in E. Aerts, B. Henau, P. Janssens, and R. Van Uytven (eds.), *Studia Historica Economica. Liber Amicorum Herman Van der Wee*, Leuven: Leuven University Press, pp. 157–172.

Lamfalussy, A. (1959), "Essai sur la croissance économique et la balance des paiements de la Belgique 1948–1957," *Bulletin de l'institut de Recherches Economiques et Sociales*, 2 (March), pp. 43–74.

—— (1961), *Investment and Growth in Mature Economies*, London: Macmillan.

Léon, P. (1977), "Guerres et crises 1914–1947," (G. Dupeux dir.), in *Histoire économique et sociale du monde*, vol. V, Paris: A. Colin.

Masoin, M. (1951), "Salaires et charges sociales en Belgique et dans les pays voisins," *Industrie*, January, pp. 7–12.

Milward, A. (1984), *The Reconstruction of Western Europe, 1945–51*, London: Methuen.

——— (1987), "Belgium and Western European Interdependence in the 1950s: Some Unexplained Problems," in M. Dumoulin (ed.), *La Belgique et les débuts de la construction européenne. De la guerre aux traités de Rome*. Louvain-la-Neuve: Ciaco, pp. 145–152.

——— (1992), *The European Rescue of the Nation-State*, London: Routledge.

Ministère des Affaires Economiques (1955), *L'économie belge en 1954*.

OEEC (1956, 1961, 1962), *Statistical Bulletins*.

Scholliers, P. (1993), "Strijd rond de koopkracht, 1939–1945," in *1940. Belgique, une société en crise, un pays en guerre*, Bruxelles, Centre de Recherches et d'Etudes Historiques de la Deuxième Guerre Mondiale, pp. 245–276.

Snoy et d'Oppuers, J.C. (1953), "Une révolution économique: la Belgique pays à hauts salaires," *Comptes rendus des travaux de Société Royale d'Economie Politique de Belgique*, 8–12.

Triffin, R. (1957), *Europe and the Money Muddle. From Bilateralism to Near-Convertibility, 1947–1956*, New Haven: Yale University Press.

Van Audenhove, M. (1990), *Histoire des finances communales dans l'évolution économique, financière et sociale de la Belgique: 1919–1985*, vols. I and II, Crédit Communal.

van der Rest, P. (1961), "Réalisations et perspectives de l'industrie belge," *Revue de la Société Royale Belge des Ingénieurs et des Industriels*, January, pp. 18–29.

Van Rijckeghem, W. (1982), "Benelux," in A. Boltho (ed.), *The European Economy: Growth and Crisis*, Oxford: Clarendon Press, pp. 581–609.

Waelbroeck, J. and E. Rosselle (1961), "La position de la Belgique vis à vis de ses concurrents du Marché Commun, essai de diagnostic économétrique," *Cahiers économiques de Bruxelles*, 9 (Janvier): 115–122.

11 France: real and monetary aspects of French exchange rate policy under the Fourth Republic

GILLES SAINT-PAUL

1 Introduction

French international economic policy after World War II was torn between principle and practice. The principles were provided by a set of newly established international institutions which sought to constrain the conduct of trade and exchange rate policy. The Articles of Agreement of the International Monetary Fund committed France to the maintenance of fixed exchange rates. As a signatory of the GATT and a member of the OEEC, post-war France was committed to the restoration of free trade.

Practice was based on urgency and, with hindsight, diverged markedly from principle. Given the burdens of reconstruction and two colonial wars, the French economy had to cope with exceptional challenges: chronic inflation and budget deficits, shortages of consumer goods, social strife, wage pressure, and the threat of capital flight. These problems led to a succession of balance of payments crises in 1948, 1951, and 1957.

As a result, France was faced with the choice of compromising its commitment to either free trade or exchange rate stability. It opted for devaluation between 1945 and 1949 and for trade controls in the subsequent period.

This experience suggests a number of questions which may be relevant to other contexts including that of the transition economies of Eastern Europe and the former Soviet Union today. What is the best international monetary arrangement for a period of reconstruction and reform? What is the optimal level for the real exchange rate? What is the most effective policy for defending the exchange rate? With what frequency should

I thank Barry Eichengreen and Georges de Ménil for comments and suggestions, Charlie Bean and Guy Laroque for data, and Moïses Orellana for research assistance. Financial support from the French Ministry of Research under grant "Analyse de l'Europe" is gratefully acknowledged.

devaluation be resorted to? What are the costs and benefits of trade controls? To what extent should foreign borrowing be relied upon?

These questions are among the most difficult in all of macroeconomics. The present chapter only attempts to provide some elements of an answer. It argues that there was little virtue to the pegged exchange rate system that prevailed during the reconstruction period. Pegged rates were incapable of preventing inflation, while the instruments used to defend them (capital and trade controls) hindered the resumption of growth. A higher level of foreign borrowing was feasible and would have substantially increased output and enhanced welfare. Reconstruction policy was "sub-optimal" in the sense that there was inadequate intertemporal consumption smoothing and private investment was too low. Simply eliminating capital and trade controls would not have been sufficient to insure that the optimal scenario obtained, however. Borrowing and investment still would have been depressed unless independent solutions were found to problems of political and monetary instability and inefficient financial markets.

Section 2 describes the balance of payments crises of the period. Using the theory of collapsing exchange rate regimes, it assesses the relative importance of various factors in these episodes. Section 3 takes a different approach to the problem of the balance of payments, asking what were the most appropriate paths for the balance of payments and the real exchange rate given the needs of reconstruction and the development of productivity.

Section 4 investigates the extent to which the restoration of free trade was hampered by controls. It compares France's experience with that of its neighbors and attempts to quantify the costs of French trade restrictions. Section 5 concludes by considering the political factors which conditioned the course of French international economic policy.

2 The anatomy of post-war balance of payments crises

Post-war France experienced three major balance of payments crises: the 1948 devaluation, the 1951–2 "Korean" crisis, and the 1957–8 "post-Suez" devaluation. Each was characterized by a rapid loss of reserves followed by adjustment. In 1948 and 1957 devaluation ensued, while in 1952 the crisis instead provoked a tightening of exchange controls and the suspension of trade liberalization measures.

We can consider these crises from the point of view of the literature on "collapsing exchange rate regimes" (also known as the "speculative attack" literature). Despite differences between the institutional setting it considers and the one which prevailed in post-war France, this approach remains useful for understanding the forces underlying these crises.

The theory of collapsing exchange rate regimes

The speculative-attack approach to balance of payments crises was pioneered by Krugman (1979) and subsequently developed by Flood and Garber (1984) and Buiter (1987), among others. Its basic insight is that a fixed exchange rate regime is bound to collapse so long as domestic monetary policy is inconsistent with the currency peg. If monetary policy is more expansionary at home than abroad, the country will lose reserves as the real exchange rate appreciates and/or spending exceeds income. When reserves are exhausted, it is no longer possible for the central bank to sustain the currency peg, and the economy shifts to a floating rate. A prediction of this literature is that speculators will not wait for the exhaustion of reserves to attack the currency. Recognizing that the exchange rate peg will ultimately be abandoned, they will attack the reserves of the central bank prior to their exhaustion. The timing of this attack depends on the relationship between the actual exchange rate and its "shadow" value. The shadow exchange rate is that which would prevail if there was an immediate shift to floating. As soon as the shadow rate exceeds the pegged rate, a speculative attack will occur, exhausting the remaining reserves of the central bank. The timing is determined by the fact that arbitrage in asset markets requires that the shadow exchange rate not jump when the transition to floating occurs.

How useful is this theory for understanding France's post-war experience? It suggests that the two main forces underlying the depletion of international reserves were trade deficits due to the appreciation of the real exchange rate and speculative capital flows attributable to differences in expected yields.

This theory makes two assumptions which do not fit the facts. First, capital controls remained in place after World War II. One should therefore expect trade deficits to exercise a more powerful role than capital flows. Moreover, restrictions on capital mobility might make it possible for the shadow exchange rate to exceed the actual rate without immediately leading to the exhaustion of reserves. A second assumption at variance with the post-war facts is that the attack on the currency peg causes a shift to floating. In fact, France's post-war balance of payments crises were not followed by floating (since such an arrangement would have been incompatible with the IMF Articles of Agreement) but rather by a devaluation or a tightening of controls. Wyplosz (1986) has shown how the standard speculative-attack model can be modified to accommodate repeated devaluations in an environment of capital controls. As he demonstrates, the relationship between the actual and shadow exchange rates remains the relevant criterion for determining whether a collapse will ultimately occur.

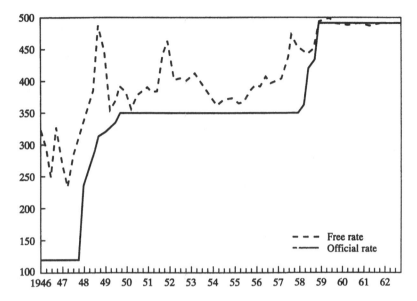

Figure 11.1   Official and free dollar rates
Source: Statistique et Etudes Financières.

Asset markets and exchange rate crises

In practice, capital controls were far from fully effective, allowing speculative capital movements to play a role in the country's monetary crises. This raises the question of the channels through which speculation occurred.

The idea that capital controls were not fully effective is evident in the behavior of the parallel market for foreign exchange and the money market. Despite regulations restricting movements in prices and quantities, prices in these markets still reflected underlying supplies and demands to a considerable extent. Figure 11.1 plots the black market rate for the US dollar along with the official rate. It suggests that the black market, despite its thinness, was an efficient predictor of subsequent changes in monetary policy. Each balance of payments crisis was preceded by a sharp rise in the black market rate. In the case of the 1948 crisis, the increase persisted beyond the devaluation by fully three quarters.

An alternative measure of market expectations is the interest rate. Figure 11.2 plots the French short-term rate and the US discount rate. It suggests that capital controls were less than completely effective in isolating French monetary policy from the outside world. Each of the three crises was preceded by a sharp rise in the interest differential, as if significant capital

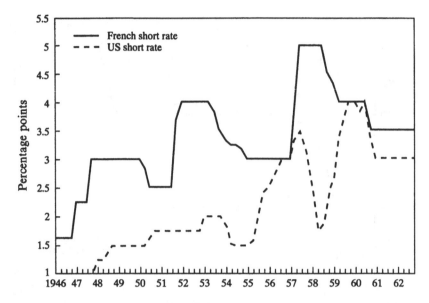

Figure 11.2   US and French interest rates
Source: Bank of England.

mobility occurred in response to a rising probability of devaluation. However, the interest differentials are smaller than if full capital mobility prevailed. Assume that if a devaluation takes place, the new official rate equals the pre-devaluation free rate. It is then possible to compute the implicit probability of devaluation by dividing the interest differential by the black market premium. This produces implausibly low estimates of devaluation probabilities, which never exceed 10 percent per quarter. This implies that capital mobility must have been imperfect.

Another fact emerging from figure 11.2 is that the French government had to maintain domestic interest rates above world levels for considerable periods following stabilization. Following the 1948 crisis, the increase lasted two years. This may reflect the expectation that the franc would have to be devalued a second time, assuming that sterling and other European currencies were eventually devalued themselves, as in fact occurred in 1949. In 1951–2, interest differentials remain high for a full year after the crisis. This fact may reflect the large budget deficits of 1952 and uncertainty about the effectiveness of trade controls. In 1958, in contrast, the interest differential drops at the time devaluation was announced, perhaps reflecting the greater transparency and consistency of the accompanying policies.

The free rate and the shadow rate

The free market for US dollars can supply us with a measure of the "shadow" exchange rate used by speculators to launch speculative attacks. Figure 11.1 suggests that crises were triggered by a rise in the free/official differential beyond a critical threshold. The question is what economic fundamentals were responsible for the movement of the free rate.

In Appendix I an econometric model is developed to explain the movement of the free rate. The results there support the view that the free rate responded to fundamentals in predictable ways. An extra point of inflation in France relative to the US tended to produce a 1 percent appreciation of the dollar on the black market. Faster money growth in France had an additional effect on the free rate, leading to an immediate depreciation of the franc even before showing up in faster domestic inflation. US interest rates also affected the black market premium in predictable ways.

These results can be used to gauge the relative importance of trade and capital flows in the genesis of speculative attacks. If capital controls had been fully effective, thus eliminating capital flows, the shadow exchange rate would be determined by the condition that trade would be balanced once the economy shifted to a regime of floating exchange rates and official intervention ceased. Only inflation differentials would drive the black market rate. In fact, the results tell us that there was also a speculative mechanism at work, since higher interest rates abroad and expectations of higher future inflation due to looser monetary policy also raised the black market premium. The model allows us to compute a time series for the shadow rate, which is plotted in figure 11.3. While each crisis was preceded by a rise in the shadow rate, this rise was smaller than the rise in the free rate, in accordance with the predictions of the theory.

Reserve losses and the shadow exchange rate

The theory of collapsing exchange rate regimes has the strong implication that when the shadow rate exceeds the actual rate, all reserves of the central bank will be eliminated. This was not the case in post-war France. The shadow rate was always above the official rate, and only when the difference between the two exceeded a critical threshold did a crisis occur.

Reserve losses, in other words, were more gradual than predicted by theory. As shown in figure 11.4, there was a negative correlation between the change in reserves and the premium of the shadow rate over the official rate. While this pattern is consistent with theory, there is no evidence of the kind of sharp non-linearity predicted by speculative-attack models with

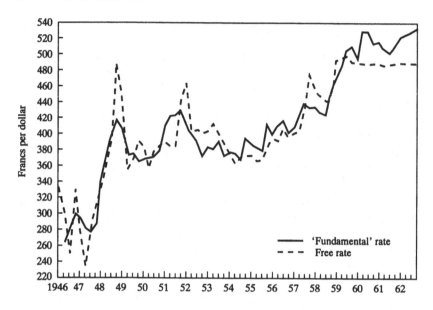

Figure 11.3   Free and "fundamental" rates
Source: Statistique et Etudes Financières.

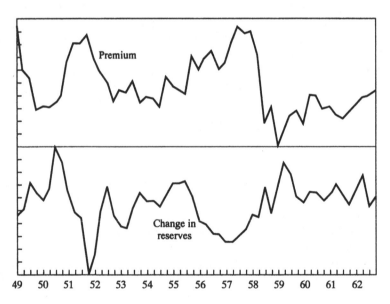

Figure 11.4   Reserve loss and premium
Sources: Statistique et Etudes Financières; Patat (1986).

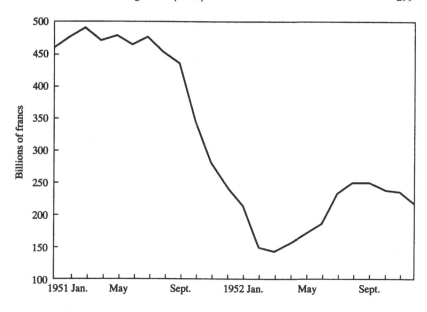

Figure 11.5   Reserve levels during 1951 crisis
Source: Patat (1986).

perfect capital mobility. This is hardly surprising given the extent of capital controls.

Using monthly data from 1950, figure 11.5 plots the level of reserves during the 1951–2 crisis. It shows that reserve exhaustion was in fact quite rapid. Again, this suggests that capital controls were far from fully effective. In comparison, the depletion of reserves was much more gradual during the Suez crisis but persisted for a longer period.

Factors contributing to the crises

There was no shortage of shocks to contribute to these crises: the Korean War, the Suez conflict, colonial wars, etc. While the gap between the free and shadow rates might be interpreted in terms of the impact of these events on confidence, I abstract from these considerations and focus on the contribution of the underlying economic factors suggested by the model in Appendix I.

Table 11.1 shows the change in the fundamental rate from peak to trough during each episode, along with the contribution of the variables considered by the model. It suggests that the 1947–8 crisis was due mainly to the sharp divergence between inflation at home and abroad. There is also a

Table 11.1. *Change in the "fundamental" rate and contributing factors during monetary crises*

	Change in fundamental rate	% contribution of		
		relative prices	money growth	US interest rate
I. 1947–8 crisis				
47.3 to 48.4	0.410796	82.11733	12.85766	5.024759
48.4 to 49.2	−0.11822	49.38252	50.61739	0
II. 1951–2 crisis				
50.3 to 51.4	0.150312	65.69842	32.01351	2.288718
51.4 to 52.4	−0.148350	69.96261	30.03803	0
III. 1956–8 crisis				
56.1 to 57.2	0.062771	32.60205	12.59230	54.805464
57.2 to 58.1	0.022823	367.5942	−131.932	−135.657

small contribution of money growth and of a rising US interest rate, but the behavior of inflation is key. Inflation continued, albeit at a slower rate, even after the devaluation. It was fueled by large budget deficits which were financed in significant part by money creation. Money financing was important because of the lack of an adequate fiscal infrastructure (the main administrative body for collecting taxes only having been established in 1948) and the difficulty the government experienced in issuing debt after the various capital levies that had been applied following the war.

Marshall aid was instrumental in slowing the post-war inflation by helping to underwrite government spending and thereby reducing the need for money creation. The first inflow of Marshall aid in the spring of 1948 was accompanied by a drop in the quarterly inflation rate, which had reached 25 percent in the first quarter, to 8 percent. Inflation did not fall further because there were lags and countervailing forces at work. Uncertainties about the evolution of monetary and exchange rate policy arose due to the fact that the 1948 devaluation violated the provisions of the IMF Articles of Agreement and interrupted France's access to Fund resources. This limited the government's capacity to defend the exchange rate, and in response a complex system of multiple exchange rates was established. Transactions occurred at a weighted average of different rates, with weights varying according to the type of transaction. In October 1948 free rates were given a higher weight compared to official rates, an initiative tantamount to devaluation. These policies were a source of considerable uncertainty, which by undermining confidence delayed stabilization.

Stabilization was marked by an appreciation of the shadow exchange rate. The inflation differential moved in France's favor and the rate of money growth slowed; together these developments account for about half of the underlying appreciation.

The factors which triggered the Korean crisis were an increase in the rate of money growth and a loss of competitiveness. They account for 30 and 70 percent of the deterioration in the shadow exchange rate, respectively. Their impact on the shadow rate was reversed by the Pinay stabilization of 1952, despite the persistence of a sizeable budget deficit. It is often argued that the Korean crisis was due to a rise in world prices (see, for example, De Lattre, 1959). Table 11.1 suggests that this view is incorrect: the crisis was due to the loosening of French monetary policy.

The real appreciation that occurred during this period reflected a relatively high inflation rate in 1951: inflation rose from 9 percent in 1950 to 23 percent in 1951. Only a portion of this acceleration can be attributed to the rise in world prices. The budget deficit, at 3 percent of GDP, was small by contemporary standards. But cyclical factors contributing to a high level of aggregate demand were important in explaining the inflation. After three years of real growth at a rate of 6 percent per annum, capacity constraints began to bind. Figure 11.6 plots the Beveridge curve (the relationship between vacancy and unemployment rates) as a measure of labor-market tightness. The vacancy rate peaked and the unemployment rate declined to its lowest level in 1951, indicating a very tight labor market which fueled demand-driven inflationary pressures. In addition, supply factors were important: March 1951 saw strikes in the metals industry and the public sector, which intensified the underlying wage pressure. Figure 11.7 plots an index of the "wage gap," i.e., the ratio of real wages relative to total factor productivity. This ratio increased sharply in 1951–2 and 1951–3, confirming the existence of an inflation problem.

The Suez crisis should be split into two phases. The first, from early 1956 to the *de facto* devaluation of October 1957, was characterized by a sharp increase in US interest rates. This was the main factor contributing to the franc crisis. In the second phase, there was a monetary contraction in France, accompanied by falling US interest rates. Even together, however, these two factors are inadequate to explain the contemporaneous movement in the shadow exchange rate.

Inflation picked up less quickly during the Suez crisis: it rose from 2.5 percent in 1955 to 5 percent in 1956, 8 percent in 1957, and 9 percent in 1958. As in 1951, cyclical factors were important: the budget deficit widened from 3 percent of GDP in 1955 to 4.5 percent in 1956 and 1957. The economy was at an extremity on the Beveridge curve, with very low

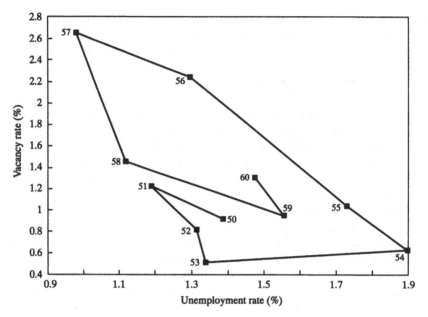

Figure 11.6   The Beveridge curve in the 1950s
Source: OECD.

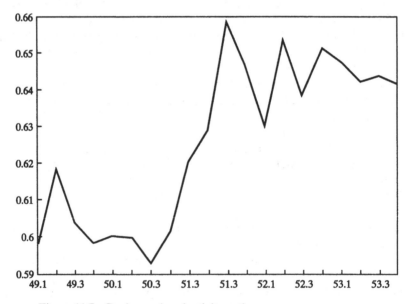

Figure 11.7   Real wage/productivity ratio
Source: OECD.

unemployment and high vacancy rates. In contrast, supply factors were less important than in 1951: wage push was less powerful. All this suggests that demand played a larger role in 1957 than 1951.

We conclude that while domestic inflation was the most important factor in the French balance of payments crises of the period, monetary factors giving rise to expectations of future difficulties also played a role. The question is through what channels the speculative pressures to which these expectations gave rise ultimately operated.

Channels of speculation

Despite the maintenance of capital controls, there was still scope for speculation on the capital account. Non-residents could decide whether or not to repatriate their assets. French firms could reduce their foreign borrowing if they expected a devaluation to occur. There was also French investment abroad: while these investments were subject to administrative authorization, authorization was generally granted, although the investor had to provide the foreign exchange. If this was earned by selling assets abroad, it had no implications for the central bank's balance sheet. But if it came from export revenues, it caused a reserve loss at the central bank. Furthermore, foreign currency was sometimes provided by the central bank for such transactions, as in 1951. While these investments were generally small, this was not the case in 1947 when they rose from $23 million to $120 million.

There was room for speculation on the current account as well. It was possible to disguise capital transactions as current account transactions by overinvoicing imports and underinvoicing exports. It was also possible to alter the terms of payment in foreign currency, while an importer would pay in francs.[1] De Lattre (1959) reports that the terms of payment reacted sharply to the 1957 devaluation.

Figure 11.8 plots the evolution of the terms of trade (the ratio of the import price deflator to the export price deflator) during the 1951 crisis. There is a deterioration in the terms of trade, which is consistent with over- and underinvoicing. While a similar terms of trade deterioration occurred during the 1957–8 crisis, it is explained by an increase in energy prices.

In a situation where there is reason to anticipate that the authorities will respond to speculative pressures by tightening trade controls rather than devaluing, importing durable goods is a better strategy than speculating on the foreign exchange market. In fact, each crisis was preceded by a sharp

[1] While this is in fact part of the capital account, it is difficult to put controls on this channel without restricting trade; capital controls were therefore ineffective in preventing speculation through the terms of payment.

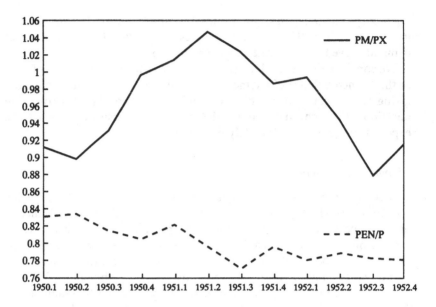

Figure 11.8   Import price/export price ratio versus relative price of energy
Source: *Statistique et Etudes Financières* for consumer durables; Laroque *et al.* (1990) for total imports.

increase in the share of consumer durables in total imports, followed by a drop as stabilization occurred. This spike is most pronounced around the 1957 crisis. Thus, the evidence supports the notion that imports of consumer durables were a major channel of speculation.[2]

3 Post-war reconstruction: a counterfactual simulation

Standard models predict that a war should be followed by an investment boom. Because the stock of capital has been depleted, its marginal product is high, thus encouraging investment. Consumption should drop only slightly, since expected future income exceeds current income, and consumption depends on permanent income. Consumption and investment in excess of current income should be financed by capital inflows from abroad, as the country runs a temporary balance of payments deficit. When

---

[2] A last point should be noted before we conclude this section: the fact that balance of payments crises were synchronized with the business cycle. The French economy was subject to a fairly standard business cycle during the period: three years of expansion followed by one to two years of recession. Interestingly, each balance of payments crisis occurred at the end of an expansion.

reconstruction is complete, consumption and investment decline relative to income. The nation repays its external debt by running a balance of payments surplus.

While this pattern is evident in France between 1945 and 1948, the extent of foreign borrowing was inadequate. No investment boom took place in the aftermath of the war: the requisite investment surge was delayed until the end of the 1950s. Consumption followed output too closely: there was inadequate consumption smoothing, particularly in the immediate post-war years.

Low investment was attributable to fears of expropriation created by the uncertain political climate, widespread nationalization, and an inefficient financial market (see Saint-Paul, 1993). Low consumption due to inadequate intertemporal smoothing reflected the stunted development of financial markets, which limited households' access to consumer credit. Little foreign borrowing took place, largely as a result of self-imposed restrictions: foreign borrowing by French firms was heavily restricted by government regulation, for example.

I quantify the losses caused by these distortions by comparing the historical evolution of the French economy to that of an "optimal" economy free of barriers to investment, capital inflows, and borrowing. I compute the optimal investment path, derive the corresponding paths for output and the capital stock, and compute the corresponding optimal level of consumption, the trade balance, and the real exchange rate.

Optimal investment

Investment following World War II was not particularly low by historical standards, but it was low in light of the fact that a significant share of the capital stock had been destroyed in the course of hostilities. To infer what investment should have been in an economy free of distortions, I estimate an investment equation for the years 1962–89 and simulate it over the preceding period (1946–59). Details of the estimation procedure are described in Appendix II.

Figure 11.9 plots optimal investment and compares it to the historical record. Optimal investment is always above actual investment. (The close coincidence of these two in the immediate post-war years is largely attributable to the presence in the specification of a lagged dependent variable.)[3]

---

[3] Since there is no accelerator effect in the neo-classical investment model on which the estimated equation is based (employment and total factor productivity are taken as given), the model predicts that investment should not have dropped in the 1952–3 and 1959 recessions.

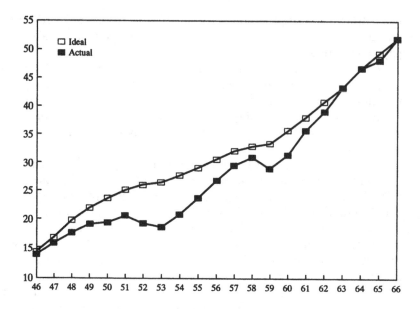

Figure 11.9   Actual and ideal investment (% of GNP)
Source: Laroque *et al.* (1990).

Optimal output, capital stock, and consumption

Given optimal investment, I compute the paths that output and the capital stock should have followed. The gap between the optimal and actual values peaks in 1956, when the capital stock was 15 percent below what it should have been and output is 4 percent below its optimal value. The gap subsequently declines as the end of the sample period is approached.

The addition to welfare that corresponds to the optimal investment strategy is the present discounted value of the additional output net of the present discounted cost of the additional investment. Assuming a real interest rate of 5 percent, this value is positive. The additional investment pays for itself, in other words. More precisely, the net present value of the optimal investment scenario in 1946 is equal to 20 percent of 1946 GDP. By way of comparison, the net present value of American aid over the same period amounted to 15 percent of 1946 GDP. That is to say, France would have been better off if instead of having the Marshall Plan it had created a post-war environment as conducive to investment as that of the 1960s.

Optimal consumption differs from actual consumption for two reasons. First, the economy would have been richer if the optimal level of investment

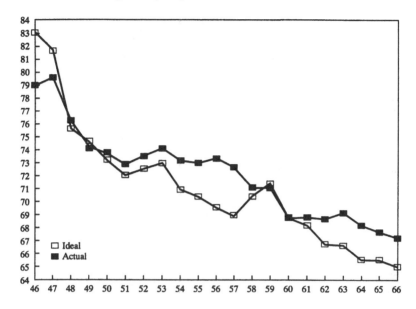

Figure 11.10   Actual and ideal consumption (% of GNP)
Sources: Laroque *et al.* (1990)

had been undertaken. This alone would have financed an increase in consumption of 1 percent per annum over the period 1946–66. Second, consumption smoothing was inadequate; consumption was too low in the early years relative to the later ones. In Appendix II I derive the optimal level of consumption, which is plotted in figure 11.10. It shows that consumption was too low in the immediate post-war years: consumption should have been 82 percent of GDP, even greater than the already high levels of 79–80 percent. Thereafter, actual and simulated consumption ratios track one another until 1952; note that this implies a higher absolute level of consumption in the optimal scenario, since output is higher in the optimal case. The optimal consumption/GDP ratio is 2 to 4 percent lower than the actual values from 1954 to 1966, with the exception of 1958–60.

The trade deficit, the real exchange rate, and debt

The optimal scenario implies higher levels of spending than those that actually obtained. If this higher level of spending had taken place, France would have run larger trade deficits at the beginning of the period and larger surpluses toward its end. Higher levels of spending would have

Table 11.2. *Difference between ideal and actual scenarios*

	Trade balance (% of GDP)	Real exchange rate (%)
1946	−4.97	−11.11
1947	−3.24	−7.11
1948	−0.98	−2.31
1949	−2.39	−5.76
1950	−2.23	−5.60
1951	−1.73	−4.63
1952	−2.92	−7.73
1953	−3.02	−8.25
1954	−0.76	−3.10
1955	0.77	0.52
1956	3.06	5.98
1957	3.83	7.82
1958	0.79	0.63
1959	−1.36	−4.69
1960	−0.77	−3.59
1961	0.82	0.49
1962	2.41	4.50
1963	3.48	7.25
1964	3.63	7.76
1965	2.66	5.47
1966	3.02	6.44

Sources: Figures 11.9, 11.10, Laroque *et al.* (1990).

strengthened the real exchange rate. (Because increased spending creates an incipient excess demand for non-traded goods, their relative price has to rise to clear commodity markets.)

The results in table 11.2 imply that France should have run larger deficits from 1946 to 1954 and larger surpluses thereafter. The deficit in 1946, for example, should have been 15 rather than 10 percent of GDP. In 1950 France should have run a deficit of 0.9 percent of GDP rather than a surplus of 1.3 percent. This implies that the real exchange rate was undervalued from 1946 through 1954. The extent of the undervaluation was small, however: it peaked in 1946 at 11 percent.

Trade deficits would have been financed by foreign borrowing. Despite the magnitude of the reconstruction task, actual foreign borrowing was limited: external debt peaked at 15 percent of GDP in 1949 and declined thereafter. Marshall aid was used to stabilize and reduce the debt as well as to replenish reserves. The optimal scenario implies larger but still moderate levels of external debt, which rise to 28 percent of GDP in 1950 and peak at 30 percent in 1953 before declining. Due to consumption smoothing, debt should rise in recessions and decline in expansions; hence the countercyclical swings of 1951 and 1957.

Welfare

Finally, one may ask by how much welfare would have been higher in the optimal scenario. It is possible to answer this question using the social welfare function of Appendix II. The estimate there is 160 percent of 1946 GDP.[4] Of this 160 percent, 20 percent is due to the net returns to optimal investment, while 140 percent is due to additional consumption smoothing.[5] This indicates large welfare losses due to restrictions on the availability of consumer credit and access to foreign borrowing. If relaxing these restrictions was feasible, doing so would have made the French as happy as a ten-fold increase in American aid.[6]

4 Trade and growth in the 1950s

A prominent characteristic of the post-war period was the worldwide rise in trade. As we have seen, France was constantly lagging in its participation, due to its reliance on trade controls to defend the exchange rate. There was no increase in the openness of the French economy over the 1946–59 period (see Saint-Paul, 1993).

Comparisons with other European countries complicate the picture somewhat. Here it is important to distinguish levels of openness and changes in that level. Table 11.3 shows the rise in openness to trade from

---

[4] This can be done as follows: first compute the utility level associated with the actual path of consumption, second compute the wealth level which would give the same utility level under consumption smoothing, third subtract it from the PDV of consumption expenditures in the ideal scenario.

[5] It is even possible to argue that the 140 percent figure is an underestimate: this is because the calibrated value of the intertemporal elasticity of substitution is high compared to what is suggested by econometric studies of consumption (see Hall, 1988; Deaton, 1992). This tends to underestimate the effect of consumption smoothing on utility; under perfect intertemporal substitutability, the intertemporal allocation of the gains from ideal investment would be irrelevant, so that the total welfare gains would drop from 160 percent to just the 20 percent associated with investment.

[6] It may be argued that the 5 percent value used for real interest rates was too large: real rates were typically negative during the period. With a lower rate, the net PDV of investment would be higher, consumption would be flatter, trade deficits and indebtedness would be higher. However, these negative rates prevailed in a period of highly regulated international capital flows. Given the large demand for world savings generated by reconstruction needs, 5 percent is not an unreasonable estimate.

Table 11.3. *Openness index in the four main European countries*

Year	UK	FRANCE	ITALY	GERMANY
1950	48.3	27.1	19.0	19.3
1951	58.5	30.8	22.2	23.2
1952	50.5	27.3	20.8	23.6
1953	45.9	25.4	20.8	24.1
1954	45.1	25.4	20.2	27.7
1955	46.5	25.1	20.6	29.6
1956	45.5	25.2	22.0	31.5
1957	45.2	25.0	24.3	34.1
1958	41.9	24.0	21.8	32.6
1959	41.7	25.0	22.1	33.7
1960	43.2	26.9	26.5	35.4

Note: openness index constructed as imports plus exports divided by GDP.
Source: OECD

1950 to 1960 for the four largest European countries. Openness is defined in the standard way, as the ratio of exports plus imports to GDP.

Judged by the level of openness, France did not do badly at liberalizing compared to Germany and Italy: its index is higher than that of either country in 1950. In terms of rates of change, however, the picture is different: whereas France's index declined, Italy's remained unchanged and Germany's rose markedly. The UK's openness index also declined but nonetheless remained considerably higher than that of the other three countries. One may conjecture that if trade controls had not been in place, France's index would have risen rather than fallen.

The question is how much was lost in the process. It is often argued that openness has favorable effects on growth (see Olson 1982, Grossman and Helpman 1991, Rivera-Batiz and Romer 1991a, b).[7] Table 11.4 presents cross-country growth regressions for the period 1950–60. The sample consists of twenty-two OECD countries. Iceland and Turkey are excluded, which reduces the number of observations but increases the homogeneity of the sample, thus reducing the likelihood of bias due to omitted variables. Several interesting results emerge. Changes in openness were important for growth in the 1950s, even after controlling for other determinants such as the investment rate. The level of openness, in contrast, does not appear to

---

[7] Whether this is a robust relationship remains to be established; it does not show up in Barro's (1991) regressions and is not included as a "robust" variable by Levine and Renelt (1992). This makes it all the more useful to investigate whether trade openness was an important determinant of French growth during the 'fifties.

Table 11.4. *Growth regressions, 1950–60. (Dependent variable: mean growth rate per employee, 1950–60)*

Independent variable	(1)	(2)
Constant	0.09	0.1
	(2.4)	(2.5)
LYW50	−0.0175	−0.0173
	(5.2)	(−5.3)
LOPN	−0.0022	—
	(0.7)	
DLOPN	0.12	0.14
	(1.6)	(2.2)
LI	0.022	0.021
	(2.7)	(2.6)
LG	0.009	0.01
	(2.1)	(2.3)
R^2	0.79	0.79

Notes: Both equations were estimated with OLS. *t*-statistics in parentheses.
LYW50 = Log of GDP per worker in 1950, at constant 1985 international prices. LOPN = Log of exports plus imports divided by GDP.
DLOPN = Average yearly change in LOPN between 1950 and 1960.
LI = Average log of investment rate during the period. LG = Log of consumption share in GDP.
Sources: For openness, OECD; for all other data, Summers and Heston (1991).

have exercised an impact. This is not surprising since most of the cross-country variation in the level may be due to the scale of the national economy and to geographical factors, neither of which is obviously a fundamental determinant of growth. The coefficient on initial income is similar to that obtained by Barro and Sala-i-Martin (1990). Government consumption appears to have had a positive impact on growth. This last result contradicts the findings in Barro (1991) and suggests that there are conditions under which government expenditure can enhance growth. (This would be the case, for example, if a large share of public expenditure is devoted to education.)

According to table 11.3, France was as open to trade in 1950 as in 1960, a period over which Germany's openness increased by 80 percent (or about 6 percent a year). Suppose that French openness had increased at 3.9 percent a year, with imports plus exports reaching 40 percent of GDP in 1960. According to the coefficients in the second column of table 11.4, the French economy would have grown by an additional 0.6 percent per annum.

Combining this with the gains from the optimal investment policy derived in the previous section (which implied an additional 0.38 percent of growth per annum), the results imply that France would have been 10 percent richer in 1960 if barriers to trade and investment had not existed.

5 Conclusion

What are the implications of this discussion of French international economic policy after World War II? First, there is little evidence that French monetary policy following the war was tightly constrained by the maintenance of a fixed exchange rate. Although monetary restriction was in fact used to defend the franc's fixed parity (as shown in figure 11.2), this was only one of a range of instruments on which the government relied. Not only were capital controls in place, but the authorities could supplement them with quantitative trade restrictions and even resort to unilateral devaluation, as in 1948. The availability of these instruments reduced the costs of inflation. As a result, monetary discipline was limited. This is not to say that monetary policy was no different than it would have been in the absence of a pegged exchange rate. French governments hesitated to resort to devaluation too often. They were aware that excessive reliance on trade controls reduced the economy's efficiency and slowed reconstruction. Thus, a pegged exchange rate served as a modest, but incompletely effective, restraint on domestic monetary excesses.

At the same time, policymakers faced a dilemma in choosing the appropriate level for the real exchange rate. Monetary considerations suggested fixing it at a low level in order to enhance competitiveness, accumulate international reserves, and minimize the danger of a speculative attack. This is evidenced by the gap between the "fundamental" and official rates depicted in figures 11.1 and 11.3. It was also argued that it was useful to have an undervalued exchange rate in order to develop the export sector as an engine of growth. On the other hand, intertemporal models of the balance of payments suggest that the real exchange rate should have been set at levels high enough to encourage consumption smoothing and cheapen the imports of capital goods needed for reconstruction. This view suggests that the exchange rate was excessively undervalued between 1946 and 1955.

A higher real exchange rate would have implied larger trade deficits, which France should have financed through foreign borrowing. It might be argued that there was no scope for further borrowing, given that most external finance in this period was negotiated directly between the French government and the US Import–Export Bank. Indeed, one of the aims of the Marshall Plan was to relax the borrowing constraint. But the French government was itself at least partially responsible for these constraints through its maintenance of restrictions on private borrowing. In addition, communist participation in the government increased the riskiness of lending money to France.[8] Whether self-imposed or not, limits on foreign borrowing severely constrained the pace of reconstruction and pushed the real exchange rate to unnecessarily low levels.

While this suggests that many of the problems analyzed in section 2 could have been avoided had France engaged in additional foreign borrowing, the dilemma may not have been so easily finessed. Given the inflationary problems that typically plague transition economies, it is important for policymakers to establish a reputation for preferring tough monetary and fiscal policies. A problem with the optimal policy described in section 3, which involves large trade deficits financed by foreign indebtedness, is that it resembles the strategy that an undisciplined policymaker would choose to pursue. This makes it difficult for the public to distinguish a temporary real appreciation generated by the imperatives of reconstruction from a chronic overvaluation caused by excessive spending by a lax government. The cost to the policymaker of establishing his reputation for monetary and fiscal probity may therefore be a relatively low level of spending and an undervalued real exchange rate during the transition period, like those which in fact obtained in France after World War II.

Appendix I A model of exchange rate determination

Consider a simple model of exchange rate determination under floating:

$$m_t = m_{t-1} + \mu + \varepsilon_t \tag{1}$$

$$p_{t+1} - p_t = -\phi(p_t - e_t - p^*) \tag{2}$$

$$m_t - p_t = -\gamma i_t \tag{3}$$

$$i_t = i^* + E_t(e_{t+1} - e_t) \tag{4}$$

where m_t is the log of the money stock, p_t is the log domestic price level, e_t is the log nominal exchange rate, and i_t is the domestic interest rate. Asterisks denote foreign variables. Equation (1) is a stochastic process for the money supply, which follows a random walk with drift. Equation (2) describes price formation. Prices are sluggish, and price changes tend to correct deviations from purchasing power parity. (One can obtain (2) by assuming that

[8] There was an unsuccessful attempt by the French government to borrow from the Americans in 1947. See Bossuat (1984). The riskiness associated with French loans is evident from the conditions imposed by the Americans on the use of Marshall funds. See DeLong and Eichengreen (1993).

aggregate demand depends on the real exchange rate through exports and imports and that prices rise when aggregate demand exceeds the equilibrium level of output.) (3) is a money demand function, where I have excluded output for simplicity. (4) is the uncovered interest parity condition.

This stylized model is not meant to be a realistic description of the French economy but to illustrate how different factors affect the shadow rate. One can solve it for the exchange rate using the method of undetermined coefficients:

$$e_t = (m_t^* - p^*) + a_0(m_t - p_t) + a_1 i^* + a_2 \mu \tag{5}$$

where $a_0 = (\sqrt{1 + 4/\phi\gamma} - 1)/2;$ $a_1 = 2\phi/(\sqrt{1 + 4/\phi\gamma} - 1);$ and

$a_2 = (\sqrt{1 + 4/\phi\gamma} + 1)/\phi(\sqrt{1 + 4/\phi\gamma} - 1).$

Theory predicts that speculators will compare the shadow exchange rate as determined by (5) with the official rate in order to determine whether or not to attack the currency. The shadow rate will depreciate whenever there is an increase in the money stock m, an increase in the price level p, an increase in world interest rates i^*, a fall in world prices p^*, or an increase in the rate of money growth μ.

The values which would prevail after the speculative attack has occurred are m and μ.[9] The attack is characterized by a discrete loss of reserves and consequently by a monetary contraction. In most theoretical analyses it is assumed that this reserve loss is not sterilized, i.e., that the money stock after the attack equals domestic credit. The appropriate fundamental for the shadow rate in (5) is therefore not the money stock but the level of domestic credit dc_t. Here I take another route and assume that reserve losses will be sterilized. This is the assumption consistent with the historical facts. After the attack the government will set the money stock according to a target in terms of real balances:

$$m_s = p_s + c \tag{6}$$

where s is the date immediately after the attack. I also assume that money growth will proceed at the same rate u after the attack. (6) then implies that at each date t the shadow rate is determined by:

$$\tilde{e}_t = p_t - p^* + a_1 i^* + a_2 \mu + a_0 c. \tag{7}$$

---

[9] This implies that there can be multiple equilibria if the attack is triggered by self-fulfilling expectations of a looser monetary policy under floating (see Obstfeld (1986)).

Table A1. *Regressions for the free rate (sample period: 1946.2–1958.1)*

	(1)	(2)	(3)
Constant	8.10	8.33	8.18
	(19.14)	(30.18)	(140.7)
LP	0.98	1.06	1.00
	(6.46)	(9.7)	
LP*	−0.91	−1.06	−1.00
	(3.95)	(9.7)	
GLM	2.34	1.99	1.85
	(2.66)	(2.75)	(2.77)
IUS	0.031	0.036	0.041
	(1.30)	(1.64)	(2.10)
R^2	0.8	0.798	0.751
DW	1.67	1.65	1.63
SSR	0.212	0.215	0.217

Notes: Dependent variable: log of the free rate; LP: log of French GDP deflator; LP*: log of an index of world wholesale prices; GLM: money growth; IUS: US discount rate. Regression (2) constrains the coefficients on LP and LP* to add up to zero. Regression (3) constrains them to be equal to 1 and −1, respectively. *t*-statistics in parentheses.
Sources: Bournay and Laroque (1979), Laroque *et al.* (1990) for LP and GLM, Jeanneney (1959) for world wholesale prices, Bank of England.

Equation (7) suggests that speculative attacks can be triggered by movements in home and foreign price levels, the foreign interest rate, or the domestic rate of money creation.

Equation (7) can be estimated using the free rate. Table A.1 reports regression results for the 1946.2–1958.1 period.[10] The first column reports results when the coefficients on home and foreign prices are allowed to differ. In column (2) these coefficients are constrained to sum to zero. In column (3) they are set equal to 1 and –1, respectively.

The coefficients on p and p^* are close to 1 and –1, and the sum of squared residuals indicates that the hypothesis that they are equal to 1 and −1 cannot be rejected by an F-test at conventional levels of significance. This suggests that deviations from purchasing power parity were used by participants to price the franc in the free market. Money growth and US interest rates display the anticipated signs, although the coefficient on the

---

[10] Extending the sample until 1962.4 gives very similar results.

latter is significant only when the constraint that coefficients on prices are 1 and –1 is imposed.

Appendix II The optimal scenario

Optimal investment

Our investment equation is based on the neo-classical model, which predicts that firms will invest so as to bring the capital stock gradually to its "desired," or optimal, level. This level is such that the marginal product of capital is equal to its rental cost. Investment therefore depends positively on the desired level of capital and negatively on its current level. Assuming a fixed interest rate r and a Cobb–Douglass production function, the desired level of capital is:

$$K^* = L(\alpha A/r)^{1/(1-\alpha)}$$

where α is capital's share of income, L is employment, and A is total factor productivity. The estimated equation (with t-statistics in parentheses) is:

$$I/K = -0.00087 + 0.4457Z/K + 0.7997(I/K)_{-1} \qquad (3.1)$$
$$\quad\ \ (3.5) \qquad\ (2.8) \qquad\quad\ (4.3)$$

where $Z = A^{1/(1-\alpha)}L$, and I have taken $\alpha = 0.3$. "Optimal" investment is computed by simulating this equation over the 1947–66 period, taking employment and total factor productivity as given.

Optimal consumption

We compute the optimal path of consumption by maximizing an intertemporal utility function of the form:

$$\sum_{t=0}^{T} u(C_t/N_t)/(1 + \theta)^t \qquad (3.2)$$

where N_t is population. Maximization takes place subject to the intertemporal budget constraint:

$$\sum_{t=0}^{T} (Y_t - I_t - C_t)/(1 + r)^t + W_0 \geq 0 \qquad (3.3)$$

where W_0 is financial wealth as of $t = 0$ (1946), i.e., the sum of net assets and the present discounted value of American aid. Under the assumption that u is isoelastic, the solution is such that consumption satisfies the Euler equation:

$$\Delta C_t/C_t - \Delta N_t/N_T = \sigma(r - \theta) \tag{3.4}$$

where σ is the intertemporal elasticity of substitution. The growth rate of consumption is unrelated to the growth rate of output. Empirically, however, consumption growth is equal to output growth and not correlated with interest rates (see Carroll and Summers, 1990). If one solves the preceding problem for given values of r, θ, and σ, consumption and output will diverge indefinitely. Since this is implausible, I calibrate the model so that consumption growth per capita as implied by (3.4), is equal to its actual average value over the 1946–66 period (3.8 percent a year). Setting r to 5 percent, this determines the relation between θ and σ. I set θ at 2.5 percent, implying a value of σ of approximately 1.7. This assumption will generate an optimal path for consumption which is not too different from the actual path.

In the actual data there is no reason to expect that the budget constraint (3.3) will be satisfied with equality. I therefore assume that W_0 reflects a "target" level of foreign assets as of the end of the period ($T = 1966$): that is, net foreign assets in 1966 must be the same as their actual value. Taking differences between the optimal and actual scenarios, the budget constraint can be rewritten:

$$\sum_{t=0}^{T} (\hat{Y}_t - \hat{I}_t - \hat{C}_t)/(1 + r)^t \geq 0 \tag{3.5}$$

where a hat stands for the difference between the optimal and actual. Optimal consumption is then determined by maximization of (3.2) subject to (3.5) with $\sigma = 1.7$ and $\theta = 0.025$.

The optimal exchange rate

The change in the trade balance is equal to $\hat{Y} - \hat{I} - \hat{C}$ and can be obtained from the preceding computations. The change in the real exchange rate can be derived with an estimate of the effect of the real exchange rate on the trade balance. The following equation was estimated by ordinary least squares for the 1946.2–1962.4 period:[11]

---

[11] *t*-statistics in parentheses and AR(1) correction for serial autocorrelation.

$$\text{Log(RER)} = -4.29 - 2.13 \, \text{Log(SPR)} \quad R^2 = 0.51 \quad DW = 1.95$$
$$(5.3) \quad (5.85)$$

where RER is the real exchange rate and SPR is the spending ratio (consumption plus investment divided by GDP). The coefficients are almost identical if (3.6) is estimated by two-stage least squares instead of OLS, using money growth as an instrument for SPR. -2.13 is taken as our estimate of the elasticity of the real exchange rate with respect to spending.[12] To compute the gap between the actual and optimal levels of the real exchange rate, I multiply the gap between the optimal and actual spending ratios by this elasticity.

References

Banque de France, *Statistique et Etudes Financières*, all years.

Barro, R.J. (1991) "Economic Growth in a Cross-Section of Countries," *Quarterly Journal of Economics*, 106(2): 407–44.

Barro, R.J. and X. Sala-i-Martin (1990), "Convergence," *Journal of Political Economy*, 100(2): 223–51.

Bossuat, G. (1984), "Le poids de l'aide américaine sur la politique économique et financière de la France en 1948," *Relations Internationales*, 37: 17–36.

Bournay, J. and G. Laroque (1979), *Comptes Trimestriels 1949–1959*, les collections de l'INSEE, C 70, March.

Buiter, W. (1987), "Borrowing to Defend the Exchange Rate and the Timing and Magnitude of Speculative Attacks," *Journal of International Economics*, 23: 221–39.

Carroll, C. and L. Summers (1990), "Consumption Growth Parallels Income Growth: Some New Evidence," mimeo, Harvard.

Deaton, A. (1992), *Consumption*, Oxford: Oxford University Press.

De Lattre, A. (1959), *Les Finances Extérieures de la France*, Paris: PUF.

DeLong, B. and B. Eichengreen (1993), "The Marshall Plan: History's Most Successful Structural Adjustment Program," in R. Dornbusch, R. Layard, and W. Nölling (eds.), *Post-War Economic Reconstruction and Lessons for the East Today*, Cambridge, Mass.: MIT Press, pp. 189–230.

Flood, R. and P. Garber (1984), "Collapsing Exchange Rate Regimes: Some Linear Examples," Journal of International Economics, 117: 1–13.

Grossman, G. and E. Helpman (1991), *Innovation and Growth in the Global Economy*, Cambridge, Mass.: MIT Press.

Hall, R.E. (1988), "Intertemporal Substitution in Consumption," *Journal of Political Economy*, 96: 339–57.

[12] Again, this tends to minimize deviations between the actual and optimal scenarios because the residuals from equation (3.6) are embodied in the implied series for the ideal exchange rate.

INSEE (1949) *Mouvement Economique de 1938 à 1948.*
(1959) *Mouvement Economique en France de 1944 à 1957.*
Bulletin Mensuel de Statistique.

Jeanneney, J.M. (1959), *Tableaux Statistiques pour la France et le Reste du Monde,* Paris: Fondation Nationale des Sciences Politiques.

Kindleberger, C. (1967), *Europe's Post-war Growth,* Cambridge Mass: Harvard University Press.

Krugman, P. (1979), "A Model of Balance-of-Payments Crises," *Journal of Money, Credit and Banking,* 11: 311–25.

Laroque, G., P. Ralle, B. Salanié, and J. Toujas-Bernate (1990), "Description d'une base de donn es trimestrielles longues," mimeo, INSEE.

Levine, R. and D. Renelt (1992), "A Sensitivity Analysis of Cross-country Growth Regressions," *American Economic Review,* 82: 942–64.

Obstfeld, M. (1986), "Rational and Self-fulfilling Balance of Payments Crises," *American Economic Review,* 76: 72–81.

Olson, M. (1982), *The Rise and Decline of Nations,* New Haven: Yale University Press.

Patat, J.P. (1986), *Histoire Monétaire de la France,* Paris: Economica.

Rivera-Batiz, L.A. and P. Romer (1991a), "Economic Integration and Endogenous Growth," *Quarterly Journal of Economics,* 106(2): 531–56.

(1991b), "International Trade with Endogenous Technical Change," *European Economic Review,* 35: 971–1004.

Saint-Paul, G. (1993), "Economic Reconstruction in France: 1945–1958," in R. Dornbusch, R. Layard, and W. Nölling (eds.), *Post-War Economic Reconstruction and Lessons for the East Today,* Cambridge, Mass.: MIT Press, pp. 83–114.

Summers, R. and A. Heston (1991), "The Penn World Table (mark 5): An Expanded Set of International Comparisons, 1950–88," *Quarterly Journal of Economics,* 106(2): 327–68.

Wyplosz, C. (1986), "Capital Controls and Balance of Payment Crises," *Journal of International Money and Finance,* 5: 167–79.

Part V

Synthesis

12 Post-war Germany in the European context: domestic and external determinants of growth

HOLGER C. WOLF

1 Introduction

In 1945 much of Western Europe resembled an economic shambles: bombed out factories and houses, a heavily destroyed infrastructure, and raw material shortages combined with dysfunctional monies to create a grim picture of the economic future. Experts viewed a rapid recovery to prewar consumption levels as optimistic: "The probable improvements over the next five years, or even in the coming decade, are not likely to bring about a solution of the basic economic problem of Europe – the severe poverty in which the majority of the European peoples live" (United Nations, 1948, p. 212).

In retrospect, the initial pessimism was unjustified, and spectacularly so: growth rates during the first post-war decade remain among the highest on historical record. Among the recovering countries, West Germany, initially written off as an all but hopeless case, turned in one of the most impressive performances (table 12.1), rebounding sprightly from post-war depths to more than double prewar production levels by the end of the 1950s, while integrating some ten million propertyless and homeless newcomers from the East. In the contemporary view the strong recovery was all the more surprising as the German government, under the liberal economics minister Ludwig Erhard, favored supply-side policies that often were the direct antithesis of the post-war Keynesian recipe for rapid growth (Wankel, 1979; Sohmen, 1959).

"Economic miracles" are again in strong demand today as the post-socialist economies of Eastern Europe embark on the long march toward a market economy. Many of the maladies haunting post-war Europe have returned to plague the new capitalist nations: large-scale unemployment, distorted production patterns, trade imbalances, and monetary disequilib-

I thank José Campa, Rudiger Dornbusch, Barry Eichengreen, Bruno Frey, Robert Kavesh, Karl-Hienz Paqué, Rudolf Richter, and Richard Sylla for helpful comments on this and earlier drafts.

Table 12.1. *Industrial production (1938–100)*

	1946	1948	1949	1950	1955
Austria	47	92	122	144	226
Belgium	89	122	123	125	156
Denmark	94	120	127	144	164
Finland	70	132	135	145	223
France	85	102	112	120	157
Greece	57	76	89	112	187
Ireland	109	134	140	172	202
Italy	54	102	109	126	195
Netherlands	72	114	129	141	190
Norway	100	124	132	148	198
Spain	125	128	130	145	159
Sweden	102	142	145	152	177
UK	105	110	118	124	148
Average	92	112	120	128	161
Germany	28	51	72	94	167

Sources: United Nations, Monthly Bulletin of Statistics, various years; IMF, International Financial Statistics, various years.

ria are providing a repeat performance. Faced with an old malady, there is a natural temptation to take a gulp of the old medicine. The German model in particular has been proposed as a panacea for the childhood illnesses of the transition economies. A solid application of the "classical medicine," the argument goes, will do much to revitalize the moribund economies. This chapter examines the prescription in more detail, starting with a look at some of the popular explanations of post-war German growth before discussing their applicability to the Eastern Europe of the 1990s.

The relative merit of rival views attributing a major effect to some factor x are difficult to assess in a single-country context. The historical discussion of Germany is hence framed throughout in the context of the broader experience of post-war Europe, using a cross-sectional data base covering Austria, Belgium, Denmark, Finland, France, Germany, Italy, the Netherlands, Norway, Spain, Sweden, and the United Kingdom. The cross-country perspective raises the question how much of recorded growth rates in various countries can be meaningfully attributed to the policies adopted there. The following section is devoted to this issue, arguing – in line with a substantial literature – for the need to distinguish between "soft" recovery-related growth in the initial post-war period and "hard" growth commencing in the early 1950s. "Soft growth" reflected the return to the prewar production levels and took place throughout Europe largely irrespective of the particular policies in place, with countries suffering particularly large production declines enjoying particularly substantial rebounds. Once recovery was completed, "hard" growth expanded the production possibility set. In preparation for the comparative study of the role of policies the growth data are hence purged of – to an approximation – the policy independent soft component to derive policy dependent hard growth rates.

The study of comparative policies begins with a look at internal factors, concentrating on two areas – the labor market and the capital market – of particular relevance for Eastern Europe. I then turn to both idiosyncratic and systemic external determinants before concluding with a discussion of the transferability of the experiences of the 1950s to the transition economies of the 1990s.

2 Soft versus hard growth

Writing after World War II, Keynes cautioned against excessive pessimism regarding wartime economic damage: "Popular opinion attributes . . . too much to the war . . . Fortunately, the accumulations of man's wealth are not in such shape that they can be quickly squandered. War exhausts contemporary effort, but it cannot destroy knowledge, or make an overdraft on the bounty of nature" (Keynes, 1922).[1] Some forty years later, Milton Friedman pushed the idea further, suggesting the following recipe for rapid growth: "Destroy the greater part of a nation's fixed capital in war activity and dislocate the whole economic structure. Eventual recovery from this chaotic state of affairs will be rapid, giving a growth rate of 8–10 percent annually."[2]

The likelihood of a rebound effect suggests a fruitful distinction between two types of post-war economic growth. *Soft growth* takes an economy from a state of underemployed resources back to full employment. *Hard growth* expands the full-employment production level itself. Soft growth is brought about by better coordination and use of existing resources; hard growth requires additional resource accumulation or additional advances in productivity.

Germany enjoyed a particularly large potential for soft growth: in 1946 output stood at 27 percent of the 1938 level while the available production resources had actually increased during the war. Annual net investment of 1.7 percent of GDP between 1935 and 1939 and 5.8 percent between 1940

---

[1] Keynes's remarks pick up earlier observations in the aftermath of the Napoleonic wars and the civil war in the United States.

[2] Cited in Klein (1961: 291). See also Janossy and Hollo (1969), Abelshauser (1975, 1983), Ambrosius (1977), Borchard (1982), and in particular Dumke (1990).

and 1945 exceeded bombing and demolition losses, while inward migration offset wartime population losses. By 1946 the capital stock exceeded its 1938 level by almost 16 percent with only limited reductions in the labor force.[3]

In contrast to direct productive capacity, the transportation and communication infrastructure suffered disabling if localized damage. The failure of these networks caused a major fall in production. The investment required to repair this damage was however small. Reconstruction proceeded rapidly (OMGUS, 1946; United Nations, 1947, 1948), and by 1947 the major constraint on production had shifted to the monetary system: a persistent monetary overhang, price controls, and quantitative restrictions rendered production of many goods unprofitable. On the eve of the 1948 reforms, the productive *capability* of the West German economic engine thus considerably exceeded its actual production, yielding the potential for extraordinary growth once incentives were restored. The reform program – combining a drastic monetary reform implemented by the Allies with a supply-side package encompassing price liberalization and a sizeable reduction in tax rates implemented by Ludwig Erhard – succeeded in eliciting the desired supply response: "It was as if money and markets had been invented afresh as reliable media of the division of labor" (Mendershausen, 1949).

Germany's particularly low starting point generated particularly rapid soft growth: in the first two post-reform years, industrial production soared by 42.8 percent and 26.6 percent respectively. While the 1948 reforms made this recovery possible, the *rate* of growth – as contrasted with the existence of a recovery per se – predominantly reflected the low starting point rather than the policy measures. The same stylized fact holds for most other European countries in this period, rendering the use of actual growth rates in a cross-country comparison of policies potentially misleading. Figure 12.1 plots labor productivity growth in 1946–50 and 1950–60 against the growth rate from 1938 to 1946 for the cross section of countries. The figure suggests the importance of soft growth in the immediate post-war period: countries suffering large output losses during the war experienced above average growth rates in the following five years, with a weaker link for the following decade. As a preliminary step toward assessing the contribution of policies to post-war growth, it is thus helpful to purge the growth rate of the soft component to derive an estimate of hard growth.

I calculate hard growth as the residual of a regression of actual productivity growth in industry on a constant term, on the growth rate

---

[3] See Krengel (1958), Kaldor (1945), and Roskamp (1964).

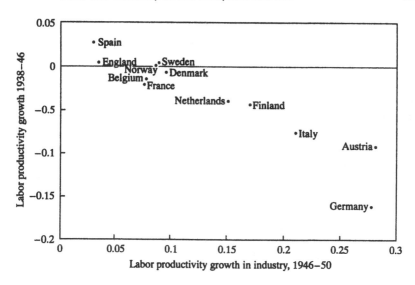

Figure 12.1a   The rebound effect, 1946–50

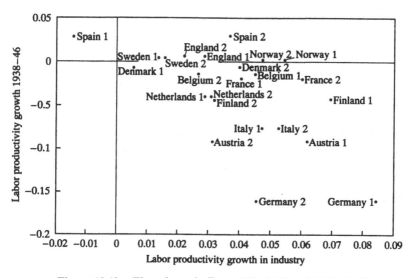

Figure 12.1b   The rebound effect, 1950–5 (1) and 1955–60 (2)

Table 12.2. *Hard growth rates (annual %)*

Country	1945–50	1950–5	1955–60
Austria	4.5	−1.5	−2.5
Belgium	−1.4	1.7	0.1
Denmark	0.4	−2.8	0.4
Finland	0.8	0.9	−1.9
France	−2.9	0.7	2.8
Italy	0.9	−1.3	0.8
Netherlands	1.9	−0.4	0.4
Norway	0.7	2.3	1.3
Sweden	1.0	−1.6	−2.1
UK	−2.8	0.6	−0.4
Germany	−3.3	1.2	1.0

Source: See text.

between 1938 and 1945, and on the initial relative productivity level. The former variable captures the rebound effect; the latter allows for catch-up of the initially less productive economies. The regressions (reported in table 1B in Appendix B) confirm the visual impression: the convergence and recovery effects explain a full 95 percent of cross-sectional variation in growth rates in the initial five-year period. Both effects however rapidly lose importance: the explained fraction of cross-sectional growth rate differences drops to 55 and 10 percent for the next two five-year periods.

Table 12.2 reports the estimated hard growth rates, calculated relative to the mean of all sample economies. Controlling for recovery and catch-up effects substantially alters the ranking. Norway, the Netherlands, and France exhibit above average hard growth rates, while the hard growth rates of Denmark, the United Kingdom, and Sweden lag behind the average. Germany's performance throughout the 1950s remains above average but is no longer extraordinary: both Norway and France enjoyed higher hard growth rates over the decade.

3 Hard growth: Germany in the European context

Post-war governments confronted many of the same maladies now plaguing the transition economies of Eastern Europe. Governments were challenged to convert industrial production from military to civilian use and to find employment for millions of workers released from the armed forces. Trade had collapsed and increasingly reflected political influences rather than comparative advantage. Years of price control and monetized deficits had distorted relative prices and brought about monetary disequilibrium.

Policy discussions took place against the background of the perceived failure of the capitalist system during the 1930s and the apparent success of the socialist model in Russia. A return to the prewar status quo hence held small attraction, regardless of political outlook. With some simplification, the reconstruction approaches eventually adopted grouped around two poles. The British and French model sought salvation in a greater role of the state in organizing and shepherding economic life. In this model, the government centrally coordinated investment – helped by the nationalization of key industries – used demand management to guarantee full employment, employed trade restrictions to insulate the domestic economy from external shocks, and used price controls to check the inflationary consequences of demand stimulation.

The alternative, the German model, de-emphasized the role of the government as a macroeconomic agent. Instead, the intellectual leaders of the ordo-liberal school around Eucken, Müller-Armack and – on the political side – Ludwig Erhard, dominated early post-war economic thinking in Germany and envisaged a return to the competitive ideal of the nineteenth century, though tempered by the provision of social support for those less favored by the market processes. To prevent a repeat of interwar disasters attributed to the erosion of competition, the government was to assume a new function as guarantor of competitive market structures. Yet it would shun demand stabilization and direct investment planning, limiting its activities to the provision of a stable environment facilitating private long-term decisionmaking. It was neither to engage in activist policies nor to offset the sanctions of the market. The ordo-liberals welcomed free trade as an additional source of competitive pressures for domestic producers and for the same reasons rejected restrictions on current account convertibility (Clay, 1950; Hohmann *et al.*, 1989).

The combination of Germany's high growth rate with the apparently sharp differences between German economic policy and the European norm spawned a rich literature attributing Germany's relative growth performance to her adoption of one or another supply-side policy. This interpretation raises some concerns. First, Germany's relative growth performance loses some of its luster if hard rather than total growth is the yardstick. Indeed, after controlling for the rebound effect the "competitive" German economy lags behind the "planned" French economy, suggesting caution regarding the laudability of supply-side policies. Second, disentangling the contribution of alternative supply-side measures is quite difficult in a single-country framework.

In the next sections I reinvestigate theories of post-war German growth, focusing on two domestic policy areas of particular concern to Eastern Europe – labor and capital markets – before turning to the external sector. To reduce the data problem, I use the hard growth rates constructed in the previous section as the basis of comparison. To mitigate the identification issue, I analyze the performance of the German economy relative to a cross section of post-war economies.

3.1 Internal determinants

Domestic explanations of the German miracle fall into two broad groups. The first focusses on the behavior of labor. In this view, an ethic of hard work and forward-looking union policies provided a climate conducive to investment. Labor behavior, in turn, reflected both exogenous factors – in particular large-scale immigration – and the government's refusal to adopt Beveridgean full-employment policies. The second set of hypotheses focuses directly on the incentives for investment, arguing that generous tax incentives coupled with a government philosophy encouraging competition and accepting a deterioration of the income distribution as the price of rapid reconstruction created the investment boom of the 1950s.

3.1.1 LABOR-BASED EXPLANATIONS

A number of authors have turned to the labor market to find explanations of Germany's growth. With some simplification, two groups of theories can be distinguished. The first line of argument focuses on the availability of a particularly skilled, motivated, and mobile labor force, enabling a rapid expansion of the German economy into the growth sectors of the 1950s. The second related group of arguments focuses on the effect of union and wage behavior on investment incentives. The next paragraphs examine both strands of the literature in turn.

From 1945 to 1953 the West German population increased by a quarter. Initially, the inflow was regarded with alarm: in an economy already close to collapse the inflow of some 10 million homeless and propertyless people further strained resources. Ten years – and eight million new jobs – later, the pendulum of expert opinion had swung 180 degrees; researchers viewed the availability of a large pool of qualified workers, willing to work hard to re-obtain their previous standard of living, as a boon to the West German economy. A number of specific contributions have been suggested:

> **Labor quality** Most of the newly arriving workers had passed through two self-selection processes: the initial decision to migrate and the second decision, upon reaching East Germany, to forego the social security of the socialist East for the social Darwinism of

Table 12.3. *Occupational structure*

	Absolute (thousands)			Percent of total labor force		
	1950	1960	Change	1950	1960	Change
Agriculture	5,191	3,544	−1,646	22.1	13.3	−8.8
Industry	10,499	12,900	2,401	48.4	48.4	+3.7
Commerce	3,734	5,303	1,569	15.9	19.9	4.0
Services	4,040	4,904	864	17.2	18.4	1.2
Total	23,489	26,653	3,164	100	100	0.0

Note: Percent totals may not sum to 100 due to rounding.

the West. These two selection processes implied a preponderance of skilled and motivated individuals among the immigrants entering the West German labor market. While quantification of the quality effect is difficult, Abelshauser estimates that the total inward transfer of human capital amounted to about 30 billion DM.

Structural adjustment The high sectoral and geographic mobility rates of the immigrants compared with the traditionally migration averse established workers significantly facilitated structural and geographical adjustment from a wartime to a peacetime economy and the ongoing reorientation toward industry during the 1950s (table 12.3), assuring potential investors of the availability of skilled labor.

Effort Wallich (1955) cites "hard work" as one of the causes of rapid growth in post-war Germany. The effort level was presumably particularly strong among newcomers aiming to re-attain their previous living standards. In terms of hours worked, the evidence on this point however remains rather weak: while average weekly working hours in industry increased from 39.1 in 1947 to 48.2 in 1950, they remained below prewar standards and did not significantly exceed those in other European countries. A more important but hard-to-measure factor might have been the effect on effort of the threat of unemployment, a sanctioning device lacking in the full-employment economies of Western Europe.

These arguments trace the German miracle to the availability of a particularly well-skilled, motivated, and flexible labor force. A second –

related – strand of labor-based explanations focuses on the impact of union behavior on investment: the 1948 reforms aimed to elicit supply responses by raising the return to investment, a strategy crucially dependent upon union acquiescence.

One line of argument (Kindleberger, 1967) views the willingness of the West German union movement to accept wage moderation and to strive for progress through growth rather than through redistribution as a major factor in Germany's post-war performance. The different behavior of German unions has been attributed to a range of factors. At the political level, the contribution of class struggle during the Weimar Republic to the emergence of National Socialism prompted a less combative bargaining stance. Second, while unions in victorious countries – in particular the United Kingdom – had "expectations of better things" (Cairncross, 1991), Germany, in the face of defeat and substantial destruction, could not offer such rewards, motivating instead a mentality of belt-tightening and sacrifice. Third, German unions may have faced constraints on their ability to bargain aggressively. A substantially higher unemployment rate (table 12.5) reflecting continued inward migration and the government's explicit refusal to stimulate demand by fiscal expansion created a buyer's market for labor, reducing union bargaining power. Lastly, the institutional reforms undertaken by Germany and the prevalence of comprehensive, powerful unions and employer federations facilitated the coordination necessary to make a forward-looking, low-wage, high-growth strategy feasible (Olson, 1982; Batstone, 1986).

Does the German labor market indeed stand out in the European comparison? Figure 12.2 plots the shares of wages in income and consumption in GDP against growth, documenting a negative relationship for both.[4] While the German wage share in income is close to the European average, the consumption share is the lowest for all three five-year periods. Table 12.4 examines the evolution of various wage measures. The nominal wage in Germany is seen to have increased at the European average. The low German inflation rate, however, translated equal nominal wage growth into a considerably faster growth of the real consumption wage of 53 percent compared to an European average of 26 percent. At the same time, the 88 percent growth in productivity more than offset the 53 percent rise in producer wages. Germany's labor share in GDP, while somewhat below the average, displays an above-average increase, suggesting a relative as well as an absolute gain for German workers.

Table 12.5 provides information on labor market characteristics. The

---

[4] A univariate regression of the hard growth rate on the wage and consumption shares yields coefficients of -6.04 and -10.43 respectively.

Table 12.4. *Consumption and product wages, 1960 (1948=100)*

Country	Wages	Cost of living	Wholesale prices	Consum. wage	Produc. wage	Productivity	[Labor's Share] 1951	1960	Change
Austria	206	167	138	123	149	159	72.2	73.1	+0.9
Belgium	154	121	110	127	140	143	69.1[a]	72.1	+3.0
Denmark	173	142	122	121	142	126	71.5	73.6	+2.1
Finland	196	170	170	115	115	166	74.6	73.4	-1.2
France	253	177	167	142	151	164	77.0[b]	72.3	-4.7
Italy	164	141	106	116	155	165	65.9	68.3	+2.4
Netherlands	164	138	120	118	137	135	68.2	67.5	-0.7
Norway	194	155	145	125	134	165	75.3	81.9	+6.6
Sweden	204	158	147	129	139	117	70.9	73.2	+2.3
UK	165	147	135	112	122	130	77.7	77.5	-0.2
Europe	187	149	135	126	139	151	71.8	73.0	+1.2
Germany	187	122	122	153	153	188	68.3	70.6	+2.3

Note: [a] 1953, [b] 1952.
Sources: See Appendix A.

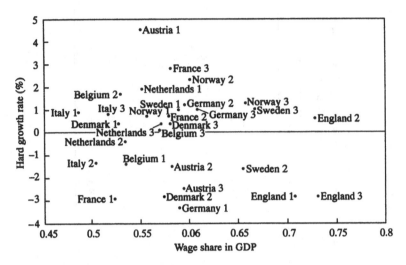

Figure 12.2a Wage share and growth, 1945–50 (1), 1950–5 (2), and 1955–60(3)

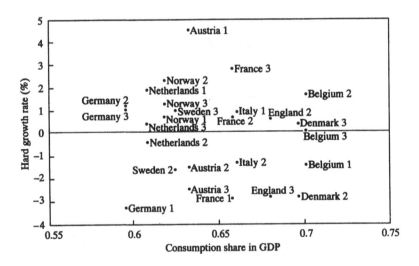

Figure 12.2b Consumption share and growth, 1945–50 (1), 1950–5 (2), and 1955–60 (3)

Table 12.5. *Industrial relations*

Country	Sclerosis index 0–100	Union power 0 or 1	Employer power 1–5	Strikes: days lost per worker 1950–60	Unemployment rate 1950, 1955
Austria	36	1	4	0.061	5.8
Belgium	61	1	3	0.462	7.4
Denmark	58	0	5	0.048	9.2
Finland	40	1	4	1.287	0.7
France	44	0	2	0.361	0.8
Italy	44	0	2	0.564	8.0
Netherlands	63	1	4	0.026	1.7
Norway	57	1	5	0.162	2.6
Spain	60	1	5	0.066	1.2
Sweden	63	0	4	0.160	2.4
UK	90	0	2	0.296	1.3
Europe	55	—	—	0.283	4.1
Germany	46	1	4	0.063	7.7

Sources: See Appendix A.

sclerosis index measures the age of institutions, taking a low value for defeated countries having undergone substantial institutional reform. The union power index takes a value of 1 if unions have *both* substantial coverage and power. Employer power, defined between 1 and 5, similarly measures the bargaining strength of employer groups. The strike intensity index measures the average days per year and per worker lost due to strikes.

In the European comparison, Germany is characterized by mild institutional sclerosis, powerful unions and employer groups, high unemployment, and one of the lowest strike intensities, providing some support for views attributing Germany's relative growth performance to particularly placid labor markets. The cross-country perspective also provides moderate support for the coordination view: two of the top three performers (Austria and Germany) have both strong unions and strong employer groups; their strike losses (0.061 and 0.063) lie substantially below the group average of 0.283, as does their sclerosis index (36 and 46 versus 55).

The comparative importance of these factors is further examined by regression analysis. Table 2B in Appendix B reports a cross-sectional

Table 12.6. *Savings and investment rates*

	Savings rate 1950–8			Investment rate average of 1950, 1955, 1960
	Total	Households	Firms	
Austria	21.4	13.6	7.8	20.7
Belgium	17.6	7.6	10.0	16.8
Denmark	18.6	11.1	7.5	17.1
Finland	26.7	19.6	7.1	NA
France	18.1	7.0	11.1	17.3
Italy	19.3	NA	NA	19.9
Netherlands	25.5	11.2	14.3	22.0
Norway	27.3	NA	NA	28.2
Sweden	21.2	9.5	11.7	20.2
UK	15.2	4.0	11.2	14.5
Europe	21.5	10.4	10.6	19.9
Germany	25.9	10.8	15.1	21.9

Note: NA: Not available.
Source: United Nations (1964: IV: 8).

regression of real wage growth on labor market characteristics.[5] Productivity growth is strongly correlated with real wage growth, with a coefficient substantially below unity. In contrast, neither union coverage nor union power exerts a significant influence. The negative although insignificant link between real wage growth and the investment share provides some support for the view of a wage-restraint–investment social contract. The coefficients on institutional sclerosis, unemployment, and the dummy for defeated countries have the predicted signs although they are insignificant.

3.1.2 CAPITAL-BASED EXPLANATIONS

Capital-based explanations of German growth experience fall into two complementary groups. The first focuses on the specific incentives for investment set by the government; the second regards the world view underlying specific policy decisions as an important independent contributor to a healthy investment climate.

The first strand of the argument points to the role of low tax rates on

---

[5] The sample divides into three subsamples (1945–50, 1950–5, 1955–60), yielding a total of thirty-six potential observations for the twelve-country dataset. Both this and the following regressions are potentially plagued by endogeneity of right-hand side variables. Lack of data precluded IV estimation.

reinvested profits and high rates on disbursed profits, special tax breaks for replacement of war damaged capital, subsidies for investment in key sectors, tax exemptions for employee capital formation, and life insurance premia in encouraging both investment and savings rates that, although not exceptional, were among the highest in Europe (table 12.6).

The second strand argues that current incentives by themselves were insufficient to elicit long-term investment responses, pointing to the importance of a stable macroeconomic framework as an additional major stimulant of investment. The importance of long-term stability was particularly pronounced in Germany because domestic and international capital markets proved unable to satisfy financing needs, making sensitive retained earnings the main source of funds: in 1948–9 retained earnings financed a full 83.5 percent of investment, a fraction declining slowly to 54 percent by 1953 (table 12.7). Stringent fiscal policies and the pursuit of hard money, constitutional constraints on borrowing,[6] and the independence of the central bank provided the necessary assurance of long-term financial stability conducive to investment decisions. Finally, the competitive economic philosophy espoused by the government, favoring medium size enterprises and opting for unilateral liberalization, is held to have complemented incentives by facilitating challenges from new entrants and raising the potential cost of underinvestment.

In this view, competitive pressures in a stable environment created the incentive for innovation and exploitation of new profit opportunities, permitting Germany to move rapidly into new markets.[7]

The regressions reported in table 2B in Appendix B go some way toward disentangling the various effects.[8] While the relative few degrees of freedom and the likely endogeneity of several explanatory variables suggest caution in interpreting the regressions, the results are suggestive of substantial supply-side and institutional effects. Other than the (insignificant) corporate tax rate, the variables enter with the expected sign. Higher real interest rates, a higher degree of institutional sclerosis, and political fractionalization all reduce the investment ratio. A fall in unit labor costs and a higher debt service ratio – proxying the development of the domestic capital market – raise the investment share. The labor market view, emphasizing the long-term horizon of the unions, finds less support: higher union power and coverage are found to reduce investment, while a higher level of employer power increases investment, suggesting a relative bargaining power explanation.

[6] Article 115 of the Basic Law restricts new borrowing to the level of public investment.
[7] Boarman (1964), Reuss (1963), Sohmen (1959).
[8] Missing information, in particular on the real long-term interest rate, reduced the effective number of observations to nineteen.

Table 12.7. *Investment and savings (% of total)*

Source	1948–9	1949	1950	1951	1952	1953	6.4–53
			Investment: sources of funds				
Capital market	4.4	9.5	12.0	8.7	12.0	20.6	12.1
Budget funds	11.1	18.0	17.0	18.8	21.1	22.8	18.9
Public programs	1.0	3.1	12.1	3.7	2.9	2.6	4.0
Self-financing	83.5	69.0	58.9	68.8	64.0	54.0	65.0
			Savings: composition				
Private household			17.5	12.1	20.0	23.2	
Retained earnings			44.3	57.5	48.6	38.2	
Public household			26.0	25.9	30.5	38.7	
External finance			12.2	4.5	0.8	−0.1	

Note: First column June 1948 to June 1949.
Second column June 1949 to December 1949.

Table 12.8. *Trade volume per capita (1936 = 100)*

	Import	Export
1950	88	74
1952	107	112
1954	144	151
1956	196	200
1958	230	230

Source: Gleitze (1960: 178).

3.2 External determinants

Previous sections identified a number of suggestive internal causes of German post-war growth. Most students of post-war German economic history emphasize external factors as important additional determinants of growth (Wallich, 1955; Giersch *et al.*, 1991, 1992). A first glance at the data indeed suggests a link between rapidly growing trade (table 12.8) and production.

However, a simple export-led-growth explanation does little justice to the complex web of factors fueling Germany's post-war growth. First, external trade, like production, experienced a strong rebound effect. Second, while absolute trade grew rapidly, the trade share remained below interwar levels: in 1938 Germany accounted for 9.4 percent of world trade, in 1952 for only 5.4 percent. Third, cross-country comparisons do not suggest a pronounced link between export performance and growth. Figure 12.3 plots export shares against growth, revealing a much weaker relationship than that observed for investment shares.[9] Nevertheless, external developments undoubtedly played a major role in determining Germany's post-war growth. In evaluating the role of external factors, it is useful to distinguish between features specific to Germany and systemic factors affecting all of Europe.

3.2.1 IDIOSYNCRATIC FACTORS

In the first post-war decade, Germany was twice favored by fortune. First, Germany's long-standing specialization in investment goods met a pent up demand for such goods once the post-war reconstruction got underway, generating a trend improvement in the terms of trade. Second, the Korean boom, coming at a time when the other European economies had reached

---

[9] A univariate regression of hard growth against the export and investment shares yields coefficients of 1.58 and 9.41, respectively.

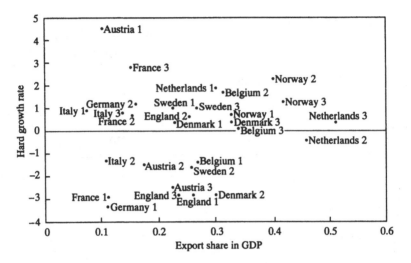

Figure 12.3a   Export share and growth, 1945–50(1), 1950–5(2), and 1955–60(3)

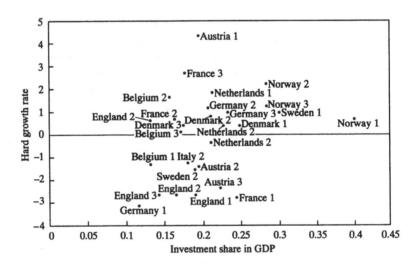

Figure 12.3b   Investment share and growth, 1945–50(1), 1950–5(2), and 1955–60(3)

their goal of full employment, provided a major stimulus to a German economy plagued by excess capacity.

While these two developments were exogenous, the ability of German enterprises to exploit fortune's offerings were significantly enhanced by government policy. The decision to forego full-employment policies forced German firms to seek external markets, a challenge spared enterprises in the full-employment economies. On the monetary side, tight money policies produced low inflation and hence a real depreciation throughout the 1950s *vis-à-vis* Germany's trading partners. The willingness of the German government to pursue unilateral trade liberalization meanwhile increased competition for domestic enterprises and encouraged complementary trade liberalization by Germany's main trading partners.

3.2.2 SYSTEMIC FACTORS

Domestic policies and fortuitous external shocks go some way toward explaining comparative German performance. However, a second feature deserves attention: while German growth in the post-war decade was above the European average, so was the European average itself above the historical norm. A sizeable literature attributes this performance at least partly to the role played by international institutions, in particular to the adjustment assistance provided by the European Recovery Program (ERP), to the trade-creating function played by the European Payments Union (EPU), and to the trade liberalization progress made under the GATT.

In one prominent line of analysis (Hogan, 1987; Maier, 1987), the ERP acted as the catalyst shifting a Europe increasingly mired in recession onto the growth path of the 1950s by financing the import of bottleneck resources, providing funds for additional private and public-sector investment, and revitalizing European trade. The revisionist view points to the timing and small absolute amount of ERP aid to argue against a major role. DeLong and Eichengreen (1993) concur on the small quantitative influence of the ERP but contend that the ERP nevertheless played a major role by providing an initial boost and critical income support during painful reform and more importantly by shifting the political equilibrium in Europe from economic nationalism and interventionism to the acceptance of (relatively) free markets and trade.

In the end, the European Recovery Program probably played a rather minor role for Germany along both of these avenues. The relatively small amount of aid received, and the late date at which deliveries arrived (table 12.9) limited the significance of the resource transfer: as a fraction of imports, ERP aid amounted to 37 percent in 1949 but declined rapidly to 18 percent in 1950, 12 percent in 1951, and 3 percent in 1952. On the liberalization front, the German authorities needed little prodding by the

Table 12.9. *Composition of ERP/Mutual Security Act imports* (*$ millions*)

	Foodstuff fodder, seeds	Industrial raw materials	Machinery, vehicles	Freight
1948/9	213	135	8	32
1949/50	175	202	9	29
1950/1	196	240	13	31
1951/2	76	100	8	26
1952/3	24	38	2	4
Total	683	719	36	121

Source: Bundesminister für den Marshallplan.

Allies to adopt free-market policies. Indeed, external opinion often attempted to slow or reverse the liberalization process in Germany, in particular during the 1949/50 crisis (UNECE, 1949).

Rather, Germany may have benefitted by the ERP through more indirect channels. By prodding more interventionist governments toward liberalization, the ERP increased the payoff to the liberal policies adopted by Germany: "A genuine market economy cannot stop short at the national frontiers: it tends to abolish its own frontiers and thus provides powerful inducements to others to reciprocate. A market economy cannot flourish as an island in a sea of controlled economies." (Erhard, 1954, p. 26). Second, by providing particularly generous support to France and the United Kingdom, the ERP facilitated an early resolution of the reparations question. Third and perhaps most importantly, the ERP served to reintegrate "outcast" Germany into Western Europe, with strong beneficial effects on the long-term outlook for potential investors.

Much the same argument applies to the European Payments Union and the GATT. Following the free trade tenet of the ordo-liberal approach, the German government had opted to pursue unilateral liberalization and was committed to early convertibility. The benefit for Germany from participating in the EPU and the GATT may thus again be found in the significance it attached to the liberalization process in the more intervention-prone economies and in the political benefits of European integration.

By ensuring a *coordinated* return to a liberal economic system, the EPU and the ERP almost certainly raised European growth rates relative to the levels likely had bilateral clearing and interventionism continued. Yet the appropriate yardstick for evaluating the contribution of the ERP is the growth path under the institutions that would have been adopted in the absence of the ERP and the EPU. While an assessment of the likelihood and potential success of an uncoordinated liberalization is necessarily highly speculative, two points deserve mention.

First, despite some setbacks, performance during 1945–7 compares favorably with that during 1918–20, suggesting that stagnation may well be the wrong yard stick against which to evaluate the performance of the ERP (Milward, 1984). Second, while the United States used the leverage provided by ERP aid to achieve substantial liberalization in some fields, the financial support provided by the ERP and the credits provided by the EPU weakened the incentive for reform in other sectors. Internally, counterpart funds permitted continued expansion in the bottleneck industries coal, steel, and transportation. Yet the scarcity of domestic investment in these sectors reflected continued price controls rendering investment unprofitable; the ERP thus acted as a brake on further liberalization in these sectors.

Externally the EPU exerted one-sided pressure on surplus countries to unilaterally liberalize while granting resources to debtor countries, facilitating the postponement of unpopular reforms; hence the ERP may have postponed current account convertibility.

4 Germany 1948: a role model for the 1990s?

Nothing of the swindle of the past should be allowed to survive – even the last illusion had to be destroyed. Ludwig Erhard[10]

The starting conditions facing Western Europe in 1945 and Eastern Europe today share many common elements, notably pervasive government intervention in production and exchange, dysfunctional monetary systems, and managed external trade. The similarity of the afflictions tempts one to prescribe the same medicine. Indeed, the standard recipe for successful transition in the 1990s is remarkably similar to the ordo-liberal prescription of 1948 – liberalization, privatization, fiscal stringency, and monetary orthodoxy. The prescription is problematic on several counts.

First, the similarity of the symptoms hides substantial differences in the underlying affliction. The immediate challenge facing Western Europe in 1945 was to revive temporarily dysfunctional but fundamentally sound market economies. The challenge confronting today's transition economies is more daunting. A large part of the inherited industrial structure is obsolete, requiring extensive structural adjustment, including the shrinkage of inefficient sectors. While Western Europe could achieve growth by

---

[10] Commenting on the 1948 reforms, cited in Domes and Wolffsohn (1978).

bringing mothballed or slightly damaged factories back on stream, Eastern Europe will have to construct entire sectors from scratch. While Western Europe already operated close to best practice, Eastern Europe has to overcome decades of technological backwardness. While Western Europe could rely on established market-experienced administrations, Eastern Europe must rebuild institutions. While Western Europe could revive long-standing trade links, Eastern Europe must build foreign market positions from scratch.

Second, the free-market mystique surrounding the German economic miracle hides substantial – though limited in the European context – intervention. Among other measures the German government maintained restrictions on current account convertibility for a decade after the 1948 monetary reform, retained controls in key industrial sectors – notably coal and steel – and used counterpart funds as an instrument of industrial policy.

Going beyond this *ex post* filtering of the post-war success stories, a prior that policies proven successful in reviving temporarily dysfunctional market economies are automatically also conducive to achieving a successful transition from planned to market economies is unwarranted. Questioning this assumption raises several issues for the current reform debate.

Balanced policies Post-war reconstruction saw a tendency for relatively one-sided policies. While the economies following supply-side policies on average outperformed their demand-oriented neighbors, with hindsight their success depended crucially on the fortuitous presence of positive demand shocks.

Looking back, one cannot help being struck by the uneasy balance between recovery and growth objectives. Governments advocating full-employment policies succeeded in bringing about a rapid return to full capacity utilization, in marked contrast to the post-World War I experience that hampered structural change. The more liberal economies in contrast found the return to full employment to be more difficult but experienced somewhat higher growth once the Korean boom fortuitously delivered the initial demand boost their governments refused to provide.

The costs of equality In the 1990s as in the 1950s, limited external funds imply that domestic savings will constrain capital accumulation. Backlogs of postponed consumption will limit consumer savings. A desire for high investment then requires accumulation by the wealthy, confronting society with the choice between equality and growth. The 1948 reform was a deliberate attempt to create incentives for the economically strong to accumulate, in the expectation that they would pull along the weak. While a social safety net ensured survival, payments were small: the German reform was a harsh social experiment. The outcome suggests, however, that rapid increases in absolute income can, at least temporarily, mitigate social conflicts arising from a worsening distribution.

Capital markets Today's standard recipe for Eastern European revival places substantial emphasis on the creation of sophisticated financial markets. Inadequate market depth and assorted information problems will however severely restrict the potential role of capital markets in the foreseeable future. The German experience suggests that reliance on traditional finance sources, in particular retained earnings and short-term bank credit, can successfully bridge the period until financial markets can fulfill their role.

Speed of reforms The last years have seen a spirited debate on the merits of gradual versus radical reform. The received wisdom in the early post-war years viewed radical reform as an invitation for disaster, advocating instead a gradual relaxation of controls. The expectations for Germany's 1948 reforms were thus muted at best: "When we changed course in 1948 almost nobody believed in the success of the measures. The statistics, the calculations and all planning considerations suggested incontrovertibly that it would be impossible to introduce, from today to tomorrow, economic freedom in an economy and a market which had nothing left to offer."[11] The *ex post* success of the German package thus illustrates the power of incentives.

Coordination In uncertain political situations, coordination problems may hamper investment: the individual wealthholder refrains from committing irretrievable funds to real investment until reasonably certain of the success of the program, yet this very success in turn depends on the amount of new investment.[12] Most Western European governments chose to address the coordination problem by interventionist measures ranging from nationalization of key sectors to indicative plans with investment incentives. Erhard chose the market mechanism, attempting to achieve coordination by concentrating the systemic change on a single date to achieve a shift in "animal spirits." The strategy succeeded, yet it was fraught with risk: what if enterprises had adopted a wait-and-see attitude on 21 June? What if union leaders had been more

---

[11] Speech by Erhard in Stockholm, November 2, 1953, cited in Hunold (1957).
[12] See Laban and Wolf (1993).

militant in the fall of 1948? What if the Korean War had not occurred? While answers to these questions are necessarily conjectures, they point to the risk of exclusive reliance on the market.

Political support A closer look at German reform experience throws a somewhat more positive light on the performance of today's reformers. The German "miracle" has become inextricably intertwined with the spectacular change occurring on the weekend of the currency reform: the sudden abundance of goods in previously empty shop windows has entered economic lore. The focus on June 1948 renders the contrast with today's reforming economies sobering. The view of German post-war growth as a linear process commencing with the currency reform is however misleading. The reconstruction period is better described as a time of repeated setbacks and confidence crises interspersed with timely interventions of fortune, with a shift toward steady growth not occurring before 1952, some four years after the initial rebound.

Nor is the current skepticism of Eastern European populations regarding the merits of the market a novel feature. Inflation and rising unemployment rapidly eroded popular support for the continuation of the Erhard reforms. Asked in December of 1948 whether price controls should be re-instituted, 70 percent of the respondents answered yes, and only 20 percent endorsed free prices (Noelle and Neumann, 1956, p. 155). Table 12.10 reveals that public esteem for Erhard remained quite limited until 1953, reflecting the lagged effect of the reforms on (perceived?) living standards.

What, then, does post-war experience suggest for the fate of the transition economies of Eastern Europe? Not unlike 1945, a significant part of the current decline in production reflects temporary disorganization rather then permanent loss of factor supplies, a consequence of the near complete depreciation of organizational capital after the switch to markets. Charles Kindleberger's assessment of post-war Germany's malaise: "Most fundamental and general, overshadowing the more specific causes, is a failure of organization"[13] describes Eastern Europe well. Now as then, a limited "recovery" will occur and is indeed on the way in Poland and east Germany and beginning in the Czech Republic. Whether matters will stop there – as they did in 1950s Britain – will depend on the structural policies adopted in the near future.

What advice can be given to the reforming country searching for the

[13] Kindleberger (1947).

Table 12.10. *Public opinion in post-war Germany*

Date	Opinion of Erhard		⌈Perceived change in living standard[a]⌉		
	Good	Not good	Better	Worse	Same
1951	14	49	12	56	32
1952	26	29	21	30	49
1953	37	18	24	19	57
1954	45	13	29	20	51
1955	46	12	25	16	59

Note: [a]Change measured relative to previous year.
Source: Noelle and Neumann (1956).

"best" system to lubricate the painful transition from planning to markets? The evidence presented above argues against the existence of a holy grail. In particular, fashionable systemic explanations lack support. While it is tempting to link West German growth performance to her role as the sole extoller of the virtues of unbridled competition, the economic performance of France, the archetype of sophisticated planning, cautions against such a view.

In the end, *consistency* may provide a more relevant criterion for judging growth prospects than fundamental philosophy: France and Germany adopted diametrically opposite, but consistently applied, strategies. France provides a case study of the capabilities of sophisticated planning while Germany illustrates the growth potential of (relatively) free markets under a stable policy framework, emphasizing incentives for the Schumpeterian entrepreneur. Against this background, the United Kingdom provides a negative role model, illustrating the potential danger of full-employment policies cum pointillist interventions without the guiding light of a consistent global strategy, "the untenable middle course between a liberal and a collectivist economic system."[14]

Appendix A Data

The data used in the regressions were drawn from a variety of sources. The

[14] Ropcke (1950). *The Economist*, in comparing France and the United Kingdom, likewise concluded that "The parts [of the Monnet Plan] consequently fit together into a whole, and M. Monnet has an industrial policy where Sir Stafford Cripps will have, at best, only a collection of unrelated expedients."

GNP shares are taken from the OECD historical statistics. Industrial production figures are predominantly from the United Nations Economic Survey of Europe (UNESE) augmented by the IMF International Financial Statistics. Employment figures are likewise from UNESE.

The data on institutional sclerosis are drawn from Batstone (1986) and Choi (1983). Batstone classifies unions according to their scope (broad or narrow), defined in terms of their coverage and according to their sophistication (high or low), proxied by the central union's control over strikes, their level of income and staffing. An index of employers organization power (1 to 5) is similarly based on their membership, their role in bargaining, the existence of strike funds, and the control of the central organization, including sanctions. Choi (1983) develops a continuous index of sclerosis depending upon the time since the last institutional upheaval.

Political fragmentation data are from Banks (1971). The seats held by the communist party are from Flora (1983), as are the strike data, the labor share, and the wage-to-profit ratio. The corporate tax rate, computed as the ratio of corporate taxes as a fraction of GDP to the share of GNP going to capital, is based on OECD statistics (taxes) and Flora (shares). The change in q, computed as the difference in the growth rates of the stock price index and the wholesale price index, is based on variables taken from International Financial Statistics. The two real interest rates are both measured relative to the wholesale price index and are also both taken from the IFS. The first measure uses the discount rate, the second measure the rate on long-term government bonds.

Appendix B Regression results

Table 1B. *Recovery and convergence effects*

Explanatory variables	[1] 1945–50	[2] 1950–55	[3] 1955–60
Growth 1938–46	−1.20 (8.59)	−0.29 (2.33)	−0.09 (0.90)
Productivity level 1938	−0.15 (4.27)	−0.02 (0.61)	0.01 (0.20)
R^2	0.95	0.55	0.10

Notes: Dependent variable is annual labor productivity growth. All equations include a constant (not reported). *t*-statistics in parentheses.

Table 2B. *Determinants of real wage growth*

Variable	Coefficient	t-statistic
Constant	0.12	2.62
Change in productivity	0.24	2.51
Defeat in war	−0.01	1.01
Institutional sclerosis	−9.4E − 04	1.91
Coverage of unions	2.8E + 03	0.20
Union power	1.9E − 05	0.00
Unemployment rate	−0.51	1.39
CPI inflation	−0.37	4.33
Investment share	−0.12	1.45
R^2	0.57	
Number of obs.	30	
Degrees of freedom	21	
Standard error	0.022	
Mean of dep. variable	0.027	

Sources: See Appendix A.

Table 3B. *Determinants of Investment*

Variable	Coefficient	t-statistic
Constant	1.59	2.74
Real interest rate	−0.63	2.42
Corporate tax rate	1.60	1.40
Wage share	−1.16	2.10
Growth of real share prices	0.38	2.43
Growth of unit labor costs	0.004	0.01
Union power	−0.20	3.04
Employer power	0.10	3.94
Coverage of unions	−0.06	1.58
Debt service (% of GDP)	12.58	2.74
Sclerosis index	−0.01	2.72
Fragmentation of parliament	−0.83	2.90
R^2	0.84	
Number of obs.	19	
Degrees of freedom	7	
Standard error	0.027	
Mean of dep. variable	0.196	

Sources: See Appendix A.

References

Abelshauser, W. (1975), *Wirtschaft in Westdeutschland 1945–1948*, Stuttgart: DVA.
(1983), *Wirtschaftsgeschichte der Bundesrepublik Deutschland*, Stuttgart: DVA.
Ambrosius, G. (1977), *Die Durchsetzung der Sozialen Marktwirtschaft in West-deutschland 1945–49*, Stuttgart: DVA.
Banks, A. (1971), *Cross-Polity Time-Series Data*, Cambridge, Mass.: MIT Press.
Batstone, E. (1986), "Labour and Productivity," *Oxford Review of Economic Policy*, 2(3): 32–46
Boarman, Patrick (1964), *Germany's Economic Dilemma: Inflation and the Balance of Payments*, New Haven: Yale University Press.
Borchardt, Knut (1982), "Trend, Zyklus, Strukturbruche, Zufalle: Was bestimmt die Deutsche Wirtschaftsgeschichte des 20. Jahrhunderts?" in K. Borchard (ed.) *Wachstum, Krisen, Handlungsspielraume der Wirtschaftspolitik*, Göttingen: Vanderhoock & Ruprecht, pp. 100–124.
Cairncross, Alec (1991), "Reconversion, 1945–51," in N. F. R. Crafts and M. Woodward (eds.), *The British Economy since 1945*, Oxford: Clarendon Press.
Clay, H. (1950), "Planning and Market Economy: Recent British Experience," *American Economic Review*, 40(1): 1–10.
DeLong, J. Bradford and Barry Eichengreen (1993), "The Marshall Plan: History's Most Successful Structural Adjustment Program," in Rudiger Dornbusch, Willem Nölling and Richard Layard (eds.), *Postwar Economic Reconstruction and Lessons for the East Today*, Cambridge, Mass.: MIT Press, pp. 189–230.
Domes, J. and M. Wolffsohn (1978), "Setting the Course for the Federal Republic of Germany," in Rudolf Richter (ed.), *Currency and Economic Reform: West Germany after World War II*; Special issue of *Journal of Institutional and Theoretical Economics*, 135(3): 332–351.
Dumke, J. (1990), "Reassessing the Wirtschaftswunder: Reconstruction and Postwar Growth in West Germany in an International Context," *Oxford Bulletin of Economics and Statistics*, 52(2): 451–91.
Erhard, Ludwig (1954), *Germany's Comeback in the World Market*, London: George Allen & Unwin.
Flora, Peter (1983), *State, Economy and Society in Western Europe 1815–1975*, Frankfurt: Campus Verlag.
Giersch, H. and H. Schmieding (1991), "The Economic Reconstruction of West Germany 1948–1959," mimeo.
Giersch, Herbert, Karl-Heinz Paqué, and Holger Schmieding (1992), *The Fading Miracle*, Cambridge University Press.
Gleitze, Bruno (1960), *Wirtschafts- und sozialstatistisches Handbuch*, Cologne: Wirtschaftswissenschaftliches Institut der Gewerkschaften.
Hicks, J. (1947), "The Empty Economy," *Lloyds Bank Review*, 1: 1–13.
Hogan, Michael (1987), *The Marshall Plan*, Cambridge University Press.
Hohmann, K., W. Stutzel, C. Watrin, and H. Willgerodt (eds.) (1989), *Standard Texts on the Social Market Economy*, Bonn: Ludwig Erhard Stiftung.
Hunold, Alfred (1957), "Sir Robert Peel und Ludwig Erhard: Bahnbrecher Einer Neuen Liberalen Aera," in Von Beckerath, Erwin, Fritz Meyer, and Alfred

Müller-Armack (eds.), *Wirtschaftsfragen der Freien Welt*, Frankfurt: Knapp, pp. 57–72.

Janossy, F. and M. Hollo (1969), *Das Ende der Wirtschaftswunder*, Frankfurt: Verlag Neve Kritik.

Kaldor, N. (1945), "The German War Economy," *Review of Economic Studies*, 13(33): 33–52.

Keynes, J. (1922), "Reconstruction in Europe: An Introduction," *Manchester Guardian Commercial*, 18.5.1922, reprinted in *Collected Works*, vol. 17, pp. 426–454.

Kindleberger, C. (1947), "Cleveland-Moore-Kindleberger Memorandum," in *Marshall Plan Days*, (1987), Boston: Allen & Unwin.

(1967), *Europe's Postwar Growth*, Cambridge, Mass: Harvard University Press.

Klein, L. (1961), "A Model of Japanese Economic Growth," *Econometrica*, 29: 277–292.

Kramer, Alan (1991), *The West German Economy 1945–1955*, New York: St. Martin's Press.

Krengel, Rolf (1958), *Anlagevermogen, Produktion und Beschaftigung im Gebiet der Bundesrepublik von 1924 bis 1956*, DIW Sonderhefte Neue Folge, no. 52, Berlin.

(1963), "Some Reasons for the Rapid Growth of the German Federal Republic," *Banca Nazionale del Lavoro Quarterly Review*, 64: 121–150.

Laban, Raul and Holger Wolf (1993), "Large-Scale Privatization in Transition Economies," *American Economic Review*, 83: 1199–1210.

Maier, Charles (1987), *In Search of Stability*, Cambridge University Press.

Mendershausen, H. (1949), "Prices, Money and the Distribution of Goods in Post War Germany," *American Economic Review*, 39: 646–72.

Milward, Alan S. (1984), *The Reconstruction of Western Europe 1945–51*, Berkeley: University of California Press.

Noelle, E. and E. Neumann (eds.) (1956), *Jahrbuch der Offentlichen Meinung 1947–1955*, Allensbach.

Office of Military Government For Germany (US) (OMGUS) (1946), "Appendixes to a Plan for the Liquidation of War Finance and the Financial Rehabilitation of Germany," mimeo.

Olson, M. (1982), *The Rise and Decline of Nations*, New Haven: Yale University Press.

Reuss, Frederick (1963), *Fiscal Policy for Growth without Inflation: The German Experiment*, Baltimore: Johns Hopkins University Press.

Ropcke, W. (1950), "Is the German Economic Policy the Right One?" in Hohmann *et al.* (1989).

Roskamp, Karl (1964), *Capital Formation in West Germany*, Detroit: Wayne State University Press.

Sohmen, Egon (1959), "Competition and Growth: The Lesson of West Germany," *American Economic Review*, 49 (December): 986–1003.

United Nations (UNECE), *Economic Survey of Europe*, various issues.

United Nations (1964), *Some Factors in Economic Growth in Europe during the 1950s*, Geneva: United Nations.

Wallich, H. (1955), *Mainsprings of the German Revival*, New Haven: Yale University Press.

Wankel, E. (1979), "Historical Developments Prior to the German Currency Reform of 1948," *Zeitschrift für die gesamte Staatswissenschaft*, 135: 320–31.

Index